# The Linux Philosophy for SysAdmins

## And Everyone Who Wants To Be One

David Both

Apress®

## The Linux Philosophy for SysAdmins

David Both
Raleigh, North Carolina, USA

ISBN-13 (pbk): 978-1-4842-3729-8          ISBN-13 (electronic): 978-1-4842-3730-4
https://doi.org/10.1007/978-1-4842-3730-4

Library of Congress Control Number: 2018952337

Managing Director, Apress Media LLC: Welmoed Spahr
Acquisitions Editor: Louise Corrigan
Development Editor: James Markham
Coordinating Editor: Nancy Chen

Cover designed by eStudioCalamar

Cover image designed by Freepik (www.freepik.com)

Distributed to the book trade worldwide by Springer Science+Business Media New York, 233 Spring Street, 6th Floor, New York, NY 10013. Phone 1-800-SPRINGER, fax (201) 348-4505, e-mail orders-ny@springer-sbm.com, or visit www.springeronline.com. Apress Media, LLC is a California LLC and the sole member (owner) is Springer Science + Business Media Finance Inc (SSBM Finance Inc). SSBM Finance Inc is a **Delaware** corporation.

For information on translations, please e-mail rights@apress.com, or visit http://www.apress.com/rights-permissions.

Apress titles may be purchased in bulk for academic, corporate, or promotional use. eBook versions and licenses are also available for most titles. For more information, reference our Print and eBook Bulk Sales web page at http://www.apress.com/bulk-sales.

Any source code or other supplementary material referenced by the author in this book is available to readers on GitHub via the book's product page, located at www.apress.com/9781484237298. For more detailed information, please visit http://www.apress.com/source-code.

Printed on acid-free paper

*This book is dedicated to all of the amazing and hard-working "lazy Admins" who take the young SysAdmins under your wings. It is your work as mentors that make it possible for us to learn and grow into our full potential.*

*I had some amazing mentors who understood what it takes to learn. You are my heroes. Here's to you, Alyce, BRuce, Vern, Dan, Chris, Heather, Ron, Don, Dave, Earl, and Pam. And to all of you unsung mentors out there – You rock! Thanks for your support and guidance.*

# Table of Contents

# About the Author

**David Both** is an Open Source Software and GNU/Linux advocate, trainer, writer, and speaker. He has been working with Linux and Open Source Software for more than 20 years and has been working with computers for over 45 years. He worked for IBM for 21 years and, while working as a Course Development Representative in Boca Raton, Florida, in 1981, wrote the training course for the first IBM PC. He has taught RHCE classes for Red Hat and has worked at MCI Worldcom, Cisco, and the State of North Carolina. In most of the places he has worked since leaving IBM, he has taught classes on Linux ranging from Lunch'n'Learns to full five-day courses.

David prefers to purchase the components and build his own computers from scratch to ensure that each new computer meets his exacting specifications. His latest build is an ASUS TUF X299 motherboard and an Intel i9 CPU with 16 processors (32 threads) and 64GB of RAM in a ThermalTake Core X9 case.

He has written articles for magazines including, *Linux Magazine* and *Linux Journal*. He currently writes prolifically and is a volunteer Community Moderator for OpenSource. com. He particularly enjoys learning new things while researching his articles.

David currently lives in Raleigh, North Carolina, with his very supportive wife, Alice, and a strange rescue dog that is mostly Jack Russell. David also likes reading, travel, the beach, and spending time with his two children, their spouses, and four grandchildren.

# About the Technical Reviewer

 **Ben Cotton** is a meteorologist by training and a high-performance computing engineer by trade. Ben has over a decade of experience supporting Linux, Windows, and macOS systems for academia and high-performance computing. Ben co-founded a local tech meetup group and is a member of the Open Source Initiative and supporter of the Software Freedom Conservancy. He has written for Sysadvent, Opensource.com, *The Next Platform*, as well as his blog at funnelfiasco.com.

# Acknowledgments

Writing a book is not a solitary activity and *The Linux Philosophy for System Administrators* is no exception. It takes a team to produce a book as well as some personal cheerleaders. The most important person in this effort has been my awesome wife, Alice, who has been my head cheerleader throughout this process. I could not have done this without the support of you gave me, my best friend, my sweetheart.

Many times the hardest part of publishing a book of any kind is selling it to a publisher. I already had about 20,000 words written when I went to All Things Open (ATO) in Raleigh, North Carolina, in October of 2017 with the intent of picking people's brains for publishers that they would recommend. I had already asked the smart and talented Rikki Endsley, community manager and editor at Opensource.com for whom I write frequent articles, if she could help me out. Rikki gave me a short list of people she knew from her years in technical publishing and two of the publishers on the list were at ATO. I owe many thanks to Rikki for her support over the time I have been writing for Opensource.com, for pointing me to Apress, and for being an understanding friend. Thanks also for being a fantastic cheerleader, not just for me, but also for many of the authors who write for Opensource.com.

On the first day of ATO in 2017, I was browsing through the vendors' exhibits and ran across one of the names on the list that Rikki had given me, Louise Corrigan, a senior editor for open source at Apress. She was staffing the Apress both and when I picked up her card I said to her, "I have a book for you." She expressed immediate interest and as I told her of my vision for this book, she became quite enthusiastic about it. It was her enthusiasm and the fact that she liked my vision without suggesting any changes to it that sold me on Apress. Thank you, Louise, for believing in me and my vision.

To Nancy Chen and James Markham, the editors at Apress who shepherded the creation of this book from beginning to end, have provided guidance, answered my questions, and just been there for me. Thanks to both of you for helping me through the process of writing my first book.

Despite the fact that this is a book about a philosophy, it is also a very technical book. Ben Cotton has done a fantastic job as my technical reviewer. He has ensured the technical accuracy of the experiments and other technical sections of this book. Ben also made some excellent suggestions about the content where it needed further clarification and when I had simply forgotten or missed covering some salient points. This book is much better for your contributions, Ben. Thank you very much for your splendid work.

I want to thank all the editors at Opensource.com for the work they do on the articles I submit there and also for the gentle way they helped me learn about the editorial process. They also helped me earn my chops as a writer. Thanks to you all, Jason Hibbits, Rikki Endsley, Jen Wike Huger, Jason Baker, Bryan Behrenshausen, and Alex Sanchez.

I also need to thank all the volunteer community moderators who contribute so much to Opensource.com. One of the highlights of my year is always at ATO when as many of us as possible manage to get together from all over the world. I am honored to be a member of such a community of brilliant people and I always learn so much from you.

# PART I

# Introduction

Part 1 of *The Linux Philosophy for System Administrators* introduces you to the Unix Philosophy and the original Linux Philosophy, which was derived directly from the Unix Philosophy. You will learn a little about the history and participants in the development of Unix and Linux and how they brought first the Unix Philosophy and then the Linux Philosophy into being.

You will also learn about my reasons and motivation for setting down my own Philosophy. In large part this is due to the inadequacy of the original Linux Philosophy when it is applied to the System Administrator.

Throughout this book you will find hands-on experiments to enable the type of learning that most SysAdmins like best – learning by doing. In Part 1, you will prepare for those experiments. You will be provided with a set of minimum specifications for a Linux computer on which the experiments should be run, and you will prepare a USB memory stick that will be used in some of the experiments.

The experiments in this book are intended to be short and simple. Their main purpose is to help you understand the Linux Philosophy for System Administrators.

# PART I

# Introduction

# CHAPTER 1

# Introduction to the Linux Philosophy

The Unix Philosophy is an important part of what makes Unix[1] unique and powerful. Much has been written about the Unix Philosophy. And the Linux philosophy is essentially the same as the Unix philosophy because of its direct line of descent from Unix.

The original Unix Philosophy was intended primarily for system developers. In fact, the developers of Unix, led by Ken Thompson[2] and Dennis Ritchie,[3] designed Unix in a way that made sense to them, creating rules, guidelines, and procedural methods, then designing them into the structure of the operating system. That worked well for system developers and that also – partly, at least – worked for SysAdmins (System Administrators). That collection of guidance from the originators of the Unix operating system was codified in the excellent book, *The Unix Philosophy*, by Mike Gancarz, and then later updated by Mr. Gancarz as *Linux and the Unix Philosophy*.[4]

Another fine book, *The Art of Unix Programming*,[5] by Eric S. Raymond, provides the author's philosophical view of programming in a Unix environment. It is also somewhat of a history of the development of Unix as it was experienced and recalled by the author. This book is also available in its entirety at no charge on the Internet.[6]

---

[1]https://en.wikipedia.org/wiki/Unix

[2]https://en.wikipedia.org/wiki/Ken_Thompson

[3]https://en.wikipedia.org/wiki/Dennis_Ritchie

[4]Mike Gancarz, *Linux and the Unix Philosophy*, Digital Press – an imprint of Elsevier Science, 2003, ISBN 1-55558-273-7

[5]Eric S. Raymond, *The Art of Unix Programming*, Addison-Wesley, September 17, 2003, ISBN 0-13-142901-9

[6]Eric S. Raymond, "The Art of Unix Programming," http://www.catb.org/esr/writings/taoup/html/

© David Both 2018

D. Both, *The Linux Philosophy for SysAdmins*, https://doi.org/10.1007/978-1-4842-3730-4_1

I learned a lot from all three of those books. They all have great value for Unix and Linux programmers. In my opinion, *Linux and the Unix Philosophy* and *The Art of Unix Programming*" should be required reading for Linux programmers, System Administrators, and DevOps personnel.

I have been working with computers for over 45 years in total. Holy cow – that is a long time! It was not until I started working with Unix and Linux and started reading some of the articles and books about Unix, Linux, and the common philosophy they share that I understood the reasons why many things in the Linux and Unix worlds are done as they are.

Having worked with Unix and Linux for over 20 years as of this writing, I have found that the Linux philosophy has contributed greatly to my own efficiency and effectiveness as a SysAdmin. I have always tried to follow the Linux philosophy because my experience has been that a rigorous adherence to it, regardless of the pressure applied by a legion of Pointy-Haired-Bosses (PHB), will always pay dividends in the long run.

The original Unix and Linux philosophy was intended for the developers of those operating systems. Although System Administrators could apply many of the tenets to their daily work, many important tenets that address things unique to SysAdmins were missing.

I was very fortunate to have had a couple excellent mentors during my Unix and Linux careers. They helped me to gain the confidence to fail. When I failed, I learned far more than when things went right because they made me fix the problems I had inflicted on myself. These experts, people who had many years more experience than I at being a SysAdmin, never berated me or punished me for failing – their credo was, "if you fail you learn." And I learned a lot. A significant part of what they taught me was the Linux philosophy, but they also taught me their own philosophies, ones that helped to fill in the missing sections of the original.

So, over the years I have been working with Linux and Unix, I have formulated my own philosophy – one which applies more directly to the everyday life and tasks of the System Administrator. My Philosophy is based in part upon the original Unix and Linux Philosophy, as well as the philosophies of my mentors. When I decided to write my own book, one that is aimed at and that addresses the needs of today's System Administrator, I started with those tenets, but as I progressed and the structure of this book revealed itself to me, the structure and nature of the Philosophy became clearer than ever. As it turns out, this Philosophy is significantly different from the original Linux Philosophy. It was only then that I realized just how much a new philosophy was needed, one that was intended specifically for the SysAdmin. Naturally I call this new philosophy, "The Linux Philosophy for the System Administrator."

This book is the result of my creation of the new philosophy – it provides a unique hands-on approach to becoming a better SysAdmin. This book and the philosophy it reveals is my attempt to give back to the community that nurtured me as I grew and helped me to became more confident.

Because the name "Linux Philosophy for System Administrators" is a bit long, most of the time I will refer to it in this book as the "Philosophy" for simplicity.

# Am I a SysAdmin?

Since this book is intended for SysAdmins it would be helpful for you to know whether you are one or not. Wikipedia[7] defines a System Administrator as "a person who is responsible for the upkeep, configuration, and reliable operation of computer systems; especially multi-user computers, such as servers." In my experience, this can include computer and network hardware, software, racks and enclosures, computer rooms or space, and much more.

The typical SysAdmin's job can include a very large number of tasks. In a small business a SysAdmin may be responsible for doing everything computer related. In larger environments, multiple SysAdmins may share responsibility for all of the tasks required to keep things running. In some cases, you may not even know you are a SysAdmin; your manager may have simply told you to start maintaining one or more computers in your office – that makes you a SysAdmin, like it or not.

There is also a term, "DevOps," that is used to describe the intersection of the formerly separate development and operations organizations. In the past, this has been primarily about teaching SysAdmins to write code, but the focus is now shifting to teaching programmers how to perform operational tasks.[8] Attending to SysAdmin tasks makes these folks SysAdmins, too, at least for part of the time. While I was working at Cisco, I had a DevOps type of job. Part of the time I wrote code to test Linux appliances and the rest of the time I was a SysAdmin in the lab where those appliances were tested. It was a very interesting and rewarding time in my career.

---

[7]https://en.wikipedia.org/wiki/System_administrator

[8]Charity, "Ops: It's everyone's job now," https://opensource.com/article/17/7/ state-systems-administration

I have created this short list to help you determine whether you are a SysAdmin. You know you are a SysAdmin if...

1. You think this book might be a fun read.

2. People frequently ask you to help them with their computers.

3. You check the servers every morning before you do anything else.

4. You write shell scripts to automate even simple tasks.

5. You share your shell scripts.

6. Your shell scripts are licensed with an Open Source license.

7. You know what Open Source means.

8. You document everything you do.

9. You have hacked the wireless router to install Linux software.

10. You find computers easier to interact with than most humans.

11. You understand `:(){ :|:&};:`

12. You think the command line is fun.

13. You like to be in complete control.

14. You are root.

15. You understand the difference between "free as in beer," and "free as in speech," when applied to software.

16. You have installed a computer in a rack enclosure.

17. You have replaced the standard CPU cooling fan with one that dissipates more heat.

18. You purchase the parts and build your own computers.

19. You use liquid cooling for your CPU.

20. You install Linux on everything you can.

21. You have a Raspberry Pi connected to your television.

22. You use a Raspberry Pi as a firewall for your home network.

23. You run your own Email, DHCP, NTP, NFS, DNS, and/or SSH servers.

24. You have hacked your home computer to replace the processor with a faster one.

25. You have upgraded the BIOS in a computer.

26. You leave the covers off your computer because you replace components frequently.

27. The router provided by your ISP is in "pass through" mode.

28. You use a Linux computer as a router.

29. ...etc...

You get the idea. I could list a lot more things that might make you a SysAdmin, but there would be hundreds of items. I am sure you can think of plenty more that apply to you.

# The Structure of the Philosophy

There are three layers to the Linux Philosophy for System Administrators in a way that is similar to Maslow's hierarchy of needs.[9] These layers are also symbolic of our growth through progressively higher levels of enlightenment.

The bottom layer is the foundation – the basic commands and knowledge that we as SysAdmins need to know in order to perform the lowest level of our jobs. The middle layer consists of those practical tenets that build on the foundation and inform the daily tasks of the SysAdmin. The top layer contains the tenets that fulfill our higher needs as SysAdmins and which encourage and enable us to share our knowledge.

This book is structured in three parts that correspond to the layers of the Philosophy as shown in Figure 1-1. In the first and most basic layer of the Philosophy, the foundation is laid. We will be introduced to "The Linux Truth," data streams, Standard IO (STDIO), transforming data streams, and the meaning of "everything is a file." As enlightenment begins to dawn in our work life, we find ourselves learning many new commands, how to use them effectively in simple command-line programs, and how to make use of the fact that everything is a file. This foundational layer of our Philosophy is explored in Part 2 of this book.

---

[9]Wikipedia, "Maslow's hierarchy of needs," https://en.wikipedia.org/wiki/ Maslow%27s_hierarchy_of_needs

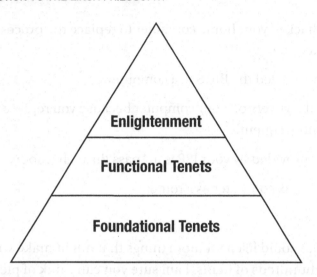

*Figure 1-1.*  *The hierarchy of the Linux Philosophy for SysAdmins*

Our journey then extends beyond simply pounding out commands at the keyboard, and we begin to explore the middle layer where the functional aspects of the Philosophy become our guides. Embracing the command line to better advantage, we begin to expand our command-line programs to create tested and maintainable shell programs that we save and can use repeatedly, and even share. We become the "lazy admin" and begin to automate everything. We use the Linux filesystem hierarchy appropriately and store data in open formats. The functional portions of the Philosophy are found in Part 3.

At the top layer of the Philosophy, which is covered in Part 4, we move into enlightenment. As we begin to progress beyond merely performing our SysAdmin tasks and just getting the job done, our understanding of the elegance and simplicity in the design of Linux is perfected. We begin striving for doing our own work elegantly, keeping solutions simple, simplifying existing but complex solutions, and creating usable and complete documentation. We begin to explore and experiment simply for the sake of gaining new knowledge. At this stage of enlightenment, we begin to pass our knowledge and methods to those new to the profession and we actively support our favorite open source projects.

As in real life, the layers of the Philosophy are seldom clear-cut. How we work and apply the tenets of the Philosophy may vary depending upon circumstances, Pointy-Haired-Bosses, our level of training, and our current understanding of the Philosophy.

# Who Should Read This Book

If you are or want to be a SysAdmin, you should read this book. If you are performing at least some of the duties of a SysAdmin even if that is not your job title, you should read this book. If you work in DevOps you should read this book. If you are root on one or more Linux computers, you should read this book. If you regularly use and like the command line, you should read this book. If you think that the command line is fun and powerful, you should read this book. And check out the cow in the following figure who also wants you to read this book.

```
 ------------------------------
/ If you want to know why there \
| is a cow in a book about the  |
| Linux Philosophy for System   |
| Administrators, you should    |
\ read this book.               /
 ------------------------------
        \   ^__^
         \  (oo)_____
            (__)\       )\/\
                ||----w |
                ||     ||
```

If you want to learn the secrets that make the best Linux SysAdmins powerful far beyond that of mere mortals; if you want to understand the concepts that unlock those secrets; if you want to be the SysAdmin that everyone else turns to when the bytes hit the CPU cooling fan – then this book is for you.

This book is not about learning new commands. Rather, it is about using the common and well-known commands with which you should already be familiar to illuminate the underlying structure of Linux at the command line. Think of this book and the commands you will use in the exercises like the X-rays, CT scans, and MRI's that a doctor uses to reveal the inside of a human body. This book will show you how to use some simple Linux commands to reveal the underlying structure of GNU/Linux.

The Linux Philosophy for System Administrators is intended to reveal and illustrate the awesome power and flexibility of the command line along with the design and usage philosophies that support those traits. This understanding of how to extract the most from the Linux command line can help you become a better SysAdmin.

I assume that readers of this book have at least a full year of constant experience with the Linux command-line interface, preferably with the bash shell but any shell will do. You should be comfortable with many Linux commands.

My expectation is that you already know how to perform a large part of the SysAdmin's job using the appropriate commands and making adjustments for use of the proper devices. So when I tell you, for example, to "mount the USB device on /mnt," you will know what I mean and be able to determine which device file to mount, use the mount command to perform the mount, and access the mounted device as needed to create or view the contents.

You should also have root access on one or more Linux computers and have performed at least some SysAdmin duties for at least six months. If you have installed Linux on one or more computers at home, you meet this requirement and should read this book.

## But I Don't Meet Those Requirements

Perhaps you do not meet any of the previously stated requirements but would like to read this book anyway. Whether you want to become a SysAdmin or just because you think it might be interesting, if you still want to read this book, then do so.

If you have the kind of interest in learning about the Linux Philosophy for System Administrators that you want to continue with this book despite what I have just said above, well – just do it. In that case I have tried to provide enough information to make it possible for you to perform most of these experiments. If you do get stuck, contact your local Linux users group. There are many of these around the world and I have found that the members of these LUGs tend to be very helpful.

There are three books I recommend if you are interested in learning more about working on the Linux command line and learning System Administration skills. They will make good references as you proceed through the experiments in this book.

1. *Pro Linux System Administration*; Matotek, Dennis, Turnbull,
   James, LIEVERDINK, PETER; Apress; ISBN 978-1-4842-2008-5

2. *Beginning the Linux Command Line*; van Vugt, Sander; Apress;
   ISBN 978-1-4302-6829-1

3. *A Practical Guide to Linux Commands, Editors, and Shell*
   *Programming* Third Edition; Sobell, Prentice Hall;
   ISBN 978-0-13-308504-4

These three books should get you started on the Linux command line and help you
learn system administration. But the best way is to just get as much hands-on as you can.

## Who Should Not Read This Book

If you just want to use your web browser, send email, and perhaps use the LibréOffice
Writer program to create a few documents, if you do not care about what happens
behind the scenes with Linux, if you rely on someone else to fix problems with your
computer, this book is not for you. Read no further.

If your sole purpose is that you want to learn about advanced commands and how to
use them – an admirable goal itself – this is not the book for you.

## The Linux Truth

The amazing power of the Linux command line is hinted at in the following quote that
originally referenced Unix. It also applies to Linux.

> *Unix was not designed to stop its users from doing stupid things, as that*
> *would also stop them from doing clever things.*

—Doug Gwyn

This quote summarizes the overriding truth of Unix and Linux – that the operating
system must trust the user. It is only by extending this full measure of trust that allows the
user to access the full power made possible by the operating system. This truth applies to
Linux because of its heritage as a direct descendant of Unix.

# Restrictive Operating Systems

Operating systems that shield their users from the power they possess were developed starting with the basic assumption that the users are not smart or knowledgeable enough to be trusted with the full power that computers can actually provide. These operating systems are restrictive and have user interfaces – both command line and graphical – that enforce those restrictions by design. These restrictive user interfaces force regular users and SysAdmins alike into an enclosed room with no windows and then slam the door shut and triple lock it. That locked room prevents them from doing any of those clever things alluded to by Mr. Gwyn.

The command-line interfaces of such limiting operating systems offer a relatively few commands, providing a de facto limit on the possible activities in which anyone might engage. Some users find this a comfort. I do not and, apparently, neither do you to judge from the fact that you are reading this book.

# Linux Is Open and Free

Linux was designed from the beginning as open and free in the sense that users and SysAdmins should have full access within their own realm to all aspects of the operating system. The result is that we can do those very clever things with Linux. There are other meanings to open and free, such as Free Libré Open Source Software (FLOSS), and free beer, but that discussion is one for other books.

Even the most experienced users can do "stupid things" using Linux. My experience has been that recovery from my own not-so-infrequent stupidity has been made much easier by the open access to the full power of the operating system. I find that most times a few commands can resolve the problem without even a reboot. On a few occasions, I have had to switch to a lower runlevel to fix a problem. I have only very Infrequently needed to boot to recovery mode in order to edit a configuration file that I managed to damage so badly, it caused serious problems including failure to boot. It takes knowledge of the underlying philosophy, the structure, and the technology of Linux to be able to fully unleash its power, especially when things are broken. Linux just requires a bit of understanding and knowledge on the part of the SysAdmin to fully unlock its potential.

# Real Knowledge

Anyone can memorize or learn commands and procedures but rote memorization is not true knowledge. Without the knowledge of the philosophy and how that is embodied in the elegant structure and implementation of Linux, applying the correct commands as tools to resolve complex problems is not possible. I have seen smart people who had a vast knowledge of Linux be unable to resolve a relatively simple problem because they were unaware of the elegance of the structure beneath the surface.

As a SysAdmin, part of my responsibility in many of my jobs has been to assist with hiring new employees. I participated in many technical interviews of people who had passed many Microsoft certifications and who had fine resumes. I also participated in many interviews in which we were looking for Linux skills but very few of those applicants had certifications. This was at a time when Microsoft certifications were the big thing but during the early days of Linux in the data center and few applicants were yet certified.

We usually started these interviews with questions designed to determine the limits of the applicant's knowledge. Then we would get into the more interesting questions, ones that would test their ability to reason through a problem to find a solution. I noticed some very interesting results. Few of the Windows certificate owners could reason their way through the scenarios we presented while a very large percentage of the Linux applicants were able to do so.

I think that result was due in part to the fact that obtaining the Windows certificates relied upon memorization rather than actual hands-on experience, and the fact that Windows is a closed system that prevents SysAdmins from truly understanding how it works. I think that the Linux applicants did so much better because Linux is open on multiple levels, and logic and reason can be used to identify and resolve any problem. Any SysAdmin who has been using Linux for some time has had to learn about the architecture of Linux and has had a decent amount of experience with the application of knowledge, logic, and reason to the solution of problems.

# Enlightenment

Much of this book takes place on the Linux command line, but it is not about the commands themselves. In this book the commands are the tools through which the beauty of the underlying structure of Linux shines if you know how to illuminate it. This book will help you to achieve enlightenment by showing you how to use those common commands to explore that beauty.

You should already be familiar with all except perhaps one or two of the commands that appear in this book. This book will enable you to use those common commands to explore the underlying layers of Linux and discover for yourself the Linux Truth.

Don't forget – It should be **FUN!**

# CHAPTER 2

# Getting Ready

This book defines a philosophy, but it is also intended to illuminate the practical aspects of that philosophy with experiments that you can perform. Because we SysAdmins are a hands-on group of individuals, this book provides a number of simple experiments that you can perform in order to more fully appreciate and understand the tenets of the philosophy. Most experiments usually consist of a one-line bash shell command or program. Some of the experiments do use more than one line.

This chapter will tell you more about what to expect from the experiments. It will describe the optimum configuration for the Linux computer on which to apply these experiments, and it will give you an opportunity to prepare a USB thumb drive for use in some of the experiments.

## The Experiments

As a hands-on SysAdmin, I like to experiment with the command line in order to learn new commands and new ways to perform tasks. Most of the experiments I have devised for this book are ones that I have performed in my own explorations with perhaps some minor changes to accommodate their use here.

Please note that some of the tenets do not lend themselves to experiments; so not every tenet you read about in this book will be illustrated with an experiment, but as many as possible have experiments. Many of the experiments are illustrative of more tenets than just the one in which they appear.

All SysAdmins are hands-on people even though we have different ways of learning. I think it is helpful for SysAdmins to have hands-on experience with these tenets in order to fully visualize and appreciate the truths they embody. That is what the experiments are for – to provide an opportunity to go beyond the theoretical and apply the tenets in a practical way. Although some of the experiments are a bit contrived in order to illustrate a particular point, they are nevertheless valid.

15

© David Both 2018
D. Both, *The Linux Philosophy for SysAdmins*, https://doi.org/10.1007/978-1-4842-3730-4_2

These enlightening experiments are not tucked away at the end of each chapter, or the book, where they can be easily ignored – they are embedded in the text and are an integral part of the flow of this book. I recommend that you perform the experiments as you proceed through the book.

The commands and sometimes the results for each experiment will appear in "experiment" sections as shown below. Many experiments need only a single command, and so will have only one "experiment" section. Other experiments may be more complex and so split among two to more experiment sections.

---

### EXPERIMENT EXAMPLE

This is an example of an experiment. Each experiment will have instructions and code for you to enter end run on your computer.

Many experiments will have a series of instructions in a prose format like this paragraph. Just follow the instructions and the experiments will work just fine.

1.   Some experiments will have a list of steps to perform.

2.   Step 2.

3.   etc…

**Code that you are to enter for the experiments will look like this.**

This is the end of the experiment.

---

Most of these experiments can be performed as a non-root user; that is much safer than doing everything as root. However you will need to be root for some of these experiments.

These experiments are considered safe for use on a computer or VM designated for training. Regardless of how benign they may seem, you should not perform any of these experiments on a production system.

---

**Warning!**    You should not use a production computer for these experiments. You should use a computer or virtual machine that is designated for training.

---

There are times when I want to present code that is interesting but which you should not run as part of one of the experiments. For such situations I will place the code and any supporting text in a **CODE SAMPLE** section as shown below.

---

**CODE SAMPLE**

---

Code that is intended to illustrate a point but which you should not even think about running on any computer will be contained in a section like this one.

```
echo "This is sample code which you should never run."
```

---

# System Requirements

You will need a computer with Linux installed on it to perform these experiments. The specifications of this computer are relatively unimportant because even the smallest Linux computers provide terminal emulators or console sessions to access the command line. For best results, the minimum you might consider is Intel or AMD hardware with at least 2GB of RAM and an i3 processor or the equivalent. In a pinch a Raspberry Pi 3B with the latest version of Raspbian installed will work, too.

The computer you use for the experiments in this book should have a recent, mainstream distribution such as Fedora, Ubuntu, Mint, RHEL, or CentOS. Whichever distro that you use should have a GUI desktop installed and available for use. Some experiments require having multiple terminal emulation sessions open on the desktop.

You will also need a USB thumb drive on which to perform some of the more dangerous experiments that involve reading and writing data on hard drives. A USB thumb drive is a suitable replacement for, and will work exactly the same way, as a real hard drive with a spinning disk and moving heads and all.

I strongly suggest that you use a host computer that is not being used for anything else, such as a system designated for training, or a virtual machine running on free open source software like VirtualBox to install Linux and perform these experiments. That will significantly reduce the possibility of damage to a production computer.

You should have root access on the computer or VM you are using for these experiments. If you do not have root on any computer, you will be unable to perform some of these experiments. You will be informed for the experiments in which root access is required.

You should use an account such as a "student" account to try most of these experiments. That further reduces the danger of damaging your own files. In fact, most of these experiments assume that you are logged in as the non-privileged user, student.

---

**Warning!**    Do not perform the experiments presented in this book on a production system.

---

# How to Access the Command Line

All of the modern mainstream Linux distributions provide at least three ways to access the command line.

If you use a graphical desktop, most distributions come with multiple terminal emulators from which to choose. I prefer Krusader and Tilix but you can use any terminal emulator that you like.

Linux also provides the capability for multiple virtual consoles to allow for multiple logins from a single keyboard and monitor. Virtual consoles can be used on systems that don't have a GUI desktop, but they can be used even on systems that do have one.

Each virtual console is assigned to a Function Key corresponding to the console number. So vc1 would be assigned to function key F1, and so on. It is easy to switch to and from these sessions. On your computer you can hold down the Ctrl and Alt keys and press F2 to switch to vc2. Then hold down the Ctrl and Alt keys and press F1 to switch to vc1 and the graphical interface.

The last method to access the command line on a Linux computer is via a remote login. Secure Shell (SSH) is the most common method of remote access.

If the computer to which you have local access is not acceptable on which to run these experiments but you have access to a remote computer that is, you can SSH into that computer to run the experiments. For some of the experiments you will need to log in more than once.

We will go into much more detail about terminal emulators and console sessions in Chapter 7.

# Create the Student User

As root, you should go ahead right now and create a new user on the computer you will be using for these experiments with the user ID of "student" – without the quotes. Set the password to anything reasonably secure that you can remember.

---

**PREPARATION 2-1**

---

Enter the commands below to create the student user and assign a password.

```
[root@testvm1 ~]# useradd -c "Student User" student
[root@testvm1 ~]# passwd student
Changing password for user student.
New password: <Enter password>
Retype new password: <Enter password again>
passwd: all authentication tokens updated successfully.
```

---

# Preparing the USB Thumb Drive

You can perform many of the experiments safely with a USB thumb drive that is not being used for anything else. Of course, you will have to re-create the partition and filesystem on it in order to make it usable again when we are finished.

I found an old USB 2.0 64MB – yes MB – thumb drive that I have no other current use for, so I set it up to use with these experiments. You can use any size USB stick that you have on hand, but a small one is perfectly fine.

---

**PREPARATION 2-2**

---

Prepare the USB device for use with these experiments.

1. Open a terminal session on the computer you will be using for this experimentation and log in as root.

2. Insert the USB device in a USB slot on your Linux computer.

3. Use the dmesg command to determine which device file the kernel has assigned to the USB drive. It will probably be something like /dev/sdb. The dmesg output should show at least one partition /dev/sdb1. The drive letter – b in this example – may be a different letter on your Linux computer.

---

**Caution**   The following steps may cause the complete destruction of data on a production system if the wrong device is specified in the commands. Be sure to use a non-production system for this experiment.

---

4. Mount the drive's partition on /mnt.

5. Change the PWD to /mnt.

6. Delete any preexisting files.

7. Enter and run the following command to create some files with content on the drive.

    **for I in 0 1 2 3 4 5 6 7 8 9 ; do dmesg > file$I.txt;done**

8. Verify that there are now at least 10 files on the drive with the names file0.txt through file9.txt.

9. Change the PWD to root's home directory.

10. Unmount the USB drive and remove it from the computer until it is needed.

The USB drive is now ready for use in our experiments.

---

# What to Do if the Experiments Do Not Work

These experiments are intended to be self-contained and not dependent upon any setup, except for the USB thumb drive, or the results of previously performed experiments. Certain Linux utilities and tools must be present, but these should all be available on a standard Fedora Linux workstation installation or any other mainstream general use distribution.

Therefore, all of these experiments should "just work." We all know how that goes, right? So when something does fail, the first things to do are the obvious.

1.  Verify that the commands were entered correctly. This is the most common problem I encounter for myself.

2.  You may see an error message indicating that the command was not found. The bash shell shows the bad command; in this case I made up badcommand. It then gives a brief description of the problem. This error message is displayed for both missing and misspelled commands. Check the command spelling and syntax multiple times to verify that it is correct.

    ```
    [student@testvm1 ~]$ badcommand
    bash: badcommand: command not found...
    ```

3.  Use the man command to view the manual pages (man pages) in order to verify the correct syntax and spelling of commands.

4.  Ensure that the required command is, in fact, installed. Install them if they are not already installed.

5.  For experiments that require you to be logged in as root, ensure that you have done so. There should be only a few of these, but performing them as a non-root user will not work.

There is not much else that should go wrong – but if you encounter a problem that you cannot make work using these tips, contact me at LinuxGeek46@both.org and I will do my best to help figure out the problem.

# PART II

# Foundation

There is a great deal of power in the Linux command line that can be tapped to great advantage by its users. The graphical user interfaces (GUI) of today make using the command line unnecessary for many people who just want to use a few relatively simple tools to browse the Web, use email, and perhaps read or write documents. Most Linux users cannot conceive of the power hidden behind the GUI. However, the GUI that allows easy access to computer power for many more users than would otherwise be the case hides a large portion of the power that those same computers put into our hands.

One group of people in particular tend to be the main users of the command line: System Administrators, aka SysAdmins. SysAdmins are the ultimate power users of the command line because it provides direct access to the full extent of the available power.

That is not to say that regular, non-root users do not use the command line. Many do, but usually for those times when a GUI does not have the capability to meet their needs. Most Linux distributions have graphical tools for installing programs; managing users and groups and their permissions; moving and managing files; handling email; browsing the Web; managing processes and CPU functions; limiting access to system resources for some users; and much more. But if the casual users of the Command-Line Interface (CLI) were to explore deeply enough, they would find that Linux provides many text-mode and command-line tools to perform every task that can be performed in a GUI – and many tasks that cannot – usually faster and with more features and functions.

My needs as a SysAdmin include power, speed, flexibility, and total control over the operating system. The only means of meeting all of those needs is to have unfettered access to the Linux command line where all of that power and speed are exposed. As a SysAdmin, I find myself using the CLI far more often than I use the GUI for administrative tasks. In large part this is because I prefer the CLI, but there are also many Linux computers that do not have any type of GUI installed, and even those that do can be very slow when attempting to perform remote administration through any of the remote desktop tools. Those remote GUI tools can be useful if you have a very fast Internet connection to the remote computer, but they will never be as fast as a good old-fashioned terminal session because the network overhead for the GUI data just sucks up bandwidth.

I am not saying that I don't use a GUI desktop and that they are "bad." In fact, I find that the GUI desktop can improve my productivity on the CLI. I use the GUI to leverage my CLI access by opening multiple terminal sessions simultaneously, thus providing me with simultaneous access to the CLI for multiple users on multiple Linux hosts.

I use graphical tools on my GUI desktop. I am using LibreOffice Writer, a powerful, graphical, free, open source word processing program to write this book. I appreciate and use the CLI and the GUI for their respective strengths. However, the Linux Truth is that the CLI offers the most power to those willing to use it.

This section of *The Linux Philosophy for System Administrators* will introduce you to the foundational tenets of the philosophy. These tenets are the developmental embodiment of those tenets of the Unix/Linux Philosophy recorded in the Gancarz book that we will see more of in this part. That philosophical approach to the basic design of Unix, and thus to Linux, contributed to the stability, elegance, simplicity, and the power intrinsic to both operating systems.

This is no accident. Linus Torvalds first developed Linux as a hobby but intentionally based it on Unix. He took the freely available GNU Utilities, recompiled then for Linux, and added them to his operating system, which, when taken together in combination, is known by purists as GNU/Linux.

The personality and usability of any operating system is a function of the assumptions made by the designers. Linux is no exception. It was designed from the beginning to be Unix-like and the Unix developers had decided that Unix would allow its users to access every bit of the power that was designed into it. Not only that, they provided users with the tools needed to access that power. After all, what good is it to design an operating system – or anything else for that matter – and then limit access to it? GNU/Linux is Free Libre Open Source Software – FLOSS – that is much like Unix in its philosophy and implementation.

Because of their importance and far-ranging impact on the personality of Linux, I spend a great deal of space in this book explaining these Foundational tenets in words and illustrating them with hands-on experiments. I believe that it is only with a firm understanding of these tenets that the Functional tenets can be appreciated and their applicability to the daily tasks of the SysAdmin more completely realized.

In Part 2 of this book, our enlightenment begins with the most basic layer of the Philosophy. We will be introduced to "The Linux Truth," data streams, Standard IO (STDIO), transforming data streams, and the meaning of "everything is a file." As enlightenment begins to dawn in our work life, we find ourselves learning many new commands, how to use them effectively in simple command-line programs, and how to make use of the fact that everything is a file.

# CHAPTER 3

# Data Streams

Everything in Linux revolves around streams of data – particularly text streams.

I recently Googled "data stream" and most of the top hits are concerned with processing huge amounts of streaming data in single entities such as streaming video and audio, or financial institutions processing streams consisting of huge numbers of individual transactions. This is not what we are talking about here although the concept is the same, and a case could be made that current applications use the stream processing functions of Linux as the model for processing many types of data.

In the Unix and Linux worlds, a stream is a flow text data that originates at some source; the stream may flow to one or more programs that transform it in some way, and then it may be stored in a file or displayed in a terminal session. As a SysAdmin your job is intimately associated with manipulating the creation and flow of these data streams. In this chapter we will explore data streams – what they are, how to create them, and a little bit about how to use them.

## Text Streams – A Universal Interface

The use of Standard Input/Output (STDIO) for program input and output is a key foundation of the Linux way of doing things. STDIO was first developed for Unix and has found its way into most other operating systems since then, including DOS, Windows, and Linux.

> *This is the Unix philosophy: Write programs that do one thing and do it well. Write programs to work together. Write programs to handle text streams, because that is a universal interface.*
>
> — Doug McIlroy, *Basics of the Unix Philosophy*[1,2]

---

[1]Eric S. Raymond, *The Art of Unix Programming*, http://www.catb.org/esr/writings/taoup/html/ch01s06.html

[2]Linuxtopia, *Basics of the Unix Philosophy*, http://www.linuxtopia.org/online_books/programming_books/art_of_unix_programming/ch01s06.html

D. Both, *The Linux Philosophy for SysAdmins*, https://doi.org/10.1007/978-1-4842-3730-4_3

STDIO was developed by Ken Thompson[3] as a part of the infrastructure required to implement pipes on early versions of Unix. Programs that implement STDIO use standardized file handles for input and output rather than files that are stored on a disk or other recording media. STDIO is best described as a buffered data stream, and its primary function is to stream data from the output of one program, file, or device to the input of another program, file, or device.

# STDIO File Handles

There are three STDIO data streams, each of which is automatically opened as a file at the startup of a program – well those programs that use STDIO. Each STDIO data stream is associated with a file handle that is just a set of metadata that describes the attributes of the file. File handles 0, 1, and 2 are explicitly defined by convention and long practice as STDIN, STDOUT, and STDERR, respectively.

**STDIN**, File handle 0, is standard input that is usually input from the keyboard. STDIN can be redirected from any file including device files instead of the keyboard. It is less common to redirect STDIN than STDOUT or STDERR, but it can be done just as easily.

**STDOUT**, File handle 1, is standard output that sends the data stream to the display by default. It is common to redirect STDOUT to a file or to pipe it to another program for further processing.

**STDERR** is associated with File handle 2. The data stream for STDERR is also usually sent to the display.

If STDOUT is redirected to a file, STDERR continues to be displayed on the screen. This ensures that when the data stream itself is not displayed on the terminal, that STDERR is, thus ensuring that the user will see any errors resulting from execution of the program. STDERR can also be redirected to the same or passed on to the next transformer program in a pipeline.

STDIO is implemented as a C library, stdio.h, which can be included in the source code of programs so that it can be compiled into the resulting executable.

---

[3]Wikipedia, *Ken Thompson*, https://en.wikipedia.org/wiki/Ken_Thompson

# Generating Data Streams

Most of the Core Utilities use STDIO as their output stream and those that generate data streams, rather than acting to transform the data stream in some way, can be used to create the data streams that we will use for our experiments. Data streams can be as short as one line or even a single character, and as long as needed.[4]

Let's try our first experiment and create a short data stream.

---

## EXPERIMENT 3-1

If you have not done so already, log in to the host you are using for these experiments as the user "student." If you have logged in to a GUI desktop session, start your favorite terminal emulator; if you have logged in to one of the virtual consoles or a terminal emulator you are ready to go.

Use the command shown below to generate a stream of data. The command is in boldface.

```
[student@f26vm ~]$ ls -la
total 28
drwx------   3 student student 4096 Oct 20 01:25 .
drwxr-xr-x. 10 root    root    4096 Sep 21 10:06 ..
-rw-------   1 student student 1218 Oct 20 20:26 .bash_history
-rw-r--r--   1 student student   18 Jun 30 11:57 .bash_logout
-rw-r--r--   1 student student  193 Jun 30 11:57 .bash_profile
-rw-r--r--   1 student student  231 Jun 30 11:57 .bashrc
drwxr-xr-x   4 student student 4096 Jul  5 18:00 .mozilla
```

The output from this command is a short data stream that is displayed on STDOUT, the console or terminal session that you are logged in to.

---

In Chapter 4, "Transforming Data Streams," we will pipe the STDOUT data streams like this one to STDIN of some transformer programs in order to perform some manipulation of the data in the stream. For now, we are just generating streams of data.

Some GNU core utilities are designed specifically to produce streams of data.

---

[4]A data stream taken from special device files random, urandom, and zero, for example, can continue forever without some form of external termination such as the user entering Ctrl-C, a limiting argument to the command or a system failure.

---

## EXPERIMENT 3-2

The yes command produces a continuous data stream that consists of repetitions of the data string provided as the argument. The generated data stream will continue until it is interrupted with a Ctrl-C, which is displayed on the screen as ^C.

Enter the command as shown and let it run for a few seconds. Press Ctrl-C when you get tired of watching the same string of data scroll by.

```
[student@f26vm ~]$ yes 123465789-abcdefg
123465789-abcdefg
123465789-abcdefg
123465789-abcdefg
123465789-abcdefg
123465789-abcdefg
123465789-abcdefg
123465789-abcdefg
1234^C
```

---

"What does this prove?," you ask. Just that there are many ways to create a data stream that might be useful. For example, you might wish to automate the process of responding to the seemingly interminable requests for "y" input to from the fsck program to fix a problem on the hard drive. This solution can result in saving a lot of presses on the "y" key.

---

## EXPERIMENT 3-3

To see how the yes generates a string of "y" characters, try the yes command again without a string argument as in Experiment 3-2, and you get a string of "y" characters as output.

```
[student@f26vm ~]$ yes
y
y
y
y
y
y
y
^C
```

---

And now, here is something that you should most definitely not try. When run as root, the rm * command will erase every file in the present working directory (pwd) – but it asks you to enter "y" for each file to verify that you actually want to delete that file. This means more typing.

---

**CODE SAMPLE 3-1**

---

I haven't talked about pipes yet but as a SysAdmin, or someone who wants to become one, you should already know how to use them. The CLI program below will supply the response of "y" to each request by the rm command and will delete all of the files.

```
yes | rm *
```

---

**Warning!** Do not run this command because it will delete all of the files in the present working directory.

---

Of course you could also use rm -f *, which would also forcibly delete all of the files in the PWD. The -f means "force" the deletions. That is also something you should not do.

# Test a Theory with Yes

Another option for using the yes command is to fill a directory with a file containing some arbitrary and pretty much irrelevant data in order to – well – fill up the directory. I have used this technique to test what happens to a Linux host when a particular directory becomes full. In the specific instance where I used this technique, I was testing a theory because a customer was having problems and could not log in to their computer.

---

**Note**   I assume in this series of experiments that the USB drive is on /dev/sdb and its partition is /dev/sdb1 – as it is on my VM – be sure you verify the device it has been assigned on your computer as it might – and probably will – be different. Use the correct device file[5] for your situation.

---

[5]We will learn more about device files and the /dev directory in Chapter 5, "Everything Is a File."

```
                          EXPERIMENT 3-4
```

This experiment should be performed as root.

In order to prevent filling your root filesystem, this experiment will use the USB device that you should have prepared in advance. This experiment will not affect the existing files on the device.

You did prepare that USB drive, did you not? If not, then go back to Chapter 1 and do so now. I will wait…

Ready? Great!

1. Now insert the USB drive into one of the USB slots on your computer.

2. Use the **dmesg** command to view the information about the USB drive and determine its assigned device file. It should be /dev/sdb or something similar to that. Be sure to use the correct device file for your device.

3. Mount the USB devices filesystem partition, /dev/sdb1, on my system, on /mnt.

4. Run the commands shown below in bold. Some of the results shown here have wrapped due to the limited width of the page, but you get the idea.

Depending upon the size of your USB filesystem, the time to fill it may vary but it should be quite fast.

```
[root@testvm1 ~]# yes 123456789-abcdefgh >> /mnt/testfile.txt
yes: standard output: No space left on device
[root@testvm1 ~]# df -h /mnt
Filesystem                    Size  Used Avail Use% Mounted on

/dev/sdb1                      62M   62M  2.0K 100% /mnt
[root@testvm1 ~]# ls -l /mnt
total 62832
-rwxr-xr-x 1 root root     37001 Nov  7 08:23 file0.txt
-rwxr-xr-x 1 root root     37001 Nov  7 08:23 file1.txt
-rwxr-xr-x 1 root root     37001 Nov  7 08:23 file2.txt
-rwxr-xr-x 1 root root     37001 Nov  7 08:23 file3.txt
-rwxr-xr-x 1 root root     37001 Nov  7 08:23 file4.txt
-rwxr-xr-x 1 root root     37001 Nov  7 08:23 file5.txt
-rwxr-xr-x 1 root root     37001 Nov  7 08:23 file6.txt
```

```
-rwxr-xr-x 1 root root     37001 Nov  7 08:23 file7.txt
-rwxr-xr-x 1 root root     37001 Nov  7 08:23 file8.txt
-rwxr-xr-x 1 root root     37001 Nov  7 08:23 file9.txt
-rwxr-xr-x 1 root root  63950848 Dec  7 13:16 testfile.txt
```

Your results will look somewhat different but they should definitely be similar to mine.

Be sure to look at the line from the **df** output that refers to the /dev/sdb1 device. This shows that 100% of the space on that filesystem is used.

Now delete testfile.txt from /mnt and unmount that filesystem.

---

I used the simple test in Experiment 3-4 on the /tmp directory of one of my own computers as part of my testing to assist me in determining my customer's problem. After /tmp filled up users were no longer able to log in to a GUI desktop, but they could still log in using the consoles. That is because logging into a GUI desktop creates files in the /tmp directory and there was no room left so the login failed. The console login does not create new files in /tmp so they succeeded. My customer had not tried logging into the console because they were not familiar with the CLI.

After testing this on my own system as verification, I used the console to login to the customer host and found a number of large files taking up all of the space in the /tmp directory. I deleted those and helped the customer determine how the files were being created, and we were able to put a stop to that.

# Exploring the USB Drive

It is now time to do a little exploring, and to be as safe as possible you will use the USB thumb drive that you prepared earlier. In this experiment we will look at some of the filesystem structures.

Let's start with something simple. You should be at least somewhat familiar with the **dd** command. Officially known as "disk dump," many SysAdmins call it "disk destroyer" for good reason. Many of us have inadvertently destroyed the contents of an entire hard drive or partition using the **dd** command. That is why we will use the USB drive to perform some of these Experiments.

The **dd** command is a powerful tool that allows us to generate data streams using any file or device like a hard drive, disk partitions, RAM memory, virtual consoles, terminal emulation sessions, STDIO, and much more as both a source and target. Because the **dd** command does not modify these data streams, it gives us access to the raw data so we can view and analyze it.

Data streams generated by **dd** can be used for many different purposes as you will see as we progress through this series of experiments. It is one of my favorite tools for exploring files and devices.

---

## EXPERIMENT 3-5

It is not necessary to mount the USB drive for this experiment; in fact this Experiment is more impressive if you do not mount the device. If the USB device is currently mounted, unmount it. Log in to a terminal session as root.

As root in a terminal session, use the dd command to view the boot record of the USB drive, assuming it is assigned to the /dev/sdb device. The bs= argument is not what you might think; it simply specifies the block size, and the count= argument specifies the number of blocks to dump to STDIO. The of= argument specifies the source of the data stream, in this case, the USB device.

```
[root@f26vm ~]# dd if=/dev/sdb bs=512 count=1
•>•MSWIN4.1P•} •••)L•ONO NAME     FAT16    •}•3•••{••x•vVU•"•~•N•
•••|•E••F•E••8f$|•r<•F••fFVF•PR•F•V•• •v••^
•H••F•N•ZX••••rG8-t•
V•v>•^tJNt
••F•V••S••[r•?MZu•••BJu••pPRQ••3••v••vB•••v••V$•••••••••t<•t       •••••}•
•}••3••^••D•••}•}••r••HH•N       /
•YZXr    @uB^
•••'
Invalid system disk•
Disk I/O error•
Replace the disk,!••U•

1+0 records in
1+0 records out
512 bytes copied, 0.0116131 s, 44.1 kB/s
```

This prints the text of the boot record, which is the first block on the disk – any disk. In this case, there is information about the filesystem and, although it is unreadable because it is stored in binary format, the partition table. If this were a bootable device, stage 1 of GRUB or some other boot loader would be located in this sector. I have added a couple of line feeds after the boot record itself in order to clarify the end of the data in the sector and the information printed by the dd command itself. The last three lines contain data about the number of records and bytes processed.

Now let's do the same Experiment, but on the first record of the first partition.

## EXPERIMENT 3-6

The USB device should still be inserted and unmounted, and you should still be logged in as root.

1.  Run the following command.

```
[root@f26vm ~]# dd if=/dev/sdb1 bs=512 count=1
●<●mkfs.fat●|●●)●GR●NO NAME    FAT16   ●[|●"●t
                                    V●●●^●●2●●●●●●This is not
a bootable disk.  Please insert a bootable floppy and
press any key to try again ...
U●1+0 records in
1+0 records out
512 bytes copied, 0.0113664 s, 45.0 kB/s
```

This Experiment shows the that there are differences between a boot record and the first record of a partition. It also shows that the dd command can be used to view data in the partitions as well as for the disk itself.

Let's see what else is out there on the USB drive. Depending upon the specifics of the USB device you are using for these Experiments, you may have different results from mine. I will show you what I did and you can modify that if necessary to achieve the desired result.

What we are attempting to do is use the dd command to locate the directory entries for the files we created on the USB drive and then some of the data. If we had enough knowledge of the metadata structures, we could interpret them directly to find the locations of this data on the drive, but we don't so we will have to do this the hard way – print out data until we find what we want.

So let's start with what we do know and proceed with a little finesse. We know that the data files we created during the USB device preparation were in the first partition on the device. Therefore, we don't need to search the space between the boot record and the first partition, which contains lots of emptiness. At least that is what it should contain.

Starting with the beginning of /dev/sdb1, let's look at a few blocks of data at a time to find what we want. The command in Experiment 3-7 is similar to the previous one except that we have specified a few more blocks of data to view. You may have to specify fewer blocks if your terminal is not large enough to display all of the data at one time, or you can pipe the data through the less utility and use that to page through the data. Either way works. Remember we are doing all of this as root user because non-root users do not have the required permissions.

---

## EXPERIMENT 3-7

Enter the same command as you did in the previous Experiment, but Increase the block count to be displayed to 10 as shown below in order to show more data.

```
[root@f26vm ~]# dd if=/dev/sdb1 bs=512 count=10
•<•mkfs.fat•|••)•GR•NO NAME     FAT16   •[|•"•t
                                  V•••^••2••••••This is not a
bootable disk.  Please insert a bootable floppy and
press any key to try again ...
U••••••

•• !"#$%&'(••*+,-./0123456789:;••=>?@ABCDEFGHIJKLMN••PQRSTUVWXYZ[\]
^_`a••cdefghijklmnopqrst••vwxyz{|}~••••••••••••••••••••••••••••••••
••••••••••••••••••••••••••••••••••••••••••10+0 records in
10+0 records out
5120 bytes (5.1 kB, 5.0 KiB) copied, 0.019035 s, 269 kB/s
```

There is not a lot different here, but let's look a little further.

---

Let's look at a new option for the dd command, one which gives us a little more flexibility.

---

**EXPERIMENT 3-8**

---

We still want to display about 10 blocks of data at a time, but we don't want to start at the beginning of the partition, we want to skip the blocks we have already looked at.

Enter the following command and add the `skip=10` argument, which skips the first 10 blocks of data and displays the next 10.

```
[root@f26vm ~]# dd if=/dev/sdb1 bs=512 count=10 skip=10
10+0 records in
10+0 records out
5120 bytes (5.1 kB, 5.0 KiB) copied, 0.01786 s, 287 kB/s
```

---

We see in Experiment 3-8 that the second 10 blocks of the partition are empty; that is. they contain nulls, which do not print because they are null – nothing. We could continue to skip more and more blocks at the beginning of the partition or use larger increments in the count and the skip arguments, such as 20 and 20. But I will hopefully save you some time. I have found that the directory entries are displayed if I skip 250 blocks. This may not be the case for you if your USB drive is a different size or is formatted differently but it should be a good place to start.

---

**EXPERIMENT 3-9**

---

Now enter the **dd** command and skip 250 blocks.

```
[root@f26vm ~]# dd if=/dev/sdb1 bs=512 count=10 skip=250
Afile0•.txt•••••••FILE0    TXT •jgKgK•jgK••Afile1•.txt•••••••FILE1TXT
•jgKgK•jgK••Afile2•.txt•••••••FILE2    TXT •jgKgK•jgK)••Afile3•.txt•••••••FILE3
TXT •jgKgK•jgK<••Afile4•.txt•••••••FILE4    TXT •jgKgK•jgKO••Afile5•.txt•••••••FILE5
TXT •jgKgK•jgKb••Afile6A.txt•••••••FILE6    TXT •jgKgK•jgKu••Afile7E.txt•••••••FILE7
TXT •jgKgK•jgK•••Afile8•.txt•••••••FILE8    TXT •jgKgK•jgK•••Afile9M.txt•••••••FILE9
TXT •jgKgK•jgK•••10+0 records in
10+0 records out
5120 bytes (5.1 kB, 5.0 KiB) copied, 0.0165904 s, 309 kB/s
```

If you do not see the directory similar to that shown above on the first attempt, try changing the number of blocks to skip and run the experiment again. Our technical reviewer did locate the directory but using a much different skip count.

The output from this command shows the data contained in the directory of the /dev/sdb1 partition. This shows that directories are just data on the partition just like any other data.

I also found that skipping 500 blocks displays the data from one of the files as shown in Experiment 3-10, below.

---

## EXPERIMENT 3-10

This time enter the dd command and skip 500 blocks with a count of 5 to display only 5 blocks. Note that these results are line-wrapped but each line in dmesg starts with the timestamp.

```
[root@f26vm ~]# dd if=/dev/sdb1 bs=512 count=5 skip=500
msg='unit=systemd-journald comm="systemd" exe="/usr/lib/systemd/systemd"
hostname=? addr=? terminal=? res=success'
[    6.430317] audit: type=1131 audit(1509824958.916:49): pid=1 uid=0
    auid=4294967295 ses=4294967295 msg='unit=systemd-journald comm="systemd"
    exe="/usr/lib/systemd/systemd" hostname=? addr=? terminal=? res=success'
[    6.517686] audit: type=1305 audit(1509824959.007:50): audit_enabled=1
    old=1 auid=4294967295 ses=4294967295 res=1
[    6.665314] audit: type=1130 audit(1509824959.154:51): pid=1 uid=0
    auid=4294967295 ses=4294967295 msg='unit=systemd-journald comm="systemd"
    exe="/usr/lib/systemd/systemd" hostname=? addr=? terminal=? res=success'
[    6.671171] audit: type=1130 audit(1509824959.160:52): pid=1 uid=0
    auid=4294967295 ses=4294967295 msg='unit=kmod-static-nodes
    comm="systemd" exe="/usr/lib/systemd/systemd" hostname=? addr=?
    terminal=? res=success'
[    6.755493] audit: type=1130 audit(1509824959.244:53): pid=1 uid=0
    auid=4294967295 ses=4294967295 msg='unit=systemd-sysctl comm="systemd"
    exe="/usr/lib/systemd/systemd" hostname=? addr=? terminal=? res=success'
[    9.782860] RAPL PMU: hw unit of domain pp0-core 2^-0 Joules
[    9.783651] RAPL PMU: hw unit of domain package 2^-0 Joules
[    9.784427] RAPL PMU: hw unit of domain pp1-gpu 2^-0 Joules
```

```
[    9.785611] ppdev: user-space parallel port driver
[    9.948408] Adding 4177916k swap on /dev/mapper/fedora_f26vm-
   swap.  Priority:-1 extents:1 across:4177916k FS
[   10.082485] snd_intel8x0 0000:00:05.0: white list rate for 1028:0177 is 48000
[   10.441113] EXT4-fs (sda1): mounted filesystem with ordered data mode.
   Opts: (null)
[   11.456654] kauditd_printk_skb: 15 callbacks suppressed
[   11.457548] audit: type=1130 audit(1509824963.942:69): pid=1 uid=0
   auid=4294967295 ses=4294967295 msg='unit=lvm2-pvscan@8:2 comm="systemd"
   exe="/usr/lib/systemd/systemd" hostname=? addr=? terminal=? res=success'
[   11.523286] audit: type=1130 audit(1509824964.012:70): pid=1 uid=0
   auid=4294967295 ses=4294967295 msg='unit=systemd-fsck@dev-mapper-fedora_
   f26vm\x2dhome co5+0 records in
5+0 records out
2560 bytes (2.6 kB, 2.5 KiB) copied, 0.0223881 s, 114 kB/s
```

I have no idea which file the data is from. We could figure it out if we really wanted to, but that is not necessary for the purposes of this book. Note that the locations of the directory and the files themselves may be different on your drive. You may have to search a bit in order to find them, but this is where they were on my device.

You should definitely take some time on your own to explore the contents of the USB drive. You might be surprised at what you find.

# Streams of Randomness

It turns out that randomness is a desirable thing in computers. Who knew. There are a number of reasons that SysAdmins might want to generate a stream of random data. Data streams generated from other sources such as a file or device like a hard drive partition should be expected to contain non-random data that could be used by black-hat hackers to obtain private or classified data. Using a stream of data that is guaranteed to be random provides a safer alternative.

A stream of random data is sometimes useful to overwrite the contents of a complete partition, such as /dev/sda1, or even the entire hard drive as in /dev/sda.

Although deleting files may seem permanent, it is not. Many forensic tools are available and can be used by trained forensic specialists to easily recover files that have supposedly been deleted. It is much more difficult to recover files that have been overwritten by random data. I have frequently needed not just to delete all of the data on a hard drive but to overwrite it so it cannot be recovered. I do this for customers and friends who have "gifted" me with their old computers for reuse or recycling.

Regardless of what ultimately happens to the computers, I promise the persons who donate the computers that I will scrub all of the data from the hard drive. I remove the drives from the computer, put them in my plug-in hard drive docking station, and used a command similar to the one in Experiment 3-11 to overwrite all of the data, but instead of just spewing the random data to STDOUT as in this Experiment. I redirect it to the device file for the hard drive that needs to be overwritten – but don't do that.

---

## EXPERIMENT 3-11

Enter this command to print an unending stream of random data to STDOUT.

```
[student@testvm1 ~]$ cat /dev/urandom
```

Use Ctrl-C to break out and stop the stream of data.

---

If you are extremely paranoid, the shred command can be used to overwrite individual files as well as partitions and complete drives. It can write over the device as many times as needed for you to feel secure, with multiple passes using both random data as well as specifically sequenced patterns of data designed to prevent even the most sensitive equipment from recovering any data from the hard drive. As with other utilities that use random data, the random stream is supplied by the /dev/urandom device.

Random data is also used as the input seed to programs that generate random passwords and random data and numbers for use in scientific and statistical calculations. I will cover randomness and other interesting data sources in a bit more detail in Chapter 4: "Everything Is a File."

# Summary

In this chapter you learned that STDIO is nothing more than streams of data. This data can be almost anything from the output of a command to list the files in a directory, or an unending stream of data from a special device like /dev/urandom, or even a stream that contains all of the raw data from a hard drive or a partition. You learned some different and interesting methods to generate different types of data streams and how to use the dd command to explore the contents of a hard drive.

Any device on a Linux computer can be treated like a data stream. You can use ordinary tools like dd and cat to dump data from a device into a STDIO data stream that can be processed using other ordinary Linux tools.

So far we have not done anything with these data streams except to look at them. But wait – there's more! Read on.

# Summary

# CHAPTER 4

# Transforming Data Streams

This chapter introduces the use of pipes to connect streams of data from one utility program to another using STDIO. You will learn that the function of these programs is to transform the data in some manner. You will also learn about the use of redirection to redirect the data to a file.

I use the term "transform" in conjunction with these programs because the primary task of each is to transform the incoming data from STDIN in a specific way as intended by the SysAdmin and to send the transformed data to STDOUT for possible use by another transformer program or redirection to a file.

The standard term, "filters," implies something with which I don't agree. By definition, a filter is a device or a tool that removes something, such as an air filter removes airborne contaminants so that the internal combustion engine of your automobile does not grind itself to death on those particulates. In my high school and college chemistry classes, filter paper was used to remove particulates from a liquid. The air filter in my home HVAC system removes particulates that I don't want to breathe.

Although they do sometimes filter out unwanted data from a stream, I much prefer the term "transformers" because these utilities do much more. They can add data to a stream, modify the data in some amazing ways, sort it, rearrange the data in each line, perform operations based on the contents of the data stream, and so much more.

Feel free to use whichever term you prefer, but I prefer transformers.

© David Both 2018
D. Both, *The Linux Philosophy for SysAdmins*, https://doi.org/10.1007/978-1-4842-3730-4_4

# Data Streams as Raw Materials

Data streams are the raw materials upon which the Core Utilities and many other CLI tools perform their work. As its name implies, a data stream is a stream of data being passed from one file, device, or program to another using STDIO.

Data streams can be manipulated by inserting transformers into the stream using pipes. Each transformer program is used by the SysAdmin to perform some operation on the data in the stream, thus changing its contents in some manner. Redirection can then be used at the end of the pipeline to direct the data stream to a file. As has already been mentioned, that file could be an actual data file on the hard drive, or a device file such as a drive partition, a printer, a terminal, a pseudo-terminal, or any other device[1] connected to a computer.

The ability to manipulate these data streams using these small yet powerful transformer programs is central to the power of the Linux command line interface. Many of the Core Utilities are transformer programs and use STDIO.

# Pipe Dreams

Pipes are critical to our ability to do the amazing things on the command line, so much so that I think it is important to recognize that they were invented by Douglas McIlroy[2] during the early days of Unix. Thanks, Doug! The Princeton University web site has a fragment of an interview[3] with McIlroy in which he discusses the creation of the pipe and the beginnings of the Unix Philosophy.

Notice the use of pipes in the simple command-line program shown in Experiment 4-1 that lists each logged-in user a single time no matter how many logins they have active.

---

[1]In Linux systems, all hardware devices are treated as files. More about this in Chapter 5, "Everything Is a File."

[2]Wikipedia, Biography of Douglas McIlroy, http://www.cs.dartmouth.edu/~doug/biography

[3]Princeton University, Interview with Douglas McIlroy, https://www.princeton.edu/~hos/frs122/precis/mcilroy.htm

```
┌─────────────────────────────────────────────────────────────────┐
│                        EXPERIMENT 4-1                           │
└─────────────────────────────────────────────────────────────────┘
```

If you have not done so already, open one terminal session and log in as the student user and a second terminal session as root.

Enter the command shown below on one line.

```
[student@testvm1 ~]$ w | tail -n +3 | awk '{print $1}' | sort | uniq
root
student
```

You could also use **sort  -u** instead of the **uniq** transformer to ensure that only one instance of each logon ID is printed. Try it by entering the command below.

```
[student@testvm1 ~]$ w | tail -n +3 | awk '{print $1}' | sort -u
root
student
```

The results from these commands produce two lines of data that show that the users root and student are both logged in. It does not show how many times each user is logged in.

Both of the command pipelines in Experiment 4-1 produce the same result. There is at least one other way of changing the command pipeline in this experiment while still generating the same result. Can you find it? There can be many ways to accomplish the same task. None are right or wrong – just different. Using the second form is, in my opinion, both simpler and more elegant. We will cover those attributes in Chapter 17, Strive for elegance," and Chapter 18, "Find the Simplicity."

Pipes – represented by the vertical bar ( | ) – are the syntactical glue, the operator, that connects these command line utilities together Pipes allow the Standard Output from one command to be "piped", that is, streamed from Standard Output of one command to the Standard Input of the next command.

```
/ Pipes were invented by Doug \
\ McIlroy. Thanks, Doug.       /
--------------------------------
        \   ^__^
         \  (oo)_____
            (__)\       )\/\
             ||----w |
             ||     ||
```

A string of programs connected with pipes is called a pipeline, and the programs that use STDIO are referred to officially as filters, but I prefer the term transformers.

Think about how this program would have to work if we could not pipe the data stream from one command to the next. The first command would perform its task on the data and then the output from that command would have to be saved in a file. The next command would have to read the stream of data from the intermediate file and perform its modification of the data stream, sending its own output to a new, temporary data file. The third command would have to take its data from the second temporary data file and perform its own manipulation of the data stream and then store the resulting data stream in yet another temporary file. At each step the data file names would have to be transferred from one command to the next in some way.

I cannot even stand to think about that because it is so complex. Remember that simplicity rocks!

# Building Pipelines

When I am doing something new, solving a new problem, I usually do not just type in a complete bash command pipeline from scratch, as in Experiment 4-1 off the top of my head. I usually start with just one or two commands in the pipeline and build from there by adding more commands to further process the data stream. This allows me to view the state of the data stream after each of the commands in the pipeline and make corrections as they are needed.

In Experiment 4-2 you should enter the command shown on each line and run it as shown to see the results. This will give you a feel for how you can build up complex pipelines in stages.

```
┌─────────────────────────────────────────────────────────────────────┐
│                          EXPERIMENT 4-2                              │
└─────────────────────────────────────────────────────────────────────┘
```

Enter the commands as shown on each line. Observe the changes in the data stream as each new transformer utility is appended to the data stream using the pipe. For the first pass at this, use the **uniq** tool. The final result of this experiment will be the same as that from Experiment 4-1.

```
[student@f26vm ~]$ w

[student@f26vm ~]$ w | tail -n +3

[student@f26vm ~]$ w | tail -n +3 | awk '{print $1}'

[student@f26vm ~]$ w | tail -n +3 | awk '{print $1}' | sort

[student@f26vm ~]$ w | tail -n +3 | awk '{print $1}' | sort | uniq
```

Now let's also use the alternate form of this last command.

```
[student@f26vm ~]$ w | tail -n +3 | awk '{print $1}' | sort -n
```

The results of this Experiment illustrate the changes to the data stream performed by each of the transformer utility programs in the pipeline.

It is possible to build up very complex pipelines that can transform the data stream using many different utilities that work with STDIO.

# Redirection

Redirection is the capability to redirect the STDOUT data stream of a program to a file instead of to the default target of the display. The "greater than" ( > ) character, aka "gt," is the syntactical symbol for redirection. Experiment 4-3 shows how to redirect the output data stream of the df -h command to the file diskusage.txt.

---

## EXPERIMENT 4-3

Redirecting the STDOUT of a command can be used to create a file containing the results from that command.

```
[student@f26vm ~]$ df -h > diskusage.txt
```

There is no output to the terminal from this command unless there is an error. This is because the STDOUT data stream is redirected to the file and STDERR is still directed to the STDOUT device, which is the display. You can view the contents of the file you just created using this next command.

```
[student@f26vm ~]$ cat diskusage.txt
```

| Filesystem | Size | Used | Avail | Use% | Mounted on |
|---|---|---|---|---|---|
| devtmpfs | 2.0G | 0 | 2.0G | 0% | /dev |
| tmpfs | 2.0G | 0 | 2.0G | 0% | /dev/shm |
| tmpfs | 2.0G | 988K | 2.0G | 1% | /run |
| tmpfs | 2.0G | 0 | 2.0G | 0% | /sys/fs/cgroup |
| /dev/mapper/fedora_f26vm-root | 49G | 11G | 36G | 24% | / |
| tmpfs | 2.0G | 0 | 2.0G | 0% | /tmp |
| /dev/sda1 | 976M | 158M | 752M | 18% | /boot |
| /dev/mapper/fedora_f26vm-home | 25G | 45M | 24G | 1% | /home |
| tmpfs | 396M | 0 | 396M | 0% | /run/user/991 |
| tmpfs | 396M | 0 | 396M | 0% | /run/user/1001 |

When using the > symbol for redirection, the specified file is created if it does not already exist. If it already does exist, the contents are overwritten by the data stream from the command. You can use double greater than symbols, >>, to append the new data stream to any existing content in the file as illustrated in Experiment 4-4.

---

### EXPERIMENT 4-4

---

This command appends the new data stream to the end of the existing file.

```
[student@f26vm ~]$ df -h >> diskusage.txt
```

You can use cat and/or less to view the diskusage.txt file in order to verify that the new data was appended to the end of the file.

---

The < (less than) symbol redirects data to the STDIN of the program. You might want to use this method to input data from a file to STDIN of a command that does not take a filename as an argument but that does use STDIN. Although input sources can be redirected to STDIN, such as a file that is used as input to grep, it is generally not necessary as grep also takes a filename as an argument to specify the input source. Most other commands also take a filename as an argument for their input source.

One example of using redirection to STDIN is with the **od** command as shown in Experiment 4-5. The -N 50 option prevents the output from continuing forever. You could use Ctrl-C to terminate the output data stream if you don't use the -N option to limit it.

---

### EXPERIMENT 4-5

---

This Experiment illustrates the use of redirection as input to STDIN.

```
[student@f26vm ~]$ od -c -N 50 < /dev/urandom
0000000 331 203   _ 307   ]   { 335 337   6 257 347       $   J   Z   U
0000020 245  \0   `  \b   8 307 261 207   K   :   }   S   \ 276 344   ;
0000040 336 256 221 317 314 241 352   ` 253 333 367 003 374 264 335   4
0000060   U  \n 347   (   h 263 354 251   u   H   ] 315 376   W 205  \0
0000100 323 263 024   % 355 003 214 354 343   \   a 254   #   `   {   _
0000120   b 201 222   2 265   [ 372 215 334 253 273 250   L   c 241 233
<snip>
```

The size of the font for this Experiment has been reduced so that the lines would fit without wrapping. It is much easier to understand the nature of the results.

---

Redirection can be the source or the termination of a pipeline. Because it is so seldom needed as input, redirection is usually used as termination of a pipeline.

# Redirecting STDERR

STDERR is designed to be printed on the STDERR device – usually the same terminal session as STDOUT – in order to ensure that error messages are displayed and can be viewed by the SysAdmin rather than being passed through the pipeline and possibly lost. Even when STDOUT is redirected or piped to the next stage of a pipeine, STDERR is normally displayed on the terminal.

Experiment 4-6 illustrates the default behavior for the STDERR data stream and then moves on to show how to create alternative behaviors.

---

**EXPERIMENT 4-6**

Let's start this experiment by creating some test files in your home directory. Enter the following command on a single line.

```
[student@testvm1 ~]$ for I in 0 1 2 3 4 5 6 7 8 9;do echo "This is file $I" >
file$I.txt;done
```

Now use the cat command to concatenate the content of three of these files. At this point we are still not expecting any errors, just setting the stage.

```
[student@testvm1 ~]$ cat file0.txt file4.txt file7.txt > test1.txt
[student@testvm1 ~]$ cat test1.txt
This is file 0
This is file 4
This is file 7
```

So far everything is working as it should. Now let's change the command to generate a simple error by specifying a nonexistent file. Instead of file4.txt, we specify filex.txt, which does not exist.

```
[student@testvm1 ~]$ cat file0.txt filex.txt file7.txt > test1.txt
cat: filex.txt: No such file or directory
[student@testvm1 ~]$ cat test1.txt
This is file 0
This is file 7
```

---

The error message generated by the cat command appears on the terminal while the data is still redirected to test1.txt. We can redirect STDERR data to the file, too.

```
[student@testvm1 ~]$ cat file0.txt filex.txt file7.txt &> test1.txt
[student@testvm1 ~]$ cat test1.txt
This is file 0
cat: filex.txt: No such file or directory
This is file 7
```

In the command above, both STDOUT and STDERR are redirected to the file test1.txt. Now let's make an assumption that we want the STDOUT to continue to be sent to the terminal while we do not care about the error messages. To do this we redirect STDERR to /dev/null.[4] First we ensure that test1.txt is empty so that there is no data stored in it to confuse the results.

```
[student@testvm1 ~]$ echo "" > test1.txt
[student@testvm1 ~]$ cat test1.txt

[student@testvm1 ~]$ cat file0.txt filex.txt file7.txt 2> /dev/null
This is file 0
This is file 7
[student@testvm1 ~]$ cat test1.txt

[student@testvm1 ~]$
```

We can also redirect STDERR to the test1.txt file while still sending STDOUT to the terminal.

```
[student@testvm1 ~]$ cat file0.txt filex.txt file7.txt 2> test1.txt
This is file 0
This is file 7
[student@testvm1 ~]$ cat test1.txt
cat: filex.txt: No such file or directory
[student@testvm1 ~]$
```

We may also find it useful to redirect STDOUT to one file and STDERR to a different file. That looks like the command below.

---

[4]We will learn more about device special files like /dev/null in Chapter 5, "Everything is a File."

```
[student@testvm1 ~]$ cat file0.txt filex.txt file7.txt 1> good.txt 2> error.txt
[student@testvm1 ~]$ cat good.txt
This is file 0
This is file 7
[student@testvm1 ~]$ cat error.txt
cat: filex.txt: No such file or directory
[student@testvm1 ~]$
```

The flexibility offered by redirection makes it possible for us to perform some amazing things in a very elegant way. For example, I have some scripts that spew large amounts of output that make it difficult to determine whether any errors have occurred. By redirecting STDOUT to one log file and STDERR to a different log file, I can readily determine whether there were any errors or not without having to search nearly a megabyte of data.

# The Pipeline Challenge

I write prolifically for Opensource.com[5] and a couple of years ago I posed a challenge for our readers, one that involves pipes as a required component of the solution. It is a simple problem with a solution that I use frequently.

# The Problem

I have a number of computers configured to send administrative emails to my own email account. I have configured procmail on my email server to move most of these administrative emails into a single folder to make it easy to find them all. Over the previous couple of years, I had collected over 50,000 emails in that folder. Those emails consisted of output from rkhunter (Rootkit hunter), logwatch, cron jobs, and Fail2Ban, among others.

---

[5]http://opensource.com

The messages I am interested in are from Fail2Ban, which is Free Open Source Software that dynamically bans IP addresses of hosts that attempt to maliciously access my own hosts, primarily the firewalls on the Internet. Fail2Ban does this by adding rules to IPTables. Each time an IP address is banned for multiple failure attempts at SSH login, Fail2Ban sends an email.

The objective of the challenge was to create a single command-line program to count the number of emails from each IP Address that has attempted to access my hosts using SSH. Entrants would download the admin.index file containing CSV data exported from my email client with more than 50,000 subject lines extracted from the emails. All of the subject lines were included in the data available to the entrants, so part of the task would be to extract only the subject lines pertaining to banned SSH connections. A tiny sample of the data that entrants had available to work with is shown in Figure 4-1. Note that some lines are wrapped in the figure, but you get the idea.

```
"[Fail2Ban] SSH: banned 186.101.2.130 from wally2.","Fail2Ban
<fail2ban@example.com>","root@wally2.example.org",06/11/2015 14:59, ,
<fail2ban@example.com>","root@wally2.example.org",06/12/2015 0:10, ,
"[Fail2Ban] SSH: banned 91.200.12.21 from smwally","Fail2Ban
<fail2ban@church-ral.org>","root@smwally.church-ral.org",06/12/2015 0:31, ,
"Cron <root@david> time /usr/local/bin/rsbu -vubd1","(Cron Daemon)
<root@david1.example.org>","david@example.org",06/12/2015 1:01, ,
"Cron <root@office1> /usr/local/bin/dbu -bu","root@office1.church-ral.org
(Cron Daemon)","david@example.org",06/12/2015 1:07, ,
"Logwatch for wally1.example.org
(Linux)","logwatch@wally1.example.org","root@wally1.example.org",06/12/2015 3:11, ,
"rkhunter Daily Run on david.example.org","root
<root@david1.example.org>","root@david1.example.org",06/12/2015 3:12, ,
"rkhunter Daily Run on office1.church-ral.org","root <root@office1.church-
ral.org>","root@office1.church-ral.org",06/12/2015 3:12, ,
"Logwatch for alice1.example.org
(Linux)","logwatch@alice1.example.org","root@alice1.example.org",06/12/2015 3:48, ,
"[Fail2Ban] SSH: banned 212.118.132.162 from smwal","Fail2Ban
<fail2ban@church-ral.org>","root@smwally.church-ral.org",06/12/2015 5:04, ,
"[Fail2Ban] SSH: banned 82.187.240.70 from smwally","Fail2Ban
<fail2ban@church-ral.org>","root@smwally.church-ral.org",06/12/2015 5:12, ,
"[Fail2Ban] SSH: banned 132.248.173.10 from smwall","Fail2Ban
<fail2ban@church-ral.org>","root@smwally.church-ral.org",06/12/2015 5:22, ,
```

*Figure 4-1.* *A sample of the CSV data used in the challenge*

The rules stated that the command-line program should be only one line long and must use pipes to channel the flow of data from one command to the next. For extra credit the results could include the name of the country of each IP address.

# The Solutions

We received entries from Opensource.com readers residing in many countries around the world. Some people submitted multiple solutions but the contest rules stated that only the entrant's first solution would be considered. So some good entries had to be disqualified because they were a second or third entry by the same person.

I have my own very simple solution shown in Figure 4-2. It would not have been a winner, however, even if I had been eligible. In fact, many of the contest entries provided much better solutions than my own.

```
grep -i banned admin.index | grep SSH | awk '{print $4}' | sort
-n | uniq -c | sort -n
```

***Figure 4-2.*** *My own solution to the problem*

My own solution provides a list sorted in ascending order of IP Addresses with the most entries with the source data taken from the admin.index file. That last sort in my solution was not a requirement to win the contest, but it is something I like to do to see from where the most attacks are emanating.

My solution produced 5,377 lines of output, so there are about that number of unique IP addresses. However, my solution does not take into account some anomalous entries that have no IP addresses in them. As I was thinking about the objectives for the command-line program in this challenge, I decided not to specify the number of lines that should be produced as I felt that might be too restrictive and would place an unnecessary constraint on the entries. I think that was a good idea because many of the entries we received produce somewhat different numbers. So a winning solution need not produce the same number of lines of data as my solution.

## First Entry with Solution

Michael DiDomenico of Hamilton, NJ, USA, submitted the very first entry of the contest and it was also a working one. I particularly like Michael's use of the sort command to ensure that the output is sorted in order by IP Address.

Michael's entry, shown in Figure 4-3, produces 5,295 lines of output, which is not very different from my own result. This is also the number of lines of output that many of the other entries produced.

```
grep "SSH: banned" admin.index | sed 's/","/ /g'| cut -f4 -d" " | grep "^[0-9]"
| sort -k1,1n -k2,2 -k3,3n -k4,4n -t. | uniq -c
```

***Figure 4-3.*** *Michael DiDomenico submitted the first entry with a correct solution*

## Shortest Solutions

The shortest solution that was eligible to win a prize was submitted by Víctor Ochoa Rodríguez of Madrid, España. His 65-character solution in Figure 4-4 is very elegant and uses egrep to select only the lines that contain SSH along with an IP address while only printing that portion of each line that matches the expression. I learned about the -o option from this entry, so thanks to Víctor for that bit of new knowledge.

```
egrep -o '".F.*H.*\.[0-9]+' admin.index|cut -d\ -f4|sort|uniq -c
```

***Figure 4-4.*** *Víctor Ochoa Rodríguez submitted this solution, which is the shortest one that was eligible for a prize*

Figure 4-5 shows another entry that was actually shorter than Víctor's. Teresa e Junior submitted an entry that is 58 characters in length. She was not eligible to win a prize in the contest, but her solution deserved to be recognized at least informally in this category.

```
grep SSH admin.index|grep -Po '(\d+\.){3}\d+'|sort|uniq -c
```

***Figure 4-5.*** *This submission by Teresa e Junior was the shortest of all*

Both of these solutions also produce 5,295 lines of output.

# Most Creative Solution

The first two categories can be judged on purely objective criteria so I wanted to have this category to provide an additional opportunity to recognize folks who came up with more creative answers. The results in this category were based on my purely subjective opinion, and in my opinion there was a tie in this category.

Przemo Firszt of Co. Cork, Ireland, submitted the entry in Figure 4-6, which is very interesting and creative for its use of the tee and xargs commands. It is also unique because, in addition to using pipes, it also stores intermediate data in a file using the tee command, which also passes the data on to STDOUT, and the final output is redirected to another file rather than being allowed to go to STDOUT. It even cleans up at the end by deleting the temporary file.

```
grep SSH admin.index | awk '{print $4}' | grep -E '[0-9]{1,3}\.[0-9]{1,3}\.[0-9]{1,3}\.[0-9]{1,3}' | sed 's/\".*//' | tee ips | xargs -I % sh -c "echo -ne '%\t' ; grep -o % ips | wc -w" | sort | uniq > results ; rm ips
```

***Figure 4-6.*** *Przemo Firszt submitted this creative entry that uses tee and xargs*

This solution produces 7,403 lines of output. That appears to be because there are multiple lines for many of the IP addresses. So although this is not a perfect solution, it would take very little modification to produce only a single line of output for each IP Address.

Tim Chase of Frisco, TX, US., was the other winner in this category. Tim's entry, seen in Figure 4-7, is unique in its use of the curl command to download the file from the server, and then it uses the awk command to both select the desired lines in the file and select only the IP Address from each line. Tim's solution is the only one that included code to perform the file download. It results in 5,295 lines of output.

```
curl -s http://www.millennium-technology.com/downloads/admin.index|awk -F, '$1~/SSH: banned/{print $1}'|grep -o '[0-9]\+\.[0-9]\+\.[0-9]\+\.[0-9]\+'|sort|uniq -c
```

***Figure 4-7.*** *Tim Chase's solution is creative in its use of curl to download the file*

## Extra Credit Solution

A number of entries were aimed at the extra credit solution requirement to provide the country names for each IP Address. I found two of the entries that especially piqued my interest. Both of these entries use the GeoIP package to provide a local database for obtaining the country information. A couple of other entries used the `whois` command but, among other issues, `whois` uses a remote database and, when accessed too rapidly from a single IP address, is subject to blocking. The GeoIP package is available in the standard Fedora repository and the EPEL repository for CentOS.

Gustavo Yzaguirre, from Argentina, submitted the entry in Figure 4-8, which I like because it gives first a bare-bones listing of IP addresses with a count and then lists the countries. It produces 16,419 lines of output, many of which are duplicates. Gustavo says it is not optimized, but that was not one of the requirements.

```
awk '/SSH: banned/ && $4 ~ /^[0-9]/ {print $4}' admin.index | sed 's/[^0-9.]*//g'
| sort | uniq -c | awk '{printf $1 " " $2 " "; system("geoiplookup "$2)};' | sort
-gr | sed 's/ GeoIP Country Edition: / /g'
```

***Figure 4-8.*** *Gustavo Yzaguirre submitted this entry that lists the country name for each IP address*

Dejan Bogdanovic, of Belgrade, Serbia, also submitted a very interesting entry for the extra credit solution. His entry in Figure 4-9 lists the IP addresses in descending order of frequency along with the country information. Dejan's entry produces 5,764 lines of output.

```
cat admin.index | egrep -o '([0-9]*\.){3}[0-9]*' | sort -n | uniq -c | sort -nr |
awk '{ORS=" "} {print $1} {print $2} {system("geoiplookup " $2 "| cut -d: -f 2 |
xargs")}'
```

***Figure 4-9.*** *This extra credit entry was submitted by Dejan Bogdanovic*

# Thoughts on the Solutions

I was amazed at the many different solutions to this problem that Opensource.com readers were able to come up with. In part, I think that this is because many of the entrants interpreted the desired results with a bit of freedom, in many cases adding more information than was asked for in the original specifications.

There was also a good bit of creativity in all of the solutions. No two solutions were alike, which underscores the fact that everyone approaches problem solving differently. And even when some solutions appeared to start out from the same perspective, each had its own personality and bit of flair that can only be the product of the unique perspectives brought to the table by SysAdmins who are diverse, smart, knowledgeable, and very creative.

Let's take this contest as a metaphor for the real world. The contest rules are the specifications for this project. Each SysAdmin, even the ones that were not winners in the contest, took those specifications and crafted solutions that met the requirements and which were also insanely creative. Each solution illustrates the use of transformer programs and the use of STDIO to transform a data stream in a manner that ultimately provides meaningful information to the SysAdmin.

This contest also beautifully illustrates that "There is no should." There is no one way in which you "should" do anything. It is the results that count. You know, this sounds so good that I should make it one of the tenets. I had not up to this point in my writing thought of this as a tenet, but it is and so I will create that chapter right now.

# Summary

It is only with the use of pipes and redirection that many of the tenets of the Linux Philosophy for SysAdmins make sense. It is the pipes that transport STDIO data streams from one program or file to another. In this chapter you have learned that the use of piping streams of data through one or more transformer programs supports powerful and flexible manipulation of data in those streams.

Each of the programs in the pipeline demonstrated in the Experiments, and in all of the contest entries showcased here, is small and each does one thing well. They are also transformers, that is. they take Standard Input, process it in some way, and then send the output to Standard Output. Implementation of these programs as transformers to send processed data streams from their own Standard Output to the Standard Input of the other programs is complementary to and necessary for the implementation of pipes as a Linux tool.

# CHAPTER 5

# Everything Is a File

This is one of the most important concepts that makes Linux especially flexible and powerful: Everything is a file. That is, everything can be the source of a data stream, the target of a data stream, or in many cases both. In this chapter you will explore what "everything is a file" really means and learn to use that to your advantage as a SysAdmin.

> *The whole point with "everything is a file" is ... the fact that you can use common tools to operate on different things.*
>
> —Linus Torvalds in an email

## What Is a File?

Here is a trick question for you. Which of the following are files?

- Directories
- Shell scripts
- Running terminal emulators
- LibreOffice documents
- Serial ports
- Kernel data structures
- Kernel tuning parameters
- Hard drives - /dev/sda
- /dev/null
- Partitions - /dev/sda1

© David Both 2018
D. Both, *The Linux Philosophy for SysAdmins*, https://doi.org/10.1007/978-1-4842-3730-4_5

- Logical Volumes (LVM) - /dev/mapper/volume1-tmp

- Printers

- Sockets

To Unix and Linux, they are all files and that is one of the most amazing concepts in the history of computing. It makes possible some very simple yet powerful methods for performing many administrative tasks that might otherwise be extremely difficult or impossible.

Linux handles almost everything as a file. This has some interesting and amazing implications. This concept makes it possible to copy an entire hard drive, boot record included, because the entire hard drive is a file, just as are the individual partitions.

"Everything is a file" is possible because all devices are implemented by Linux as these things called device files. Device files are not device drivers; rather they are gateways to devices that are exposed to the user.

# Device Files

Device files are technically known as device special files.[1] Device files are employed to provide the operating system and, even more importantly in an open operating system, the users, an interface to the devices that they represent. All Linux device files are located in the /dev directory, which is an integral part of the root (/) filesystem because they must be available to the operating system during early stages of the boot process – before other filesystems are mounted.

# Device File Creation

The udev daemon is designed to simplify the chaos that has overtaken the /dev directory with huge numbers of mostly unneeded devices. Understanding how udev works is key to dealing with devices, especially hotplug devices and how they can be managed.

The /dev/directory has always been the location for the device files in all Unix and Linux operating systems. In the past, device files were created at the time the operating system was created. This meant that all possible devices that might ever be used on a

---

[1]Wikipedia, Device File, https://en.wikipedia.org/wiki/Device_file

system needed to be created in advance. In fact, tens of thousands of device files needed to be created to handle all of the possibilities. It became very difficult to determine which device file actually related to a specific physical device, or if one was missing.

# udev Simplification

udev is designed to simplify this problem by creating entries in /dev only for those devices that actually currently exist at boot time or which have a high probability of actually existing on the host. This significantly reduces the total number of device files required.

In addition, udev assigns names to devices when they are plugged into the system, such as USB storage and printers, and other non-USB types of devices as well. In fact, udev treats all devices as plug and play, or plug'n'pray as some like to say, even at boot time. This makes dealing with devices consistent at all times, whether at boot time or when they are hot-plugged later.

Let's use an experiment to see how this works.

---

**EXPERIMENT 5-1**

---

Perform this experiment as root.

Plug in the USB thumb drive you prepared earlier. If you are using a VM you may also have to make the device available to the VM.

Enter these commands.

```
[root@testvm1 dev]# cd /dev ; ls -l sd*
brw-rw---- 1 root disk 8,  0 Nov 22 03:50 sda
brw-rw---- 1 root disk 8,  1 Nov 22 03:50 sda1
brw-rw---- 1 root disk 8,  2 Nov 22 03:50 sda2
brw-rw---- 1 root disk 8, 16 Nov 28 14:02 sdb
brw-rw---- 1 root disk 8, 17 Nov 28 14:02 sdb1
```

Look at the date and time on the USB device, which in my host is /dev/sdb and /dev/sdb1, respectively. The creation date and time of the device files for the USB drive and partitions on that drive should be just at the time the device was inserted into the USB port, and different from the timestamp on the other devices that would have been created at boot time. The specific results you see will be different from mine.

---

It is not necessary for us as SysAdmins to do anything else for the device files to be created. The Linux kernel takes care of everything. It is only possible to mount the partition in order to access its contents after the device file /dev/sdb1 has been created.

Greg Kroah-Hartman, one of the creators of udev, has written a paper[2] that provides some insight into the details of udev and how it is supposed to work. Note that udev has matured since the article was written and some things have changed, such as the udev rule locations and structure. Regardless, this paper provides some deep and important insight into udev and current device naming strategies.

# Naming Rules

In modern versions of Fedora and CentOS, udev stores its default naming rules in files in the /usr/lib/udev/rules.d directory, and its local rules and configuration files in the /etc/udev/rules.d directory. Each file contains a set of rules for a specific device type. CentOS 6 and earlier stored the global rules in /lib/udev/rules.d/. The location of the udev rules files may be different on your distribution.

In earlier versions of udev, there were many local rulesets created, including a set for network interface card (NIC) naming. As each NIC was discovered by the kernel and renamed by udev for the very first time, a rule was added to the ruleset for the network device type. This was initially done to ensure consistency before names had changed from "ethX" to more consistent ones.

---

**RULE CHANGE BLUES**

One of the main consequences of using udev for persistent plug'n'play naming is that it makes things much easier for the average nontechnical user. This is a good thing in the long run; however there have been migration problems and many SysAdmins were – and still are – not happy with these changes.

The rules changed over time, and there were at least three significantly different naming conventions for network interfaces cards. That naming disparity caused a great deal of confusion and many configuration files and scripts had to be rewritten multiple times during the period of these changes.

---

[2]Greg Kroah-Hartman, Linux Journal, Kernel Korner – udev – Persistent Naming in User Space, http://www.linuxjournal.com/article/7316

For example, the name of a NIC that was originally eth0 would have changed from that to em1 or p1p2, and finally to eno1. I wrote an article[3] on my technical web site that goes into some detail about these naming schemes and the reasons behind them.

Now that udev has multiple consistent default rules for determining device names, especially for NICs, storing the specific rules for each device in local configuration files is no longer required to maintain that consistency.

# Device Data Flow

Let's look at the data flow of a typical command to visualize how device special files work. Figure 5-1 illustrates a simplified data flow for a simple command. Issuing the cat /etc/resolv.conf command from a GUI terminal emulator such as Konsole or xterm causes the resolv.conf file to be read from the disk with the disk device driver handling the device specific functions such as locating the file on the hard drive and reading it. The data is passed through the device file and then from the command to the device file and device driver for pseudo-terminal 6 where it is displayed in the terminal session.

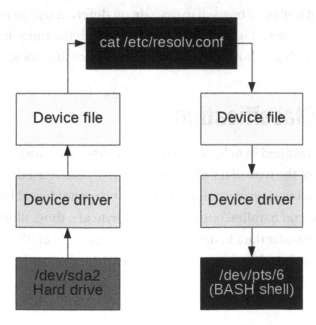

*Figure 5-1.* *Simplified data flow with device special files*

---

[3]David Both, Network Interface Card (NIC) name assignments, http://www.linux-databook.info/?page_id=4243

Of course the output of the `cat` command could have been redirected to a file in the following manner, `cat /etc/resolv.conf > /etc/resolv.bak` in order to create a backup of the file. In that case the data flow on the left side of Figure 5-1 would remain the same while the data flow on the right would be through the /dev/sda2 device file, the hard drive device driver, and then back onto the hard drive in the /etc directory as the new file, resolv.bak.

These device special files make it very easy to use Standard Streams (STDIO) and redirection to access any and every device on a Linux or Unix computer. They provide a consistent and easy to access interface to every device. Simply directing a data stream to a device file sends the data to that device.

One of the most important things to remember about these device special files is that they are not device drivers. They are most accurately described as portals or gateways to the device drivers. Data is passed from an application or the operating system to the device file, which then passes it to the device driver, which then sends it to the physical device.

By using these device files that are separate from the device drivers, it is possible for users and programs to have a consistent interface to every device on the host computer. This is how common tools can be used to operate on different things as Linus says.

The device drivers are still responsible for dealing with the unique requirements of each physical device. That is, however, outside the scope of this book.

# Device File Classification

Device files can be classified in at least two ways. The first and most commonly used classification is that of the type of data stream commonly associated with the device. For example, tty and serial devices are considered to be character based because the data stream is transferred and handled one character or byte at a time. Block type devices such as hard drives transfer data in blocks, typically a multiple of 256 bytes.

Let's take a look at the /dev/directory and some of the devices in it.

---

**EXPERIMENT 5-2**

This experiment should be performed as the user student.

Open a terminal session and display a long listing of the /dev/directory.

```
[student@f26vm ~]$ ls -l /dev | less
<snip>
brw-rw----  1 root disk      8,   0 Nov  7 07:06 sda
brw-rw----  1 root disk      8,   1 Nov  7 07:06 sda1
brw-rw----  1 root disk      8,  16 Nov  7 07:06 sdb
brw-rw----  1 root disk      8,  17 Nov  7 07:06 sdb1
brw-rw----  1 root disk      8,  18 Nov  7 07:06 sdb2
<snip>
crw--w----  1 root tty       4,   0 Nov  7 07:06 tty0
crw--w----  1 root tty       4,   1 Nov  7 07:06 tty1
crw--w----  1 root tty       4,  10 Nov  7 07:06 tty10
crw--w----  1 root tty       4,  11 Nov  7 07:06 tty11
<snip>
```

The results from this command are too long to show here in full, but you will see a list of device files with their file permissions and their major and minor identification numbers.

The voluminous output of the `ls -l` command is piped through the `less` transformer utility to allow you to page through the results; use the Page Up, Page Down, and up and down arrow keys to move around. Type **q** to quit and get out of the `less` display.

---

The pruned listing of device files shown in experiment 5-1 are just a few of the ones in the /dev/directory on my Fedora workstation. They represent disk and tty type devices among many others. Notice the leftmost character of each line in the output. The ones that have a "b" are block type devices and the ones that begin with "c" are character devices.

The more detailed and explicit way to identify device files is by using the device major and minor numbers. The disk devices have a major number of 8 that designates them as SCSI block devices. Note that all PATA and SATA hard drives have been managed by the SCSI subsystem because the old ATA subsystem was many years ago deemed as not maintainable due to the poor quality of its code. As a result, hard drives that would previously been designated as "hd[a-z]" are now referred to as "sd[a-z]".

You can probably infer the pattern of disk drive minor numbers in the small sample shown above. Minor numbers 0, 16, 32, and so on up through 240 are the whole disk numbers. So major/minor 8/16 represents the whole disk /dev/sdb and 8/17 is the device file for the first partition, /dev/sdb1. Numbers 8/34 would be /dev/sdc2.

The tty device files in the list above are numbered a bit more simply from tty0 through tty63. I find the number of tty devices a little incongruous because the whole point of the new udev system is to create device files for only those devices that actually exist; I am not sure why it is being done this way. However you can also see from the listing in Figure 5-2 that all of these device files were created at the 07:06 on November 7, which was when the host was booted. The device files on your host should also have a timestamp that is the same as the last boot time.

The Linux Allocated Devices[4] file at Kernel.org is the official registry of device types and major and minor number allocations. It can help you understand the major/ minor numbers for all currently defined devices.

# Fun with Device Files

Let's take a few minutes now and have some fun with some of these device files. We will perform a couple of fun experiments that illustrate the power and flexibility of the Linux device files.

Most Linux distributions have multiple virtual consoles, 1 through 7, that can be used to log in to a local console session with a shell interface. These can be accessed using the key combinations Ctrl-Alt-F1 for console 1, Ctrl-Alt-F2 for console 2, and so on.

---

**EXPERIMENT 5-3**

In this experiment we will show that simple commands can be used to send data between devices, in this case, different console and terminal devices. Perform this experiment as the student user.

Press **Ctrl-Alt-F2** to switch to console 2. On some distributions, the login information includes the tty (Teletype) device associated with this console, but many do not. It should be tty2 because you are in console 2. You might need to use a different key combination if you are using a local instance of a VM.

---

[4]https://www.kernel.org/doc/html/v4.11/admin-guide/devices.html

Log in to console 2 as student. Then use the who am i command—yes, just like that, with spaces—to determine which tty device is connected to this console.

```
[student@f26vm ~]$ who am i
student   tty2        2017-10-05 13:12
```

This command also shows the date and time that the user on the console logged in.

Before we proceed any further with this experiment, let's look at a listing of the tty2 and tty3 devices in /dev. We do that by using a set [23] so that only those two devices are listed.

```
[student@f26vm ~]$ ls -l /dev/tty[23]
crw--w---- 1 root tty 4, 2 Oct  5 08:50 /dev/tty2
crw--w---- 1 root tty 4, 3 Oct  5 08:50 /dev/tty3
```

There are a large number of tty devices defined at boot time, but we do not care about most of them for this experiment, just the tty2 and tty3 devices. As device files, there is nothing special about them, they are simply character type devices; note the "c" in the first column of the results. We will use these two TTY devices for this experiment. The tty2 device is attached to virtual console 2 and the tty3 device is attached to virtual console 3.

Press **Ctrl-Alt-F3** to switch to console 3 and log in again as the student user. Use the who am i command again to verify that you really are on console 3 and then enter the echo command.

```
[student@f26vm ~]$ who am i
student   tty3        2017-10-05 13:18
[student@f26vm ~]$ echo "Hello world" > /dev/tty2
```

Press **Ctrl-Alt-F2** to return to console 2. The string "Hello world" (without quotes) should displayed on console 2.

This experiment can also be performed with terminal emulators on the GUI desktop. Terminal sessions on the desktop use pseudo terminal devices in the /dev tree, such as /dev/pts/1, where pts stands for "pseudo terminal session."

Open at least two terminal sessions on the GUI desktop using Konsole, Tilix, Xterm or your other favorite graphical terminal emulator. You may open several if you wish. Determine which pseudo-terminal device files they are connected to with the **who am i** command and then choose one pair of terminal emulators to work with for this experiment. Use one to send a message to the another with the echo command.

```
[student@f26vm ~]$ who am i
student   pts/9        2017-10-19 13:21 (192.168.0.1)
[student@f26vm ~]$ w
13:23:06 up 14 days,  4:32,  9 users,  load average: 0.03, 0.08, 0.09
USER       TTY         LOGIN@   IDLE   JCPU   PCPU WHAT
student   pts/1       05Oct17  4:48m  0.04s  0.04s -bash
student   pts/2       06Oct17  2:16   2.08s  2.01s screen
student   pts/3       07Oct17  12days 0.04s  0.00s less
student   pts/4       07Oct17  2:16   0.10s  0.10s /bin/bash
root      pts/5       08:35    4:08m  0.05s  0.05s /bin/bash
root      pts/6       08:35    4:47m  1:19   1:19  htop
root      pts/7       08:35    4:40m  0.05s  0.05s /bin/bash
root      pts/8       08:50    4:32m  0.03s  0.03s /bin/bash
student   pts/9       13:21    0.00s  0.04s  0.00s w
[student@f26vm ~]$ echo "Hello world" > /dev/pts/4
```

On my test host, I sent the text "Hello world" from /dev/pts/9 to /dev/pts/4. Your terminal devices will be different from the ones I have used on my test VM. Be sure to use the correct devices for your environment for this experiment.

---

Another interesting experiment is to print a file directly to the printer using the cat command.

---

## EXPERIMENT 5-4

This experiment should be performed as the student user.

You may need to determine which device is your printer. If your printer is a USB printer, which almost all are these days, look in the /dev/usb directory for lp0, which is usually the default printer. You may find other printer device files in that directory as well.

I used LibreOffice Writer to create a short document that I then exported as a PDF file, test.pdf. Any Linux word processor will do so long as it can export to the PDF format.

We will assume that your printer device is /dev/usb/lp0, and that your printer can print PDF files directly, as most can. Be sure to use a PDF file and change the name test.pdf in the command to the name of your own file.

```
[student@f26vm ~]$ cat test.pdf > /dev/usb/lp0
```

This command should print the PDF file test.pdf on your printer.

The /dev directory contains some very interesting device files that are portals to hardware that one does not normally think of as a device like a hard drive or display. For one example, system memory – RAM – is not something that is normally considered as a "device," yet /dev/mem is the device special file through which direct access to memory can be achieved.

---

**EXPERIMENT 5-5**

---

This experiment must be run as the root user. Because you are only reading the contents of memory, this experiment poses little danger.

---

**Note**    Some testers have reported that this experiment does not work for them. I have not found any problems on several physical and virtual hosts. Just be aware that this experiment may produce a permissions error instead of the desired output.

---

If a root terminal session is not already available, open a terminal emulator session and log in as root. The next command will dump the first 200K of RAM to STDOUT.

```
[root@f26vm ~]# dd if=/dev/mem bs=2048 count=100
```

It may not look like that much and what you do see will be unintelligible. To make it a bit more intelligible – to at least display the data in a decent format that might be interpreted by an expert – pipe the output of the previous command through the **od** utility.

```
[root@f26vm ~]# dd if=/dev/mem bs=2048 count=100 | od -c
```

Root has more access to read memory than a non-root user, but most memory is protected from being written by any user, including root.

The dd command provides significantly more control than simply using the cat command to dump all of memory, which I have also tried. The dd command provides the ability to specify how much data is read from /dev/mem and would also allow me to specify the point at which to start reading data from memory. Although some memory was read using the cat command, the kernel eventually responded with the error in Figure 5-2.

You can also login as a non-root user, student, and try this command. You will get an error message because the memory you are trying to access does not belong to your user. This is a memory protection feature of Linux that keeps other users from reading or writing memory that does not belong to them.

```
ff•<f•••f<•lfffl••bhxhb••bhxh`•<f•••f>•••••••x00000x••x•flxlf••```bf•••
•••••••••••••8l•••18•ff|``•x•••••x•ff|lf•x••p•x•0000x•••••••••••••x0•••••••
•••188l••••x00x••2f•x``````x•`0xx81••00x|•v•``|ff•x•••x|••vx•••x8l`•``•v
••|••`lvff•0p000x••x•`flxl•p00000x•••••••••••x•••x•ff|`•v••|•vf`•|•x•0|0
04••••v•••x0••••l•18l••••|••0d•00•00•0000•v•8l••••••u•f`•r•fa•`•••sa•XM•
fPR•@••f•lf@f=•rf3••pf•l•@
•t••@u•••$•••••Q•ZfX•XMXMOracle VM VirtualBox
BIOSXM•••••••••_SM_}•_DMI_Y•
%XM•[••06/23/99•cat: /dev/mem: Operation not permitted
```

***Figure 5-2.*** *The error on the last line was displayed when the **cat** command attempted to dump protected memory to STDOUT*

These memory errors mean that the kernel is doing its job by protecting memory that belongs to other processes, which is exactly how it should work. So, although you can use /dev/mem to display data stored in RAM memory, access to most memory space is protected and will result in errors. Only that virtual memory that is assigned by the kernel memory manager to the bash shell running the dd command should be accessible without causing an error. Sorry, but you cannot snoop in memory that does not belong to you unless you find a vulnerability to exploit.

Many types of malware depend upon privilege escalation to allow them to read the contents of memory that they would not normally be able to access. This allows the malware to find and steal personal data such as account numbers, user ID, and stored passwords. Fortunately Linux protects against memory access by non-root users. It also protects against privilege escalation.

But even Linux security is not perfect. It is important to install security patches to protect against vulnerabilities that allow privilege escalation. You should also be aware of human factors such as the tendency people have to write down their passwords, but that is all another book.[5]

You can now see that memory is also considered to be a file and can be treated as such using the memory device file.

# Randomness, Zero, and More

There are some other very interesting device files in /dev. The device special files null, zero, random, and urandom are not associated with any physical devices. These device files provide sources of zeros, nulls, and random numbers.

The null device /dev/null can be used as a target for the redirection of output from shell commands or programs so that they are not displayed on the terminal.

---

**EXPERIMENT 5-6**

I frequently use /dev/null in my bash scripts to prevent users from being presented with output that might be confusing to them. Enter the command below to redirect the output to the null device. Nothing will be displayed on the terminal. The data is just dumped into the big bit bucket in the sky.

```
[student@f26vm ~]$ echo "Hello world" > /dev/null
```

Look at /dev/null as a source for "null" characters.

```
[student@testvm1 ~]$ cat /dev/null
[student@testvm1 ~]$ dd if=/dev/null
0+0 records in
0+0 records out
0 bytes copied, 5.2305e-05 s, 0.0 kB/s
```

There is really no visible output from the /dev/null because the null device simply returns an end of file (EOF) character. Note that the byte count is zero. The null device is much more useful as a place to redirect unwanted output so that it is removed from the data stream.

---

[5]Apress has a number of good books on security at https://www.apress.com/us/security

The /dev/random and /dev/urandom devices are both useful as data stream sources. As their names imply, they both produce random output – not just numbers but any and all byte combinations. The /dev/urandom device produces deterministic[6] random output and is very fast.

---

**EXPERIMENT 5-7**

Use this command to view typical output from /dev/urandom. You can use Ctrl-c to break out.

```
[student@f26vm ~]$ cat /dev/urandom
,3••VwM
N•g•/•l•ç•!••'⚖'•:••|R••[•t••Z••F.:H•7•,••
••z/••|•7q•Sp•"•(l_c••π••-•••••••ś•Y•••D^5•i8••"%•••&ŋ|C9!y•••f•5bPp;••C
••x••1•••U••3~•••
<snip>
```

I have shown only a part of the data stream from the command but it should give you a sense for what you should see on your system.

---

You could also pipe the output of experiment 5-6 through the od command to make it a little more human readable just for this experiment. That makes little sense for most real-world applications because it is, after all, random data.

The man page for od shows that it can be used to obtain data directly from a file as well as specify the amount of data to be read.

---

[6]Deterministic means the output is determined by a known algorithm and uses a seed string as a starting point. Each unit of output is dependent upon the previous output and the algorithm, so if you know both the seed and the algorithm, the entire data stream can be reproduced. As a result it is possible, although difficult, for a hacker to reproduce the output if the original seed is known.

```
                          EXPERIMENT 5-8
```

In this case I have used -N 128 to limit the output to 128 Bytes.

```
[student@f26vm ~]$ od /dev/urandom -N 128
0000000 043514 022412 112660 052071 161447 057027 114243 061412
0000020 154627 105675 154470 110352 135013 127206 103057 136555
0000040 033417 011054 014334 040457 157056 165542 027255 121710
0000060 125334 065600 165447 165245 020756 101514 042377 132156
0000100 116024 027770 000537 014743 170561 011122 173454 102163
0000120 074301 104771 123476 054643 105211 151753 166617 154313
0000140 103720 147660 012644 037363 077661 076453 104161 033220
0000160 056501 001771 113557 075046 102700 043405 132046 045263
0000200
```

The dd command could also be used to specify a limit to the amount of data taken from the [u]random devices but it cannot directly format the data.

The /dev/random device file produces non-deterministic[7] random output but it produces output more slowly. This output is not determined by an algorithm that is dependent only upon the previous number that was generated, but it is generated in response to keystrokes and mouse movements. This method makes it far more difficult to duplicate a specific series of random numbers. Use the cat command to view some of the output from the /dev/random device file. Try moving the mouse to see how it affects the output.

The random data generated from /dev/random and /dev/urandom, regardless of how it is read from those devices, is usually redirected to a file on some storage media or to STDIN of another program. Random data seldom needs to be viewed by the SysAdmin, developer, or the end user. But it does make a good demonstration for this experiment.

As its name implies, the /dev/zero device file produces an unending string of zeroes as output. Note that these are Octal zeroes and not the ASCII character zero (0).

---

[7]Non-deterministic results are not dependent upon the previous data in the random data stream. Thus they are more truly random than if they were deterministic.

---

**EXPERIMENT 5-9**

Use the dd command to view some output from the /dev/zero device file. Note that the byte count for this command is non-zero.

```
[student@f26vm ~]$ dd if=/dev/zero  bs=512 count=500 | od -c
0000000  \0  \0  \0  \0  \0  \0  \0  \0  \0  \0  \0  \0  \0  \0  \0  \0
*
500+0 records in
500+0 records out
256000 bytes (256 kB, 250 KiB) copied, 0.00126996 s, 202 MB/s
0764000
```

---

# Back Up the Master Boot Record

Consider, for example, the simple task of making a backup of the Master Boot Record (MBR) of a hard drive. I have had, on occasion, needed to restore or re-create my MBR, particularly the partition table. Re-creating it from scratch is very difficult. Restoring it from a saved file is easy. So let's back up the boot record of the hard drive.

Note that all of the experiments in this section must be performed as root.

---

**EXPERIMENT 5-10**

We are going to create a backup of your master boot recod (MBR), but we will not attempt to restore it.

The dd command must be run as root because for security reasons non-root users do not have access to the hard drive device files in the /dev directory. The bs value is not what you might think; it stands for Block Size. Count is the number of blocks to read from the source file.

```
[root@f26vm ~]# dd if=/dev/sda of=/tmp/myMBR.bak bs=512 count=1
```

This command creates a file, myMBR.bak in the /tmp directory. The file is 512 bytes in size and contains the contents of the MBR including the bootstrap code and partition table.

Now look at the contents of the file you just created.

```
[root@testvm1 ~]# cat /tmp/myMBR.bak
•c•••••••••••|••••!••8u
Z•••••••}•f••d•@f•D••••••••@•••••f•f•`|fL••uNf•\|f1•f•4••1•f•t;}7•••O••••Z••p
••1••r••`•••1••••••••a•&Z|••}•••}•4••}•.•••GRUB GeomHard DiskRead Error
••••<u••}•••• !••( •)•••• ••U•[root@testvm1 ~]#
```

Because there is no end-of-line character at the end of the boot sector, the command prompt is on the same line as the end of the boot record.

If the MBR were damaged, it would be necessary to boot to a rescue disk and use the command in Code Sample 5-1 that would perform the reverse operation of the one above. Notice that it is not necessary to specify the block size and block count as in the first command because the dd command will simply copy the backup file to the first sector of the hard drive and stop when it reaches the end of the source file.

---

## CODE SAMPLE 5-1

The following code would restore the backup master boot record to the first sector on the hard drive.

```
[root@testvm1 ~]#  dd if=/tmp/myMBR.bak of=/dev/sda
```

Do not run this code because it may damage your system if entered improperly.

---

So now that you have performed a backup of the boot record of your hard drive and verified the contents of that backup, let's move to a safer environment to destroy the boot record and then restore it.

---

### EXPERIMENT 5-11

---

This is a rather long experiment and it must be performed as root. You are going to make a backup of the MBR for the USB device, damage the MBR on the device, try to read the device, and then restore the MBR. Do not mount the USB drive.

Ensure that the USB drive is inserted in your computer and verify the device file name. In my case it is still /dev/sdb.

First we look at the partition table with fdisk to provide a basis for later comparison, and then we back up the MBR of the USB device and verify the content of the backup file. As in previous similar experiments, the warning messages are part of the content of the MBR.

```
[root@testvm1 ~]# fdisk -l /dev/sdb
Disk /dev/sdb: 62.5 MiB, 65536000 bytes, 128000 sectors
Units: sectors of 1 * 512 = 512 bytes
Sector size (logical/physical): 512 bytes / 512 bytes
I/O size (minimum/optimal): 512 bytes / 512 bytes
Disklabel type: dos
Disk identifier: 0x73696420

Device     Boot Start    End Sectors  Size Id Type
/dev/sdb1        2048 127999  125952 61.5M  c W95 FAT32 (LBA)

[root@f26vm ~]# dd if=/dev/sdb of=/tmp/myMBR.bak bs=512 count=1
1+0 records in
1+0 records out
512 bytes copied, 0.012374 s, 41.4 kB/s
[root@f26vm ~]# cat /tmp/myMBR.bak
•>•MSWIN4.1P•} •••)L•ONO NAME    FAT16    •}•3•••{•x•vVU•"•~•N•
•••|•E••F•E••8f$|•r<•F••fFVF•PR•F•V•• •v••^
•H••F•N•ZX••••rG8-t• V•v>•^tJNt
••F•V••S••[r•?MZu•••BJu••pPRQ••3••v••vB•••v••V$•••••••••t<•t
   ••••••}••}••3••^••D•••}•}••r••HH•N ••YZXr   @uB^
        •••'
Invalid system disk•
Disk I/O error•
Replace the disk,!••U•
```

So now comes the fun part in which we overwrite the MBR of the USB device with one 512 Byte block of random data, then view the new content of the MBR to verify the change. Notice that the warning messages are no longer there because they have been overwritten.

```
[root@f26vm ~]# dd if=/dev/urandom of=/dev/sdb bs=512 count=1
1+0 records in
1+0 records out
512 bytes copied, 0.0195473 s, 26.2 kB/s
[root@f26vm ~]# dd if=/dev/sdb bs=512 count=1
6••••%•w••pI!8k••••••$••Q••¯••••gO••\••AT••KQ•••••• ••"5•oW-•••;••
•••⌒r3••oiP•d•q••••••a••%••••N••#••&F•_•••y••?•\•••)••K••?•fa••+.••••F•'
F••~•H•••XbS•••BA•V•^••z[S•jy••••••••=aPs:••N_[◡••••b••#%•;/•••,4•}9
0••7•••◡F85••L•g••\•R4••••q••Kn|M••cy••ç••m•\••••yi{_o^•i•j
K•nry2MMSeA••••p•^E•n•v•u2•/•A•Zb•••1••I•K5•3•x•K•ia•K?•Iw••••^•1f•••
{3•p&E•••M••rbʃ•••••••••• p••K•1+0 records in
1+0 records out
512 bytes copied, 0.0137811 s, 37.2 kB/s
```

Let's try a couple more things to test out this state of affairs before we move on to restoring this MBR  First we use fdisk to verify that the USB drive no longer has a partition table, which means that the MBR has been overwritten.

```
[root@f26vm ~]# fdisk -l /dev/sdb
Disk /dev/sdb: 62.5 MiB, 65536000 bytes, 128000 sectors
Units: sectors of 1 * 512 = 512 bytes
Sector size (logical/physical): 512 bytes / 512 bytes
I/O size (minimum/optimal): 512 bytes / 512 bytes
```

An attempt to mount the original partition will fail. The error message indicates that the special device does not exist. This shows that most of the special device files are created and removed as necessary, on demand.

```
[root@f26vm ~]# mount /dev/sdb1 /mnt
mount: /mnt: special device /dev/sdb1 does not exist.
```

It is time to restore the boot record you backed up earlier. Because you used the dd command to carefully overwrite with random data only the MBR that contains the partition table for the drive, all of the other data remains intact. Restoring the MBR will make it available again. Restore the MBR, view the MBR on the device, then mount the partition and list the contents.

```
[root@f26vm ~]# dd if=/tmp/myMBR.bak of=/dev/sdb
1+0 records in
1+0 records out
512 bytes copied, 0.0738375 s, 6.9 kB/s

[root@testvm1 ~]# fdisk -l /dev/sdb
Disk /dev/sdb: 62.5 MiB, 65536000 bytes, 128000 sectors
Units: sectors of 1 * 512 = 512 bytes
Sector size (logical/physical): 512 bytes / 512 bytes
I/O size (minimum/optimal): 512 bytes / 512 bytes
Disklabel type: dos
Disk identifier: 0x73696420

Device     Boot Start    End Sectors  Size Id Type
/dev/sdb1       2048 127999  125952 61.5M  c W95 FAT32 (LBA)

[root@f26vm ~]# mount /dev/sdb1 /mnt
[root@f26vm ~]# ls -l /mnt
total 380
-rwxr-xr-x 1 root root 37001 Nov  7 08:23 file0.txt
-rwxr-xr-x 1 root root 37001 Nov  7 08:23 file1.txt
-rwxr-xr-x 1 root root 37001 Nov  7 08:23 file2.txt
-rwxr-xr-x 1 root root 37001 Nov  7 08:23 file3.txt
-rwxr-xr-x 1 root root 37001 Nov  7 08:23 file4.txt
-rwxr-xr-x 1 root root 37001 Nov  7 08:23 file5.txt
-rwxr-xr-x 1 root root 37001 Nov  7 08:23 file6.txt
-rwxr-xr-x 1 root root 37001 Nov  7 08:23 file7.txt
-rwxr-xr-x 1 root root 37001 Nov  7 08:23 file8.txt
-rwxr-xr-x 1 root root 37001 Nov  7 08:23 file9.txt
```

Wow – how cool is that! This series of experiments is designed to illustrate that you can use the fact that all devices can be treated like files and therefore use some very common but powerful CLI tools in some very interesting ways.

It is not necessary to specify the amount of data to be copied with the sb= and count= parameters because the dd command only copies the amount of data available, in this case a single 512 Byte sector.

Unmount the USB device because we are finished with it for now.

# Implications of Everything Is a File

The implications of "Everything is a file" are far-reaching and much greater than can be listed here. You have already seen some examples in the preceding experiments. But here is a short list that encompasses those and more.

- Clone hard drives.

- Back up partitions.

- Back up the master boot record (MBR).

- Install ISO images onto USB thumb drives.

- Communicate with users on other terminals.

- Print files to a printer.

- Change the contents of certain files in the /proc pseudo filesystem to modify configuration parameters of the running kernel.

- Overwrite files, partitions, or entire hard drives with random data or zeros.

- Redirect unwanted output from commands to a null device where it disappears forever.

- etc., etc., etc.

There are so many possibilities here that any list can really only scratch the surface. I am sure that you have – or will – figure out many ways to use this tenet of the Philosophy far more creatively than I have discussed here.

# Summary

It is all part of the filesystem. Everything on a Linux computer is accessible as a file in the filesystem space. The whole point of this is to be able to use common tools to operate on different things – common tools such as the standard GNU/Linux utilities and commands that work on files will also work on devices – because, in Linux, they are files.

# Using the Linux FHS

The Linux Filesystem Hierarchical Standard (FHS) defines the structure of the Linux directory tree. It names a set of standard directories and designates their purposes.

This standard has been put in place to ensure that all distributions of Linux are consistent in their directory usage. Such consistency makes writing and maintaining shell and compiled programs easier for SysAdmins because the programs, their configuration files, and their data, if any, should be located in the standard directories. This chapter is about storing programs and data in the standard and recommended locations in the directory tree and the advantages of doing so. You will learn how to refer to the Linux FHS documentation and use that knowledge in problem solving.

## Definitions

Before we get too deep into this subject, let's put some definitions of the word "filesystem" in place to try and sort some of the confusion you are likely to find about terminology. You may hear people talk about filesystems in a number of different and confusing ways. The word itself can have multiple meanings, and you may have to discern the correct meaning from the context of a discussion or document.

I will attempt to define the various meanings of the word "filesystem" based on how I have observed it being used in different circumstances. Note that, while attempting to conform to standard "official" meanings, my intent is to define the term based on its various usages.

© David Both 2018
D. Both, *The Linux Philosophy for SysAdmins*, https://doi.org/10.1007/978-1-4842-3730-4_6

1.  The entire Linux directory structure starting at the top (/) root
    directory.

2.  A specific type of data storage format such as EXT3, EXT4, BTRFS,
    XFS, and so on. Linux supports almost 100 types of filesystems
    including some very old ones, as well as some of the newest.
    Each of these filesystem types uses its own metadata structures to
    define how the data is stored and accessed.

3.  A partition or logical volume formatted with a specific type of
    filesystem that can be mounted on a specified mount point – a
    directory – on a Linux filesystem.

I will be using the term "filesystem" in the context of all of these definitions at some
point in this chapter.

# The Standard

As SysAdmins our tasks include everything from fixing problems to writing CLI programs
to perform many of our tasks for us and for others. Knowing where data of various types
are intended to be stored on a Linux system can be very helpful in resolving problems as
well as preventing them.

The latest Filesystem Hierarchical Standard (3.0)[1] is defined in a document
maintained by the Linux Foundation.[2] The document is available in multiple formats
from their web site as are historical versions of the FHS.

Table 6-1 provides a brief list of the standard, well known, and defined top-level
Linux directories and their purposes. These directories are listed in alphabetical order. I
suggest that you read the entire document in order to understand the roles played by the
many subdirectories of these top-level ones.

---

[1]http://refspecs.linuxfoundation.org/fhs.shtml

[2]The Linux Foundation maintains documents defining many Linux standards. It also sponsors the
  work of Linus Torvalds.

Note column 2, the middle column, in Table 6-1. All of the directories with a "Yes" in this column must be an integral part of the root (/) filesystem. None of these directories can be located on separate partitions or logical volumes; they must all be located in the same partition or logical volume as the root filesystem because they are an integral part of it. These directories must all be mounted at the beginning of the boot process as a single unit with the root filesystem.

The directories that have a "No" in column 2 can be created on separate partitions or logical volumes – they do not have to be separate, but they can be. These filesystems, when they are separate from the root filesystem, are mounted later in the startup sequence based on the information contained in the /etc/fstab file. There are some very good reasons for mounting these directories as separate filesystems and I will discuss those later in this chapter.

***Table 6-1.*** *The Top Level of the Linux Filesystem Hierarchical Standard*

| Directory | Part of / | Description |
| --- | --- | --- |
| / (root filesystem) | Yes | The root filesystem is the top-level directory of the filesystem. It must contain all of the files required to boot the Linux system before other filesystems are mounted. After the system is booted, all other filesystems are mounted on standard, well-defined, mount points as subdirectories of the root filesystem. |
| /bin | Yes | The /bin directory contains user executable files. |
| /boot | No | Contains the static bootloader and kernel executable and configuration files required to boot a Linux computer. |
| /dev | Yes | This directory contains the device files for every hardware device attached to the system. These are not device drivers, rather they are files that represent each device on the computer and facilitate access to those devices. |
| /etc | Yes | Contains a wide variety of system configuration files for the host computer. |
| /home | No | Home directory storage for user files. Each human user usually has a subdirectory in /home. Some organizations may choose other locations for the users' home directories. Some service or sever applications may also use different locations for home directories. For example, the Apache web server uses /var/www. You can look at the /etc/passwd file to view the home directory locations for those users. Installations that use a central file server may also have those remote home directories located on mount points other than /home. |

*(continued)*

*Table 6-1.* (*continued*)

| Directory | Part of / | Description |
|---|---|---|
| /lib | Yes | Contains shared library files that are required to boot the system. |
| /media | No | A place to mount external removable media devices such as USB thumb drives that may be connected to the host. |
| /mnt | No | A temporary mountpoint for regular filesystems (as in not removable media) that can be used while the administrator is repairing or working on a filesystem. |
| /opt | No | Optional files such as vendor-supplied application programs should be located here. |
| /proc | Virtual | Virtual filesystem used to expose access to internal kernel information and editable tuning parameters. |
| /root | Yes | This is not the root (/) filesystem. It is the home directory for the root user. |
| /sbin | Yes | System binary files. These are executables used for system administration. |
| /selinux | Virtual | This pseudo filesystem is only used when SELinux is enabled. When activated, this filesystem contains critical SELinux tools and files. |
| /sys | Virtual | This virtual filesystem contains information about the USB and PCI buses and the devices attached to each. |
| /tmp | No | Temporary directory. Used by the operating system and many programs to store temporary files. Users may also store files here temporarily. Note that files stored here may be deleted at any time without prior notice. |
| /usr | No | These are shareable, read-only files including executable binaries and libraries, man[ual] files, and other types of documentation. |
| /usr/local | No | These are typically shell programs or compiled programs and their supporting configuration files that are written locally and used by the SysAdmin or other users of the host. |
| /var | No | Variable data files are stored here. This can include things like log files, MySQL and other database files, web server data files, email inboxes, and much more. |

The /media and /mnt directories are mount points for temporary filesystem maintenance or for external devices such as USB thumb drives that contain filesystems.

There is actually one exception to the "top level" statement about Table 6-1. That is the /usr/local directory. I will discuss that directory in more detail a bit later in this chapter.

# Using a Well-Defined filesystem Structure

There are some excellent reasons for following the Linux Filesystem Hierarchical Standard. All of them make our lives as SysAdmins easier. Don't worry, I am not going to discuss the functions of each of the directories defined in the standard – after all, you can read what I have written and the more detailed online version just as easily as I can. What I am going to do is discuss how a couple of specific features of this FHS affect how I do my work.

The purpose of the Linux FHS is to provide a well-defined structure in which to store files, whether executables, data, or configuration files. The structure defined in the document, Filesystem Hierarchical Standard (3.0), and previously referenced, sets forth guidelines for file locations in Linux that are based in historical context dating back to the early days of Unix, as well as new, updated, and changing standards and conventions.

The fact is that usages do change. It is also true that the Filesystem Hierarchical Standard has changed with the times. Even further, not all distributions and software vendors interpret the FHS in the same way and some software vendors may just be ignorant of the standard.

Regardless of these facts, it is incumbent upon us as SysAdmins to adhere to the current standard in all the ways that are under our control. We cannot always control the usage by vendors, but we can certainly have our say. Don't misunderstand me – I see no widespread problems here, but if there is a problem I believe that as responsible SysAdmins we should report those issues to the proper vendor.

We should also adhere to these standards ourselves when we write code even when it seems to be just a small, insignificant bit of CLI programming.

# Linux Unified Directory Structure

The Linux filesystem directory structure consists of a hierarchy of mountable filesystems, item number 3 on the list at the beginning of this chapter. This results in easier and more consistent access to all of the directories in the hierarchy. It also provides some very useful side effects.

In some non-Linux PC operating systems, if there are multiple physical hard drives or multiple partitions, each disk or partition is assigned a drive letter. It is necessary to know on which hard drive a file or program is located, such as C: or D:. Then you issue the drive letter as a command, D:, for example to change to the D: drive, and then you use the cd command to change to the correct directory to locate the desired file. Each hard drive has its own separate and complete directory tree.

The Linux filesystem unifies all physical hard drives, partitions, and logical volumes into a single directory structure. It all starts at the top – the root (/) directory. All other directories and their subdirectories are located under the single Linux root directory. This means that there is only one single directory tree in which to search for files and programs.

This can work only because a filesystem, such as /home, /tmp, /var, /opt, or /usr can be created on separate physical hard drives, a different partition, or a different logical volume from the / (root) filesystem and then be mounted on a mountpoint as part of the root filesystem directory tree. Mountpoints are just empty directories with nothing special about them. Even removable drives such as a USB thumb drive, an external USB or an ESATA hard drive will be mounted onto the root filesystem and become an integral part of that directory tree.

One good reason to do this is apparent during an upgrade from one version of a Linux distribution to another, or changing from one distribution to another. In general, and aside from any upgrade utilities like dnf-upgrade in Fedora, it is wise to occasionally reformat the root and other partitions containing the operating system during an upgrade to positively remove any cruft that has accumulated over time. If /home is part of the root filesystem, it will be reformatted as well and would then have to be restored from a backup. By having /home as a separate filesystem, it will be known to the installation program as a separate filesystem and formatting of that filesystem can be skipped. This can also apply to /var where database, email inboxes, web site, and other variable user and system data are stored, and the /opt filesystem where commercial applications are intended to be stored. Thus none of that data is lost, and the applications should not require reinstallation unless the vendor is incredibly stupid.

There are other reasons for maintaining certain parts of the Linux directory tree as separate filesystems. For example, a long time ago, when I was not yet aware of the potential issues surrounding having all of the required Linux directories as part of the / (root) filesystem, I managed to fill up my home directory with a large number of very big files. Since neither the /home directory nor the /tmp directory were separate filesystems but simply subdirectories of the root filesystem, the entire root filesystem filled up. There was no room left for the operating system to create temporary files or to expand existing data files. At first the application programs started complaining that there was no room to save files, and then the OS itself started to act very strangely. Booting to single user mode and clearing out the offending files in my home directory allowed me to get going again; I then reinstalled Linux using a pretty standard multi-filesystem setup and was able to prevent complete system crashes from occurring again.

I once had a situation where a Linux host continued to run, but prevented the user from logging in using the GUI desktop. I was able to log in using the command-line interface (CLI) locally using one of the virtual consoles, and remotely using SSH. The problem was that the /tmp filesystem had filled up and some temporary files required by the GUI desktop could not be created at login time. Because the CLI login did not require files to be created in /tmp, the lack of space there did not prevent me from logging in using the CLI. In this case the /tmp directory was a separate filesystem and there was plenty of space available in the volume group of which the /tmp logical volume was a part. I simply expanded the /tmp logical volume to a size that accommodated my fresh understanding of the amount of temporary file space needed on that host and the problem was solved. Note that this solution did not require a reboot and as soon as the /tmp filesystem was enlarged, the user was able to log in to the desktop.

# Special filesystems

Linux has some special filesystems when running, two of which are particularly interesting to SysAdmins, /proc and /sys. These are virtual filesystems that exist only in RAM while the Linux host is running; they do not exist on any physical disk. Because they exist only in RAM these filesystems are not persistent like filesystems that are stored on the hard drive. They disappear when the computer is turned off and are re-created anew each time Linux starts up.

Each of the special filesystems has a unique role to play in a Linux host. The /proc filesystem is most likely the one with which you will become well acquainted as a SysAdmin, so we are going to explore it just a bit.

# The /proc filesystem

The /proc filesystem is defined by the FHS as the location for Linux to store information about the system, the kernel, and all processes running on the host. It is intended to be a place for the kernel to expose information about itself in order to facilitate access to data about the system. It is also intended to provide access to view kernel configuration parameters and to modify many of them when necessary.

When used as a window into the state of the operating system and its view of the system and hardware, it provides easy access to virtually every bit of information you might want as a SysAdmin.

---

## EXPERIMENT 6-1

For best results with this experiment it must be performed as root.

Let's first look at the top-level contents of the /proc filesystem of a running Linux host. On your host you may see color coding to differentiate files from directories.

First, look at the numeric entries. The names of these directories are PIDs, or process ID numbers. Each of those PID directories contains information about the running process that it represents.

```
[root@testvm1 proc]# cd /proc ; ls
1       26533  666  828      cpuinfo        modules
10      26561  669  83       crypto         mounts
11      27     680  84       devices        mtrr
12      29356  681  85       diskstats      net
13      30     685  86       dma            pagetypeinfo
14      30234  686  87       driver         partitions
15      31     692  9        execdomains    sched_debug
16      333    694  90       fb             schedstat
17      361    695  91       filesystems    scsi
18      4      697  927      fs             self
19      401    7    928      interrupts     slabinfo
```

| 2 | 402 | 707 | 929 | iomem | softirqs |
|---|---|---|---|---|---|
| 20 | 412 | 708 | 934 | ioports | stat |
| 21 | 413 | 740 | 937 | irq | swaps |
| 22 | 433 | 741 | 940 | kallsyms | sys |
| 23 | 434 | 749 | 941 | kcore | sysrq-trigger |
| 24 | 517 | 756 | 942 | keys | sysvipc |
| 25 | 543 | 764 | 947 | key-users | thread-self |
| 26 | 6 | 765 | 948 | kmsg | timer_list |
| 26465 | 615 | 766 | 966 | kpagecgroup | tty |
| 26511 | 616 | 771 | 990 | kpagecount | uptime |
| 26514 | 636 | 778 | acpi | kpageflags | version |
| 26521 | 637 | 780 | asound | latency_stats | vmallocinfo |
| 26522 | 639 | 783 | buddyinfo | loadavg | vmstat |
| 26524 | 641 | 8 | bus | locks | zoneinfo |
| 26526 | 647 | 80 | cgroups | mdstat | |
| 26527 | 661 | 81 | cmdline | meminfo | |
| 26532 | 664 | 82 | consoles | misc | |

Each of the files in the /proc directory contains information about some part of the kernel. Let's take a look at a couple of these files, cpuinfo and meminfo.

The cpuinfo file is mostly static. It contains the specifications for all installed CPUs.

```
[root@testvm1 proc]# cat cpuinfo
processor       : 0
vendor_id       : GenuineIntel
cpu family      : 6
model           : 58
model name      : Intel(R) Core(TM) i7-3770 CPU @ 3.40GHz
stepping        : 9
microcode       : 0x19
cpu MHz         : 3392.345
cache size      : 8192 KB
physical id     : 0
siblings        : 1
core id         : 0
cpu cores       : 1
apicid          : 0
initial apicid  : 0
fpu             : yes
```

```
fpu_exception   : yes
cpuid level     : 13
wp              : yes
flags           : fpu vme de pse tsc msr pae mce cx8 apic sep mtrr pge mca
                  cmov pat pse36 clflush mmx fxsr sse sse2 syscall nx rdtscp
                  lm constant_tsc rep_good nopl xtopology nonstop_tsc cpuid
                  pni pclmulqdq monitor ssse3 cx16 sse4_1 sse4_2 popcnt aes
                  xsave avx rdrand lahf_lm
bugs            :
bogomips        : 6784.69
clflush size    : 64
cache_alignment : 64
address sizes   : 36 bits physical, 48 bits virtual power management:
```

The data from the cpuinfo file includes the processor ID and model, its current speed in MHz, and the flags that can be used to determine the CPU features. If you run the command `ls -la cpuinfo`, you will see that the timestamp on the file is continuously changing. That indicates the file is being updated.

Now let's look at memory. First cat the meminfo file and then use the `free` command to do a comparison.

```
[root@testvm1 proc]# cat meminfo
MemTotal:        4044740 kB
MemFree:         2936368 kB
MemAvailable:    3484704 kB
Buffers:          108740 kB
Cached:           615616 kB
SwapCached:            0 kB
Active:           676432 kB
Inactive:         310016 kB
Active(anon):     266916 kB
Inactive(anon):      316 kB
Active(file):     409516 kB
Inactive(file):   309700 kB
Unevictable:        8100 kB
Mlocked:            8100 kB
SwapTotal:       4182012 kB
SwapFree:        4182012 kB
```

```
Dirty:                   0 kB
Writeback:               0 kB
AnonPages:          270212 kB
Mapped:             148088 kB
Shmem:                 988 kB
Slab:                80128 kB
SReclaimable:        64500 kB
SUnreclaim:          15628 kB
KernelStack:          2272 kB
PageTables:          11300 kB
NFS_Unstable:            0 kB
Bounce:                  0 kB
WritebackTmp:            0 kB
CommitLimit:       6204380 kB
Committed_AS:       753260 kB
VmallocTotal:   34359738367 kB
VmallocUsed:             0 kB
VmallocChunk:            0 kB
HardwareCorrupted:       0 kB
AnonHugePages:           0 kB
ShmemHugePages:          0 kB
ShmemPmdMapped:          0 kB
CmaTotal:                0 kB
CmaFree:                 0 kB
HugePages_Total:         0
HugePages_Free:          0
HugePages_Rsvd:          0
HugePages_Surp:          0
Hugepagesize:         2048 kB
DirectMap4k:         73664 kB
DirectMap2M:       4120576 kB
[root@testvm1 proc]# free
              total        used        free      shared  buff/cache   available
Mem:        4044740      304492     2935748         988      804500     3484100
Swap:       4182012           0     4182012
```

There is a lot of information in the /proc/meminfo file. A few bits of that data are used by programs like the free command. If you want the complete picture of memory usage, look in /proc/meminfo. The free command, like many other core utilities, gets its data from the /proc filesystem.

Because the data in /proc is a nearly instantaneous picture of the state of the Linux kernel and the computer hardware, the data may change rapidly. Look at the interrupts file several times in a row.

I suggest you spend a little time to compare the data in the /proc/meminfo file against the information you get when using commands like free and top. Where do you think these utility tools and many others get their information? Right here in the /proc filesystem, that's where.

Let's look a little bit deeper into PID 1. Like all of the process directories, it contains information about the process with that ID. So let's look at some of that information.

---

## EXPERIMENT 6-2

Let's enter and look at the contents of the /proc/1 directory. Then use the cat command to view the contents of the cmdline file.

```
[root@testvm1 proc]# cd 1 ; cat cmdline
/usr/lib/systemd/systemd--switched-root--system--deserialize24
```

We can see from the contents of the cmdline that this is systemd, the mother of all programs. On all older and some current versions of Linux, PID 1 will be the init program. Take some time to explore the contents of some of the other files and directories for this process.

Also take some time to explore a few of the other PID directories.

---

There is a huge amount of information available in the /proc filesystem, and it can be used to good advantage to solve problems. In fact, making changes to the running kernel on the fly and without a reboot is a powerful tool that allows you to make instant changes to the Linux kernel to resolve a problem, enable a function, or tune performance. Let's look at one example.

Linux is very flexible and can do many interesting things. One of those cool things is that any Linux host with multiple network interface cards (NICs) can act as a router. All it takes is a little knowledge, a simple command, and some changes to the iptables firewall.

Routing is a task managed by the kernel. So turning it on (or off) requires that we change a kernel configuration parameter. Fortunately we do not need to recompile the kernel, and that is one of the benefits of exposing the kernel configuration in the /proc filesystem. We are going to turn on IP forwarding, which provides the kernel's basic routing functionality.

---

### EXPERIMENT 6-3

This little command line program makes the /proc/sys/net/ipv4 directory the PWD, prints the current state of the ip_forward file that should be zero (0); sets it to "1"; and then prints its new state, which should be 1. Routing is now turned on. Be sure to enter the command on a single line.

```
[root@testvm1 ipv4]# cd /proc/sys/net/ipv4 ; cat ip_forward ;
echo 1 > ip_forward ; cat ip_forward
0
1
```

Congratulations! You have just altered the configuration of the running kernel.

---

In order to complete the configuration of a Linux host to full function as a router, additional changes would need to be made to the iptables firewall, or to whatever firewall software you may be using, and to the routing table. Those changes will define the specifics of the routing such as which packets get routed where. Although beyond the scope of this book, I have written an article[3] with some detail about configuring the routing table to which you can refer if you want more information. I also wrote an article[4] that briefly covers all of the steps required to turn a Linux host into a router, including making IP forwarding persistent after a reboot.

While you are here in the /proc filesystem look around some more – follow your own curiosity to explore different areas of this important filesystem.

---

[3]David Both, "An introduction to Linux network routing," https://opensource.com/business/16/8/introduction-linux-network-routing

[4]David Both, "Making your Linux Box Into a Router," http://www.linux-databook.info/?page_id=697

---

**Warning**    I intentionally chose to modify a kernel parameter that I am familiar
with and that won't cause any harm to your Linux host. As you explore the /proc
filesystem, you should not make any further changes.

---

## The /sys filesystem

The /sys directory is another virtual filesystem that is used by Linux to maintain specific
data for use by the kernel and SysAdmins. The /sys directory maintains the list of
hardware hierarchically for each bus type in the computer hardware.

A quick look at the /sys filesystem shows us its basic structure.

---

**EXPERIMENT 6-4**

In this experiment we look briefly at the contents of the /sys directory and then one of its
subdirectories, /sys/block.

```
[root@testvm1 sys]# cd /sys ; ls
```

```
block  bus  class  dev  devices  firmware  fs  hypervisor  kernel
module  power
[root@testvm1 sys]# ls block
dm-0  dm-1  sda  sr0
```

There are different types of disk (block) devices in /sys/block and the sda device is one of
them. This is usually the first, and in this case the only, hard drive in this VM. Let's take a quick
look at some of the contents of the sda directory.

```
[root@testvm1 sys]# ls block/sda
alignment_offset    events_async       queue       slaves
bdi                 events_poll_msecs  range       stat
capability          ext_range          removable   subsystem
dev                 holders            ro          trace
```

---

```
device              inflight        sda1        uevent
discard_alignment   integrity       sda2
events              power           size
[root@testvm1 sys]# cat block/sda/dev
8:0
[root@testvm1 sys]# ls block/sda/device
block                               ncq_prio_enable
bsg                                 power
delete                              queue_depth
device_blocked                      queue_ramp_up_period
device_busy                         queue_type
dh_state                            rescan
driver                              rev
eh_timeout                          scsi_device
evt_capacity_change_reported        scsi_disk
evt_inquiry_change_reported         scsi_generic
evt_lun_change_reported             scsi_level
evt_media_change                    state
evt_mode_parameter_change_reported  subsystem
evt_soft_threshold_reached          sw_activity
generic                             timeout
inquiry                             type
iocounterbits                       uevent
iodone_cnt                          unload_heads
ioerr_cnt                           vendor
iorequest_cnt                       vpd_pg80
modalias                            vpd_pg83
model                               wwid
[root@testvm1 sys]# cat block/sda/device/model
VBOX HARDDISK
```

For a bit more realistic information from this last command, I also performed this on my own physical hard drive rather than the VM I have been using for these experiments and that looks like this.

```
[root@david proc]# cat /sys/block/sda/device/model
ST320DM000-1BD14
```

This information is more like what you would see on one of your own hardware hosts rather than a VM. Now let's use the smartctl command to show that same bit of information and more. I used my physical host for this due to the more realistic data. I have also trimmed a large amount of output from the end of the results.

```
[root@david proc]# smartctl -x /dev/sda
smartctl 6.5 2016-05-07 r4318 [x86_64-linux-4.13.16-302.fc27.x86_64]
(local build)
Copyright (C) 2002-16, Bruce Allen, Christian Franke, www.smartmontools.org

=== START OF INFORMATION SECTION ===
Model Family:     Seagate Barracuda 7200.14 (AF)
Device Model:     ST320DM000-1BD14C
Serial Number:    Z3TT43ZK
LU WWN Device Id: 5 000c50 065371517
Firmware Version: KC48
User Capacity:    320,072,933,376 bytes [320 GB]
Sector Sizes:     512 bytes logical, 4096 bytes physical
Rotation Rate:    7200 rpm
Device is:        In smartctl database [for details use: -P show]
ATA Version is:   ATA8-ACS T13/1699-D revision 4
SATA Version is:  SATA 3.0, 6.0 Gb/s (current: 6.0 Gb/s)
Local Time is:    Wed Dec 13 13:31:36 2017 EST
SMART support is: Available - device has SMART capability.
SMART support is: Enabled
AAM level is:     208 (intermediate), recommended: 208
APM feature is:   Unavailable
Rd look-ahead is: Enabled
Write cache is:   Enabled
ATA Security is:  Disabled, frozen [SEC2]
Wt Cache Reorder: Enabled

=== START OF READ SMART DATA SECTION ===
SMART overall-health self-assessment test result: PASSED

General SMART Values:
<snip>
```

Had I not cut off the end of the results from this last command, it would also show things like failure indicators a temperature history, which can be helpful in determining the source of hard drive problems.

The `smartctl` utility obtains the data it uses from the /sys filesystem, just as other utility programs obtain their data from the /proc filesystem.

As you can see, the data in this directory contains a great deal of information about the device.

The /sys filesystem contains data about the PCI and USB system bus hardware and any attached devices. The kernel can use this information to determine which device drivers to use, for one example.

---

## EXPERIMENT 6-5

Let's look at some information about one of the buses on the computer, the USB bus. I am going to skip right to the locations of the devices in the /sys filesystem; you may need to do a little exploring on your own to find the items that interest you.

```
[root@testvm1 ~]# ls /sys/bus/usb/devices/usb2
2-0:1.0                bMaxPacketSize0      driver              quirks
authorized             bMaxPower            ep_00               removable
authorized_default     bNumConfigurations   idProduct           remove
avoid_reset_quirk      bNumInterfaces       idVendor            serial
bcdDevice              busnum               interface_authorized speed
                                            _default
bConfigurationValue    configuration        ltm_capable         subsystem
bDeviceClass           descriptors          manufacturer        uevent
bDeviceProtocol        dev                  maxchild            urbnum
bDeviceSubClass        devnum               power               version
bmAttributes           devpath              product
```

The above results show some of the files and directories that provide data about that particular device. But there is an easier way by using the core utilities so that we don't have to do all that exploration on our own.

```
[root@david ~]# lsusb
Bus 002 Device 005: ID 1058:070a Western Digital Technologies, Inc. My
Passport Essential (WDBAAA), My Passport for Mac (WDBAAB), My Passport
Essential SE (WDBABM), My Passport SE for Mac (WDBABW
```

```
Bus 002 Device 004: ID 05e3:0745 Genesys Logic, Inc. Logilink CR0012
Bus 002 Device 003: ID 1a40:0201 Terminus Technology Inc. FE 2.1 7-port Hub
Bus 002 Device 002: ID 8087:0024 Intel Corp. Integrated Rate Matching Hub
Bus 002 Device 001: ID 1d6b:0002 Linux Foundation 2.0 root hub
Bus 006 Device 005: ID 0bc2:ab1e Seagate RSS LLC Backup Plus Portable Drive
Bus 006 Device 003: ID 2109:0812 VIA Labs, Inc. VL812 Hub
Bus 006 Device 002: ID 2109:0812 VIA Labs, Inc. VL812 Hub
Bus 006 Device 001: ID 1d6b:0003 Linux Foundation 3.0 root hub
Bus 005 Device 007: ID 2109:2812 VIA Labs, Inc. VL812 Hub
Bus 005 Device 004: ID 2109:2812 VIA Labs, Inc. VL812 Hub
Bus 005 Device 006: ID 04f9:0042 Brother Industries, Ltd HL-2270DW Laser
Printer
Bus 005 Device 005: ID 04f9:02b0 Brother Industries, Ltd MFC-9340CDW
Bus 005 Device 003: ID 050d:0234 Belkin Components F5U234 USB 2.0 4-Port Hub
Bus 005 Device 002: ID 2109:3431 VIA Labs, Inc. Hub
Bus 005 Device 001: ID 1d6b:0002 Linux Foundation 2.0 root hub
Bus 001 Device 005: ID 046d:c52b Logitech, Inc. Unifying Receiver
Bus 001 Device 006: ID 17f6:0822 Unicomp, Inc
Bus 001 Device 003: ID 051d:0002 American Power Conversion Uninterruptible
Power Supply
Bus 001 Device 002: ID 8087:0024 Intel Corp. Integrated Rate Matching Hub
Bus 001 Device 001: ID 1d6b:0002 Linux Foundation 2.0 root hub
Bus 004 Device 001: ID 1d6b:0003 Linux Foundation 3.0 root hub
Bus 003 Device 010: ID 0424:4063 Standard Microsystems Corp.
Bus 003 Device 009: ID 0424:2640 Standard Microsystems Corp. USB 2.0 Hub
Bus 003 Device 008: ID 0424:2514 Standard Microsystems Corp. USB 2.0 Hub
Bus 003 Device 001: ID 1d6b:0002 Linux Foundation 2.0 root hub
```

Once again I ran this last command on my own physical host because it produces more interesting results.

The lspci command performs the same function as lsusb, but for the PCI bus. Go ahead and try the lspci command on your own.

I sometimes find it helpful to find specific hardware devices, especially newly added ones. As with the /proc directory, there are some core utilities like lsusb and lspci that make it easy for us to view information about the devices connected to the host.

# SELinux

The selinux pseudo filesystem is similar to other pseudo filesystems such as /proc. It can be located at either /selinux or at /sys/fs/selinux. This filesystem is only created and present when SELinux is enabled.

When present, the /selinux filesystem contains files that are closely related to the kernel in the same way that files in /proc are. This filesystem provides a window into the security functions of the running kernel when SELinux is enabled.

Fedora and other Red Hat-related distributions have SELinux enabled in Targeted mode by default. Your distribution may have it off or it may have been turned off as many SysAdmins do, including me. This next experiment helps us explore the selinux filesystem but we need to get to a known state first.

---

**EXPERIMENT 6-6**

---

**Caution**    Only perform this experiment on a host or VM designated for training purposes. Do not under any circumstances perform this experiment on a production host.

---

If your host has SELinux enabled, we will disable it before proceeding. First let's see if it is disabled or not.

```
[root@testvm1 ~]# sestatus
SELinux status:                 enabled
SELinuxfs mount:                /sys/fs/selinux
SELinux root directory:         /etc/selinux
Loaded policy name:             targeted
Current mode:                   enforcing
Mode from config file:          enforcing
Policy MLS status:              enabled
Policy deny_unknown status:     allowed
Memory protection checking:     actual (secure)
Max kernel policy version:      31
```

SELinux is enabled in targeted mode on my Fedora host. If this is the case on your host, note the location specified for the SELinuxfs mount point. Also make a note of the current mode, which should be enforcing or permissive.

Disable SELinux. Open the /etc/sysconfig/selinux file with your favorite editor. Change the SELINUX= line to disabled. The file should look like the one below when you are finished.

```
# This file controls the state of SELinux on the system.
# SELINUX= can take one of these three values:
#     enforcing - SELinux security policy is enforced.
#     permissive - SELinux prints warnings instead of enforcing.
#     disabled - No SELinux policy is loaded.
SELINUX=disabled
# SELINUXTYPE= can take one of these three values:
#     targeted - Targeted processes are protected,
#     minimum - Modification of targeted policy. Only selected processes are
#       protected.
#     mls - Multi Level Security protection.
SELINUXTYPE=targeted
```

Now reboot the host. It will take some time to reboot because SELinux must remove its labels from the files in the filesystem(s) it is protecting. After those labels are removed, the host will reboot again.

After your host has rebooted, log in as root. You can do this in one of the virtual consoles because there is no need for a GUI for this part of the experiment.

Everyone should perform the rest of this experiment, whether SELinux was enabled or disabled.

Try to locate the selinux filesystem in the location you noted above. It should not be present.

```
[root@testvm1 ~]# ls -l /sys/fs/selinux
ls: cannot access '/sys/fs/selinux': No such file or directory
```

Now reenable SELinux by using your editor to change the SELINUX line back to enforcing or permissive, whichever it was before we changed it the first time. Then reboot the system and wait until it has completed the second reboot.

Log in to a virtual console as root, or to the desktop whichever you prefer. If you log in to the desktop, open a terminal emulator window as root. Now try to view the selinux directory.

```
[root@testvm1 ~]# ls -l /sys/fs/selinux/
total 0
-rw-rw-rw-.  1 root root     0 Feb  3  2018 access
dr-xr-xr-x.  2 root root     0 Feb  3  2018 avc
dr-xr-xr-x.  2 root root     0 Feb  3  2018 booleans
```

```
-rw-r--r--.  1 root root     0 Feb  3  2018 checkreqprot
dr-xr-xr-x. 99 root root     0 Feb  3  2018 class
--w-------.  1 root root     0 Feb  3  2018 commit_pending_bools
-rw-rw-rw-.  1 root root     0 Feb  3  2018 context
-rw-rw-rw-.  1 root root     0 Feb  3  2018 create
-r--r--r--.  1 root root     0 Feb  3  2018 deny_unknown
--w-------.  1 root root     0 Feb  3  2018 disable
-rw-r--r--.  1 root root     0 Feb  3  2018 enforce
dr-xr-xr-x.  2 root root     0 Feb  3  2018 initial_contexts
-rw-------.  1 root root     0 Feb  3  2018 load
-rw-rw-rw-.  1 root root     0 Feb  3  2018 member
-r--r--r--.  1 root root     0 Feb  3  2018 mls
crw-rw-rw-.  1 root root 1, 3 Feb  3  2018 null
-r--r--r--.  1 root root     0 Feb  3  2018 policy
dr-xr-xr-x.  2 root root     0 Feb  3  2018 policy_capabilities
-r--r--r--.  1 root root     0 Feb  3  2018 policyvers
-r--r--r--.  1 root root     0 Feb  3  2018 reject_unknown
-rw-rw-rw-.  1 root root     0 Feb  3  2018 relabel
-r--r--r--.  1 root root     0 Feb  3  2018 status
-rw-rw-rw-.  1 root root     0 Feb  3  2018 user
--w--w--w-.  1 root root     0 Feb  3  2018 validatetrans
```

If you don't see the contents of the selinux directory, verify the correct location and try again.

# Problem Solving

One of the best reasons I can think of for adhering to the Linux FHS is that of making the task of problem solving as easy as possible. Using the Linux Filesystem Hierarchical Standard promotes consistency and simplicity, which makes problem solving easier. Knowing where to find things in the Linux filesystem directory structure has saved me from endless flailing about on more than just a few occasions.

I find that most of the Core Utilities, Linux services, and servers provided with the distributions I use are consistent in their usage of the /etc directory and its subdirectories for configuration files. This means that finding a configuration file for a misbehaving program or service supplied by the distribution should be easy to find.

I typically use a number of the ASCII text files in /etc to configure SendMail, Apache, DHCP, NFS, NTP, DNS, and more. I always know where to find the files I need to modify for those services, and they are all open and accessible because they are in ASCII text, which makes them readable to both computers and humans.

---

**Note**    There would appear to be an inconsistency with BIND DNS because its zone, reverse, and the root hints file, named.ca, are located in /var/named. This is not inconsistent because those are not configuration files, they are database files, which, as you can see in Table 6-1, is one of the functions of /var. Also, those "variable" files may be modified by external servers such as when a primary[5] name server updates the database of a secondary name server. Keeping those external servers out of the main configuration directory, /etc, on our computer is a really good idea.

The location of the BIND database files is consistent with the FHS. But it did take me a while to figure that out and why it is so, not to mention extensive research into the FHS. Sometimes my curiosity can take me on long detours, but I have always learned a great deal from those journeys that has been useful later on.

---

# Using the filesystem Incorrectly

One situation involving the incorrect usage of the filesystem occurred while I was working as a lab administrator at a large technology company in Research Triangle Park. One of our developers had installed an application in the wrong location, /var. The application was crashing because the /var filesystem was full, and the log files, which are stored in /var/log on that filesystem, could not be appended with new messages that would indicate that the /var filesystem was full because due to the lack of space in /var. However the system remained up and running because the critical / (root) and /tmp filesystems did not fill up. Removing the offending application and reinstalling it in the /opt filesystem, where it was supposed to be, resolved that problem. I also had a little discussion with the developer who did the original installation.

---

[5]I dislike the official names for the primary and secondary servers so won't use them. I think primary and secondary are more descriptive in any event.

# Email Inboxes

There have been a number of times when I needed to fix a problem with an email inbox. I have found that some spam email does not conform to proper email standards and at least some email clients have problems viewing and managing those spam emails as well as some of the ones that come after in the email inbox file.

Do you know where the email inbox is located on an email server? It is in /var/spool/mail, and each of the inbox files there has the name of the email user ID. With a little luck and a good bit of research I was able to repair the inbox by removing the offending spam email.

Even if I have never needed to make changes to the configuration file for a particular service, I know that it can almost always be found in the /etc directory. This significantly reduces the amount of searching I need to do.

# Adhering to the Standard

So how do we as SysAdmins adhere to the Linux FHS? It is actually pretty easy, and there is a hint way back in Table 6-1. The /usr/local directory is where locally created executables and their configuration files should be stored.

By local programs, the FHS means those that we create ourselves as SysAdmins to make our work or the work of other users easier. This includes all of those powerful and versatile shell programs we write.

The programs should be located in /usr/local/bin, and the configuration files, if any, in /usr/local/etc. There is also a /var/local directory in which local programs can store their own database files.

I have written a fair number of shell programs over the years and it took me at least five years before I understood the appropriate places to install my own software on host computers. In some cases I had even forgotten where I installed them. In other cases, I installed the configuration files in /etc instead of /usr/local/etc, and my file was overwritten during an upgrade. It took a few hours to track that down the first time it happened.

By adhering to these standards when writing shell programs, it is easier for me to remember where I have installed them. It is also easier for other SysAdmins to find things by searching only the directories that we as SysAdmins would have installed those programs and their files.

```
 / I have trouble remembering \
 | where to put files, too.   |
 \ The FHS can help.          /
  -----------------------------
             \   ^__^
              \  (oo)_____
                 (__)\       )\/\
                  ||----w |
                  ||     ||
```

# Where Does This File Go?

I used to install my simple Bash programs by simply copying the files to their appropriate locations on the hosts I was working on. Sometimes I forgot where they were supposed to go. And as the number of programs increased, it took ever more time to perform all of the tasks I needed to do to install the growing number of my own time-saving tools.

I found an excellent way to facilitate installation of my shell programs when I install a new computer, as well as upgrades when they need to be disseminated. I created an RPM that contains my programs and all of their configuration and other ancillary files, along with instructions for where to place each file. The RPM also contains a small Bash script that runs post-installation in order to perform certain configuration tasks, install the latest updates, and install some applications and utilities that I always like to have on my Linux hosts but that do not usually get installed by the installation program.

In one sense, creating this RPM was an act of the Lazy SysAdmin, automating the installation of a large number of programs, fonts, configuration files, and more. At one time I had so much stuff I was doing manually – by individual commands at the terminal – that I would spend three or four hours of my own time performing those tasks. After creating the RPM it now takes a couple minutes to run dnf to install the RPM. Then it takes a minute to enter the command to run a large Bash program that I have written to perform all of the other installations, modifications, and so on that I previously performed by hand. The shell program can take from 20 minutes to an hour or so to run through to completion, but I no longer need to monitor each and every command so I can be ready to run the next one by hand. I do not need to hover over the computer; I can go do other, more productive things while the automation does the work for me.

# Summary

This chapter has explored the Linux filesystems. You have learned that the hierarchical directory structure has standards applied to the usage of the directories in that structure. Adhering to the standard usage conventions as outlined in the Linux Filesystem Hierarchical Standard as maintained by the Linux Foundation provides some significant benefits to SysAdmins. This can be especially true when portions of the directory tree containing data are created as independent filesystems and mounted separately.

The Linux filesystem is not simply a place to store programs and data. It is a place where data and statistics about the operating system, running programs, and even the hardware can be found and put to good use. The Linux FHS defines the directories where this information can be found so we know it will always be there for us when we need it.

Knowledge of what is contained in the Linux filesystem and where it is located can be an indispensable tool in performing problem determination.

# PART III

# Function

In Part 3, our enlightenment extends beyond simply pounding out commands at the keyboard, and we begin to apply the basics in more advanced ways. Embracing the command line to better advantage, we begin to expand our command-line programs and create tested, portable, and maintainable shell programs that we save and can use repeatedly, and even share. We become the "lazy admin" and begin to automate everything. We use the Linux filesystem hierarchy to store data in open formats.

This part of the *Linux Philosophy for System Administrators* is about making our jobs easier. We use the functionality of the command line and apply some new tenets to leverage the things we have learned in Part 2 to automate as much as possible and to create programs that work for us.

Automation for SysAdmins is not about compiled programs as those take too much time and effort to create, test, release, and maintain. Programming for SysAdmins is about shell programs such as BASH programming, which is fast, open, and portable.

Some people in the industry would consider shell programming to be a lesser endeavor than writing programs in a compiled language. This is just not true, and although I use the terms script and scripting in places, writing shell scripts is just as much programming as is using C. The advantages of shell programming are manifold and we will discuss those in detail in this section.

Let us agree that the words "script" and "program" are interchangeable. So when I say "programs," you can take that to mean shell scripts, particularly BASH scripts because BASH is the default shell in almost every Linux distribution.

# CHAPTER 7

# Embrace the CLI

The Force is with Linux and the Force is the Command-Line Interface – the CLI. The vast power of the Linux CLI lies in its complete lack of restrictions. In this chapter we will begin to explore the command line in ways that will illuminate the power that it literally places at your fingertips.

There are many options for accessing the command line such as virtual consoles, many different terminal emulators, and other related software that can enhance your flexibility and productivity. All those possibilities will be covered in this chapter as well as some specific examples of how the command line can perform seemingly impossible tasks – or just satisfy the Pointy-Haired-Boss.

Before we get any further into our discussion about the command line, there is a little preparation we need to take care of.

---

## PREPARATION

Not all distributions install several software packages we will need during this chapter so we will install them now. If one or more of these packages are already installed, a message will be displayed to indicate that, but the rest of the packages will still install correctly. Some additional packages will be installed to meet the prerequisites of the ones we are installing.

My package manager is dnf, but you should use the package manager supplied by your distribution. Do this as root.

```
[root@testvm1 ~]# dnf -y install konsole tilix screen ksh tcsh zsh
```

On my test, VM Konsole and screen were already installed, but the command installed ksh, csh, zsh, tilix, and three other packages to meet dependencies.

---

© David Both 2018
D. Both, *The Linux Philosophy for SysAdmins*, https://doi.org/10.1007/978-1-4842-3730-4_7

# Defining the Command Line

The command line is a tool that provides a text mode interface between the user and the operating system. The command line allows the user to type commands into the computer for processing and to see the results.

The Linux command-line interface is implemented with shells such as bash (Bourne again shell), csh (C shell), and ksh (Korn shell) to name just three of the many that are available. The function of any shell is to pass commands typed by the user to the operating system that executes the commands and returns the results to the shell.

Access to the command line is through a terminal interface of some type. There are three primary types of terminal interfaces that are common in modern Linux computers, but the terminology can be confusing. So indulge me while I define those terms as well as some other terms that relate to the command line – in some detail.

## CLI Terminology

There are several terms relating to the command line that are often used interchangeably. This indiscriminate usage of the terms caused me a good bit of confusion when I first started working with Unix and Linux. I think it is important for SysAdmins to understand the differences between the terms console, virtual console, terminal, terminal emulator, terminal session, and shell.

Of course you can use whatever terminology works for you so long as you get your point across. Within the pages of this book, I will try to be as precise as possible because the reality is that there are significant differences in the meanings of these terms and it sometimes matters.

## Command Prompt

The command prompt is a string of characters like this one that sits there with a flashing cursor, waiting – prompting – you to enter a command.

```
[student@testvm1 ~]$ ▪
```

The typical command prompt in a modern Linux installation consists of the user name; the host name; and the present working directory (PWD), also known as the "current" directory, all enclosed in square braces. The tilde (~) character indicates the home directory.

# Command Line

The command line is the line on the terminal that contains the command prompts and any command you enter.

# Command-Line Interface

The Command-Line Interface is a text mode user interface to the Linux operating system that allows the user to type commands and see the results as textual output.

# Terminal

A terminal is an old bit of hardware that provides a means of interacting with a mainframe or Unix computer host. The terminal is not the computer; the terminals merely connect to the mainframes and Unix systems. Terminals – the hardware type – are usually connected to their host computer through a long serial cable. Terminals such as the DEC VT100 shown in Figure 7-1 are usually called "dumb terminals" to differentiate them from a PC or other small computer that may act as a terminal when connecting to a mainframe or Unix host. Dumb terminals have just enough logic in them to display data from the host and to transfer keystrokes back to the host. All of the processing and computing is performed on the host to which the terminal is connected.

***Figure 7-1.***  *A DEC VT100 dumb terminal. This file is licensed under the Creative Commons Attribution 2.0 Generic license. Author: Jason Scott*

111

Terminals that are even older, such as mechanical teletype machines (TTY) predate the common use of CRT displays. They used rolls of newsprint-quality paper to provide a record of both the input and results of commands. The first college course I took on computer programming used these TTY devices, which were connected by telephone line at 300 bits per second to a GE (yes, General Electric) time-sharing computer a couple of hundred miles away. Our university could not afford a computer of their own at that time.

Much of the terminology pertaining to the command line is rooted by historical usage in these dumb terminals of both types. For example, the term TTY is still in common use but I have net seen an actual TTY device in a many years. Look again in the /dev directory of your Linux or Unix computer. and you will find a large number of TTY device files.

---

**Note**    We covered device files in Chapter 5.

---

Terminals were designed with the singular purpose of allowing users to interact with the computer to which they were attached by typing commands and viewing the results on the roll of paper or the screen. The term, "terminal," tends to imply a hardware device that is separate from the computer while being used to communicate and interact with it (Figure 7-2).

*Figure 7-2.*  *Unix developers Ken Thompson and Dennis Ritchie. Thompson is sitting at a teletype terminal used to interface with the Unix computer. Peter Hamer – Uploaded by Magnus Manske*

# Console

A console is a special terminal because it is the primary terminal connected to a host. It is the terminal at which the system operator would sit to enter commands and perform tasks that were not allowed at other terminals connected the host. The console is also the only terminal on which the host would display system-level error messages when problems occurred.

There can be many terminals connected to mainframe and Unix hosts, but only one is or can act as a console. On most mainframes and Unix hosts, the console was connected through a dedicated connection that was designated specifically for the console.

Like Unix, Linux has runlevels and some of the runlevels such as runlevel 1, single user mode, and recovery mode are used only for maintenance. In these runlevels only the console is functional to allow the SysAdmin to interact with the system and perform maintenance.

---

**Note**   KVM stands for Keyboard, Video, and Mouse, the three devices that most people use to interact with their computers.

---

On a PC the physical console is usually the keyboard, monitor, and sometimes the mouse (KVM) that are directly attached to the computer. These are the physical devices used to interact with BIOS during the BIOS boot sequence, and can be used during the early stages of the Linux boot process to interact with GRUB and choose a different kernel to boot or modify the boot command to boot into a different run level.

Because of the close physical connection to the computer of the KVM devices, the SysAdmin must be physically present at this console during the boot process in order to interact with the computer. Remote access is not available to the SysAdmin during the boot process and only becomes available when the SSHD service is up and running.

# Virtual Console

Modern personal computers and servers that run Linux do not usually have dumb terminals that can be used as a console. Linux typically provides the capability for multiple virtual consoles to allow for multiple logins from a single keyboard and monitor. Red Hat Linux, CentOS, and Fedora Linux usually provide for six or seven virtual consoles for text mode logins. If a graphical interface is used, the first Virtual console, vc1, becomes the first graphical (GUI) session after the X Window System (X) starts, and vc7 becomes the second GUI session. See Figure 7-3.

```
Fedora 27 (Twenty Seven)
Kernel 4.13.12-300.fc27.x86_64 on an x86_64 (tty2)

testvm1 login: _
```

***Figure 7-3.***  *Login prompt for virtual console 2*

Each virtual console is assigned to a Function Key corresponding to the console number. So vc1 would be assigned to function key F1, and so on. It is easy to switch to and from these sessions. On your computer you can hold down the **Ctrl-Alt** keys and press **F2** to switch to vc2. Then hold down the **Ctrl-Alt** keys and press **F1** to switch to vc1 and what is usually the graphical desktop interface. If there is no GUI running, vc1 will be simply another text console.

Virtual consoles provide a means to access multiple consoles using a single physical system console, the keyboard, video display, and mouse (KVM). This gives administrators more flexibility to perform system maintenance and problem solving. There are some other means for additional flexibility, but Virtual Consoles are always available if you have physical access to the system or directly attached KVM device or some logical KVM extension such as Integrated Lights Out, or iLO. Other means such as the screen command might not be available in some environments and a GUI will probably not be available on most servers.

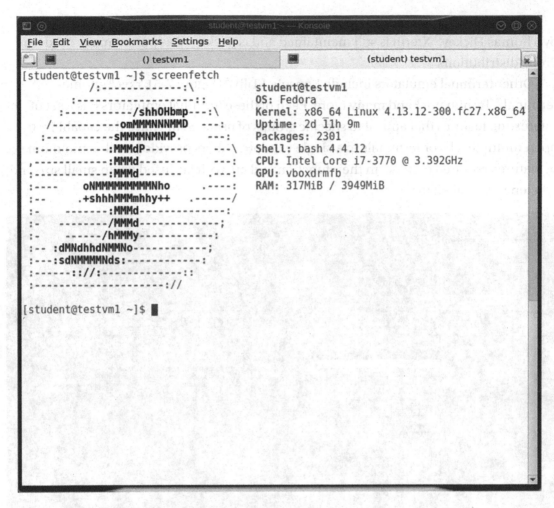

```
[student@testvm1 ~]$ screenfetch
           /:-------------:\                student@testvm1
        :-------------------::              OS: Fedora
      :-----------/shhOHbmp---:\            Kernel: x86_64 Linux 4.13.12-300.fc27.x86_64
    /-----------omMMMNNNMMD  ---:           Uptime: 2d 11h 9m
   :-----------sMMMMNMNMP.    ---:          Packages: 2301
   :-----------:MMMdP-------    ---\        Shell: bash 4.4.12
  ,------------:MMMd--------    ---:        CPU: Intel Core i7-3770 @ 3.392GHz
  :------------:MMMd-------    .---:        GPU: vboxdrmfb
  :----    oNMMMMMMMMMNho     .----:        RAM: 317MiB / 3949MiB
  :--     .+shhhMMMmhhy++   .------/
  :-     -------:MMMd--------------:
  :-    --------/MMMd-------------;
  :-     ------/hMMMy------------:
  :--  :dMNdhhdNMMNo-----------;
  :---:sdNMMMMNds:------------:
  :------::://:-------------::
  :---------------------://
[student@testvm1 ~]$ ▉
```

*Figure 7-4.*   *The Konsole terminal emulator window with two tabs open*

# Terminal Emulator

A terminal emulator is a software program that emulates a hardware terminal such as the VT100. Most of the current terminal emulators can emulate several different types of hardware terminals (Figure 7-4). Most terminal emulators are graphical programs that run on any Linux graphical desktop environment like KDE, Cinnamon, LXDE, GNOME, and others. The Linux Console[1] is the terminal emulator for the Linux virtual consoles.

---

[1]Wikipedia, Konsole, `https://en.wikipedia.org/wiki/Linux_console`

The first terminal emulator was Xterm,[2] which was originally developed in 1984 by Thomas Dickey.[3] Xterm is still maintained and is packaged as part of many modern Linux distributions.

Other terminal emulators include Konsole,[4] Tilix,[5] (Figure 7-5), rxvt,[6] gnome-terminal,[7] Terminator,[8] and many more. Each of these terminal emulators has a set of interesting features that appeal to specific groups of users. Some have the capability to open multiple tabs or terminals in a single window. Others provide just the minimum set of features required to perform their function and are typically used when small size and efficiency are called for.

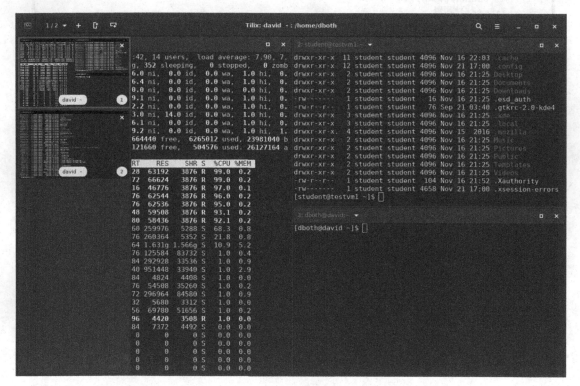

***Figure 7-5.*** *A Tilix instance with several sessions open*

[2]Wikipedia, Xterm, https://en.wikipedia.org/wiki/Xterm

[3]Wikipedia, Thomas Dickey, https://en.wikipedia.org/wiki/Thomas_Dickey

[4]Wikipedia, Konsole, https://en.wikipedia.org/wiki/Konsole

[5]Fedora Magazine, Tilix, https://fedoramagazine.org/try-tilix-new-terminal-emulator-fedora/

[6]Wikipedia, Rxvt, https://en.wikipedia.org/wiki/Rxvt

[7]Wikipedia, Gnome-terminal, https://en.wikipedia.org/wiki/Gnome-terminal

[8]Wikipedia, Terminator, https://en.wikipedia.org/wiki/Terminator_(terminal_emulator)

My favorite terminal emulators are Konsole and Tilix because they offer the ability to have many terminal emulator sessions in a single window. Konsole does this using multiple tabs that I can switch between.

Tilix offers the ability to tile multiple emulator sessions in a window session as well as providing multiple sessions. Figure 7-5 shows an instance of Tilix with two sessions displayed in the left sidebar. The visible session, though partially covered by the sidebar has three terminals running. The sidebar allows switching between sessions.

Other terminal emulator software provides these features but not as adroitly and seamlessly as Konsole and Tilix.

## Pseudo Terminal

A pseudo terminal is a Linux device file to which a terminal emulator is logically attached in order to interface with the operating system. The device files for pseudo terminals are located in the /dev/pts directory and are created only when a new terminal emulator session is launched. That can be a new terminal emulator window or a new tab or panel in an existing window of one of the terminal emulators, such as Konsole, that supports multiple sessions in a single window.

The device files in /dev/pts are simply a number for each emulator session that is opened. The first emulator would be /dev/pts/1, for example.

## Session

Session is another of those terms that can apply to different things and yet it retains essentially the same meaning.

The most basic application is a to terminal session. That is a single terminal emulator connected to a single user login and shell. So in its most basic sense a session is a single window or virtual console logged into a local or remote host with a command-line shell running in it.

The Tilix terminal emulator uses the term session to mean a window pane with one or more terminals open in it. The pane is the session in this case, and each of the sub-windows is a terminal. You can see this in Figure 7-5.

# Shell

A shell is the command interpreter for the operating system. Each of the many shells available for Linux interprets the commands typed by the user or SysAdmin into a form usable by the operating system. When the results are returned to the shell program, it displays them on the terminal.

The default shell for most Linux distributions is the bash shell. bash stands for Bourne Again Shell because the bash shell is based upon the older Bourne shell, which was written by Steven Bourne in 1977. Many other shells are available. The four I list here are the ones I encounter most frequently but many others exist.[9]

- csh – the C shell for programmers who like the syntax of the C language.

- ksh – the Korn shell, written by David Korn and popular with Unix users.

- tcsh – a version of csh with more ease of use features.

- zsh – which combines many features of other popular shells.

All shells have some built-in commands that supplement or replace the commands provided by the core utilities. Open the man page for bash and find the "SHELL BUILTIN COMMANDS" section to see the list of commands provided by the shell itself.

I have used the C shell, the Korn shell, and the Z shell. I still like the bash shell better than any of the others I have tried. Each shell has its own personality and syntax. Some will work better for you and others not so well. Use the one that works best for you, but that might require that you at least try some of the others.

You can change shells easily.

---

[9]Wikipedia, Comparison of command shells, https://en.wikipedia.org/wiki/
Comparison_of_command_shells

---

**EXPERIMENT 7-1**

---

Because most Linux distributions use the bash shell as the default, I will assume that is the one you have been using and that it is your default shell. In our preparation for this chapter we installed three other shells, ksh, tcsh, and zsh.

Do this experiment as the user student. First, look at your command prompt which should look like this:

```
[student@testvm1 ~]$
```

This is the standard bash prompt for a non-root user. Now let's change this to the ksh shell. Just enter the name of the shell.

```
[student@testvm1 ~]$ ksh
$
```

You can tell by the difference in the prompt that this is a different shell. Run a couple of simple commands such as `ls` and `free` just to see that there is no difference in how the commands work. This is because most of the commands are separate from the shell, except for the built-ins.

Try scrolling up to get a command history like bash. It does not work.

```
$ zsh
This is the Z Shell configuration function for new users,
zsh-newuser-install.
You are seeing this message because you have no zsh startup files
(the files .zshenv, .zprofile, .zshrc, .zlogin in the directory
~).  This function can help you with a few settings that should
make your use of the shell easier.

You can:

(q)  Quit and do nothing. The function will be run again next time.

(0)  Exit, creating the file ~/.zshrc containing just a comment.
     That will prevent this function being run again.

(1)  Continue to the main menu.

--- Type one of the keys in parentheses ---
```

If you continue, you will be taken through a series of menus that will help you configure the Z shell to suit your needs – as best you might know them at this stage. I chose "Q" to just go on to the prompt that looks like just a bit different from the bash prompt.

```
[student@testvm1]~%
```

Run a few simple commands while you are in the Z shell. Then type exit twice to get back to the original bash shell.

```
[student@testvm1]~% w
 14:30:25 up 3 days,  6:12,  3 users,  load average: 0.00, 0.00, 0.02
USER     TTY          LOGIN@   IDLE   JCPU   PCPU WHAT
student  pts/0        Tue08    0.00s  0.07s  0.00s w
root     pts/1        Wed06    18:48  0.26s  0.26s -bash
student  pts/2        08:14    6:16m  0.03s  0.03s -bash
[student@testvm1]~% exit
$ exit
[student@testvm1 ~]$
```

What do you think might happen if you start a bash shell while you are already in a bash shell?

```
[student@testvm1 ~]$ bash
[student@testvm1 ~]$ ls
Desktop Documents Downloads Music Pictures Public Templates Videos
[student@testvm1 ~]$ exit
exit
[student@testvm1 ~]$
```

You just get into another bash shell, is what.

This illustrates more than it might appear on the surface. First there is the fact that each shell is a layer. Starting a new shell does not terminate the previous one. When you started tcsh from bash, the bash shell remained in place; and when you exited from tcsh, you were returned to the waiting bash shell.

It turns out that this is exactly what happens when running any command or process from a shell. The command runs in its own session and the parent shell – process – waits until that sub-command returns and control is returned to it before being able to continue processing further commands.

So if you have a script that runs other commands – which is the purpose of a script – the script runs each command, waiting for it to finish before moving on to run the next command.

That behavior can be modified by appending an ampersand (&) to the end of a command, which places the called command in the background and allows the user to continue to interact with the shell, or for the script to continue processing more commands. You would only want to do this with commands that do not require further human interaction or output to STDOUT. You would also not want to run commands in the background when the results of that command are needed by other commands that will be run later, but perhaps before the background task has finished.

You can change your shell with the chsh command so that it will be persistent every time you log in and start a new terminal session.

## Secure Shell (SSH)

SSH is not really a shell. The ssh command starts a secure communication link between itself as the client and another host with the SSHD server running on it. The actual command shell used at the server end is whatever the default shell set for that account on the server side, such as the bash shell.

## Screen

You might at first think of "screen" as the device on which your Linux desktop is displayed. That is one meaning.

For geeks like us, screen is a program, a screen manager, that enhances the power of the command line. The screen utility allows launching multiple shells in a single terminal session and provides means to navigate between the running shells.

Remember when you had a remote session running a program and the communications link failed? I have had that happen many times. When that happened, the running program was terminated as well and I had to restart it from the beginning. It could get very frustrating.

The screen program can prevent that. A screen session will continue to run even if the connectivity to the remote host is broken because the network connection fails. It also allows disconnecting the screen session from the terminal session and reconnecting later from the same or a different computer. All of the CLI programs running in the screen terminal sessions will continue to run on the remote host. This means that once communications are reestablished, one can log back into the remote host and use the screen -r command at the remote command line to reattach the screen session to the terminal.

So I can start up a bunch of terminal sessions in screen, use **Ctrl-a + d** to disconnect from screen, and log out. Then I can go to another location, log in to a host, SSH to the host running screen, login, and use the `screen -r` command to reconnect to the screen session and all of the terminal sessions and their respective programs will still be running.

The screen command can be useful in some environments where physical access to a hardware console is not available to provide access to the Virtual Consoles but the flexibility of multiple shells is needed. You will probably find it convenient to use the screen program, and in some cases it will be necessary to do so in order to work quickly and efficiently.

---

### EXPERIMENT 7-2

In this experiment we explore the use of the screen program. Perform this experiment in a terminal session as the student user.

Before we begin, let's discuss how to send commands to the screen program itself in order to do things like open a new terminal and switch between running terminal sessions.

In this experiment I provide instructions such as "press **Ctrl-a + c**" to open a new terminal, for example. That means that you should hold down the Control key while you press the "a" key; at this point you can release the Control and "a" keys because you have alerted the screen program that the next keystroke is intended for it; now press the "c" key. This sequence of keystrokes seems a bit complicated, but I soon learned it as muscle memory and it is quite natural by now. I'm sure the same will be true for you, too.

For the sequence **Ctrl-a + "** (double quote) sequence that shows a list of all open terminals in that screen session, do **Ctrl-a**, release those keys and then press **shift + "**.

The only exception I have found to this procedure is the **Ctrl-a + a** sequence, which toggles between the last two terminal sessions. You must continue to hold down the Control key and press the "a" key twice in a row before releasing the Ctrl key.

1.  Enter the **screen** command that will clear the display and leave you at a command prompt. You are now in the screen display manager with a single terminal session open and displayed in the window.

2.  Type any command such as **ls** to have something displayed in the terminal session besides the command prompt.

3.  Press **Ctrl-a + c** to open a new shell within the screen session.

4.  Enter a different command, such as **df −h** in this new terminal.

5.  Type **Ctrl-a + a** to switch between the terminals.

6.  Enter **Ctrl-a + c** to open a third terminal.

7.  Type **Ctrl-a + "** to list the open terminals. Choose any one except the last one by using the up/dn arrow keys and hit the **Enter** key to switch to that terminal.

8.  To close one terminal, type **exit** and press the **Enter** key.

9.  Type the command **Ctrl-a + "** to verify that the terminal is gone. Notice that the terminal with the number you have chosen to close is no longer there and that the other terminals have not been renumbered.

10.  To reopen a fresh terminal use **Ctrl-a + c**.

11.  Type **Ctrl-a + "** to verify that the new terminal has been created. Notice that it has been opened in the place of the terminal that was previously closed.

12.  To disconnect from the screen session and all open terminals, press **Ctrl-a + d**. Note that this leaves all of the terminals and the programs in them intact and still running.

13.  Enter the command **screen -list** command on the command line to list all of the current screen sessions. This can be useful to ensure that you reconnect to the correct screen session if there are multiple ones.

14.  Use the command **screen −r** to reconnect to the active screen session. If multiple active screen sessions are open, then a list of them will be displayed and you can choose the one to which you wish to connect; you will have to enter the name of the screen session to which you want to connect.

I recommend that you not open a new screen session inside of an existing screen session. It can be difficult to switch between the terminals because the screen program does not always understand which of the embedded sessions to which to send the command.

I use the screen program all the time. It is a powerful tool that provides me with extreme flexibility for working on the command line.

# The GUI and the CLI

You may like and use any of the many graphical user interfaces, that is, desktops, which are available with almost all Linux distributions; you may even switch between them because you find one particular desktop such as KDE more usable for certain tasks, and another like GNOME better suited for other tasks. But you will also find that most of the graphical tools required to manage a Linux computer are simply wrappers around the underlying CLI commands that actually perform those functions.

A graphical interface cannot approach the power of the CLI because the GUI is inherently limited to those functions the programmers have decided you should have access to. This is how Windows and other restrictive operating systems work. They only allow you to have access to the functions and power that they decide you should have. This might be because they think you really do want to be shielded from the full power of your computer, or it might be due to the fact that they don't think you are capable of dealing with that level of power.

Just because the GUI is limited in some ways does not mean that good SysAdmins cannot leverage it to make their jobs easier. I do find that I can leverage the GUI with more flexibility for my command-line tasks. By allowing multiple terminal windows on the desktop, or by using advanced terminal emulation programs such as Tilix and Konsole that are designed for a GUI environment, I can improve my productivity. Having multiple terminals open on the desktop gives me the capability of being logged into multiple computers simultaneously. I can also be logged into any one computer multiple times, having open multiple terminal sessions using my own user ID and more terminal sessions as root.

For me, having multiple terminal sessions available at all times, in multiple ways, is what the GUI is all about. A GUI can also provide me with access to programs like LibreOffice, which I am using to write this book, graphical email and web browsing applications, and much more. But the real power for SysAdmins is in the command line.

Linux uses the GNU Core Utilities, which were written by Richard M. Stallman,[10] aka RMS, and many other contributors, as the free, open source utilities required by any free version of Unix or Unix-like operating systems. The GNU Core Utilities are the basic file, shell, and text manipulation utilities of any GNU operating system such as GNU/Linux and can be counted upon by any SysAdmin to be present on every version of Linux. In addition, every Linux distribution has an extended set of utilities that provides even more functions.

---

[10]Wikipedia, Richard M. Stallman, https://en.wikipedia.org/wiki/Richard_Stallman

You can enter the command, `info coreutils`, to view a list of the GNU Core Utilities, and select individual commands for more information. You can also use the man <command> to view the man page for each of these commands and all of the many hundreds of other Linux commands that are also standard with every distribution.

# Non-Restrictive Interface

The Linux CLI is a non-restrictive interface because it places no limits on how you use it.

A GUI is by definition a very restrictive interface. You can only perform the tasks you are allowed in a prescribed manner and all of that is chosen by the programmer. You cannot go beyond the limits of the imagination of the programmer who wrote the code or – more likely – the restrictions placed on the programmer by the Pointy-Haired Bosses.

In my opinion, the greatest drawback of any graphical interface is the suppression of any possibility for automation. No GUI offers any capability to truly automate tasks. Instead there is only repetitive mouse clicks to perform the same or similar operations multiple times on slightly different data.

The CLI, on the other hand, allows for great flexibility in performing tasks. The reason for this is that each Linux command, not just the GNU core utilities but also the vast majority of the Linux commands, were written using tenets of the Linux Philosophy such as, "everything is a file," "Always use STDIO," "Each program should do one thing well," "Avoid captive user interfaces," and so on. You get the idea and I will discuss each of these tenets later in this book, so don't worry too much if you don't yet understand what they mean.

The bottom line for the SysAdmin is that when developers follow the tenets, the power of the command line can be fully exploited.

# The Mailing List

This example highlights the power and flexibility of the CLI for its ability to automate common tasks.

I have administered several listservs during my career and still do. People send me lists of email addresses to add to those lists. In one case I received a list of names and email addresses in a Word document that were to be added to one of my lists.

The list itself was not really very long but it was very inconsistent in its formatting. An abbreviated version of that list, with name and domain changes, is shown in Figure 7-6. The original list has extra lines, characters like brackets and parentheses that need to be deleted, and some empty lines. The format required to add these emails to the list is `first last <email@example.com>`.

```
Team 1 Apr 3
Leader  Virginia Jones  vjones88@example.com
Frank Brown  FBrown398@example.com
Cindy Williams  cinwill@example.com
Marge smith   msmith21@example.com
 [Fred Mack]    edd@example.com

Team 2 March 14
leader  Alice Wonder  Wonder1@example.com
John broth  bros34@example.com
Ray Clarkson  Ray.Clarks@example.com
Kim West    kimwest@example.com
[JoAnne Blank]  jblank@example.com

Team 3 Apr 1
Leader  Steve Jones  sjones23876@example.com
Bullwinkel Moose bmoose@example.com
Rocket Squirrel RJSquirrel@example.com
Julie Lisbon  julielisbon234@example.com
[Mary Lastware) mary@example.com
```

***Figure 7-6.*** *A partial listing of the original document of email addresses to add to a listserv*

It was obvious that I needed to manipulate the data in order to mangle it into an acceptable format for inputting to the list. It is possible to use a text editor or a word processor such as LibreOffice Writer to make the necessary changes to this small file. However, people send me files like this quite often so it becomes a chore to use a word processor to make these changes. Despite the fact that Writer has a good search and replace function, each character or string must be replaced singly and there is no way to save previous searches. Writer does have a very powerful macro feature, but I am not familiar with either of its two languages, LibreOffice Basic or Python. I do know bash shell programming.

I did what comes naturally to a SysAdmin – I automated the task. The first thing I did was to copy the address data to a text file named addresses.txt so I could work on it using command-line tools. After a few minutes of work, I developed the bash command line program in Figure 7-7 that produced the desired output as the file, addresses2.txt. This command would be entered on a single line on the terminal; line wrapping is acceptable, but don't press the Enter key until the command is completely entered.

```
cat addresses.txt | grep -v Team | grep -v "^\s$" | sed -e "s/[Ll]eader//"
-e "s/\[//g" -e "s/\]//g" -e "s/)//g" | awk '{print $1" "$2" <"$3">"}' >
addresses2.txt
```

**Figure 7-7.**   *This bash command line program cleans up the email address data in Figure 7-6 and, if saved as an executable shell script, can be reused many times*

I saved the bash program in an executable file and now I can run this program any time I receive a new list. Some of those lists are fairly short, as is the one in Figure 7-6, but others have been quite long, sometimes containing up to several hundred addresses and many lines of "stuff" that do not contain addresses to be added to the list.

It is very important to realize that my solution is not the only one. There are different methods in bash for producing the same output, there are other languages like Python and Perl that can also be used. And, of course, there are always LibréOffice Writer macros. But I can always count on bash as part of any Linux distribution. I can perform these tasks using bash programs on any Linux computer, even one without a GUI desktop and that does not have LibréOffice installed.

## Solution Tenets

Using the bash shell for programs that solve problems like this one helps to ensure that the solution meets other Philosophy tenets. For example, bash shell programs are portable to other Linux and Unix environments. So here is a list of the tenets met by this particular solution.

- Embrace the CLI

- Be a Lazy SysAdmin

- Use STDIO and data streams

- Automate everything

- Always use shell programs
- Store data in flat text files
- Make programs portable
- Strive for elegance
- Find the simplicity
- Silence is golden
- Test everything

# Baffle Them with Big Data

*The value of a program is proportional to the weight of its output.*

—Laws of Computer Programming

I saw this quote on a poster in a programmer's office many years ago. For those of you who are too young to remember those "good old days," it refers back to a time when almost all output from a computer was in the form of printed reports on wide, fan-fold paper. Some programs would dump huge stacks of 11"x15" fan-fold continuous form paper[11] from the IBM 1403 printer.[12] Your rank in the company hierarchy could be determined by how many stacks of computer paper in your office and how high they were.

Despite the fact that those days are – mostly – behind us, huge amounts of data can still be a sign of … something. In my case a way to counter continuous requests for essentially meaningless data.

Here is another interesting example of using the command line. Some time in mid-1999 when I was working for the State of North Carolina, one of the PHBs asked me to create a list for the security people. As is appropriate, they wanted to know every piece of software on my "non-standard" PC, and its function. At that time I was using Red Hat Linux 6 rather than the "standard" Windows.

---

[11]Wikipedia, Continuous form paper, https://en.wikipedia.org/wiki/Continuous_stationery
[12]Wikipedia, IBM 1403 printer, https://en.wikipedia.org/wiki/IBM_1403

My dilemma was to figure out exactly what it was they wanted. Did they simply want a list like, Red Hat Linux 6.1, OpenOffice, Mozilla? or did they want more. No matter how much I requested clarification, they just said they wanted a list of "everything" that was non-standard. Knowing the people in Security, I figured that more is better.

They had said they wanted a list of every bit of software on my Linux computer and what it did so I accommodated them. I wrote a bash program that determined every RPM package installed on the computer in question, sorted them into alphabetical order, then used the RPM database to obtain the basic description of the software. The little program I wrote to accomplish this is shown in Experiment 7-3. Run it on your own computer to see the results.

Be sure to use the back-ticks as shown (`rpm -qa | sort`) or this experiment will not work. Enclosing code in back-ticks (`) is a way to execute that bit of code before evaluating the rest of the code in the statement. So the enclosed code is evaluated first and then used as the input list for the for command. This works exactly like parentheses in a math problem like $X=a*3+2*(6-3)$. The parentheses change the sequence in which the expression is evaluated.

---

**EXPERIMENT 7-3**

Perform this experiment as root.

```
[root@testvm1 ~]# for I in `rpm -qa | sort`;do echo $I; rpm -qi $I | grep Summary;done
```

This simple command-line program generates two lines of data for each RPM package that is installed on your computer. It turned out to be 4,630 lines on my testvm1 virtual machine with a fairly modest installation.

---

Once again I could have used the mailx command at the end of this program to send the data directly to the requesting PHB via email.

---

**Note**   It has been over 15 years since I had done this, and I did not have a copy of that bash program. It took me about 5 minutes to re-create it while writing this chapter.

---

The end result of this was dozens of pages of data, which was exactly what they had asked for. I knew that most of it would be meaningless to them but that was irrelevant because I gave them exactly what they wanted. It just turned out to be far more than they expected and with mostly cryptic descriptions – unless you were deeply familiar with the guts of Linux. I think they just expected a one-page listing of things like, email, browser, and office software.

However, despite the fun I used to have providing the PHBs exactly what they asked for, this experiment does illustrate that the command line can be used in some amazing and powerful ways. Let's list our "non-standard" software again but add one more command.

---

**EXPERIMENT 7-4**

Perform this experiment as root.

```
[root@testvm1 ~]# for I in `rpm -qa | sort`;do echo $I; rpm -qi $I | grep
Summary;done | text2pdf -o /tmp/non-std-software.pdf
```

The last command in the pipeline, `text2pdf` converts the ASCII text data stream directly into a text file.

---

# CLI Power

I hope you can see from these simple examples just a little of the vast power available to the SysAdmin when using the command line.

In this chapter you have discovered that Linux provides a very large number of methods to access the command line and perform your work as a SysAdmin. You can use the virtual consoles and any of a number of different terminal emulators. You can combine those with the screen program in order to further enhance the flexibility you have at the command line.

The examples in this chapter are informative in themselves, but the real power of the CLI comes from the fact that I also "Automate everything" using that CLI, which is another tenet of the philosophy. It is well known by experienced SysAdmins that if something needs to be done once, it will need to be done again, usually many times. So to make it easy later I placed those simple lines of bash code in text files and made the files executable. Whenever I was asked to provide that same information again, all I had to do was to run the appropriate bash script.

# Be a Lazy SysAdmin

Despite everything we were told by our parents, teachers, bosses, well-meaning authority figures, and hundreds of quotes about hard work that I found with a Google search, getting your work done well and on time is not the same as working hard. One does not necessarily imply the other.

I am a lazy SysAdmin. I am also a very productive SysAdmin. Those two seemingly contradictory statements are not mutually exclusive; rather they are complementary in a very positive way. Efficiency is the only way to make this possible.

This chapter is about working hard at the right tasks to optimize our own efficiency. Part of this is about automation, which I will touch on here and discuss in detail in Chapter 9. But the greater part of this chapter is about finding a few of the myriad ways to use the shortcuts already built into Linux.

## Preparation

We need to install the logwatch package in preparation for one of the experiments.

---

**PREPARATION**

We need to install the logwatch package for one of the experiments in this chapter to work properly.

---

**Note**   Be sure to use the correct package manager for your distribution. I use dnf for Fedora.

---

```
[root@testvm1 ~]# dnf -y install logwatch
```

If logwatch is already installed the preceding command will print a message to that effect.

---

© David Both 2018
D. Both, *The Linux Philosophy for SysAdmins*, https://doi.org/10.1007/978-1-4842-3730-4_8

# True Productivity

Typing away at the keyboard all day long every day to perform the tasks required by the job is probably the least productive that any SysAdmin can be. A SysAdmin is most productive when thinking – thinking about how to solve existing problems and about how to avoid future problems; thinking about how to monitor Linux computers in order to find clues that anticipate and foreshadow those future problems; thinking about how to make her work more efficient; thinking about how to automate all of those tasks that need to be performed whether every day or once a year.

This contemplative aspect of the SysAdmin job is not well known or understood by those who are not SysAdmins – including many of those who manage the SysAdmins, the Pointy-Haired-Bosses. SysAdmins all approach the contemplative parts of their job in different ways. Some of the SysAdmins I have known found their best ideas at the beach, cycling, participating in marathons, or climbing rock walls. Others think best when sitting quietly or listening to music. Still others think best while reading fiction, studying unrelated disciplines, or even while learning more about Linux. The point is that we all stimulate our creativity in different ways, and many of those creativity boosters do not involve typing a single keystroke on a keyboard. Our true productivity may be completely invisible to those around the SysAdmin.

Many PHBs, being completely ignorant of how to measure SysAdmin productivity – or anyone else's productivity for that matter – like to hear those keys being struck. Lots of keyboard noise is music to their ears. That is the worst possible measurement of a SysAdmin's productivity.

Some PHBs go so far as to install keystroke and mouse movement monitoring software on their employees' computers as a measurement of how productive they are. Google it and see for yourself the large number of programs that perform this type of keystroke counting. The more keystrokes and mouse clicks, the more productive the user must be, right? *Nope!* Perhaps that is exciting stuff for bean counters, but it is a horrible way to measure the productivity of a SysAdmin – or anyone else for that matter.

# Preventative Maintenance

One interesting experience of mine comes to mind. This took place while I was working for IBM as a Customer Engineer (CE). I was assigned to fixing broken unit record equipment[1] such as keypunches, card sorters, collators, and other devices that used the now old-fashioned punch cards.

As the new guy in town, I was assigned some of the oldest and least reliable of these mechanical devices as part of my territory. Because of the fact the person I was replacing had been gone for some time, most of these devices had been worked on just enough to fix the immediate problem but not enough to prevent the next one that was just around the corner. That IBM required preventative maintenance (PM) prescribed for those devices had been ignored for many months and the machines were wearing out.

The only way to reduce the long-term workload was to perform the required PM, which would reduce the frequency of calls on each device. So I spent a few minutes after I fixed each broken machine to perform all of the PM called for at that time. This included cleaning, lubricating, and replacing worn parts that had not yet failed but soon would. By performing this PM, I reduced the number of trouble calls on those devices and saved myself work later on, and saved IBM the cost of me or one of my coworkers from having to go out and fix a problem that could have been prevented by performing PM.

Many would say my job was to fix computer equipment. My managers at IBM understood that was only the tip of the iceberg; they – and I – knew my job was Customer Satisfaction. Although that usually meant fixing broken hardware, it also meant reducing the number of times the hardware broke. That was good for the Customer because they were more productive when their machines were working. It was good for me because I received far fewer calls from those happier customers. I also got to sleep more due to the resultant fewer emergency off-hours call-outs. I was being the Lazy CE. By doing the extra work up front, I had to do far less work in the long run.

This same tenet has become one of the functional tenets of the Linux Philosophy for SysAdmins. As SysAdmins, our time is best spent doing those tasks that minimize future workloads.

---

[1]Wikipedia, Unit Record Equipment, https://en.wikipedia.org/wiki/Unit_record_equipment

Now let's look at some ways to be lazy. Remember, these strategies are only a few of the many that can be used to reduce your workload, work more efficiently, and get all of your work done with as little effort on your part as possible. Every SysAdmin I know has their own strategies. These are just a few of mine.

# Minimize Typing

One part of being a lazy SysAdmin is the employment of strategies to reduce typing. Typing takes time and saving time is important.

I am a horrible typist. I went to high school at a time when boys did not take typing. That was for the women who were going to be secretaries. When I finally did start using a computer through a real keyboard instead of punched cards, I managed to teach myself enough to type at a fair speed with a couple fingers on each hand. It works for me but I have to make a lot of corrections. And making errors when typing a command to a CLI program is a bad thing. So reducing the amount of typing that needs to be done is important.

# Aliases

One way to reduce the amount of typing necessary is with aliases. Aliases are a method for substituting a long command for a shorter one that is easier to type because it has fewer characters. Aliases are a common way to reduce typing by making it unnecessary to type in long options that we use constantly by including them in the alias.

---

**EXPERIMENT 8-1**

---

As the student user, enter the `alias` command to view the current list of aliases.

```
[student@testvm1 ~]$ alias
alias egrep='egrep --color=auto'
alias fgrep='fgrep --color=auto'
alias glances='glances -t1'
alias grep='grep --color=auto'
alias l.='ls -d .* --color=auto'
alias ll='ls -l --color=auto'
alias ls='ls --color=auto'
```

```
alias lsn='ls --color=no'
alias mc='. /usr/libexec/mc/mc-wrapper.sh'
alias vi='vim'
alias vim='vim -c "colorscheme desert" '
alias which='(alias; declare -f) | /usr/bin/which --tty-only --read-alias --
read-functions --show-tilde --show-dot'
alias xzegrep='xzegrep --color=auto'
alias xzfgrep='xzfgrep --color=auto'
alias xzgrep='xzgrep --color=auto'
alias zegrep='zegrep --color=auto'
alias zfgrep='zfgrep --color=auto'
alias zgrep='zgrep --color=auto'
```

Your results should look similar to mine, but I have added some aliases of my own. One is for the glances utility, which is not a part of most distributions. Another is for vim to use the "desert" color scheme.

The aliases shown in Experiment 8-1 are primarily intended to set up default behavior such as color and some standard options. I particularly like the ll alias because I like the long listing of directory contents and instead of typing ls -l I can just type ll. I use the ll command a lot and it saves typing three characters every time I use it. For slow typists like me, that can amount to a lot of time.

I strongly recommend that you do not use aliases to alias Linux commands to those you used in another operating system like some people have done. You will never learn Linux that way.

In Experiment 8-1 the alias for the vim editor sets a color scheme, one which is not the default. I happen to like the desert color scheme better than the default, so aliasing the vim command to the longer command that also specifies my favorite color scheme is one way to get what I want with less typing.

You can use the alias command to add your own new aliases to the ~/.bashrc file to make them permanent between reboots and logout/in. To make the aliases available to all users on a host, add them to the /etc/bashrc file. The syntax in either case is the same as from the command line.

# Other Typing Shortcuts

Other ways to reduce typing include using short names for programs. Most of the Core Utilities have very short names – many are only two or three characters in length. This in itself reduces the amount of typing we have to do. I use short names for the Bash shell programs I create in order to keep them simple and easy to both remember and type.

# File Naming

I use my own conventions for naming files. In general, short names are good, but meaningful names that are easy to see in a list are even better.

My naming strategy for files that have similar names but that were created on different dates is in the form YYYYMMDD-filename.pdf, for example. I download many financial files from the Internet and they have names like statement.pdf and when downloaded into a directory I rename them with my own format so they are more easily discernible in a directory, such as `20170617-visa-statement.pdf`. Placing the date first in YYYYMMDD or YYYY-MM-DD format makes them automatically sort in the correct date sequence in directory listings, which makes it easy to find a particular file.

This type of naming does require some additional typing up front, but it can save a lot of time looking for specific files later.

# BASH Efficiency

Bash is only one of many shells available for Linux. Like all shells, Bash has many ways to help you become more efficient. We have already seen the aliases that can be configured in the .bashrc file.

Now let's look at some more of the fun command-line features provided by the Bash shell.

# Completion Facility

Bash provides a facility for completing a partially typed program and host names, file names, and directory names. Type the partial command or a file name as an argument to a command and press the **Tab** key. If the host, file, directory, or program exists and the remainder of the name is unique, Bash will complete entry of the name. Because the Tab key is used to initiate the completion, this feature is sometimes referred to as "Tab completion."

Tab completion is programmable and can be configured to meet many different needs. However, unless you have specific needs that are not met by the standard configurations provided by Linux, the Core Utilities, and other CLI applications, there should never be a reason to change the defaults.

---

**Note**    The Bash man page has a detailed and mostly unintelligible explanation of "programmable completion." The book "*Beginning the Linux Command Line*" has a short and more readable description[2] and Wikipedia[3] has more information, examples, and an animated GIF to aid in understanding this feature.

---

Experiment 8-2 provides a very short introduction to command completion if you are not already familiar with it.

---

**EXPERIMENT 8-2**

Perform this experiment as the student user. Your home directory should have a subdirectory named Documents for this experiment. Most Linux distributions create a Documents subdirectory for each user.

We use completion to change into the ~/Documents directory. Be sure that your home directory is the PWD. Type the following partial command into the terminal.

```
[student@testvm1 ~]$ cd D<Tab>
```

<Tab> means to press the Tab key once. Nothing happens because there are three directories that start with "D." You can see that by pressing the Tab key twice in rapid succession, which lists all of the directories that match what you have already typed.

```
[student@testvm1 ~]$ cd D<tab><Tab>
Desktop/   Documents/ Downloads/
[student@testvm1 ~]$ cd D
```

---

[2]Van Vugt, Sander. *Beginning the Linux Command Line* (Apress, 2015), 22.
[3]Wikipedia, Command Line Completion, https://en.wikipedia.org/wiki/Command-line_completion

Now add the "o" to the command and press Tab twice more.

```
[student@testvm1 ~]$ cd Do<tab><Tab>
Documents/ Downloads/
[student@testvm1 ~]$ cd Do
```

You should see a list of both directories that start with "Do." Now add the "c" to the command and press the Tab key once.

```
[student@testvm1 ~]$ cd Doc<Tab>
[student@testvm1 ~]$ cd Documents/
```

So if you type cd Doc<Tab> the rest of the directory name is completed in the command. Let's take a quick look at completion for commands. In this case the command is relatively short, but most are. Assume we want to determine the current uptime for the host.

```
[student@testvm1 ~]$ up<Tab><Tab>
update-alternatives     updatedb                       update-mime-database     upower
update-ca-trust         update-desktop-database  update-pciids                 uptime
update-crypto-policies  update-gtk-immodules     update-smart-drivedb
[student@testvm1 ~]$ up
```

We can see several commands that begin with "up" and we can also see that typing one more letter "t" will complete enough of the uptime command that the rest will be unique.

```
[student@testvm1 ~]$ upt<Tab>ime
 07:55:05 up 1 day, 10:01,  7 users,  load average: 0.00, 0.00, 0.00
```

The completion facility only completes the command, directory, or file name when the remaining text string needed is unequivocally unique.

Tab completion works for commands, some subcommands, file names, and directory names. I find that completion is most useful for completing directory and file names, which tend to be longer, and a few of the longer commands and some subcommands.

Most Linux commands are so short already that using the completion facility can actually be less efficient than typing the command. The short Linux command names are quite in keeping with being a lazy SysAdmin. So it just depends on whether you find it more efficient or consistent for you to use completion on short commands. Once you learn which commands are worthwhile for tab completion and how much you need to type, you can use those that you find helpful.

# Command-Line Recall and Editing

Command-line recall and editing are other methods to reduce the total amount of typing we do. These two features, command line recall and command-line editing, work together to enhance productivity. I use these features frequently and cannot imagine using a shell that does not have them. These features would not be possible without the Bash history feature so we will start there.

# History

Command-line recall uses the Bash history feature to maintain a list of previously entered shell commands. This feature allows us to use the command history to recall previous commands for reuse. Prior to pressing the Enter key, the recalled commands may be edited. Let's start by looking at the history for our hosts so we can see what that looks like.

---

### EXPERIMENT 8-3

Perform this experiment as the student user. Enter the `history` command and look at the results.

```
[student@testvm1 ~]$ history
    1  poweroff
    2  w
    3  who
    4  cd /proc
    5  ls -l
    6  ls
    7  cd 1 ; ls
    8  cd
    9  ls
   10  exit
   11  ls -la
   12  exit
   13  man screen
```

```
    14  ls -la
    15  badcommand
    16  clear
    17  ls -l /usr/local/bin
    18  clear
    19  screenfetch
    20  zsh
    21  ksh
    22  bash
    23  man chgsh
    24  man chsh
    25  screen
    26  history
[student@testvm1 ~]$
```

Your results will be different from mine, but you should see at least some of the commands that you entered for previous experiments.

The Bash command history is maintained in the ~/.bash_history file. Other shells keep their histories in different files. The Korn shell stores its history in .sh_history, for example. For Bash, at least, the history in the buffer is not written to the .bash_history file until you exit from the shell.

Each open terminal has its own history so you may not see the command you want in the listing. If you do not, try another terminal session. The **screen** program also maintains its own history buffers in memory for each terminal opened under it. The shell histories are maintained for a specified number of lines, the Fedora default being 1,000.

# Using the History

Now let's discover how we can use this history. There are two ways to access the contents of the history in order to reuse them. We can use the line number or we can use scroll back. Experiment 8-4 explores both of these methods.

---

## EXPERIMENT 8-4

---

First clear the existing history, then run a couple commands to add some new data to the history file and look at it again. By clearing the history file, you should have the same entries and results as I do for this experiment.

```
[student@testvm1 ~]$ history -c
[student@testvm1 ~]$ history
    1  history
[student@testvm1 ~]$ echo "This is a way to create a new file using the echo
command and redirection. It can also be used to append text to a file" >>
newfile1.txt
```

Note that I made this command a little long on purpose. Now look at the result. Just type the first part of the file name and press Tab to do the completion.

```
[student@testvm1 ~]$ cat new<Tab>file1.txt
This is a way to create a new file using the echo command and redirection. It
can also be used to append text to a file
```

Now press the **Up arrow (↑)** key once. You should see the command you just entered. Press the **Up arrow** key one more time to see the previous command. You should now be looking at the echo command. Press the **Enter** key to repeat this command and then look at the result using the Up arrow key to return to the cat command.

```
↑
[student@testvm1 ~]$ cat newfile1.txt Do not press Enter here!
↑
[student@testvm1 ~]$ echo "This is a way to create a new file using the echo
command and redirection. It can also be used to append text to a file" >>
newfile1.txt              Do press Enter here!
↑↑
[student@testvm1 ~]$ cat newfile1.txt
This is a way to create a new file using the echo command and redirection. It
can also be used to append text to a file
This is a way to create a new file using the echo command and redirection. It
can also be used to append text to a file
[student@testvm1 ~]$
```

There are now two lines of text in the file. Now look at the history.

```
[student@testvm1 ~]$ history
    1  history
    2  echo "This is a way to create a new file using the echo command
       and redirection. It can also be used to append text to a file" >>
       newfile1.txt
    3  cat newfile1.txt
    4  echo "This is a way to create a new file using the echo command
       and redirection. It can also be used to append text to a file" >>
       newfile1.txt
    5  cat newfile1.txt
    6  history
[student@testvm1 ~]$
```

Your history should be the same as mine at this point. If it is not, you can adjust the command number in the following sequence.

In addition to using the arrow keys to scroll through the Bash history, we can simply use the number of the entry we want to reuse. Let's add another line to the existing file using the command on line 4 of the history file.

```
[student@testvm1 ~]$ !4
echo "This is a way to create a new file using the echo command and
redirection. It can also be used to append text to a file" >> newfile1.txt
[student@testvm1 ~]$
```

Notice that the line number is preceded by the bang (exclamation point), which reruns the command from line 4 in the history. After you press the Enter key, Bash also displays the command that it is being executed. After you press the Enter key, though, there is no way to take it back.

---

**Note**    Be sure that you use the correct line number after the history buffer gets full. The default is 1,000 lines and until that number of entries is reached, the line numbers are constant. After that the line numbers of the historical commands change every time a new command is run.

---

Now we will do a little very simple command-line editing. Using the Up arrow key, scroll back to the following command but do not press the Enter key.

```
[student@testvm1 ~]$ echo "This is a way to create a new file using the echo
command and redirection. It can also be used to append text to a file" >>
newfile1.txt
```

Press the Left arrow key (◀) until the cursor is on the period in the file name. Then press the Backspace key to erase the "1." Type "2" to create the new filename "newfile2.txt" and press the **Enter** key.

List the files beginning with "new" to see the results of the previous command.

```
[student@testvm1 ~]$ ls -l new*
-rw-rw-r-- 1 student student 360 Dec 21 13:18 newfile1.txt
-rw-rw-r-- 1 student student 120 Dec 21 17:18 newfile2.txt
```

Command-line history, recall, and are very useful and time-saving tools for SysAdmins. One of the reasons I like the Bash shell is that it has the most usable history and recall features of all the shells I have tried. Bash is the default shell for most Linux distributions so it is probably the shell for your installation also.

By default the Bash shell has access to GNU emacs mode for editing the command line. Standard emacs commands can be used to move about and perform edits on the command contents. I prefer the vi mode because I am much more familiar with those editing keystrokes.

To set vi mode for editing on the Bash command line, add the following line to the /etc/bashrc configuration file.

```
set -o vi
```

By placing it there it becomes system-wide including for root and all other users. Shells that are currently open are not affected, but all shells opened after making this change will have vi mode set for editing. You can also enter that command on the command line for it to set vi mode in that specific instance of the Bash shell.

To enter vi command mode on the command line, press the **Esc** key just like you do when you are in vi. Then you can use the standard vi commands to move and edit the command.

## EXPERIMENT 8-5

Perform this experiment as the student user. To begin, you should open a terminal session if one is not already open. Then view the $SHELLOPTS environment variable to verify that emacs option is currently set. Then set vi editing mode and verify that it is set.

```
[student@testvm1 ~]$ echo $SHELLOPTS
braceexpand:emacs:hashall:histexpand:history:interactive-comments:monitor
[student@testvm1 ~]$ set -o vi
[student@testvm1 ~]$ echo $SHELLOPTS
braceexpand:hashall:histexpand:history:interactive-comments:monitor:vi
[student@testvm1 ~]$
```

The SHELLOPTS environment variable contains all of the options currently in effect for this instance of the shell. Now let's do something in vi mode.

1.  Scroll back to the long echo command we used in Experiment 8-4.

2.  Press the **Esc** key once to enter vi command mode.

3.  Type **23b** to go back 23 words.

4.  Type **d18w** to delete 18 words.

5.  Press the left arrow key once to place the cursor in the space at the end of the word "file."

6.  Press **r** to enter single-character replacement mode.

7.  Press the period key to replace the space.

8.  Press **^** (with the shift key) to move to the beginning of the line. Nothing to do here, just so you see that the cursor moves to the beginning of the line.

9.  Press **$** to move the cursor to the end of the line.

10. Here is something I discovered by accident. Press **Esc** and then **:w<Enter>** to save the line in the history. The line is saved without being executed and the command prompt is now empty.

11. Now scroll back to the last command, which should look like the line below. Do not press Enter.

    ```
    [student@testvm1 ~]$ echo "This is a way to create a new file."
    >> newfile2.txt
    ```

12. Use the left arrow key to move the cursor back to the "2."

13. Press **r** to enter replace mode and then **3** to replace "2" with "3." Your command line should now look like this.

    ```
    [student@testvm1 ~]$ echo "This is a way to create a new file."
    >> newfile3.txt
    ```

14. Now press **Enter**.

Verify the existence and content of the new file.

If you are already familiar with vi, the editing commands in Experiment 8-5 will already be familiar. The online Bash Reference Manual[4] has a chapter on Bash command-line editing and how to set and use both emacs and vi editing modes.

If you are not a vi user, you have just had your first lesson. But because emacs editing is the default, that mode of command-line editing is already available to you just by pressing the **Esc** key.

I won't pretend to know enough about emacs editing to be able to create an experiment that covers command-line editing in emacs mode for you. I did find an excellent source of information on the Web, Peter Krumins's blog, with more information and downloadable cheat sheets for Bash history,[5] Bash emacs editing,[6] and Bash vi editing.[7]

Many specialized tools also provide tab completion for their command-line interfaces. The names of those tools and the entries they recognize are maintained in the /etc/bash_completion.d directory.

---

[4]gnu.org, Bash Reference Manual – Command Line Editing, https://www.gnu.org/software/bash/manual/html_node/Command-Line-Editing.html

[5]Peter Krumins' Blog, Bash history, http://www.catonmat.net/blog/the-definitive-guide-to-bash-command-line-history/

[6]Peter Krumins's Blog, Bash emacs editing, http://www.catonmat.net/blog/bash-emacs-editing-mode-cheat-sheet/

[7]Peter Krumins's Blog, Bash vi editing, http://www.catonmat.net/blog/bash-vi-editing-mode-cheat-sheet/

# Logs Are Your Friend

Use the log files to help determine the source of problems and performance issues. They contain large amounts of data that can be used to track down many types of problems. The most common error I make when troubleshooting is not going to the log files sooner.

Almost all of the log files are located in /var/log and can be accessed either directly or with simple commands. The most current of each type of log file has no date as part of its name while older log files names have dates to differentiate them. In general and by default, the log files are maintained for a period of one month with each log file containing a maximum of one week of data. If the amount of data in a file passes a preconfigured threshold, the file may be rotated when it reaches that threshold rather than waiting for the full seven-day time period to pass.

The logrotate facility manages log rotation and deletion.

# SAR

My long-time favorite is System Activity Report, or SAR. SAR is an excellent place to start looking for information about a Linux computer's performance.

SAR has a daemon that runs in the background collecting data. Every 10 minutes the collected data is stored in the /var/log/sa directory. These logs are in a binary format and cannot be read directly. The `sar` command is used to view these records.

One of the advantages of SAR is the fact that it reports historical data for up to 30 days. This enables us to go back in time and see if we can locate patterns or specific periods when the load on one or more resources was very high. None of the other performance monitoring tools available for most distributions provide this type of historical data. Commands like top, iostat, vmstat, and so on all provide only instantaneous readings of the data they monitor.

---

**Note**    SAR is not installed or enabled on some distributions. Recent releases of Fedora do install and enable SAR, but older ones do not even install it.

---

---

**PREPARATION FOR EXPERIMENT 8-6**

---

Perform this preparation section as root to install SAR if it is not already installed. The package we need to install is sysstat. Use dnf or yum for RPM-based distributions or the package manager for your specific distribution.

```
[root@testvm1 ~]# dnf -y install sysstat
```

If you had to install the sysstat package, you may also need to enable and start it.

```
[root@testvm1 log]# systemctl enable sysstat
Created symlink /etc/systemd/system/multi-user.target.wants/sysstat.service
→ /usr/lib/systemd/system/sysstat.service.
Created symlink /etc/systemd/system/sysstat.service.wants/sysstat-collect.
timer → /usr/lib/systemd/system/sysstat-collect.timer.
Created symlink /etc/systemd/system/sysstat.service.wants/sysstat-summary.
timer → /usr/lib/systemd/system/sysstat-summary.timer.
[root@testvm1 log]# systemctl start sysstat
```

SAR is now installed and the system data collection processes have been started.

---

There will not be any data aggregated until after the the next 10-minute time increment, like on the hour, 10 after, 20 after, and so on. If you had to install the sysstat package, I suggest you wait for an hour or so to allow some data to accumulate. You can check the contents of /var/log/sa to verify that data is being collected. You could also check the messages file to look for entries pertaining to sysstat.

Now that you have the sysstat package installed and have waited for data to be collected, let's proceed with the experiment.

---

**EXPERIMENT 8-6**

---

In its simplest form the `sar` command displays CPU statistics in 10-minute summary increments since midnight. This task can be performed as the student user.

```
[student@testvm1 ~]# sar | head -25
Linux 4.14.5-300.fc27.x86_64 (testvm1)   12/23/2017 _x86_64_        (1 CPU)
```

| 12:00:02 AM | CPU | %user | %nice | %system | %iowait | %steal | %idle |
|---|---|---|---|---|---|---|---|
| 12:10:21 AM | all | 1.09 | 0.02 | 0.70 | 1.72 | 0.00 | 96.48 |
| 12:20:21 AM | all | 1.07 | 0.00 | 0.51 | 0.03 | 0.00 | 98.39 |
| 12:30:21 AM | all | 1.03 | 0.00 | 0.51 | 0.02 | 0.00 | 98.44 |
| 12:40:21 AM | all | 1.12 | 0.00 | 0.54 | 0.02 | 0.00 | 98.32 |
| 12:50:21 AM | all | 0.99 | 0.00 | 0.52 | 0.01 | 0.00 | 98.48 |
| 01:00:21 AM | all | 1.00 | 0.00 | 0.48 | 0.02 | 0.00 | 98.49 |
| 01:10:21 AM | all | 0.90 | 0.00 | 0.51 | 0.11 | 0.00 | 98.48 |
| 01:20:21 AM | all | 0.92 | 0.01 | 0.54 | 0.19 | 0.00 | 98.33 |
| 01:30:21 AM | all | 0.98 | 0.00 | 0.54 | 0.09 | 0.00 | 98.39 |
| 01:40:21 AM | all | 1.00 | 0.00 | 0.50 | 0.23 | 0.00 | 98.26 |
| 01:50:21 AM | all | 0.92 | 0.00 | 0.46 | 0.02 | 0.00 | 98.60 |
| 02:00:21 AM | all | 0.90 | 0.00 | 0.47 | 0.05 | 0.00 | 98.58 |
| 02:10:21 AM | all | 0.97 | 0.00 | 0.44 | 0.23 | 0.00 | 98.36 |
| 02:20:21 AM | all | 0.92 | 0.04 | 0.51 | 0.05 | 0.00 | 98.48 |
| 02:30:21 AM | all | 0.91 | 0.00 | 0.49 | 0.11 | 0.00 | 98.49 |
| 02:40:21 AM | all | 0.88 | 0.00 | 0.46 | 0.11 | 0.00 | 98.56 |
| 02:50:21 AM | all | 0.98 | 0.00 | 0.48 | 0.02 | 0.00 | 98.53 |
| 03:00:21 AM | all | 0.93 | 0.00 | 0.47 | 0.02 | 0.00 | 98.58 |
| 03:10:21 AM | all | 0.94 | 0.00 | 0.47 | 0.08 | 0.00 | 98.51 |
| 03:20:21 AM | all | 0.91 | 0.02 | 0.45 | 0.07 | 0.00 | 98.55 |
| 03:30:21 AM | all | 1.39 | 2.19 | 7.21 | 5.89 | 0.00 | 83.32 |
| 03:40:21 AM | all | 0.94 | 0.06 | 0.71 | 0.07 | 0.00 | 98.22 |

I have used the head utility to truncate the output after 25 lines for this experiment. Each line in the output displays the averages of all the data collected during each 10-minute period. So that for the period ending at 03:10:21, the idle time for the CPU was 98.51%.

Now run the sar command using the -A option to display all of the data types collected by SAR. Run it through the less utility so you can page through the data, which is far to long for me to reproduce here.

```
[student@testvm1 ~]$ sar -A | less
```

By default, the sar command shows the data collected for today, up to the current time. Data for days up to one month in the past can be located in files in the /var/log/sa directory. The files are named saXX where XX is the day of the month. To see data from a previous day, use the following command. Be sure to use the name of a file that is present in your own sa directory.

```
[root@testvm1 sa]# sar -A -f sa07 | less
```

The preceding command displays all of the data for the 7th day of the month and pipes it to the `less` command.

The large amount of data produced by SAR can be daunting to try to interpret, but I have found it to be very useful in locating various types of problems.

Many distributions still put the sysstat script in /etc/cron.d to run the data aggregation program, sa1, at specified intervals of 10 minutes. In current versions of Fedora, the data aggregation is managed by systemd and the several control files are located in the /usr/lib/systemd/system directory.

I suggest that you spend some time on a regular basis to look through the SAR results. This will provide you with some knowledge of what your system should look like when it is running correctly. That will make it easier to spot problems when they do occur.

The SAR man page has a lot of information about the data collected and how to display specific types of data such as disk, CPU, network, and others. Despite that, many of the headings in the SAR reports can be difficult to decipher at first. Much googling has turned up very little in the way of decoding keys for the SAR report column headings, but I did find one web site that has the best descriptions anywhere.[8] The best book I have found in my own Linux reference collection, one that contains many references to SAR and its use is *The Unix and Linux System Administration Handbook*.[9] Most other books that cover SAR stick to CPU statistics but SAR provides far more data than that and this book covers at least some of that.

# Mail Logs

I run my own personal mail server and frequently use the logs to resolve problems. In the case of email, problems tend to be related to the non-delivery of mail or blocking spam and other unwanted email.

I find log entries in the /var/log/maillog files that tell me whether an email was delivered or not, and sometimes enough information to tell me why it was not delivered. If you run a mail server, you should become very familiar with the maillog files.

---

[8]Computer Hope website, https://www.computerhope.com/unix/usar.htm

[9]Nemeth, Evi [et al.], *The Unix and Linux System Administration Handbook*, Pearson Education, Inc., ISBN 978-0-13-148005-6. This title is also available on Amazon in Kindle format.

# messages

The /var/log/messages log files contain kernel and other system-level messages of various types. This is another of the files I frequently use to assist me with problem determination. Entries from the kernel, systemd, and many of the running services are logged here. Each log entry begins with the date and time to make it easy to determine the sequence of events and to locate entries made at specific times in the log file.

Because it is so important, let's take a quick look at the messages file.

---

**EXPERIMENT 8-7**

Perform this experiment as the root user. Make /var/log the PWD. Use the `less` command to view the messages log file.

```
[root@testvm1 log]# less messages
```

I have not included any output from my test VM because of the large amount of data that is displayed. Browse through the contents of the messages file to get a feel for the types of messages you will typically encounter. Use **Ctrl-C** to terminate `less`.

---

The messages log files are full of interesting and useful information.

- SAR data collection

- DHCP client requests for network configuration

- The resulting DHCP configuration information

- Data logged by systemd during startup and shutdown

- Kernel data about things such as USB memory devices when they are plugged in

- USB hub information

- And much more

The messages file is usually the first place I look when working on non-performance issues. It can also be useful for performance issues, but I start with SAR for that.

# dmesg

dmesg is not a file, it is a command. There used to be a log file named dmesg that contained all of the messages generated by the kernel during boot and most messages generated during startup. The startup process begins when the boot process ends, when init or systemd take control of the host.

The dmesg command displays all of the messages generated by the kernel including massive amounts of data about the hardware it discovers during the boot process. I always start with this command when looking for bootup problems and hardware issues.

---

**Note**    Much of the hardware data found in the output from dmesg can be found in the /proc filesystem.

---

Let's look at a bit of the output from the dmesg command.

---

### EXPERIMENT 8-8

---

This experiment can be performed as the either the root or the student user.

```
[root@testvm1 log]# dmesg | less
[    0.000000] Linux version 4.14.5-300.fc27.x86_64 (mockbuild@bkernel01.
phx2.fedoraproject.org) (gcc version 7.2.1 20170915 (Red Hat 7.2.1-2) (GCC))
#1 SMP Mon Dec 11 16:00:36 UTC 2017
[    0.000000] Command line: BOOT_IMAGE=/vmlinuz-4.14.5-300.fc27.x86_64
root=/dev/mapper/fedora_testvm1-root ro rd.lvm.lv=fedora_testvm1/root rd.lvm.
lv=fedora_testvm1/swap
[    0.000000] x86/fpu: Supporting XSAVE feature 0x001: 'x87 floating point
registers'
[    0.000000] x86/fpu: Supporting XSAVE feature 0x002: 'SSE registers'
[    0.000000] x86/fpu: Supporting XSAVE feature 0x004: 'AVX registers'
[    0.000000] x86/fpu: xstate_offset[2]:  576, xstate_sizes[2]:  256
[    0.000000] x86/fpu: Enabled xstate features 0x7, context size is 832
bytes, using 'standard' format.
[    0.000000] e820: BIOS-provided physical RAM map:
[    0.000000] BIOS-e820: [mem 0x0000000000000000-0x000000000009fbff] usable
[    0.000000] BIOS-e820: [mem 0x000000000009fc00-0x000000000009ffff]
reserved
```

```
[    0.000000] BIOS-e820: [mem 0x00000000000f0000-0x00000000000fffff]
reserved
[    0.000000] BIOS-e820: [mem 0x0000000000100000-0x00000000dffeffff] usable
[    0.000000] BIOS-e820: [mem 0x00000000dfff0000-0x00000000dfffffff] ACPI
data
[    0.000000] BIOS-e820: [mem 0x00000000fec00000-0x00000000fec00fff]
reserved
[    0.000000] BIOS-e820: [mem 0x00000000fee00000-0x00000000fee00fff]
reserved
[    0.000000] BIOS-e820: [mem 0x00000000fffc0000-0x00000000ffffffff]
reserved
[    0.000000] BIOS-e820: [mem 0x0000000100000000-0x000000011fffffff] usable
```

Most of the lines in the sample data are wrapped, which makes it a bit more difficult to read. Each line of data starts with a timestamp accurate to within a microsecond. The timestamp represents the time since the kernel started.

Scroll through the data to familiarize yourself with the many different types of data to be found here.

The data displayed by the dmesg command is located in RAM rather than on the hard drive. No matter how much RAM memory you have in your host, the space allocated to the dmesg buffer is limited. When it fills up, the oldest data is discarded as newer data is added.

# secure

The /var/log/secure log file contains security-related entries. This includes information about successful and unsuccessful attempt to log in to the system. Let's look at some of the entries you might see in this file.

---

**EXPERIMENT 8-9**

This experiment must be performed as root. Use the **less** command to view the contents of the secure log file.

```
[root@testvm1 log]# less secure
Dec 24 13:44:25 testvm1 sshd[1001]: pam_systemd(sshd:session): Failed to
release session: Interrupted system call
```

Dec 24 13:44:25 testvm1 sshd[1001]: pam_unix(sshd:session): session closed for user student
Dec 24 13:44:25 testvm1 systemd[929]: pam_unix(systemd-user:session): session closed for user sddm
Dec 24 13:44:25 testvm1 sshd[937]: pam_systemd(sshd:session): Failed to release session: Interrupted system call
Dec 24 13:44:25 testvm1 sshd[937]: pam_unix(sshd:session): session closed for user root
Dec 24 13:44:25 testvm1 sshd[770]: Received signal 15; terminating.
Dec 24 13:44:25 testvm1 systemd[940]: pam_unix(systemd-user:session): session closed for user root
Dec 24 13:44:25 testvm1 systemd[1004]: pam_unix(systemd-user:session): session closed for user student
Dec 24 13:45:03 testvm1 polkitd[756]: Loading rules from directory /etc/polkit-1/rules.d
Dec 24 13:45:03 testvm1 polkitd[756]: Loading rules from directory /usr/share/polkit-1/rules.d
Dec 24 13:45:04 testvm1 polkitd[756]: Finished loading, compiling and executing 9 rules
Dec 24 13:45:04 testvm1 polkitd[756]: Acquired the name org.freedesktop.PolicyKit1 on the system bus
Dec 24 13:45:04 testvm1 sshd[785]: Server listening on 0.0.0.0 port 22.
Dec 24 13:45:04 testvm1 sshd[785]: Server listening on :: port 22.
Dec 24 13:45:09 testvm1 sddm-helper[938]: PAM unable to dlopen(/usr/lib64/security/pam_elogind.so): /usr/lib64/security/pam_elogind.so: cannot open shared object file: No such file or directory
Dec 24 13:45:09 testvm1 sddm-helper[938]: PAM adding faulty module: /usr/lib64/security/pam_elogind.so
Dec 24 13:45:09 testvm1 sddm-helper[938]: pam_unix(sddm-greeter:session): session opened for user sddm by (uid=0)
Dec 24 13:45:09 testvm1 systemd[939]: pam_unix(systemd-user:session): session opened for user sddm by (uid=0)
Dec 24 13:46:18 testvm1 sshd[961]: Accepted publickey for root from 192.168.0.1 port 46764 ssh2: RSA SHA256:4UDdGg3FP5sITB8ydfCb5JDg2QCIrsW4cfoNgFxhC5A
Dec 24 13:46:18 testvm1 systemd[963]: pam_unix(systemd-user:session): session opened for user root by (uid=0)
Dec 24 13:46:18 testvm1 sshd[961]: pam_unix(sshd:session): session opened for user root by (uid=0)

```
Dec 24 15:37:02 testvm1 sshd[1155]: Accepted password for student from
192.168.0.1 port 56530 ssh2
Dec 24 15:37:02 testvm1 systemd[1157]: pam_unix(systemd-user:session):
session opened for user student by (uid=0)
Dec 24 15:37:03 testvm1 sshd[1155]: pam_unix(sshd:session): session opened
for user student by (uid=0)
######################### <snip> #########################
Dec 26 13:02:39 testvm1 sshd[31135]: Invalid user hacker from 192.168.0.1
port 46046
Dec 26 13:04:21 testvm1 sshd[31135]: pam_unix(sshd:auth): check pass; user
unknown
Dec 26 13:04:21 testvm1 sshd[31135]: pam_unix(sshd:auth): authentication
failure; logname= uid=0 euid=0 tty=ssh ruser= rhost=192.168.0.1
Dec 26 13:04:24 testvm1 sshd[31135]: Failed password for invalid user hacker
from 192.168.0.1 port 46046 ssh2
Dec 26 13:04:27 testvm1 sshd[31135]: pam_unix(sshd:auth): check pass; user
unknown
Dec 26 13:04:29 testvm1 sshd[31135]: Failed password for invalid user hacker
from 192.168.0.1 port 46046 ssh2
Dec 26 13:04:30 testvm1 sshd[31135]: pam_unix(sshd:auth): check pass; user
unknown
Dec 26 13:04:32 testvm1 sshd[31135]: Failed password for invalid user hacker
from 192.168.0.1 port 46046 ssh2
Dec 26 13:04:32 testvm1 sshd[31135]: Connection closed by invalid user hacker
192.168.0.1 port 46046 [preauth]
Dec 26 13:04:32 testvm1 sshd[31135]: PAM 2 more authentication failures;
logname= uid=0 euid=0 tty=ssh ruser= rhost=192.168.0.1
```

Most of the data in /var/log/secure pertains to records of users' logins and logouts and information about whether a password or public key was used for authentication.

This log also contains failed password attempts as shown in the data below the line where I snipped out some of the data in this file.

My primary use for the secure log file is to identify break-in attempts from hackers. But I don't even do that – I use automation tools for that, too. In this case, the logwatch tool.

# Following Log Files

Searching through log files can be a time-consuming and cumbersome task even when using tools like grep to help isolate the desired lines. Many times while troubleshooting, it can be helpful to continuously view the contents of a text format log file especially to see the newest entries as they arrive. Using cat or grep to view log files displays the contents at the moment in time the command was entered.

I like to use the tail command to view the end of the file but it can be time consuming and disruptive to my problem determination process to rerun the tail command to see new lines. Use tail -f to enable the tail command to "follow" the file and immediately display new lines of data as they are added.

---

### EXPERIMENT 8-10

You should be using a non-production host that has little or no activity. That is perfect for performing most experiments but this one requires some activity so that you can observe the new log entries as they are added.

Perform this experiment as root. We need two terminal sessions with root logins. These terminal sessions should be in separate windows and arranged so you can see both of them at the same time. In one root terminal session, make /var/log the PWD and then follow the messages file.

```
[root@testvm1 ~]# cd /var/log
[root@testvm1 log]# tail -f messages
Dec 24 09:30:21 testvm1 audit[1]: SERVICE_STOP pid=1 uid=0 auid=4294967295
ses=4294967295 msg='unit=sysstat-collect comm="systemd" exe="/usr/lib/
systemd/systemd" hostname=? addr=? terminal=? res=success'
<snip>
Dec 24 09:37:58 testvm1 systemd[1]: Starting dnf makecache...
Dec 24 09:37:59 testvm1 dnf[29405]: Metadata cache refreshed recently.
Dec 24 09:37:59 testvm1 systemd[1]: Started dnf makecache.
Dec 24 09:40:21 testvm1 audit[1]: SERVICE_STOP pid=1 uid=0 auid=4294967295
ses=4294967295 msg='unit=sysstat-collect comm="systemd" exe="/usr/lib/
systemd/systemd" hostname=? addr=? terminal=? res=success'
```

Tail displays the last 10 lines of the log file and then sits there waiting for more data to be appended. I have deleted some of these lines for brevity.

Let's make some log entries appear. There are several ways to do this, but the easiest is to use the logger command. In the second window, enter this command as root to log a new entry to the messages file.

```
[root@testvm1 ~]# logger "This is test message 1."
```

The following line should have appeared in the other terminal at the end of the messages log file.

```
Dec 24 13:51:46 testvm1 root[1048]: This is test message 1.
```

We can also use STDIO for this.

```
[root@testvm1 ~]# echo "This is test message 2." | logger
```

And the results are the same – the message appears in the messages log file.

```
Dec 24 13:56:41 testvm1 root[1057]: This is test message 2.
```

Use Ctrl-C to terminate following the log file.

# systemd Logs

The relatively new replacement for the SystemV start scripts, systemd, has its own set of logs, many of which are replacing the traditional ASCII text files found in the /var/log directory. The journald daemon collects and manages messages for services managed by systemd. The journalctl command is used by SysAdmins to view and manipulate the systemd logs.

The intent of using systemd to manage the logs is to provide a central point of control for all of the log-producing entities in a Linux host.

Let's explore a few of the basics of using journalctl.

---

**EXPERIMENT 8-11**

This experiment must be run as root. First let's look at the output we get with no options. By default, the results are piped through the less utility.

```
[root@testvm1 ~]# journalctl
-- Logs begin at Sat 2017-04-29 18:10:23 EDT, end at Wed 2017-12-27 11:30:07
EST. --
Apr 29 18:10:23 testvm1 systemd-journald[160]: Runtime journal (/run/log/
journal/) is 8.0M, max 197.6M,
```

```
Apr 29 18:10:23 testvm1 kernel: Linux version 4.8.6-300.fc25.x86_64
(mockbuild@bkernel02.phx2.fedorapro
Apr 29 18:10:23 testvm1 kernel: Command line: BOOT_IMAGE=/vmlinuz-4.8.6-300.
fc25.x86_64 root=/dev/mappe
Apr 29 18:10:23 testvm1 kernel: x86/fpu: Supporting XSAVE feature 0x001: 'x87
floating point registers'
Apr 29 18:10:23 testvm1 kernel: x86/fpu: Supporting XSAVE feature 0x002: 'SSE
registers'
Apr 29 18:10:23 testvm1 kernel: x86/fpu: Supporting XSAVE feature 0x004: 'AVX
registers'
```

I have only shown a small portion of the output from the journalctl command. It should look familiar because it is. This is almost the same information as the dmesg command provides. The main difference is that the timestamp for dmesg is in seconds since boot and the timestamps for journalctl are in a standard date and time format.

Take some time to page through the results and explore the types of log entries located there. One of the features I learned about while researching this experiment is the ability to define a specific time frame in which to search for log entries. One example is shown here.

```
[root@testvm1 ~]# journalctl --since 2017-12-20 --until 2017-12-24
```

It is also possible to specify times of day and to use fuzzy times like "yesterday" and user names to further define the results.

```
[root@testvm1 ~]# journalctl --since yesterday -u NetworkManager
-- Logs begin at Sat 2017-04-29 18:10:23 EDT, end at Wed 2017-12-27 11:50:07
EST. --
Dec 26 00:09:23 testvm1 dhclient[856]: DHCPREQUEST on enp0s3 to 192.168.0.51
port 67 (xid=0xaa5aef49)
Dec 26 00:09:23 testvm1 dhclient[856]: DHCPACK from 192.168.0.51
(xid=0xaa5aef49)
Dec 26 00:09:23 testvm1 NetworkManager[731]: <info>  [1514264963.5813] dhcp4
(enp0s3):   address 192.168.0.101
Dec 26 00:09:23 testvm1 NetworkManager[731]: <info>  [1514264963.5819] dhcp4
(enp0s3):   plen 24 (255.255.255.0)
Dec 26 00:09:23 testvm1 NetworkManager[731]: <info>  [1514264963.5821] dhcp4
(enp0s3):   gateway 192.168.0.254
Dec 26 00:09:23 testvm1 NetworkManager[731]: <info>  [1514264963.5823] dhcp4
(enp0s3):   lease time 21600
```

```
Dec 26 00:09:23 testvm1 NetworkManager[731]: <info>  [1514264963.5825] dhcp4
(enpOs3):   nameserver '192.168.0.51'
Dec 26 00:09:23 testvm1 NetworkManager[731]: <info>  [1514264963.5826] dhcp4
(enpOs3):   nameserver '8.8.8.8'
Dec 26 00:09:23 testvm1 NetworkManager[731]: <info>  [1514264963.5828] dhcp4
(enpOs3):   nameserver '8.8.4.4'
Dec 26 00:09:23 testvm1 NetworkManager[731]: <info>  [1514264963.5830] dhcp4
(enpOs3):   domain name 'both.org'
Dec 26 00:09:23 testvm1 NetworkManager[731]: <info>  [1514264963.5831] dhcp4
(enpOs3): state changed bound -> bound
Dec 26 00:09:23 testvm1 dhclient[856]: bound to 192.168.0.101 -- renewal in
9790 seconds.
Dec 26 02:52:33 testvm1 dhclient[856]: DHCPREQUEST on enpOs3 to 192.168.0.51
port 67 (xid=0xaa5aef49)
Dec 26 02:52:33 testvm1 dhclient[856]: DHCPACK from 192.168.0.51
(xid=0xaa5aef49)
Dec 26 02:52:33 testvm1 NetworkManager[731]: <info>  [1514274753.4249] dhcp4
(enpOs3):   address 192.168.0.101
Dec 26 02:52:33 testvm1 NetworkManager[731]: <info>  [1514274753.4253] dhcp4
(enpOs3):   plen 24 (255.255.255.0)
Dec 26 02:52:33 testvm1 NetworkManager[731]: <info>  [1514274753.4255] dhcp4
(enpOs3):   gateway 192.168.0.254
Dec 26 02:52:33 testvm1 NetworkManager[731]: <info>  [1514274753.4256] dhcp4
(enpOs3):   lease time 21600
Dec 26 02:52:33 testvm1 NetworkManager[731]: <info>  [1514274753.4258] dhcp4
(enpOs3):   nameserver '192.168.0.51'
Dec 26 02:52:33 testvm1 NetworkManager[731]: <info>  [1514274753.4260] dhcp4
(enpOs3):   nameserver '8.8.8.8'
Dec 26 02:52:33 testvm1 NetworkManager[731]: <info>  [1514274753.4262] dhcp4
(enpOs3):   nameserver '8.8.4.4'
Dec 26 02:52:33 testvm1 NetworkManager[731]: <info>  [1514274753.4263] dhcp4
(enpOs3):   domain name 'both.org'
```

It is possible to list the previous boots for the system and to view only log entries from the current or a previous boot.

```
[root@testvm1 ~]# journalctl --list-boots
-24 f5c1c24249df4d589ca8acb07d2edcf8 Sat 2017-04-29 18:10:23 EDT—Sun 2017-04-30
07:21:53 EDT
-23 ca4f8a71782246b292920e92bbdf968e Sun 2017-04-30 07:22:13 EDT—Sun 2017-04-30
08:41:23 EDT
-22 ca8203a3d32046e9a96e301b4c4b270a Sun 2017-04-30 08:41:38 EDT—Sun 2017-04-30
09:21:47 EDT
-21 1e5d609d89a543708a12f91b3e94350f Tue 2017-05-02 04:32:32 EDT—Tue 2017-05-02
08:51:42 EDT
-20 74b2554da751454f9f75c541d9390fc0 Sun 2017-05-07 05:35:44 EDT—Sun 2017-05-07
09:43:27 EDT
-19 4a6d9f2f34aa49a7bfba31368ce489e5 Fri 2017-05-12 06:11:48 EDT—Fri 2017-05-12
10:14:34 EDT
-18 bf8d02a57d0f4e9b849405ede1ffc80b Sat 2017-05-13 05:42:07 EDT—Sat 2017-05-13
12:20:36 EDT
-17 2463e2f48dd04bbfa03b72df90367990 Wed 2017-11-15 07:41:42 EST—Wed 2017-11-15
12:43:14 EST
-16 7882d4c7ff5c43a7b9404bb5aded31f1 Wed 2017-11-15 07:43:28 EST—Wed 2017-11-15
15:39:07 EST
-15 b19061d077634733b3ef5d54a8034665 Wed 2017-11-15 15:39:25 EST—Wed 2017-11-15
16:44:25 EST
-14 3c3c73161a0540d6b02ac14a3fe96fd2 Wed 2017-11-15 16:44:43 EST—Wed 2017-11-15
18:24:38 EST
-13 5807bb2932794fd18bb5bf74345e6586 Thu 2017-11-16 09:06:49 EST—Thu 2017-11-16
21:46:54 EST
-12 1df2c5a7500844a18c692a00ad834a5e Thu 2017-11-16 21:51:47 EST—Tue 2017-11-21
17:00:22 EST
-11 fe65766e48484d6bb45e450a1e46d257 Wed 2017-11-22 03:50:03 EST—Fri 2017-12-01
06:50:03 EST
-10 d84cf9eb31dc4d0886e1e474e21f7e45 Sat 2017-12-02 11:45:45 EST—Mon 2017-12-04
17:01:53 EST
 -9 d8234499519e4f4689acc326035b5b77 Thu 2017-12-07 07:52:08 EST—Mon 2017-12-11
06:40:44 EST
 -8 ec50e23f7ffb49b0af06fb0a415931c2 Tue 2017-12-12 03:17:36 EST—Fri 2017-12-15
21:42:09 EST
 -7 de72447d9eea4bbe9bdf29df4e4ae79c Sun 2017-12-17 11:13:43 EST—Sun 2017-12-17
21:30:54 EST
```

```
-6 a8781fdba6cc417dbde3c35ed1a11cc0 Sun 2017-12-17 21:31:11 EST-Tue 2017-12-19
21:57:23 EST
-5 6ed3997fc5bf4a99bbab3cc0d3a35d80 Wed 2017-12-20 16:54:01 EST-Fri 2017-12-22
10:48:30 EST
-4 c96aa6518d6d40df902fb85f0b5a9d5b Fri 2017-12-22 10:48:39 EST-Sun 2017-12-24
13:44:28 EST
-3 ad6217b027f34b3db6215e9d9eeb9d0b Sun 2017-12-24 13:44:44 EST-Mon 2017-12-25
15:26:28 EST
-2 aca68c1bae4741de8d38de9a9d28a72e Mon 2017-12-25 15:26:44 EST-Mon 2017-12-25
15:29:39 EST
-1 23169c91452645418a22c553cc387f99 Mon 2017-12-25 15:29:54 EST-Mon 2017-12-25
15:31:40 EST
 0 3335b2cb0d124ee0a93d2ac64537aa54 Mon 2017-12-25 15:31:55 EST-Wed 2017-12-27
11:50:07 EST
```

`[root@testvm1 ~]# journalctl -b ec50e23f7ffb49b0af06fb0a415931c2`

The identifier for the boot that this command would list is from line 8 in the boot list. Be sure to use an identifier from your own system for this last command.

I don't show any of the output from the last command because it is long. Be sure to spend some time looking through the data from this last command.

As you can see in Experiment 8-11, the systemd logging facilities collect data from the beginning of the boot process to the end of the shutdown. All types of logs are located in the journal database. You can use the search facility of the less utility to locate specific entries or you can use the options available within journalctl itself.

If you are interested in finding out more about managing systemd logs, you can start with the man page for journalctl. Digital Ocean has an excellent discussion of journalctl.[10]

# logwatch

Using tools like grep and tail to view a few lines from a log file while working on a problem is fine. But what if you need to search through a large number of log files? That can be tedious even when using those tools.

---

[10]Digital Ocean, "How To Use Journalctl to View and Manipulate Systemd Logs," https://www.digitalocean.com/community/tutorials/how-to-use-journalctl-to-view-and-manipulate-systemd-logs

Logwatch is a tool that can analyze the system log files and detect anomalous entries that the SysAdmin should look at. It generates a report every night around midnight. The daily report is triggered by a file in /etc/cron.daily.

The default configuration is for Logwatch to email a report of what it finds in the log files to root. There are various methods for ensuring that the email gets sent to someone and someplace other than root on the local host. One option is to call set the mailto address in the configuration file in the /etc/logwatch directory.

Logwatch can also be run from the command line and the data is sent to STDOUT. That sounds like it might be fun to explore.

---

### EXPERIMENT 8-12

This experiment must be performed as root. Our objective is to run Logwatch from the command line and view the results.

```
[root@david ~]# logwatch | less
################### Logwatch 7.4.3 (04/27/16) ###################
        Processing Initiated: Wed Dec 27 09:43:13 2017
        Date Range Processed: yesterday
                             ( 2017-Dec-26 )
                             Period is day.
        Detail Level of Output: 10
        Type of Output/Format: stdout / text
        Logfiles for Host: david
################################################################
-------------------- Disk Space Begin -----------------------
```

| Filesystem | Size | Used | Avail | Use% | Mounted on |
|---|---|---|---|---|---|
| devtmpfs | 32G | 0 | 32G | 0% | /dev |
| /dev/mapper/david1-root | 9.1G | 444M | 8.2G | 6% | / |
| /dev/mapper/david1-usr | 46G | 14G | 31G | 31% | /usr |
| /dev/sdc1 | 1.9G | 400M | 1.4G | 24% | /boot |
| /dev/mapper/vg_david2-stuff | 128G | 107G | 16G | 88% | /stuff |
| /dev/mapper/david1-var | 19G | 5.4G | 12G | 32% | /var |
| /dev/mapper/david1-tmp | 29G | 12G | 15G | 44% | /tmp |
| /dev/mapper/vg_david2-home | 50G | 27G | 20G | 58% | /home |
| /dev/mapper/vg_david2-Pictures | 74G | 18G | 53G | 25% | /home/dboth/Pictures |

```
/dev/mapper/vg_david2-Virtual    581G   402G   153G   73% /Virtual
/dev/mapper/vg_Backups-Backups   3.6T   2.9T   597G   83% /media/Backups
/dev/sdd1                        3.6T   1.6T   1.9T   45% /media/4T-Backup

-------------------- Disk Space End --------------------

-------------------- Fortune Begin ---------------------
If we do not change our direction we are likely to end up where we are
headed.
-------------------- Fortune End -----------------------
-------------------- lm_sensors output Begin -----------------------
coretemp-isa-0000
Adapter: ISA adapter
Package id 0:   +50.0 C   (high = +95.0 C, crit = +105.0 C)
Core 0:         +46.0 C   (high = +95.0 C, crit = +105.0 C)
Core 1:         +49.0 C   (high = +95.0 C, crit = +105.0 C)
Core 2:         +45.0 C   (high = +95.0 C, crit = +105.0 C)
Core 3:         +50.0 C   (high = +95.0 C, crit = +105.0 C)
Core 4:         +48.0 C   (high = +95.0 C, crit = +105.0 C)
Core 5:         +46.0 C   (high = +95.0 C, crit = +105.0 C)
Core 6:         +44.0 C   (high = +95.0 C, crit = +105.0 C)
Core 7:         +46.0 C   (high = +95.0 C, crit = +105.0 C)
Core 8:         +50.0 C   (high = +95.0 C, crit = +105.0 C)
Core 9:         +49.0 C   (high = +95.0 C, crit = +105.0 C)
Core 10:        +50.0 C   (high = +95.0 C, crit = +105.0 C)
Core 11:        +45.0 C   (high = +95.0 C, crit = +105.0 C)
Core 12:        +47.0 C   (high = +95.0 C, crit = +105.0 C)
Core 13:        +45.0 C   (high = +95.0 C, crit = +105.0 C)
Core 14:        +45.0 C   (high = +95.0 C, crit = +105.0 C)
Core 15:        +47.0 C   (high = +95.0 C, crit = +105.0 C)

radeon-pci-6500
Adapter: PCI adapter
temp1:          +39.0 C   (crit = +120.0 C, hyst = +90.0 C)

asus-isa-0000
Adapter: ISA adapter
cpu_fan:        0 RPM
-------------------- lm_sensors output End -----------------------
```

Page through the data produced by Logwatch and be sure to look for the Kernel, Cron, Disk Space, and Systemd sections. If you have a physical host on which to run this experiment, and if the lm_sensors package is installed, you may also see a section showing temperatures in various parts of the hardware, including that for each CPU.

I have only included a few sections of the output because Logwatch produces over 1,400 lines on my workstation.

---

The sections that appear in the Logwatch output depends upon the software packages you have installed on your Linux computer. So if you are looking at the output from Logwatch for a basic installation rather than a primary workstation or even a server, you will see far fewer entries.

Since 2014, Logwatch does have the ability to search the journald database for log entries.[11] This compatibility with the systemd logging facility ensures that a major source of log entries is not ignored.

# Success as a Lazy SysAdmin

By now you have figured out that this chapter is not really about being lazy in the usual sense of the term. The successful lazy SysAdmin is not lazy – just efficient. As it was with my time as a CE at IBM, preventing problems by anticipating them and doing the necessary work to ensure that they do not occur or that they can be resolved efficiently pays dividends in the long run.

The strategies I have discussed here are not the only ones that can be used to enhance our own efficiency. I am certain that you already have found many of your own ways to work smarter.

There is one way to greatly leverage our skill and knowledge that I have not discussed yet in any detail though I have mentioned it many times. In Chapter 9, we will explore the tenet "Automate Everything" and what that really means.

---

[11]SourceForge, Logwatch repository, https://sourceforge.net/p/logwatch/patches/34/

# CHAPTER 9

# Automate Everything

My question is, "What is the function of computers?" The right answer is, "to automate mundane tasks in order to allow us humans to concentrate on the tasks that the computers cannot – yet – do." For SysAdmins, those of us who run and manage the computers most closely, we have direct access to the tools that can help us work more efficiently. We should use those tools to maximum benefit.

In this chapter, we explore using automation to make our own lives as SysAdmins easier.

## Why I Use Scripts

In Chapter 8, "Be a Lazy SysAdmin", I state, "A SysAdmin is most productive when thinking – thinking about how to solve existing problems and about how to avoid future problems; thinking about how to monitor Linux computers in order to find clues that anticipate and foreshadow those future problems; thinking about how to make her job more efficient; thinking about how to automate all of those tasks that need to be performed whether every day or once a year."

SysAdmins are next most productive when creating the shell programs that automate the solutions that they have conceived while appearing to be unproductive. The more automation we have in place, the more time we have available to fix real problems when they occur and to contemplate how to automate even more than we already have.

I have learned that, for me at least, writing shell programs – also known as scripts – provides the best strategy for leveraging my time. Once having written a shell program, it can be rerun as many times as needed.

I can update my shell scripts as needed to compensate for changes from one release of Linux to the next. Other factors that might require making these changes are the installation of new hardware and software, changes in what I want or need to accomplish with the script, adding new functions, removing functions that are no longer needed, and fixing the not-so-rare bugs in my scripts. These kinds of changes are just part of the maintenance cycle for any type of code.

Every task performed via the keyboard in a terminal session by entering and executing shell commands can and should be automated. SysAdmins should automate everything we are asked to do or that we decide on our own needs to be done. Many times I have found that doing the automation up front saves time the first time.

One bash script can contain anywhere from a few commands to many thousands. In fact, I have written bash scripts that have only one or two commands in them. Another script I have written contains over 2,700 lines, more than half of which are comments.

# How I Got Here

How did I get to the point of "automate everything?"

Have you ever performed a long and complex task at the command line thinking, "Glad that's done – I never have to worry about it again."? I have – very frequently. I ultimately figured out that almost everything that I ever need to do on a computer, whether mine or one that belongs to my employer or one of my consulting customers, will need to be done again sometime in the future.

Of course I always think that I will remember how I did the task in question. But the next time I need to do it is far enough out into the future that I sometimes even forget that I have ever done it at all, let alone how to do it. For some tasks I used to do, I started writing down the steps required on a bit of paper. I thought, "How stupid of me!" So I then transferred those scribbles to a simple note pad type application on my computer. Suddenly one day I thought again, "How stupid of me!" If I am going to store this data on my computer, I might as well create a shell script and store it in a standard location so that I can just type the name of the shell program and it does all of the tasks I used to do manually.

My personal main reason for automating everything is that any task that must be performed once will certainly need to be done again. By collecting the commands required to perform the task into a file to use as a shell program, it becomes easy to run that exact same set of commands at a later time.

For me automation also means that I don't have to remember or re-create the details of how I performed that task in order to do it again. It takes time to remember how to do things and time to type in all of the commands. This can become a significant time sink for tasks that require typing large numbers of long commands. Automating tasks by creating shell scripts reduces the typing necessary to perform my routine tasks.

Shell programs can also be an important aid to newer SysAdmins to enable them to keep things working while the senior SysAdmin is out on vacation or ill. Because shell programs are inherently open to view and change, they can be an important tool for less experienced SysAdmins to learn the details of how to perform these tasks when they need to be responsible for them.

# Scripting Repetitive Tasks

I have always had several – sometimes as many as 14 or 15 – computers at one time, although I am currently down to 8 or 9, and a similar number of virtual machines that I use for testing. I also install Linux on customer systems. As a result, I do frequent installations of Linux. Sometimes several a day. This results in the need to do fast, repeatable installations.

For example, I have a favorite set of configurations that I do for things like Midnight Commander (mc), a powerful file manager with a text mode user interface, and other configurable tools. I also have a number of fonts that I like to install that are not part of most default installations. I could install each font manually using DNF, and I could make the configuration changes to Midnight Commander manually each time I do an install, but that take a lot of time and gets to be very tedious and boring.

When I was doing all of this manually, I forgot things so I started keeping lists of things to do but that was still very time consuming. So over the years I have developed a process that ensures that installations are done quickly and reliably, and that I don't forget to install or configure anything.

My old process was to first do a pretty basic installation. I would configure the disk partitioning and logical volumes the way I want. I did not go through the entire list of available packages or groups and try to remember which ones I wanted to install to get just exactly the right tools I wanted on my computers. It was very cumbersome to go through the options offered by the installer and select the ones I wanted and cost a lot of time.

# Making It Easier

I developed what was at first a fairly simple bash script that I ran to do the configurations and installation of the other RPM packages that I wanted. After performing a basic installation, I would log in to a terminal session as root and run my script.

As time went on, that simple script evolved to include command-line options that allow me to tailor that standard installation for differing needs based on whether they were to be desktops, servers, customer systems, or classroom systems. As I learned about tools that I found to be helpful, I added them to the list of packages to install.

I created various configuration files that needed to be installed and determined that the best way to do that was to create an RPM package that included those files. Some of those files were more scripts that I have created over the years to perform various other repetitive tasks, as well as my post-installation script.

The RPM package is in itself a form of automation because it relieved me of the need to remember which files to install and where. The RPM package now installs about a dozen files of my own creation and ensures that certain prerequisite RPM packages are installed from various Fedora and CentOS repositories. I have been improving the post-installation script for about 10 years and it is up to over 1,500 lines of code, and more than 1,100 comment lines for a total of over 2,600 lines.

Even using the RPM and the post-installation script, it can still take more than an hour to complete all of the work required to get each one of many computers I install up to my standards. I certainly don't miss the days of typing all of those instructions by hand and waiting for each to complete before typing in the next one. All I need to do now is install the RPM and then type one command to install all of the other packages and configure them.

# From Desirable to Necessity

Everything was going along nicely and although I could have done all of that work manually, it has been much easier to use my automation. When Fedora 21 appeared on the scene, the automation I created over the years became a necessity.

For those of you who are not familiar with Fedora 21, the installation program changed dramatically with that release. Instead of a single ISO image, there were then three separate installation ISO images: Desktop, Server, and Cloud.

I have used both Desktop and Server ISOs for installation and I dislike them both intensely. I think the new installations are terribly limiting for the vast majority of Fedora users. There is no simple install image. The Desktop ISO is a live image. There are no options for installing any packages during the installation except those that are in the live image ISO. None. If I want to install the KDE – or any other – desktop instead of GNOME (which I do), I have to download the KDE spin or install KDE after the initial installation. I cannot do it from the primary installation medium, the live image.

I cannot even choose to install LibreOffice. There is no way to do that during installation. I have to install that and many other things after the initial installation. In my opinion this is a huge stumbling block to many would-be Linux users, especially the noobs. And, of course I always install updates immediately after performing a new Fedora installation because there are always updates.

Fortunately my post-installation RPM and post-install script allow me to do all of those things with very little fuss. And, yes, I have had to make a few adjustments to my script – as I have with every new release – to accommodate some of the changes between releases.

My penchant for following the Linux Philosophy for SysAdmins has paid off exceedingly well for me. Because I take the time to "Automate everything," I have personally experienced very little disruption due to a major change in the way Fedora Linux handles installations.

So here is what I have gained by automating my installations.

- Save time on every installation.

- Installations are consistent.

- Updates are always installed.

- Minimal or no disruption when major changes to distribution installation are introduced.

- Easy to create identical installations.

There are other ways to do the automation of a Linux installation and configuration, and many tools that can be applied to that task such as Kickstart, Puppet, Satellite Server, and others. I have used Kickstart extensively. See the article I wrote with a colleague for Linux Magazine, "Complete Kickstart" – I keep a copy of on my own web site.[1]

My script works very well for me in my current environment and meets my needs – and that is the name of the game in Linux.

# Updates

Another task I do frequently is to install updates on all of my computers. In fact I have been doing updates this morning. This is a task that requires only a couple of decisions and can be easily automated. "But that is so simple, why automate a task that requires only a command or two?" It turns out that updates are not so simple. Let's think about this for a minute.

---

[1]David Both, Linux DataBook, "Complete Kickstart," http://www.linux-databook.info/?page_id=9

First I must determine whether any updates are available. Then I need to determine whether a package that requires a reboot is being updated, such as the kernel or glibc. At this point I can install the update. Before I do a reboot, assuming one is required, I run the `mandb` utility to update the man pages; if this is not done, new and replacement man pages won't be accessible and old ones that have been removed will appear to be there even though they are not. Figure 9-1 shows the partial results of the updating the man database after doing updates this morning. Then, if the kernel has been updated, I need to rebuild the grub boot loader configuration file so that it will include recovery options for each installed kernel. Finally, if a reboot is needed, I do that.

```
Checking for stray cats under /var/cache/man/local...
134 man subdirectories contained newer manual pages.
8908 manual pages were added.
0 stray cats were added.
0 old database entries were purged
```

***Figure 9-1.*** *The partial results of running mandb after performing an upgrade*

That is a non-trivial set of individual tasks and commands that requires some decisions. Doing those tasks manually requires paying attention and intervention to enter new commands when the previous ones complete. Because of the need to babysit while waiting to enter the next command, this would take a great deal of my time to monitor each computer as it went through the procedures. There was room for error as I was reminded occasionally when I would enter the wrong command on a host.

```
 _____
/ You do create a set of \
\ requirements, right?    /
 - - - - - - - - - - - - - - - - - - - - - - - -
        \   ^__^
         \  (oo)_____
            (__)\       )\/\
             ||----w |
             ||     ||
```

Using the statement of requirements I created above, because that is what that paragraph really is, it was easy to automate this to eliminate all of those issues. I wrote a little script that I call doUpdates. It is a little over 400 lines in length and provides options like help, verbose mode, printing the current version number, and an option to reboot only if the kernel or glibc had been updated.

Over half of the lines in this program are comments so I can remember how the program works the next time I need to work on it to fix a bug or add a little more function. Much of the basic function is copied from a template file that maintains all of the standard components that I use in every script I write. Because the framework for new scripts is always there, it is easy to start new ones.

Figure 9-2 is a listing of the doUpdates bash script. To prevent most of the longer lines from wrapping, I have set the font size a bit smaller than usual. Nevertheless, a few very long lines are wrapped. I apologize if it is too small to read comfortably. I have also removed some blank lines and empty comment lines to shorten the listing as much as possible but it remains about 8 pages in length.

```
#!/bin/bash
################################################################################
#                              doUpdates                                       #
#                                                                              #
# This is a simple program to perform updates on a Linux computer. If a new    #
# kernel is installed, it will build a new grub.cfg to create the recovery     #
# mode kernel boot options, and then reboot the computer.                      #
#                                                                              #
# Change History                                                               #
```

*Figure 9-2.* A listing of the doUpdates script

```
# 04/12/2017   David Both    Original code. Suitable only for testing.      #
# 04/13/2017   David Both    Tested code. V1.0.0.                           #
# 04/13/2017   David Both    Added messages for rebooting or not at end.    #
# #                          Added check for new glibc for doing reboot.    #
# 04/14/2017   David Both    Completion message includes hostname.          #
# 04/28/2017   David Both    Add GPL2 statement.                            #
# 05/12/2017   David Both    Added the code I forgot that rebuilds the grub.cfg #
# #                          file. Duh.                                     #
# 06/30/2017   David Both    Test for glibc separately then change the logic so #
# #                          we only rebuild grub.conf when replacing the   #
# #                          kernel.                                        #
# 08/08/2017   David Both    Add -r option so that reboots only occur if -r is #
# #                          used and the kernel or glibc is updated.       #
# 08/11/2017   David Both    Redo logic for reboots just a bit. Add message to #
# #                          manually reboot if kernel or glibc updated but the #
# #                          -r option was not selected.                    #
# #                          Add -c option to check and report on whether   #
# #                          updates are needed and whether reboot is needed. #
#####################################################################################
#####################################################################################
#  Copyright (C) 2007, 2018 David Both                                       #
#  LinuxGeek46@both.org                                                      #
#  This program is free software; you can redistribute it and/or modify      #
#  it under the terms of the GNU General Public License as published by       #
#  the Free Software Foundation; either version 2 of the License, or          #
#  (at your option) any later version.                                       #
#                                                                            #
#  This program is distributed in the hope that it will be useful,           #
#  but WITHOUT ANY WARRANTY; without even the implied warranty of             #
#  MERCHANTABILITY or FITNESS FOR A PARTICULAR PURPOSE.  See the              #
#  GNU General Public License for more details.                              #
#                                                                            #
#  You should have received a copy of the GNU General Public License         #
#  along with this program; if not, write to the Free Software               #
#  Foundation, Inc., 59 Temple Place, Suite 330, Boston, MA  02111-1307  USA  #
#####################################################################################
#####################################################################################
# Help                                                                       #
#####################################################################################
Help()
{
   # Display Help
   echo "doUpdates - Performs all updates, builds new GRUB2, and"
   echo "reboots if a new kernel or glibc was installed."
   echo
   echo "Syntax: doUpdates --[g|h|c|V|rv]"
   echo "options:"
   echo "g      Print the GPL license notification."
   echo "c      Check to see if updates are available and whether reboot would be
needed."
   echo "        Does not actually do the update or reboot."
```

*Figure 9-2.* (*continued*)

```
    echo "h      Print this Help."
    echo "r      Reboot if the kernel or glibc or both have been updated."
    echo "v      Verbose mode."
    echo "V      Print software version and exit."
    echo
}

#############################################################################
# Print the GPL license header                                              #
#############################################################################
gpl()
{
echo
echo
"#############################################################################"
echo "#  Copyright (C) 2007, 2016  David Both
#"
echo "#  LinuxGeek46@both.org                                              #"
echo "#                                                                    #"
echo "#  This program is free software; you can redistribute it and/or modify #"
echo "#  it under the terms of the GNU General Public License as published by  #"
echo "#  the Free Software Foundation; either version 2 of the License, or     #"
echo "#  (at your option) any later version.                                  #"
echo "#                                                                    #"
echo "#  This program is distributed in the hope that it will be useful,   #"
echo "#  but WITHOUT ANY WARRANTY; without even the implied warranty of    #"
echo "#  MERCHANTABILITY or FITNESS FOR A PARTICULAR PURPOSE.  See the     #"
echo "#  GNU General Public License for more details.                      #"
echo "#                                                                    #"
echo "#  You should have received a copy of the GNU General Public License #"
echo "#  along with this program; if not, write to the Free Software       #"
echo "#  Foundation, Inc., 59 Temple Place, Suite 330, Boston, MA  02111-1307 USA #"
echo "#############################################################################"
echo
}

#############################################################################
# Quit nicely with messages as appropriate                                  #
#############################################################################
Quit()
{
   if [ $verbose = 1 ]
     then
     if [ $error = 0 ]
        then
        echo "Program terminated normally"
     else
        echo "Program terminated with error ID $ErrorMsg";
     fi
   fi
   exit $error
}
```

*Figure 9-2.* (*continued*)

```
################################################################################
# Display verbose messages in a common format                                  #
################################################################################
PrintMsg()
{
   if  [ $verbose = 1 ] && [ -n "$Msg" ]
   then
      echo "########## $Msg ##########"
      # Set the message to null
      Msg=""
   fi
}


################################################################################
# Define the $PkgMgr variable based on distro and release                      #
################################################################################
SelectPkgMgr()
{
   # get the Distribution, release and architecture.
   GetDistroArch
   if [ $NAME = "Fedora" ] && [ $RELEASE -ge 20 ]
   then
      PkgMgr="dnf"
   elif [ $NAME = "Fedora" ] && [ $RELEASE -lt 20 ]
   then
      PkgMgr="yum"
   elif [ $NAME = "CentOS" ]
   then
      PkgMgr="yum"
   else
      Msg="Unknown distrubution and release. Unable to define Package Manager."
      PrintMsg
      error=7
      Quit $error
   fi
   Msg="Using $PkgMgr Package Manager"
   PrintMsg
} # End SelectPkgMgr

################################################################################
# Get Distribution and architecture 64/32 bit                                  #
################################################################################
GetDistroArch()
{
   #-------------------------------------------------------------------------
   # Get the host physical architecture
   HostArch=`echo $HOSTTYPE | tr [:lower:] [:upper:]`
   Msg="The host physical architecture is $HostArch"
   PrintMsg
```

*Figure 9-2.* (*continued*)

```
#-------------------------------------------------------------------------
# Get some information from the *-release file. We care about this to give
# us Fedora or CentOS version number and because some group names change between
# release levels.
#-------------------------------------------------------------------------
# First get the distro info out of the file in a way that produces consistent
results
# Due to the different ways distros keep info in the release files we have to do
this
# a bit harder than we would otherwise.
# Switch to /etc for now
cd /etc
# Start by looking for Fedora
if grep -i "NAME=Fedora" os-release > /dev/null
then
    # This is Fedora
    NAME="Fedora"
    # Define the Distribution
    Distro=`grep PRETTY_NAME  os-release | awk -F= '{print $2}' | sed -e "s/\"//g"`
    # Get the full release number
    FULL_RELEASE=`grep VERSION_ID os-release | awk -F= '{print $2}'`
    # The Release version is the same as the full release number, i.e., no minor
versions for Fedora
    RELEASE=$FULL_RELEASE
    #---------------------------------------------------------------------
    # Verify Fedora release $MinFedoraRelease= or above. This is due to the lack
    # of Fedora and Fusion repositories prior to that release.
    #---------------------------------------------------------------------
    if [ $RELEASE -lt $MinFedoraRelease ]
    then
        Msg="Release $RELEASE of Fedora is not supported. Only releases
$MinFedoraRelease and above are supported."
        PrintMsg
        error=2
        Quit $error
    fi
elif grep -i CentOS centos-release > /dev/null
then
    # This is CentOS
    NAME="CentOS"
    Distro=`cat centos-release`
    # Get the full release number
    FULL_RELEASE=`echo $Distro | sed -e "s/[a-zA-Z() ]//g"`
    # Get the CentOS major version number
    RELEASE=`echo $FULL_RELEASE | awk -F. '{print $1}'`

    #---------------------------------------------------------------------
    # Verify CentOS release $MinCentOSRelease= or above. This is due to the lack
    # of testing for this program prior to that release.
    #---------------------------------------------------------------------
    if [ $RELEASE -lt $MinCentOSRelease ]
```

***Figure 9-2.*** (*continued*)

175

```
        then
            Msg="Release $RELEASE of CentOS is not supported. Only releases
$MinCentOSRelease and above are supported."
            PrintMsg
            error=4
            Quit $error
        fi
    else
        Msg="Unsupported OS: $NAME"
        PrintMsg
        error=2
        Quit $error
    fi

    Msg="Distribution = $Distro"
    PrintMsg
    Msg="Name = $NAME   Release = $RELEASE Full Release = $FULL_RELEASE"
    PrintMsg
    # Now lets find whether Distro is 32 or 64 bit
    if uname -r | grep -i x86_64 > /dev/null
    then
        # Just the bits
        Arch="64"
    else
        # Just the bits
        Arch="32"
    fi
    if [ $verbose = 1 ]
    then
        Msg="This is a $Arch bit version of the Linux Kernel."
        PrintMsg
    fi
} # end GetDistroArch

################################################################################
################################################################################
# Main program                                                                 #
################################################################################
################################################################################
# Set initial variables
badoption=0
check=0
doReboot=0
error=0
MinCentOSRelease="6"
MinFedoraRelease="22"
NeedsReboot=0
newKernel=0
newglibc=0
PkgMgr="dnf"
RC=0
```

***Figure 9-2.***  (*continued*)

```
UpdatesAvailable=0
verbose=0
version=01.02.03


#--------------------------------------------------------------------------
# Check for root

if [ `id -u` != 0 ]
then
   echo ""
   echo "You must be root user to run this program"
   echo ""
   Quit 1
fi


################################################################################
# Process the input options                                                    #
################################################################################
# Get the options
while getopts ":gchrvV" option; do
   case $option in
      g) # display GPL
         gpl
         Quit;;
      v) # Set verbose mode
         verbose=1;;
      V) # Set verbose mode
         echo "Version = $version"
         Quit;;
      c) # Check option
         verbose=1
         check=1;;
      r) # Reboot option
         doReboot=1;;
      h) # display Help
         Help
         Quit;;
     \?) # incorrect option
         badoption=1;;
   esac
done

if [ $badoption = 1 ]
then
   echo "ERROR: Invalid option"
   Help
   verbose=1
   error=1
   ErrorMsg="10T"
   Quit $error
fi
```

***Figure 9-2.*** (*continued*)

```
# What package manager should we be using?
SelectPkgMgr

# Are updates available? Just quit with message if not
# RC from dnf check-update = 100 if available and 0 if none available.
$PkgMgr check-update > /dev/null
UpdatesAvailable=$?
if [ $UpdatesAvailable = 0 ]
then
   Msg="Updates are NOT available for host $HOSTNAME at this time."
   # Turn on verbose so message will print
   verbose=1
   PrintMsg
   Quit
else
   Msg="Updates ARE available for host $HOSTNAME."
   # Turn on verbose so message will print
   PrintMsg
fi

# Does the update include a new kernel
if $PkgMgr check-update | grep ^kernel > /dev/null
then
   newKernel=1
   NeedsReboot=1
fi
# Or is there a new glibc
if $PkgMgr check-update | grep ^glibc > /dev/null
then
   newglibc=1
   NeedsReboot=1
fi

# Are we checking or doing?
if [ $check = 1 ]
then
   # Checking: Report results and quit
   if [ $NeedsReboot = 1 ]
   then
     Msg="A reboot will be required after these updates are installed."
     PrintMsg
   else
     Msg="A reboot will NOT be required after these updates are installed."
     PrintMsg
   fi
   Quit
else
   # Do the update
   $PkgMgr -y update
   # Preserve the return code
```

***Figure 9-2.*** (*continued*)

```
    RC=$?
    # Message and quit if error =3 occurred
    if [ $RC -eq 1 ]
    then
        Msg="An error ocuurred during the update but it was handled by $PkgMgr."
        PrintMsg
    elif [ $RC -eq 3 ]
    then
        Msg="WARNING!!! An uncorrectable error ocuurred during the update."
        PrintMsg
        Quit
    fi
fi


# Update man database
mandb

# If new kernel rebuild grub.cfg and reboot
if [ $newKernel = 1 ]
then
    # Generate the new grub.cfg file
    Msg="Rebuilding the grub.cfg file on $HOSTNAME."
    PrintMsg
    grub2-mkconfig > /boot/grub2/grub.cfg
fi

if [ $doReboot = 1 ] && [ $NeedsReboot = 1 ]
then
    # reboot the computer because the kernel or glibc have been updated
    # AND the reboot option was specified.
    Msg="Rebooting $HOSTNAME."
    PrintMsg
    reboot
    # no need to quit in this fork
elif [ $doReboot = 0 ] && [ $NeedsReboot = 1 ]
then
    Msg="This system, $HOSTNAME, needs rebooted but you did not choose the -r option
to reboot it."
    PrintMsg
    Msg="You should reboot $HOSTNAME manually at the earliest opportunity."
else
    Msg="NOT rebooting $HOSTNAME."
fi

PrintMsg
Quit

################################################################################
# End of program
################################################################################
```

The doUpdates script should be located in /usr/local/bin in accordance with the Linux FHS. It can be run with the command **doUpdates -r** that will cause it to reboot the host only if one or both of the conditions for that is met.

I won't deconstruct the entire doUpdates program for you but there are some things to which I want to call your attention. First notice the number of comments; these are to help me remember what each section is supposed to do. The first lines of the program after the she-bang (#!/bin/bash) contain the name of the program, a short description of its function, and a maintenance or change history. This first section is based on some practices I was taught and followed while I worked at IBM. Other comments delineate the various procedures and major sections and provide a short description of each. Finally, shorter comments embedded in the code describe the function or objective of shorter bits of code such as flow control structures.

I have a large number of procedures at the beginning of the script. This is where they go for bash. These procedures are from my template script and I use them whenever possible in new scripts to save the effort of rewriting them.

The procedure and variable names are meaningful and some use uppercase for one or two characters. This makes easier reading and helps the programmer (me) and any future maintainers (also me) understand the functions of the procedures and variables. Yes, this does seem to be contrary to one of the other tenets of the Philosophy but making the code more readable saves far more time in the long run. I know this from several past experiences with code of my own and that of others.

One organization I did some consulting work for started me with the task of fixing some bugs in a number of scripts. I took one look at the scripts and knew it would take a lot of work to fix the actual bugs because I first had to fix the readability of the scripts. I started by adding comments to the scripts because there were none. I then started renaming variables and procedures so that it was easier to understand the purpose of those variables and the nature of the data they held. It was only after making those changes that I could begin to understand the nature of the bugs they were experiencing.

We will see more about this organization in Chapter 18. They really had a lot of problems with those scripts.

The doUpdates script is available for download at the Apress web site.
`https://github.com/Apress/linux-philo-sysadmins/tree/master/Ch09`

# Additional Levels of Automation

Now I have this incredibly wonderful and useful script. I have copied it to /usr/local/bin on all of my computers. All I have to do now is run it at appropriate times on each of my Linux hosts to do the updates. I can do this by using SSH to log in to each host and run the program.

But wait! There's more! Have I told you yet how absolutely cool SSH is?

The `ssh` command is a secure terminal emulator that allows one to log in to a remote computer to access a remote shell session and run commands. So I can log in to a remote computer and run the `doUpdates` command on the remote computer. The results are displayed in the ssh terminal emulator window on my local host. The Standard Output (STDOUT) from the command is displayed on my terminal window.

That part is trivial and everyone does that. But the next step is a bit more interesting. Rather than maintain a terminal session on the remote computer, I can simply use a command on my local computer such as that in Figure 9-3 to run the same command on the remote computer with the results being displayed on the local host. This assumes that SSH public/private keypairs[2] (PPKP) are in use and I do not have to enter a password each time I issue a command to the remote host.

```
ssh hostname doUpdates -r
```

***Figure 9-3.*** *This command runs the doUpdates program on a remote host using Public/Private KeyPairs for authentication*

So now I run a single command on my local host that sends a command through the SSH tunnel to the remote host. OK, that is good, but what does it mean?

It means that what I can do for a single computer I can also do for several – or several hundred. The bash command-line program in Figure 9-4 illustrates the power I now have.

```
for I in host1 host2 host3 ; do ssh $I doUpdates -r ; done
```

***Figure 9-4.*** *This bash command-line program runs the doUpdates program on three remote hosts*

---

[2]How to Forge, https://www.howtoforge.com/linux-basics-how-to-install-ssh-keys-on-the-shell

Think we're done? No, we are not! The next step is to create a short bash script of this CLI program so we don't have to retype it every time we want to install updates on our hosts. This does not have to be fancy; the script can be as simple as the one in Figure 9-5.

```
#!/bin/bash
for I in host1 host2 host3 ; do ssh $I doUpdates -r ; done
```

**Figure 9-5.** *This bash script contains the command-line program that runs the doUpdates program on three remote hosts*

This script could be named "updates" or something else depending on how you like to name scripts and what you see as its ultimate function. I think we should call this script, "`doit.`" Now we can just type a single command and run a smart update program on as many hosts as we have in the list of the `for` statement. Our script should be located in the /usr/local/bin directory so it can be easily run from the command line.

Our little `doit` script looks like it could be the basis for more general application. We could add more code to doit that would enable it to take arguments or options such as the name of a command to run on all of the hosts in the list. This enables us to run any command we want on a list of hosts and our command to install updates might be **doit doUpdates -r** or **doit myprogram** to run "myprogram" on each host.

The next step might be to take the list of hosts out of the program itself and place them in a doit.conf file locate in /usr/local/etc – again in compliance with the Linux FHS. That command would look like Figure 9-6 for out simple `doit` script. Notice the back tics (`) that create the list used by the `for` structure from the results of the `cat` command.

```
#!/bin/bash
for I in `cat /usr/local/etc/doit.conf` ; do ssh $I doUpdates ; done
```

**Figure 9-6.** *We have now added a simple external list that contains the host names on which the script will run the specified command*

By keeping the list of hosts separate, we can allow non-root users to modify the list of hosts while protecting the program itself against modification. It would also be easy to add an -f option to the `doit` program so that the users could specify the name of a file containing their own list of hosts on which to run the specified program.

Finally, we might want to set this up as a cron job so that we don't have to remember to run it on whatever schedule we want. Setting up cron jobs is worthy of its own section in this chapter so that is coming up next.

# Using cron for Timely Automation

There are many tasks that need to be performed off-hours when no one is expected to be using the computer or, even more importantly, on a regular basis at specific times. I don't want to have to get up at oh-dark-hundred to start a backup or major update, so I use the cron service to schedule tasks on a repetitive basis, such as daily, weekly, or monthly. Let's look at the cron service and how to use it.

I use the cron service to schedule obvious things like regular backups that occur every day at 2:00 a.m. I also do a couple of less obvious things. All of my many computers have their system times, that is the operating system time, set using NTP – the Network Time Protocol. NTP sets the system time; it does not set the hardware time which can drift and become inaccurate. I use cron to set the hardware time using the system time. I also have a bash program I run early every morning that creates a new "message of the day" (MOTD) on each computer that contains information such as disk usage that should be current in order to be useful. Many system processes use cron to schedule tasks as well. Services like logwatch, logrotate, and rkhunter all use the cron service to run programs every day.

The crond daemon is the background service that enables cron functionality.

The cron service checks for files in the /var/spool/cron and /etc/cron.d directories and the /etc/anacrontab file. The contents of these files define cron jobs that are to be run at various intervals. The individual user cron files are located in /var/spool/cron, and system services and applications generally add cron job files in the /etc/cron.d directory. The /etc/anacrontab is a special case that will be covered a bit further on.

## crontab

Each user, including root, can have a cron file. By default no file exists, but using the crontab -e command as shown in Figure 9-7 to edit a cron file creates them in the /var/spool/cron directory. I strongly recommend that you not use a standard editor such as vi, vim, emacs, nano, or any of the many other editors that are available. Using the crontab command not only allows you to edit the command, it also restarts the crond daemon when you save and exit from the editor. The crontab command uses vi as its underlying editor because vi is always present on even the most basic of installations.

```
# crontab -e
SHELL=/bin/bash
MAILTO=root@example.com
PATH=/bin:/sbin:/usr/bin:/usr/sbin:/usr/local/bin:/usr/local/sbin

# For details see man 4 crontabs
# Example of job definition:
# .---------------- minute (0 - 59)
# |  .------------- hour (0 - 23)
# |  |  .---------- day of month (1 - 31)
# |  |  |  .------- month (1 - 12) OR jan,feb,mar,apr ...
# |  |  |  |  .---- day of week (0-6)(Sunday=0 or 7)(sun,mon,tue,wed,thu,fri,sat)
# |  |  |  |  |
# *  *  *  *  * user-name  command to be executed

# backup using the rsbu program to the internal HDD then the external USB HDD
01 01 * * * /usr/local/bin/rsbu -vbd1 ; /usr/local/bin/rsbu -vbd2
# Set the hardware clock to keep it in sync with the more accurate system clock
03 05 * * * /sbin/hwclock --systohc
# Perform monthly updates on the first of the month
25 04 1 * * /usr/local/bin/doit
```

*Figure 9-7.* *The crontab command is used to view or edit the cron files*

All cron files are empty the first time you edit it so you must create it from scratch. I added the job definition example in Figure 9-7 to my own cron files just as a quick reference. Feel free to copy it for your own use.

In Figure 9-7 the first three lines set up a default environment. Setting the environment to that necessary for a given user is required because cron does not provide an environment of any kind. The SHELL variable specifies the shell to use when commands are executed. In this case it specifies the bash shell. The MAILTO variable sets the email address to which cron job results will be sent. These emails can provide the status of backups, updates, or whatever, and consist of the output from the programs that you would see if you ran them manually from the command line. The last of these three lines sets up the PATH for this environment. Regardless of the path set here, however, I always like to prepend the fully qualified path to each executable.

There are several comment lines that detail the syntax required to define a cron job. I think that they are mostly self-explanatory, so I will use the entries in Figure 9-7 as examples, then add a few more that will show you some of the more advanced capabilities of crontab files.

The line shown in Figure 9-8 runs another of my bash shell scripts, rsbu, to perform backups of all my systems. This job is kicked off at 1 minute after 1 a.m. every day. The splat/star/asterisks (*) in positions 3, 4, and 5 of the time specification are like file globs for those time divisions; they match every day of the month, every month, and every day of the week. This line runs my backups twice; once to backup onto an internal dedicated backup hard drive, and once to backup onto an external USB hard drive that I can take to the safe deposit box.

```
01 01 * * * /usr/local/bin/rsbu -vbd1 ; /usr/local/bin/rsbu -vbd2
```

***Figure 9-8.*** *This line in /etc/crontab runs a script that performs daily backups for my systems*

The line shown in Figure 9-9 sets the hardware clock on the computer using the system clock as the source of an accurate time. This line is set to run at 3 minutes after 5 a.m. every day.

```
03 05 * * * /sbin/hwclock --systohc
```

***Figure 9-9.*** *This line sets the hardware clock using the system time as the source*

The last cron job, shown in Figure 9-10, is the one we are especially interested in. It is used to perform our updates at 04:25 a.m. on the first day of each month. This assumes we are using the very simple doit program from Figure 9-5. The cron service has no option for "The last day of the month," so we use the first day of the following month.

```
25 04 1 * * /usr/local/bin/doit
```

***Figure 9-10.*** *The cron job for running the doit command which in turn runs doUpdates*

So now all of the hosts in our network get updated each month with no intervention at all from us. This is the ultimate in being the Lazy SysAdmin.

# cron.d

There are some other options provided by the cron service that we can also use to run our doit program on a regular basis. The directory /etc/cron.d is for system-level jobs run by various users. It is where some applications install cron files when there are no users under which the programs would run, these programs need a place to locate cron files so they are placed in /etc/cron.d. Root can place other cron files in this directory as well, including cron files for non-root users. Many Linux SysAdmins prefer using the cron.d directory for cron files over the older crontab system of managing cron files located in /var/spool/cron.

The cron files located in /etc/cron.d have the same format as a regular cron file. All of the information about the regular cron files that we covered above is the same for each file located in the cron.d directory.

Files located in the cron.d directory are run in alphanumeric sort order. That is the reason that the 0hourly file has a zero at the beginning of its name, so that it runs first.

One of the drawbacks of the crontab system of managing cron jobs is the fact that some users have used a standard editor to alter the files. This method does not inform the crond daemon of the changes so the altered cron file is not activated until crond is restarted. This is not the case with the cron files located in /etc/cron.d as the file modification times are checked every minute by crond. If a change has been made to the file it is reloaded into memory by crond. This is a much more positive method for ensuring that changes to cron files get recognized immediately upon a change having been made.

Let's create a simple cron job for the /etc/cron.d directory, one that runs every minute so we don't need to wait long for the results.

---

**EXPERIMENT 9-1**

---

Perform this experiment as root. Only root can add files to cron.d.

Make /etc/cron.d the PWD and list the files already located there. On a simple training system or VM there should be three.

```
[root@david ~]# cd /etc/cron.d ; ls -l
total 12
-rw-r--r-- 1 root root 128 Aug  2 15:32 0hourly
-rw-r--r-- 1 root root  74 Mar 25  2017 atop
-rw-r--r-- 1 root root 108 Aug  3 21:02 raid-check
```

Now use your favorite editor to create a new file named myfree in cron.d with the following content.

```
# Run the free command every minute. The accumulated
# data is stored in /tmp/free.log where it can be viewed.
* * * * * root /usr/bin/free >> /tmp/free.log
```

Save the new file. It should not be made executable. No changes need to be made to its permissions. In another root terminal session, make /tmp the PWD and list the files. If you do not see the free.log file, wait until a second or so after the top of the minute and try again. When the free.log file appears use the tail command to follow the content of the file. It should look similar to my results.

```
[root@testvm1 tmp]# tail -f free.log
              total        used        free      shared  buff/cache   available
Mem:        4042112      271168     2757044        1032     1013900     3484604
Swap:       8388604           0     8388604
              total        used        free      shared  buff/cache   available
Mem:        4042112      261008     2767212        1032     1013892     3494860
Swap:       8388604           0     8388604
              total        used        free      shared  buff/cache   available
Mem:        4042112      260856     2767336        1032     1013920     3495012
Swap:       8388604           0     8388604
              total        used        free      shared  buff/cache   available
Mem:        4042112      260708     2767452        1032     1013952     3495148
Swap:       8388604           0     8388604
              total        used        free      shared  buff/cache   available
Mem:        4042112      260664     2767468        1032     1013980     3495176
Swap:       8388604           0     8388604
              total        used        free      shared  buff/cache   available
Mem:        4042112      260772     2767280        1032     1014060     3495040
Swap:       8388604           0     8388604
```

After a few cycles, delete the /etc/cron.d/myfree file or move it to another location. This will stop the execution of this job. You can also exit from the tail command using Ctrl-C.

There is an important service that is dependent on the 0hourly cron file located in /etc/cron.d, anacron that we should take a look at. There are others, but this one provides some interesting options for running scheduled tasks.

# anacron

The crond service assumes that the host computer runs all the time. What that means is that if the computer is turned off for a period of time and cron jobs were scheduled for that time, they will be ignored and will not run until the next time they are scheduled. This might cause problems if the cron jobs that did not run were critical. So there is another option for running jobs at regular intervals when the computer is not expected to be on all the time.

The anacron program performs the same function as regular cron jobs but it adds the ability to run jobs that were skipped if the computer was off or otherwise unable to run the job for one or more cycles. This is very useful for laptops and other computers that get turned off or put in sleep mode.

Soon after the computer is turned on and booted, anacron checks to see whether configured jobs have missed their last scheduled run. If they have, those jobs are run immediately, but only once no matter how many cycles have been missed. For example, if a weekly job was not run for three weeks because the system was shut down while you were away on vacation, it would be run soon after you turn the computer on, but it would be run once not three times.

The anacron program provides some easy options for running regularly scheduled tasks. Just install your scripts in the /etc/cron.[hourly|daily|weekly|monthly] directories, depending on how frequently they need to be run.

How does this work? The sequence is simpler than it first appears.

1. The crond service runs the cron job specified in /etc/cron.d/0hourly as seen in Figure 9-11.

```
# Run the hourly jobs
SHELL=/bin/bash
PATH=/sbin:/bin:/usr/sbin:/usr/bin
MAILTO=root
01 * * * * root run-parts /etc/cron.hourly
```

***Figure 9-11.*** *The contents of /etc/cron.d/0hourly cause the shell scripts located in /etc/cron.hourly to run*

2.  The cron job specified in /etc/cron.d/0hourly runs the run-parts program once per hour. The run-parts program runs all of the scripts located in the /etc/cron.hourly directory.

3.  The /etc/cron.hourly directory contains the 0anacron script that runs the anacron program using the /etdc/anacrontab configuration file shown in Figure 9-12.

```
# /etc/anacrontab: configuration file for anacron
# See anacron(8) and anacrontab(5) for details.

SHELL=/bin/sh
PATH=/sbin:/bin:/usr/sbin:/usr/bin
MAILTO=root
# the maximal random delay added to the base delay of the jobs
RANDOM_DELAY=45
# the jobs will be started during the following hours only
START_HOURS_RANGE=3-22

#period in days   delay in minutes   job-identifier   command
1         5       cron.daily                  nice run-parts /etc/cron.daily
7         25      cron.weekly                 nice run-parts /etc/cron.weekly
@monthly 45       cron.monthly                nice run-parts /etc/cron.monthly
```

*Figure 9-12.*   *The contents of /etc/anacrontab file runs the executable files in the cron.[daily|weekly|monthly] directories at the appropriate times*

4.  The anacron program runs the programs located in /etc/cron. daily once per day; it runs the jobs located in /etc/cron.weekly once per week and the jobs in cron.monthly once per month. Note the specified delay times in each line that helps prevent these jobs from overlapping themselves and other cron jobs.

Instead of placing complete bash programs in the cron.X directories, I install them in the /usr/local/bin directory, which allows me to run them easily from the command line. Then I add a symlink in the appropriate cron directory, such as /etc/cron.daily.

The anacron program is not designed to run programs at specific times. Rather, it is intended to run programs at intervals that begin at the specified times such as 3 a.m. (see the START_HOURS_RANGE in Figure 9-12) of each day, on Sunday to begin the week, and the first day of the month. If any one or more cycles are missed, then anacron will run the missed jobs one time as soon as possible.

# Scheduling Tips

Some of the times I have set in the crontab files for my various systems seem rather random and to some extent they are. Trying to schedule cron jobs can be challenging, especially as the number of jobs increases. I usually only have a couple tasks to schedule on each of my own computers so it is a bit easier than some of the production and lab environments I have worked.

One system for which I was the SysAdmin usually had around a dozen cron jobs that needed to run every night and an additional three or four that had to run on weekends or the first of the month. That was a challenge because if too many jobs ran at the same time, especially the backups and compiles, the system would run out of RAM and then nearly fill the swap file, which resulted in system thrashing while performance tanked so that nothing got done. We added more memory and were able to do a better job of scheduling tasks. Adjusting the task list included removing one of the tasks that was very poorly written and which used large amounts of memory.

# Thoughts About cron

I use most of these methods for scheduling tasks to run on my computers. All of those tasks are ones that need to run with root privileges. I have seen only a few times when users had a real need for any type of cron job, one of those being for a developer to kick off a daily compile in a development lab.

It is important to restrict access to cron functions by non-root users. However there are circumstances when it may be necessary for a user to set tasks to run at pre-specified times and cron can allow users to do that when necessary. SysAdmins realize that many users do not understand how to properly configure these tasks using cron and the users make mistakes in the configuration. Those mistakes may be harmless but they can cause problems for themselves and other users. By setting procedural policies that cause users to interact with the SysAdmin, those individual cron jobs are much less likely to interfere with other users and other system functions.

It is possible to set limits on the total resources that can be allocated to individual users or groups, but that is an article for another time.

## cron Resources

The man pages for cron, crontab, anacron, anacrontab, and run-parts all have excellent information and descriptions of how the cron system works.

# Other Automation Possibilities

I have automated many other tasks that I need to perform on the Linux computers for which I am responsible. The short list below is certainly not all-inclusive but is just intended to give you ideas for some places to start.

- Backups.

- Upgrades (dnf-upgrade).

- Distributing updates to local shell scripts to a list of hosts.

- Finding and deleting very old files.

- Creating a daily message of the day (/etc/motd).

- Checking for viruses, rootkits, and other malware.

- Change/add/delete mailing list subscriber email addresses.

- Regular checks of the host's health such as temperatures, disk usage, RAM usage, CPU usage, etc.

- Anything else repetitive.

# Some Alt Ideas

Here are a few unusual automation ideas I found on the Internet that push the boundaries of both targets for automation and propriety. The original information is from a GitHub repository and many of the programs have misogynistic and NSFW names. I leave it to you whether you want to search for this guy on the Internet but I won't help you find him.

In the references I have found, the creator of these programs would always automate every task that would take more than 90 seconds. Let's start with a couple of my favorites.

First is the shell script that works with a "smart" office coffee machine that is connected to the internal network. When this programmer ran the script it would wait 17 seconds, connect to the machine and tell it to start brewing a cup of coffee. It would wait 24 seconds and pour the coffee into a cup. Apparently this was the time it took the programmer to walk to the coffee machine.

Next is a script that enables our lazy SysAdmin to sleep late with no worries about letting the team know he will not be in. If he has not logged in to his development server by a specific time in the morning, the script sends an email to indicate that he will be working from home. The program chooses a random excuse from an array and adds it to the email before sending. This program is triggered from a cron job.

Of course what else would this guy do when he was working late? If he is still logged in at a specific time in the evening, this script sends an email with an appropriately random excuse to his wife|girlfriend.

These scripts are not directly related to his programming job. However they would make him more productive because he does not have to take the time to deal with these things every day. Personally, I would definitely not automate emails to my wife!

But the ideas here illustrate that nearly anything can be automated. Perhaps these "Alternate" ideas will give you a few time-saving automation ideas of your own.

# Deepening the Philosophy

Automation of the SysAdmin's own work is a large part of that work. Because of this, many tenets of the Linux Philosophy for SysAdmins are related to the tasks and tools that support automation using shell scripts and ad hoc command-line programming.

Computers are designed to automate various mundane tasks and why should that not also be applied to the SysAdmin's work? We lazy SysAdmins use the capabilities of the computers on which we work to make our jobs easier. Automating everything that we possibly can means that the time we free up by creating that automation can now be used to respond to some real or perceived emergency by others, especially by the PHB. It can also provide us with time to automate even more.

If you reflect on what we have done in this chapter, you can see that automation is not merely about creating a program to perform every task. It can be about making those programs flexible so that they can be used in multiple ways such as the ability to be called from other scripts and to be called as a cron job.

My programs almost always use options to provide flexibility. The `doit` program used in this chapter could easily be expanded to be more general than it is while still remaining quite simple. It could still do one thing well if its objective were to run a specified program on a list of hosts.

My shell scripts did not just spring into existence with hundreds or thousands of lines. In most cases they start as a single ad hoc command-line program. I create a shell script from the ad hoc program. Then another command-line program is added to the short script. Then another. As the short script becomes longer, I add comments, options, and a help feature.

Then, sometimes, it makes sense to make a script more general so that it can handle more cases. In this way the `doit` script becomes capable of "doing it" for more than just a single program that does updates.

# Always Use Shell Scripts

When writing programs to automate – well, everything – always use shell scripts. Because shell scripts are stored in ASCII text format, they can be easily viewed and modified by humans just as easily as they can by computers. You can examine a shell program and see exactly what it does and whether there are any obvious errors in the syntax or logic. This is a powerful example of what it means to be open.

I know some developers tend to consider shell scripts something less than true programming. This marginalization of shell scripts and those who write them seems to be predicated on the idea that the only true programming language is one that must be compiled from source code to produce executable code. I can tell you from experience that this is categorically untrue.

I have used many languages including BASIC, C, C++, Pascal, Perl, Tcl/Expect, REXX, and some of its variations including Object REXX, many shell languages including Korn and Bash, and even some assembly language. Every computer language ever devised has had one purpose – to allow humans to tell computers what to do. When you write a program, regardless of the language you choose, you are giving the computer instructions to perform specific tasks in a specific sequence.

## Definition

A shell script or program is an executable file that contains at least one shell command. They usually have more than a single command and some shell scripts have thousands of lines of code. When taken together, these commands are the ones necessary to perform a desired task with a specifically defined result.

Although an executable file containing a single line with a shell command can be run with the current shell, it is good practice to add a line called the "shebang" that defines the shell under which the program is to run. Let's try it both ways.

© David Both 2018
D. Both, *The Linux Philosophy for SysAdmins*, https://doi.org/10.1007/978-1-4842-3730-4_10

---

## EXPERIMENT 10-1

This experiment should be performed as the student user. We create a minimal script in your home directory, make it executable, and run it.

First open a new file in your home directory with vim.

```
[student@testvm1 ~]$ vim test1
```

Add one line at the beginning of the file and save the file. Do not exit from vim because we will be making more changes to the test1 script.

```
echo "Hello world!"
```

In another terminal session, do a long listing of the new program.

```
[student@testvm1 ~]$ ls -l test1
-rw-rw-r-- 1 student student 20 Dec 31 15:27 test1
```

The file permissions show that it is not executable. Make it executable for the user and the group and list it again.

```
[student@testvm1 ~]$ chmod ug+x test1
[student@testvm1 ~]$ ls -l test1
-rwxrwxr-- 1 student student 20 Dec 31 15:38 test1
```

Now let's run the program. We use ./ before the name of the file to specify that the program file is located in the current directory. Home directories are not part of the path so we must specify the path to the executable file.

```
[student@testvm1 ~]$ ./test1
Hello world!
```

Now let's add the shebang line before the echo command. This specifies that no matter which shell we are running under, the program will always run under the bash shell.

Now our program as two lines and looks like this.

```
#!/bin/bash
echo "Hello world!"
```

Run the program again. The results should not change. Exit from vim.

---

For a simple shell script like this one, it does not matter whether we add the shebang line. All of the shells in which I experimented with this script produced the same results. But there are some built-in shell commands that may not exist in other shells, or some commands may be implemented differently and the different results may affect the outcome of the program when run.

Regardless, it is always good practice to include the shebang line.

# The SysAdmin Context

Context is important and this tenet, "Always use shell scripts," should be considered in the context of our jobs as SysAdmins.

The SysAdmin's job differs significantly from those of developers and testers. In addition to resolving both hardware and software problems, we manage the day-to-day operation of the systems under our care. We monitor those systems for potential problems and make all possible efforts to prevent those problems before they impact our users. We install updates and perform full release level upgrades to the operating system. We resolve problems caused by our users. SysAdmins develop code to do all of those things and more; then we test that code; and then we support that code in a production environment.

Many of us also manage and maintain the networks to which our systems are connected. In other cases we tell the network guys where the problems are located and how to fix them because we find and diagnose them first.

We SysAdmins have been devops far longer than that term has been around. In fact, the SysAdmin job is more like dev-test-ops-net than just devops. Our knowledge and daily task lists cover all of those areas of expertise.

In this context the requirements for creating shell scripts are complex, interrelated, and many times contradictory. Let's look at some of the typical factors SysAdmins must consider when writing shell scripts.

# Requirements

This redundancy means that one requirement for creating a shell script is to obtain a set of requirements from the end user who is requesting the script. Even if we happen to be both developer and user, we should sit down and create a set of requirements before we begin to write code.

Even a short list of two or three objectives for the program will suffice as a set of requirements. The minimum I will accept is a description and sample of the input data; any formulas, logic, or other processing required; and a description of the required outputs or functional results. Of course, more is better, but with these things as a starting point, I can begin work.

Naturally the requirements will become more explicit as the project continues. Things that were not considered initially will arise. Assumptions will be changed.

## Development Speed

Programs usually must be written quickly to meet time constraints imposed by circumstances or the PHB. Most of the scripts we write are to fix a problem, to clean up the aftermath of a problem, or to deliver a program that must be operational long before a compiled program could be written and tested.

Writing a program quickly requires shell programming because it allows quick response to the needs of the customer whether that be ourselves or someone else. If there are problems with the logic or bugs in the code, they can be corrected and retested almost immediately. If the original set of requirements was flawed or incomplete, shell scripts can be altered very quickly to meet the new requirements. So, in general, we can say that the need for speed of development in the SysAdmin's job overrides the need to make the program run as fast as possible or to use as little as possible in the way of system resources like RAM.

Let's look at the BASH command-line program in Figure 10-1. It is designed to list each user ID that is currently logged into the system. We saw this program previously, but let's look at it from a different viewpoint.

```
echo `who | awk '{print $1}' | sort | uniq` | sed "s/ /, /g"
```

***Figure 10-1.*** *Revisiting our CLI program to list logged-in users*

Because users may be logged in multiple times, this one-line program only displays each ID once and separates the IDs with commas. To program this in the C language would require a significant amount of single-purpose code. Table 10-1 shows the number of lines of code in each of the CLI commands used in the above BASH program. These numbers were accurate when I found them several years ago. If they have changed since then, it would not be significant.

**Table 10-1.** *The Power of the CLI Comes from These Individual Programs*

| Command | Source Lines of Code |
|---------|----------------------|
| echo    | 177                  |
| who     | 755                  |
| awk     | 3412                 |
| sort    | 2614                 |
| uniq    | 302                  |
| sed     | 2093                 |
| TOTAL   | 9353                 |

You can see that the BASH script above uses programs that together contain over 9,000 lines of C code. All of these programs contain far more functionality than that which we actually use in our script. Yet we combine these programs that have already been written and use the parts we need.

It takes far less time to write and test the resulting BASH script than it would a compiled program to do the same thing.

# Performance Speed

Script performance in terms of speed of execution is much less relevant now than in the past. Today's CPUs are blazing fast and most computers have multiple processors. Most of my own computers have 4 cores with Hyperthreading and run at 3GHz or higher. My main workstation has an Intel Core i9 with 16 cores and 32 CPUs. I tend to have a large number of virtual machines open simultaneously while working on various projects, including research for this book.

```
 _____
/ The Lazy SysAdmin uses the \
\ tools already at hand.     /
 ----------------------------
        \   ^__^
         \  (oo)_____
            (__)\       )\/\
                ||----w |
                ||     ||
```

In general, the only question to ask is whether the job gets done in time. If it does, then no worries. If it does not, the time required to write and test the same program in a compiled language would most likely have made it even later. The time saved when the compiled program runs is less than the time saved in development when using a shell program. Remember we are considering the context of the SysAdmin's job.

Consider the example program in Figure 10-1 and the amount of C code in Table 10-1. The fact is that our example CLI program is still using large amounts of C code that has already been written and extensively tested. As lazy SysAdmins we have lots of C code already available in the form of the Linux Core Utilities and other command-line utilities. We should always use that which is already there.

This does not mean that some performance tuning might not be called for on the rare occasion. I have found the need to improve the performance of a shell script. The problems I discovered were usually more about dealing with large amounts of data than about the functional logic of the program.

Besides, the hardware will be faster next week.

# Variables

Use variables instead of hard-coded values for almost everything. Even if you think you will only use a particular value once, such as a directory name or a file name, create a variable and use the variable where you would have placed the hard-coded name.

Many times I have needed a particular value in more places in the scripts so I am already prepared if it is accessed as a variable. It can take less time to type a variable name than a complete directory name, especially if it is a long one. It is also easier to change a script if the value changes. Fixing the value of the variable in one location is much easier than replacing it in several locations.

I always have a single location in my scripts to set initial values for variables. Keeping the initial variable settings in the same place helps make them easy to find.

# Testing

Interactive testing of shell scripts can be accomplished as soon as the most basic code structure is complete, at all stages during development, when the code is complete, and when any needed changes have been made.

The test plan should be created from the requirements statements. The test plan will have lists of the requirements to test, such as, "for input X the output should be Y," and "for bad input error message X should be displayed."

Having a test plan enables me to test each new feature as it is added to the program. It helps to ensure that testing is consistent as program development proceeds from start to finish.

In Chapter 11, "Test Early, Test Often," we will explore testing in some detail but, for now, the importance of testing cannot be understated. Testing must take place right from the very start.

# Open and Open Source

By their very nature, shell scripts are open because we can read them. They are written in ASCII text format and are never compiled or altered into a binary or other format that is unreadable to humans. The bash shell, for example, reads the contents of the shell programs and interprets them on the fly. Their existence as ASCII text files also means that shell scripts can be easily modified and run immediately without having to wait through a recompile.

This open access to the code also means that we can explore shell scripts in aid of understanding their functional logic. This can be useful when writing our own scripts because we can easily include this existing code in our own scripts instead of writing our own code to perform the same task.

Of course this code sharing depends upon the open source licensing of the original code. I always include within the code itself an explicit statement of the license under which I share the code I write, usually the GPL V2. Many times I even have an option in the program to display the GPL license statement.

Making all of the code I write Open Source and properly licensed as such is just another basic requirement as far as I am concerned.

# Shell Scripts as Prototypes

I have seen a number of articles and books about the Unix philosophy in which they discuss shell scripts as a tool for prototyping large and complex programs. I think there may be some value in that for application developers rather than SysAdmins. That approach can allow for fast prototyping and early testing to ensure that the program is exactly what the customer wants.

As a SysAdmin I find that shell scripts are perfect for both prototype and the completed program. I mean, why take the extra time to translate something that is already working well into another language? Hey – we are trying to be lazy here!

# Process

We all have our own processes – ways of working that enable us to work our way through projects to completion. We are all different and our processes are different. And sometimes we have more than one process depending upon our starting point. I want to describe to you a couple of methods that work for me.

## Quick and Dirty

Most of my programming projects start as quick and dirty command-line programs that I use to perform a specific task. The doUpdates program back in Figure 9-2 is a good example. After all, installing updates is a simple yum or dnf command, right? Not so much.

For a long time, I would log in to each host, run the **dnf -y update** command, and then manually reboot if the kernel had been updated. The next step occurred when I determined in advance that the kernel was being updated. I used the compound command **dnf -y update && reboot** that rebooted the computer if the update was successful. But I was still typing the commands on the command line.

As the number of computers in my home network grew, I realized that I was also updating the man database; making a decision; and, if there was a kernel update, updating the GRUB configuration file and running the reboot command. At that point I wrote a simple script with no frills to perform those tasks.

But that script needed a couple decisions of its own and some direction from me. I did not want to have the script arbitrarily reboot the host every time it was run. So I added an option to reboot only if the kernel or glibc were updated. Well, that required that I add the case command to interpret the options. I also added a variable that contained the current version of the program and an option to display the version. A bit later I added a "verbose" option so I could get more debugging information if the program encountered problems.

With the addition of options I needed a Help facility, so I added that. Then I added an option to display the GPL statement.

A lot of that work was already done because I had included those features in my other programs and in the template I use for new programs. It was a simple matter to copy those features I needed out of the template, paste them in the doUpdates program, and modify them to meet the needs of this particular program.

Many large programs grow from those little, everyday command-line programs and become indispensable to our daily working lives. Sometimes the process is not noticeable until you realize you have a fully working script on your hands.

# Planning and Foresight

Some programs written by SysAdmins are actually planned in advance. Once again I start with a set of requirements although I try to spend a bit more time formulating them than with the quick and dirty programs.

To start coding, I make a copy of the script template and name it appropriately. The template contains all of the standard procedures and basic structure that I need to begin any project. This template includes a skeletal help facility, a procedure for ending the program with an appropriate return code (RC), and a `case` statement to enable use of options.

So the first thing I do with this template is code the help facility. Then I test to see if that is working and looks as I intend. Coding the Help facility first also begins the process of documentation. It helps me to define the function of the script as well as some of the features.

At this point I like to add comments that define specific functionality and create execution sequences within the script. If I need to write a new procedure, I create a small skeleton for that procedure with comments that contain a short description of its function. By adding these comments first, I have embedded the set of requirements I created earlier into the very fabric of the code. This makes it easy to follow and ensure that I have translated all of those requirements into code.

I then begin to add code to each section of comments. And then I test each new section to ensure that it meets the requirements stated in the comments.

Then I add a bit more and test. And add a bit more and test. Every time I test, I test everything, even the features and code segments I have tested before because new code can break existing code, too. I follow this procedure until the shell script is complete.

# Template

I have mentioned a number of times that I have a template from I like to create my programs. Let's look at that template and experiment with it. You can download the script.template.sh template file at `https://github.com/Apress/linux-philo-sysadmins/tree/master/Ch10`.

## The Code

Now that you have downloaded the template, let's look at Figure 10-2 and I will point out some of its key features. Then we will do an experiment to see how it works. Note that the font size is somewhat reduced in Figure 10-2 in an effort to reduce the number of line wraps and improve its readability.

Of course all scripts should begin with the shebang and this one is no different. Then I add a couple sections of comments.

The first comment section is the program name and description and a change history. This is a format I learned while working at IBM, and it provides a means of documenting the long-term development of the program and any fixes applied to it. This is an important start to documenting your program.

The second comment section is a copyright and license statement. I use the GPL2 and this seems to be a standard statement for programs licensed under the GPL2. If you choose to use a different open source license, that is fine, but I do suggest adding an explicit statement like this to the code in order to eliminate any possible confusion about licensing. I read an interesting article recently, "The source code is the license,[1]" that helps to explain the reasoning behind this.

The procedures section begins after these two comment sections. This is the required location for procedures in Bash. They must appear before the body of the program. As part of my own need to document everything, I place a comment before each procedure that contains a short description of what it is intended to do. I also include comments inside the procedure to provide further elaboration. Your own procedures can be added here.

I won't dissect the function of each of these procedures. Between the comments and your ability to read the code, they should be understandable. However, at the end of Figure 10-2, I will discuss some other aspects of this template.

---

[1]Scott K Peterson, "The source code is the license," Opensource.com, `https://opensource.com/article/17/12/source-code-license`

```
#!/bin/bash
################################################################################
#                         script.template.sh                                  #
#                                                                              #
# Use this template as the beginning of a new program. Place a short           #
# description of the script here.                                              #
#                                                                              #
# Change History                                                               #
# 04/12/2017  David Both    Original code. This is a template for creating     #
#                           new Bash shell scripts.                            #
#                           Add new history entries as needed.                 #
#                                                                              #
################################################################################
################################################################################
#                                                                              #
#   Copyright (C) 2007, 2016 David Both                                        #
#   LinuxGeek46@both.org                                                       #
#                                                                              #
#   This program is free software; you can redistribute it and/or modify       #
#   it under the terms of the GNU General Public License as published by        #
#   the Free Software Foundation; either version 2 of the License, or          #
#   (at your option) any later version.                                        #
#                                                                              #
#   This program is distributed in the hope that it will be useful,            #
#   but WITHOUT ANY WARRANTY; without even the implied warranty of             #
#   MERCHANTABILITY or FITNESS FOR A PARTICULAR PURPOSE.  See the              #
#   GNU General Public License for more details.                               #
#                                                                              #
#   You should have received a copy of the GNU General Public License          #
#   along with this program; if not, write to the Free Software                #
#   Foundation, Inc., 59 Temple Place, Suite 330, Boston, MA  02111-1307  USA   #
#                                                                              #
################################################################################
################################################################################
# Help                                                                         #
################################################################################
Help()
{
   # Display Help
   echo "Add description of the script functions here."
   echo
```

***Figure 10-2.*** *The script.template.sh template file I use as a starting point for new programs*

```
   echo "Syntax: template <option list here>"
   echo "options:"
   echo "g      Print the GPL license notification."
   echo "h      Print this Help."
   echo "v      Verbose mode."
   echo "V      Print software version and exit."
   echo
}

################################################################################
# Print the GPL license header                                                 #
################################################################################
gpl()
{
   echo
   echo "################################################################################"
   echo "#  Copyright (C) 2007, 2016  David Both                                        #"
   echo "#  Millennium Technology Consulting LLC                                        #"
   echo "#  http://www.millennium-technology.com                                        #"
   echo "#                                                                              #"
   echo "#  This program is free software; you can redistribute it and/or modify        #"
   echo "#  it under the terms of the GNU General Public License as published by         #"
   echo "#  the Free Software Foundation; either version 2 of the License, or            #"
   echo "#  (at your option) any later version.                                         #"
   echo "#                                                                              #"
   echo "#  This program is distributed in the hope that it will be useful,              #"
   echo "#  but WITHOUT ANY WARRANTY; without even the implied warranty of               #"
   echo "#  MERCHANTABILITY or FITNESS FOR A PARTICULAR PURPOSE.  See the                #"
   echo "#  GNU General Public License for more details.                                 #"
   echo "#                                                                              #"
   echo "#  You should have received a copy of the GNU General Public License            #"
   echo "#  along with this program; if not, write to the Free Software                  #"
   echo "#  Foundation, Inc., 59 Temple Place, Suite 330, Boston, MA  02111-1307  USA   #"
   echo "################################################################################"
   echo
}

################################################################################
# Quit nicely with messages as appropriate                                     #
################################################################################
Quit()
{
   if [ $verbose = 1 ]
      then
      if [ $error = 0 ]
         then
         echo "Program terminated normally"
      else
         echo "Program terminated with error ID $ErrorMsg";
      fi
   fi
   exit $error
}

################################################################################
# Display verbose messages in a common format                                  #
################################################################################
PrintMsg()
```

***Figure 10-2.*** (*continued*)

```
{
   if  [ $verbose = 1 ] && [ -n "$Msg" ]
   then
       echo "######### $Msg #########"
       # Set the message to null
       Msg=""
   fi
}

###############################################################################
###############################################################################
# Main program                                                                #
###############################################################################
###############################################################################
# Set initial variables
badoption=0
error=0
RC=0
verbose=0
version=01.02.03

#-----------------------------------------------------------------------------
# Check for root. Delete if necessary.

if [ `id -u` != 0 ]
then
   echo ""
   echo "You must be root user to run this program"
   echo ""
   Quit 1
fi

###############################################################################
# Process the input options. Add options as needed.                           #
###############################################################################
# Get the options
while getopts ":gchrvV" option; do
   case $option in
      g) # display GPL
         gpl
         Quit;;
      v) # Set verbose mode
         verbose=1;;
      V) # Set verbose mode
         echo "Version = $version"
         Quit;;
      h) # display Help
         Help
         Quit;;
     \?) # incorrect option
         badoption=1;;
   esac
done

if [ $badoption = 1 ]
then
   echo "ERROR: Invalid option"
   Help
```

***Figure 10-2.*** (*continued*)

```
      verbose=1
      error=1
      ErrorMsg="10T"
      Quit $error
fi

###########################################################################
###########################################################################
# The main body of your program goes here.
###########################################################################
###########################################################################

Quit

###########################################################################
# End of program
###########################################################################
```

***Figure 10-2.*** (*continued*)

The main part of the program begins after the end of the procedures section.
I usually start this section with a section to set the initial values of all the variables used
in the program. This ensures that all of the variables I use have been set to some default
initial value. It also provides a list of all of the variables used in the program.

Next I have a check to see if root is running this program and, if not, display a
message and exit. If your program can be run by non-root users, you can delete this
section.

Then I have getops and case statements that check the command line to determine
whether any options have been entered. For each option the case statement sets
specified variables or calls procedures like Help() and Quit(). If an invalid option is
entered, the last case stanza sets a variable to indicate that and the next bit of code
throws an error message and quits.

Finally the main body of the program is where most of your code will go. This
program is executable as it is without errors. But because there is no functional code, all
you can do is display the help and the GPL license statement and generate an error for
using an invalid option. Until you add some functional code to the program, it will do
nothing else at all.

Let's explore this template code with Experiment 10-2.

## EXPERIMENT 10-2

Perform this experiment as the student user. If you have not done so already, download the file script.template.sh from `https://github.com/Apress/linux-philo-sysadmins/tree/master/Ch10` into the home directory for the student user. Set the permissions to executable for user, and group, and set the ownership to student.student.

In a terminal session as the user student, ensure the PWD is your home directory. Before proceeding any further, make a working copy named test1.sh of the template.

```
[student@testvm1 ~]$ cp script.template.sh test1.sh
```

Display the help information.

```
[student@testvm1 ~]$ cd
[student@testvm1 ~]$ ./test1.sh -h
You must be root user to run this program
```

That is the bit of code telling you that you must be root. You can bypass that by using your favorite editor to comment out those lines of code. That part of the code now looks like this. Be sure to save the changes you have made.

```
#-------------------------------------------------------------------------
# Check for root. Delete if necessary.

# if [ `id -u` != 0 ]
# then
#     echo ""
#     echo "You must be root user to run this program"
#     echo ""
#     Quit 1
# fi
```

Now run the script again using the -h option to view the help.

```
[student@testvm1 ~]$ ./test1.sh -h
Add description of the script functions here.

Syntax: template <option list here>
options:
g       Print the GPL license notification.
h       Print this Help.
v       Verbose mode.
V       Print software version and exit.
```

It seems that the name of the script is not correct. Edit the test1.sh script to change the name at the top of the first comment section and in the help procedure to the new name of the script. While we are working on the help procedure, add the options list. The "Syntax" line in help should look like this.

```
echo "Syntax: test1.sh  -ghvV"
```

Save the changes and run the script again using the -h option.

```
[student@testvm1 ~]$ ./test1.sh -h
Add description of the script functions here.

Syntax: test1.sh  -ghvV
options:
g      Print the GPL license notification.
h      Print this Help.
v      Verbose mode.
V      Print software version and exit.
```

Let's see what happens when you give the program an option it does not recognize.

```
[student@testvm1 ~]$ ./test1.sh -a
ERROR: Invalid option
Add description of the script functions here.

Syntax: test1.sh  -ghvV
options:
g      Print the GPL license notification.
h      Print this Help.
v      Verbose mode.
V      Print software version and exit.

Program terminated with error ID 10T
```

That's good – it displays the help and terminates with an error message. Most people will not understand the humor of the error message ID – it is not one I would leave in any production script.

So let's at least make our little test script perform some useful work. Add the following line after the massive comment, indicating the beginning of the main body of the code, but before the Quit function call.

```
free
```

Yup – that's all, just the free command. It should look like this.

```
################################################################################
################################################################################
################################################################################
################################################################################
# The main body of your program goes here.
################################################################################
################################################################################
################################################################################
################################################################################

free

Quit

################################################################################
# End of program
################################################################################
```

Save the script and run the it again without any options.

```
[student@testvm1 ~]$ ./test1.sh
            total       used       free     shared  buff/cache   available
Mem:      4046060     248256    3384972        988      412832     3566296
Swap:     4182012          0    4182012
[student@testvm1 ~]$
```

So now you have created a working script from a fairly simple template. You have performed some simple tests to verify that the script is performing as expected.

One of the options that I like to have is a "test" mode in which the program runs and describes what it will do or prints some debugging data to STDOUT so that I can visualize how it is working. Let's add that option to our template.

The getopts statement (get options) allows us to specify option inputs to a bash script. We then use the case statement to sort through any and all of the options and set values, perform small tasks, or call longer procedures. The while statement loops until all options have been processed, unless one of the options takes a path that exits from the loop in some manner.

---

**EXPERIMENT 10-3**

---

First, let's add a new variable, Test, and set an initial value of 0 (zero). Add the following line of code in the variable initialization section of the template.

```
Test=0
```

Now let's add the new option character (t) to the getopts statement.

```
while getopts ":gchrtvV" option; do
```

Now we add a new stanza to the case statement. The finished options processing code looks like this.

```
while getopts ":gchrtvV" option; do
    case $option in
        g) # display GPL
            gpl
            Quit;;
        t) # Set test mode
            test=1;;
        v) # Set verbose mode
            verbose=1;;
        V) # Set verbose mode
            echo "Version = $version"
            Quit;;
        h) # display Help
            Help
            Quit;;
        \?) # incorrect option
            badoption=1;;
    esac
done
```

Depending upon how you write the code in the case statement stanzas, the sequence in which they appear can affect the results.

We are not yet done. You should add a line to the Help() procedure. Add the following line to the help procedure. Any place that makes sense to you is fine, but I like to place the options in alphabetical order.

```
echo "t      Set test mode. The program runs but does not perform any actions."
```

You should also add a line to the change history.

```
# 01/30/2018  David Both    Add an option for setting test mode.       #
```

Now we need to test. First let's ensure we have not broken anything, then we can add code to "test" by circumventing our `free` statement. I have only shown a few possible test modes here, but you should test every possible option and combination of options to ensure that nothing is broken.

```
[root@david development]# ./script.template.sh
              total        used        free      shared  buff/cache
available
Mem:      65626576     8896704    48397920      159924     8331952      55963460
Swap:     15626236           0    15626236
[root@david development]# ./script.template.sh -x
ERROR: Invalid option
Add description of the script functions here.

Syntax: template <option list here>
options:
g      Print the GPL license notification.
h      Print this Help.
t      Set test mode. The program runs but does not perform any actions.
v      Verbose mode.
V      Print software version and exit.

Program terminated with error ID 10T
[root@david development]# ./script.template.sh -t
              total        used        free      shared  buff/cache    available
Mem:      65626576     8895716    48399104      159924     8331756      55964424
Swap:     15626236           0    15626236
[root@david development]# ./script.template.sh -h
Add description of the script functions here.

Syntax: template <option list here>
options:
g      Print the GPL license notification.
h      Print this Help.
t      Set test mode. The program runs but does not perform any actions.
v      Verbose mode.
V      Print software version and exit.
```

Now let's add some code that prevents execution of the free statement if we set test mode.

```
# Execute the code only if this is not test mode
if [ $test ]
then
    Msg="Test mode. No action taken."
    PrintMsg
else
    free
fi
```

And we test some more.

```
[root@david development]# ./script.template.sh -t
[root@david development]# ./script.template.sh
            total        used        free      shared  buff/cache   available
Mem:     65626576     8904512    48395196      159924     8326868    55955156
Swap:    15626236           0    15626236
[root@david development]#
```

Again I only show a couple results here, but you can see there is a problem. Can you see what it is? The message does not print when we are in test mode. Can you see why? If you look at the PrintMsg() procedure, you see that the message is only printed if verbose mode is set.

There are a number of ways to fix this. One is to remove the verbose requirement from the PrintMsg() procedure. Another is to set verbose mode in the test path of the if statement. You could set verbose mode in the -t case stanza. Another choice is just to use the -v option when you run the program. The latter result looks like this.

```
[root@david development]# ./script.template.sh -tv
########## Test mode. No action taken. ##########
Program terminated normally
```

Which choice would you make to display the test message when in test mode? My preference is to set verbose mode in the case stanza so that it looks like this.

```
    t) # Set test mode
       verbose=1
       test=1;;
```

Go ahead and make whatever change you choose to ensure that test mode messages are displayed, and then test extensively until you know everything is working properly.

Remember that this is a template, a starting point for scripts that have a specific and useful purpose. Code that is not necessary, such as the bit we added in Experiment 10-3, can be safely ignored or removed.

We will use this script template as the basis for a more useful script in Chapter 11, "Test Early, Test Often."

Feel free to use this template and alter it to meet your own requirements. Because the template is open source under the GPL2, you can share it and modify it. My intention is for it to be used by you if you so choose. Remember that the Lazy Admin always uses freely available code to prevent having to duplicate the effort of writing code that already does what you need. I hope you find it useful.

# Final Thoughts

Compiled programs are necessary and fill a very important need. But for SysAdmins, there is always a better way. We should always use shell scripts to meet the automation needs of our jobs.

Shell scripts are open; their content and purpose are knowable. They can be readily modified to meet differing requirements. Personally, I have found nothing that I have ever needed to do in my SysAdmin role that could not be accomplished with a shell script.

In the very rare event that you find something a shell script cannot do, don't write the whole program in a compiled language. Write as much as possible as a shell script. Then, if – and only if – there is no possible way to do that little bit that is left by using a shell command or a series of shell commands in a pipeline, write a little program that does one thing well – that one little bit that cannot be found anywhere else.

# CHAPTER 11

# Test Early, Test Often

You know, I almost forgot to include this chapter. It was as easy to forget to write about testing the programs I write as it is to overlook testing the programs themselves.

Why is that?

I wish I had a definitive answer. In some ways it is like documentation. Once the program seems to work, we just want to get on with doing whatever task caused us to write the program in the first place.

> *There is always one more bug.*
>
> —Lubarsky's Law of Cybernetic Entomology

Lubarsky – whoever he might be – is correct. We can never find all of the bugs in our code. For every one I find there always seems to be another that crops up, usually at a very inopportune time.

In Chapter 10, "Always Use Shell Scripts," we started to talk about testing and the process I use for testing. This chapter covers testing in more detail. You will learn about how testing affects the ultimate outcome of the many tasks that SysAdmins do. You will also learn that testing is an integral part of the Philosophy.

However, testing is not just about programs. It is also about verification that problems – whether caused by hardware, software, or the seemingly endless ways that users can find to break things – that we are supposed to have resolved actually have been. These problems can be with application or utility software we wrote, system software, applications, and hardware. Just as importantly, testing is also about ensuring that the code is easy to use and the interface makes sense to the user.

217

© David Both 2018
D. Both, *The Linux Philosophy for SysAdmins*, https://doi.org/10.1007/978-1-4842-3730-4_11

# Procedures

One of the jobs I had in a previous life was as a tester for Linux-based appliances at Cisco. I developed test plans, wrote Tcl/Expect code to implement the test plan, and helped trace the root cause of the failures. I enjoyed that job and learned a lot from it.

I referred to testing briefly in Chapter 10 but more detail about my procedures is necessary here. Following a well-defined procedure when writing and testing shell scripts can contribute to consistent and high-quality results. My procedures are simple.

1. Create the test plan, at least a simple one.

2. Start testing right at the beginning of development.

3. Perform a final test when the code is complete.

4. Move to production and test more.

## Create a Test Plan

Testing is hard work and it requires a well-designed test plan based on the requirements statements. Regardless of the circumstances, start with a test plan. Even a very basic test plan provides some assurance that testing will be consistent and cover the required functionality of the code.

Any good plan includes tests to verify that the code does everything it is supposed to. That is, if you enter X and click on button Y, you should get Z as the result. So you write a test that creates those conditions and then verify that Z is the result.

The best plans include tests to determine how well the code fails. I found this out the hard way back when I got my first IBM PC in 1982.

The PC had just been announced in August of 1981 and employee purchases were not begun until early 1982. There were not a lot of programs out there, especially for kids. I wanted to introduce my young son to the PC but could find nothing appropriate so I wrote a little program in BASIC that I thought he would enjoy. Frankly, I don't even remember what it was supposed to do.

I tested that program every way I could think of. It did everything it was supposed to do. Then I turned the computer over to my son and walked out of the room. I had not gone very far when he yelled, "Dad! Is it supposed to do this?" It wasn't. I asked him what he did and he described some very strange set of keystrokes and I said, "You are not supposed to do that," and immediately realized how silly that would have sounded to him.

My problem was that I had not tested how the program would react to unexpected input. That does seem to be a common problem with programs of all kinds. But I never forgot that particular lesson. As a result, I always try to include code that tests for unexpected input and then I test to ensure that the program detects it and fails gracefully.

There are lots of different formats for test plans. I have worked with the full range from having it all in my head, to a few notes jotted down on a sheet of paper, to a complex set of forms that required a full description of each test, which functional code it would test, what the test would accomplish, and what the inputs and results should be.

Speaking as a SysAdmin who has been but is not now a tester, I try to take the middle ground. Having at least a short, written test plan will ensure consistency from one test run to the next. How much detail you need depends upon how formal your development and test procedures are.

## Test Plan Content

All of the sample test plan documents I found using Google were complex and intended for large organizations with a very formal development and test process. Although those test plans would be good for those with "Test" in their job title, they really do not apply well to System Administrators and our more chaotic and fast time-dependent working conditions. As in most other aspects of our jobs, we need to be creative. So here is a short list of things that you would want to consider including in your test plan. Modify it to suit your needs.

- The name and a short description of the software being tested.

- A description software features to be tested.

- The starting conditions for each test.

- The procedures to follow for each test.

- A description of the desired outcome for each test.

- Include specific tests designed to test for negative outcomes.

- Tests for how the program handles unexpected input.

- A clear description of what constitutes pass or fail for each test.

- Fuzzy testing, which will be described below.

This short list should give you some ideas for creating your own test plans. For most SysAdmins, this should be kept simple and fairly informal.

# Start Testing at the Beginning

I always start testing my shell scripts as soon as I complete the first portion that is executable. This is true whether I am writing a short command-line program or a script that is an executable file.

I usually start creating new programs with the shell script template that you had an opportunity to explore in Experiment 10-2. I write the code for the Help procedure and test it. This is usually a trivial part of the process, but it helps me get started and ensures that things in the template are working properly at the outset. At this point it is easy to fix problems with the template portions of the script, or to modify it to meet specific needs that the standard template cannot.

When the template and Help procedure are working, I move on to creating the body of the program by adding comments to document the programming steps required to meet the program specifications. Now I start adding code to meet the requirements stated in each comment. This code will probably require adding variables that are initialized in that section of the template – which is now becoming our shell script.

This is where testing is more than just entering data and verifying the results. It takes a bit of extra work. Sometimes I add a command that simply prints the intermediate result of the code I just wrote and verify that. Other times, for more complex scripts, I add a -t option for "test mode." In this case the internal test code is only executed when the -t option is entered at the command line.

# Final Testing

After the code is complete, I go back through a complete test of all the features and functions using known inputs to produce specific outputs. I also test for some random inputs to see if the program can handle unexpected input now that it is complete.

Final testing is intended to verify that the program is functioning essentially as intended now that it is complete. A large part of the final test is to ensure that functions that worked earlier in the development cycle have not been broken by code added or changed later in the cycle.

If you have been testing the script as you added new code to it, there should be no surprises during this final test. Wrong! There are always surprises during final testing. Always. Expect those surprises and be ready to spend some time fixing them. If there were never any bugs discovered during final testing, there would be no point in doing a final test, would there.

# Testing in Production

Huh – what?

> *Not until a program has been in production for at least six months will the most harmful error be discovered.*

—Troutman's Programming Postulates

Yes, testing in production is now considered normal and desirable. Having been a tester myself, this actually does seem reasonable. "But wait! That's dangerous," you say. My experience is that it is no more dangerous than extensive and rigorous testing in a dedicated test environment. In some cases there is no choice because there *is* no test environment – only production.

This was the case in one of my jobs, the one where I was responsible for maintenance of a large number of Perl CGI scripts that generated dynamic pages for a web site. The entire web site for this huge organization's email management interface was run on a single, very old even then, Dell desktop system. That was our critical server. I had an even older Dell desktop from which I would log in to the server to do my programming. Both of these computers ran an early version of Red Hat Linux.

The only option we had to work with was to make many critical changes on the fly in the middle of the day and then test in production. What fun that was!

Eventually we obtained a couple of additional old desktops to use as development and test environments but it was a nail biting challenge until we did. Part of the reason for lack of equipment on which to run this large email system was that it started out as a small pilot test for one department. It grew rapidly out of control with more departments asking to join as soon as they heard about it. Pilot tests are never funded and are usually lucky to be gifted with another department's old and unwanted equipment.

So SysAdmins are no strangers to the need to test new or revised scripts in production. Any time a script is moved into production, that becomes the ultimate test. The production environment itself constitutes the most critical part of that test. Nothing that can be dreamed up by testers in a test environment can fully replicate the true production environment.

The allegedly new practice of testing in production is just the recognition of what we SysAdmins have known all along. The best test is production – so long as it is not the only test.

After the final test, the program can move into production. Production is always a test of its own. Writing code in an isolated development and test environment is in no way representative of the conditions encountered in a true production environment.

Always expect new bugs to surface in production no matter how well the script was written and tested. As Troutman's postulate says, the most harmful error won't be discovered for quite some time after a program has been put in production and everyone has come to assume that the results are always correct. The most harmful bugs are not the ones that cause the programs to crash; they are the ones that quietly result in incorrect results.

Continue checking the results the script produces even after it has gone into production. Look for the next bug and you will eventually find it.

# Fuzzy Testing

This is another of those buzzwords that caused me to roll my eyes when I first heard it. I learned that its essential meaning is simple – have someone bang on the keys until something happens and see how well the program handles it. But there really is more to it than that.

Fuzzy testing is a bit like the time my son broke my code in less than a minute with his random input. Most test plans utilize very specific input that generates a specific result or output. Regardless of whether the test is for a positive or negative outcome as success, it is still controlled and the inputs and results are specified and expected, such as a specific error message for a specific failure mode.

Fuzzy testing is about dealing with randomness in all aspects of the test such as starting conditions, very random and unexpected input, random combinations of options selected, low memory, high levels of CPU contention with other programs, multiple instances of the program under test, and any other random conditions that you can think of to be applied to the tests.

I try to do some fuzzy testing right from the beginning. If the bash script cannot deal with significant randomness in its very early stages, then it is unlikely to get better as we add more code. This is also a good time to catch these problems and fix them while the code is relatively simple. A bit of fuzzy testing at each stage of completion is also useful in locating problems before they get masked by even more code.

After the code is completed I like to do some more extensive fuzzy testing. Always do some fuzzy testing. I have certainly been surprised by some of the results I have encountered. It is easy to test for the expected things, but users do not usually do the expected things with a script.

# Automated Testing

Testing can be automated, but most of the work we do as SysAdmins comes with intrinsic time pressures that preclude taking the time to write code to test our code. Those pressures are the reason most code we write is quick and dirty. So we write code and test it in a hurry.

It is possible to use tools like Tcl/Expect to write a complex test suite for our shell scripts. I never had time to do anything that formal as a SysAdmin. The most automation I have ever done in my role as a SysAdmin is to write a very short script to sequence through a set of commands to verify a few critical aspects of the script under test. Most of the time, I test manually at each step of the way and when the program is complete. Using bash history can be a reasonable substitute and provides at least some semi-automated testing.

In my role as a tester at Cisco, I wrote a lot of tests using Tcl/Expect. My task was to write the modules that would be called by the previously written test bed. The Tcl/Expect code I wrote could have been run as stand-alone tests, but the test bed provided a framework that aggregated all of the results from the individual tests and generated a nice set of reports that enabled us to see how far along we were in getting bug fixes applied to the code.

There are a lot of commercial test suites available. Many are very expensive and are not especially suitable for use by SysAdmins because of the effort required to learn them and the time necessary to prepare for the tests.

Writing Tcl/Expect programs is very time consuming, but when developing a large code base it can be quite useful. My favorite book for Tcl/Expect is *Exploring Expect*,[1] which includes plenty of information about Tcl. Wikipedia has an excellent article on software testing[2] with many links to more in-depth material.

---

[1]Libes, Don, *Exploring Expect*, O'Reilly, 2010, ISBN 978-1565920903
[2]Wikipedia, Software testing, https://en.wikipedia.org/wiki/Software_testing

# Trying It Out

In Experiment 10-2 you made some modifications to a copy of the shell script template. At each step in that experiment you tested the results of the changes you had made so you are already familiar with the basic SysAdmin development process. The experiments in this chapter will use that process to develop and test a program that will list some interesting information and statistics about your Linux host. In the end we will have a fairly long script that will have been well tested. Typical output from this script is shown in Figure 11-1.

```
################################################################################
# MOTD for Thu Jan  4 03:40:05 EST 2018
# HOST NAME:            testvm1
# Machine Type:         VM running under VirtualBox.
# Host architecture:    X86_64
# Motherboard Mfr:      Oracle Corporation
# Motherboard Model:    VirtualBox
#-------------------------------------------------------------------------------
# CPU Model:            Intel(R) Core(TM) i9-7960X CPU @ 2.80GHz
# CPU Data:             1 Single Core 64-bit
# HyperThreading:       No
#-------------------------------------------------------------------------------
# RAM:                  3.858 GB
# SWAP:                 3.987 GB
#-------------------------------------------------------------------------------
# Install Date:         Wed 15 Nov 2017 03:44:03 PM EST
# Linux Distribution:   Fedora 27 (Twenty Seven) 64-bit
# Kernel Version:       4.14.5-300.fc27.x86_64
#-------------------------------------------------------------------------------
# Disk Partition Info
# Filesystem                    Size  Used Avail Use% Mounted on
# /dev/mapper/fedora_testvm1-root   35G  9.1G   24G  28% /
# /dev/sda1                     976M  237M  673M  27% /boot
#-------------------------------------------------------------------------------
# LVM Physical Volume Info
# PV          VG              Fmt    Attr   PSize    PFree
# /dev/sda2   fedora_testvm1  lvm2   a--    <39.00g  0
################################################################################
# Note: This MOTD file gets updated automatically every day.
#       Changes to this file will be automatically overwritten!
################################################################################
```

***Figure 11-1.*** *A sample of the MOTD generated by the shell script you will create in the experiments in this chapter*

I run this script as a cron job to generate a report every day that I store as /etc/motd, which is the message-of-the-day file. Whenever anyone logs in using a remote terminal or one of the virtual consoles, the MOTD is displayed.

Before we start coding we need to create first a set of requirements and then a simple test plan.

# Requirements for MOTD Script

A simple set of requirements will help us design the program and keep on point for the specific features we want to include. These requirements should work just fine yet leave leeway for creativity.

- All output goes to STDOUT and STDERR so that it can be redirected as desired.

- Provide an option to print the script release version.

- Print the following data in a pleasing format.

  - A header with the current date

  - The host name

  - Machine type – VM or physical

  - Host hardware architecture X86_64 or i386

  - Motherboard vendor and model

  - CPU model and hyperthreading status

  - The amount of RAM (GB)

  - The amount of Swap space (GB)

  - The date Linux was installed

  - The Linux distribution

  - The kernel version

  - Disk partition information

  - LVM physical volume information

- Include comments to describe the code.

- Options should not be required to produce the desired output.

This seems like a long list, but it is quite short compared to some sets of requirements I have seen. I created the original bash script from a similar set of requirements. The script template we created in Chapter 10, "Always Use scripts," already has code that can help to meet some of these requirements.

The only issue someone might have with this list is the term "pleasing." Who knows what might be pleasing versus displeasing for whoever is going to be using this script. So for this experiment, pleasing will be what I say it is. In other environments, many pages of requirements might be needed to define the explicit format of the output. In the SysAdmin environment, pleasing is usually what works for us or for whoever asked for the program to be written.

# Test Plan for MOTD Script

Our test plan is simple and straightforward.

- Verify that the help (-h) option displays the correct help information.

- Verify that the GPL (-g) option displays the GPL license statement.

- Verify that all output data specified in the requirements are produced.

- Verify that all of the printed output is correct for the system on which testing is performed.

- Verify that the values for numeric output are correct by comparison with other sources. It is probable that some of these numbers will change between runs and when compared with other sources due to the dynamic nature of any running computer, but they should be reasonably close.

- Ensure that incorrect option selections produce an appropriate error code.

- If possible, test on multiple systems, including physical hardware and VMs to verify correct results for different conditions. Include Intel, AMD, and ARM hardware.

- If possible, test with multiple Linux distributions.

This simple test plan is everything we need to know when testing our script. We know the outputs that we need to check because they are defined in the program requirements.

The last two items may not be possible within the context of a learning environment, but it is always something to consider. Differing environments should produce different results with this script. It is helpful to test outside our actual dev/test environment to ensure that the logic and results are accurate for those other environments. Testing in production can help with this.

## Developing the Script

Remember that for SysAdmins development also means testing. Because of the amount of work required to create the complete script, I have divided it into a series of experiments in which each experiment will develop and test a section of code to meet part or all of a specific requirement.

---

**Note**    If you are not clear about how some of the commands work, and especially what the stages of pipelines do, you should research them. First look at the man pages for each command in the pipeline to understand what it does. Then build up the pipeline – one command stage – at a time to see the results. This was a very helpful way for me to figure out complicated-looking code when I was just starting as a SysAdmin. I still depend upon this approach to help me understand how some code works.

---

## The Basics

Let's start with the basics – copy the script from the revised template, change the script name internally, add a short description, and change the help procedure to match the features of our program.

---

**EXPERIMENT 11-1**

---

Make a copy of test1.sh with the new name of mymotd. You can edit this new script, mymotd, as root or as the student user but it must be run as root when testing. I do recommend editing shell scripts as a non-root user. Open two terminal sessions and su – to root in one of them. Open the mymotd script in your favorite editor in the terminal session as user student.

Be sure to save your work frequently as we edit the script.

First, let's change the script name in the header comments and add a short description of the script. The results should look like this.

```
#!/bin/bash
################################################################################
#                                  mymotd                                      #
#                                                                              #
# This bash shell extracts various interesting bits of information about       #
# the Linux host and the operating system itself. It prints this data to       #
# STDOUT in a nice looking format. The results can also be redirected to       #
# the/etc/motd file to create an informational message of the day.             #
#                                                                              #
#                                                                              #
# Change History                                                               #
# 01/08/2018  David Both    Original code.                                     #
#                                                                              #
#                                                                              #
################################################################################
```

Be sure to set the first line in the change history to the current date and your name.

Next let's work on the Help procedure. All that is needed here is to add a short description, a line to describe the syntax of the command, and a list of the possible options.

```
####################################################################
# Help                                                             #
####################################################################
Help()
{
   # Display Help
   echo "                    mymotd"
   echo "Generate an MOTD that contains information about the system"
   echo " hardware and the installed version of Linux."
   echo
   echo "Syntax:  mymotd [-g|h|v|V]"
   echo "options:"
   echo "g      Print the GPL license notification."
   echo "h      Print this Help."
   echo "v      Verbose mode."
   echo "V      Print software version and exit."
   echo
}
```

Let's do our first testing. In the terminal session as root, make /home/student the PWD, which is where the new code is located. Now run the program using one of three options for each run; -h to test the Help facility, -g to test printing the GPL statement, and -x to test for an invalid option.

```
[root@testvm1 student]# ./mymotd -h
                mymotd
Generate an MOTD that contains information about the system
 hardware and the installed version of Linux.

Syntax:  mymotd [-g|h|v|V]
options:
g      Print the GPL license notification.
h      Print this Help.
v      Verbose mode.
V      Print software version and exit.
```

```
[root@testvm1 student]# ./mymotd -g

##############################################################################
#  Copyright (C) 2007, 2016  David Both                                    #
#  Millennium Technology Consulting LLC                                    #
#  http://www.millennium-technology.com                                    #
#                                                                          #
#  This program is free software; you can redistribute it and/or modify    #
#  it under the terms of the GNU General Public License as published by    #
#  the Free Software Foundation; either version 2 of the License, or       #
#  (at your option) any later version.                                     #
#                                                                          #
#  This program is distributed in the hope that it will be useful,         #
#  but WITHOUT ANY WARRANTY; without even the implied warranty of          #
#  MERCHANTABILITY or FITNESS FOR A PARTICULAR PURPOSE.  See the           #
#  GNU General Public License for more details.                            #
#                                                                          #
#  You should have received a copy of the GNU General Public License       #
#  along with this program; if not, write to the Free Software             #
#  Foundation, Inc., 59 Temple Place, Suite 330, Boston, MA  02111-1307  USA #
##############################################################################
[root@testvm1 student]# ./mymotd -x
ERROR: Invalid option
                    mymotd
Generate an MOTD that contains information about the system
 hardware and the installed version of Linux.

Syntax: Syntax:  mymotd [-g|h|v|V]
options:
g     Print the GPL license notification.
h     Print this Help.
v     Verbose mode.
V     Print software version and exit.

Program terminated with error ID 10T
```

If you can think of any more tests to perform, such as fuzzy testing, do that now. If you see any problems while you are testing, fix them now, then test again.

# Add Sanity Checks

In Chapter 10 we commented out the sanity check to ensure that the script is being run by root so we need to restore that. We will also add a check to ensure that the script is running on a Linux host. As a bash script, it would be compatible with various Unix systems, but several of the Linux specific functions would fail.

---

**EXPERIMENT 11-2**

First remove the comment hashes from the root check. That now looks like this.

```
#-----------------------------------------------------------------------
# Check for root.

if [ `id -u` != 0 ]
then
    echo ""
    echo "You must be root user to run this program"
    echo ""
    Quit 1
fi
```

Now run two quick tests. Run the program as root to ensure that root can still use the program.

```
[root@testvm1 student]# ./mymotd
          total        used        free      shared  buff/cache   available
Mem:    4046060      254392     2947324         984      844344     3532200
Swap:   4182012           0     4182012
```

Run the program as the student user to verify that non-root users get an error.

```
[student@testvm1 ~]$ ./mymotd
```

```
You must be root user to run this program
```

If you discover any errors, fix them now before we continue.

Let's add our second sanity check to ensure that this program is run on a Linux system. This test uses the uname command to return the operating system name.

Add the following code just below the code that checks for root user.

```
#--------------------------------------------------------------------------
# Check for Linux

if [[ "$(uname -s)" != "Linux" ]]
then
    echo ""
    echo "This script runs on Linux only -- OS detected: $(uname -s)."
    echo ""
    Quit 1
fi
#--------------------------------------------------------------------------
```

We can test this only for a positive outcome – that is that we are running on Linux – but not for a negative outcome, unless we test it on a non-Linux host. But let's at least do our positive test. Just run the command and verify that you get no errors.

# Version Number

All programs should have a version number. This script already has a variable that specifies a version number, but it is the version of the script template rather than that of the new program on which we are working. Let's set our version number. Since this is early in the development process, it will not be a full version level.

I like to use three double-digit parts for my version number to allow for flexibility. So let's start with version 00.01.00 because it indicates code that is far from ready. As we get closer to releasing into the wild, that number will go up and the first full release will be 01.00.00.

---

**EXPERIMENT 11-3**

---

First set the version number in the variables section of the code. Let's also delete the RC (return code) line in this section. This is what we have in the variables section for now, but more variables will be added here as we move through the rest of the experiments in this chapter.

```
/ That little bit of new code \
\ won't break anything.       /
 -----------------------------
     \     ^__^
      \   (oo)_____
         (__)\       )\/\
             ||----w |
             ||     ||
```

```
# Set initial variables
badoption=0
error=0
verbose=0
Version=00.01.00
```

Now we test even this tiny bit of new code despite the fact that it looks simple and innocuous.

```
[root@testvm1 student]# ./mymotd -V
Version = 00.01.00
```

But you are not really done with testing. You should do some additional testing of the previously coded functions to ensure that they have not been broken by this new code.

At this point the basics are complete. We have a partial script that displays help, the GNU license statement, performs a couple of sanity checks, and displays the version number. We do not need to add any options to the case statement because everything we need is already there.

## Main Body

Now we can add the main body of the code to gather the data we want and to display it. We will gather the data in the sequence we want it and print it to STDOUT as we go. This will make early testing easy.

233

---

## EXPERIMENT 11-4

First, delete the **free** command that we used to provide some output from the script.

Now let's add some code to our program. In the main body of the program and before the **Quit** function call, add the code to perform these functions. We also add some code that will print the data we have collected. This provides a simple test while also producing the desired results.

This section of code now looks like this.

```
###################################################################
###################################################################
# The main body of your program goes here.
###################################################################
###################################################################
# Get the date
Date=`date`
# Get the hostname
host=`hostname`
###################################################################
# Start printing the data using printf to make it pretty          #
###################################################################
printf "################################################################\n"
printf "# MOTD for $Date\n"
printf "# HOST NAME: \t\t$host \n"
```

In the printf statement, \t inserts a tab into the output and \n is a newline character. It took me a while to get the entire output formatted properly when I first wrote this script. You have the advantage of my knowledge that I gained from doing this first.

Add the following variables to the initialization section.

```
host=""
Date=""
```

Now let's run the program to test just these results.

```
[root@testvm1 student]# ./mymotd
#####################################################################
# MOTD for Sat Jan 13 12:14:34 EST 2018
# HOST NAME:             testvm1
```

That looks correct for my virtual machine host. So in five lines of active code – not counting the comment lines – we have the beginnings of our script written and tested.

The code so far lends itself well to a dev/test cycle like this. We add code to obtain some data and some more code to print that data. Things are about to get more complex.

## EXPERIMENT 11-5

Now we want to add some code to determine whether the host is a physical or virtual machine and we also want some information about the motherboard. The Linux command we need to do this, **dmidecode**, is not always installed so we need to ensure that it is present on our host. The easy way to do this is to try to install it. If it is not present, it will be installed. Do this as root.

```
[root@testvm1 ~]# dnf install -y dmidecode
```

The dmidecode utility, where dmi stands for Desktop Management Interface, can access a table of hardware data maintained by the system management BIOS (SMBIOS). For example, use the following command to retrieve data about the motherboard. "-t" means "type" and type 2 is the motherboard. The dmidecode man page lists all of the data types available.

```
[root@david ~]# dmidecode -t 2
# dmidecode 3.1
Getting SMBIOS data from sysfs.
SMBIOS 3.0.0 present.

Handle 0x0002, DMI type 2, 15 bytes
Base Board Information
        Manufacturer: ASUSTeK COMPUTER INC.
        Product Name: TUF X299 MARK 2
        Version: Rev 1.xx
        Serial Number: 170807951700403
        Asset Tag: Default string
        Features:
```

```
            Board is a hosting board
            Board is replaceable
        Location In Chassis: Default string
        Chassis Handle: 0x0003
        Type: Motherboard
        Contained Object Handles: 0
```

The results of the dmidecode command above are from my main workstation rather than a test VM.

---

**Note**   This mymotd script is written for Intel processors and Fedora Linux. It will work with other chips and distributions, but the results of some sections of code may not be correct. You may want to do some experimentation on your own to make those sections work in your environment.

---

Now we have the dmidecode tool installed and we can continue adding to our program. First we want to know if the host is a VM or physical machine.

## EXPERIMENT 11-6

Now let's add some code to tell us whether the host is a physical machine of a VM. The information we need for this is part of the dmesg log buffer that is started at each boot. We just need to grep for the appropriate text strings. Add the code below immediately after the date and hostname from the previous experiment.

```
########################################################################
# Is this a VirtualBox, VMWare, or Physical Machine.                   #
########################################################################
if dmesg | grep -i "VBOX HARDDISK" > /dev/null
then
    MachineType="VM running under VirtualBox."
elif dmesg | grep -i "vmware" > /dev/null
then
    MachineType="VM running under VMWare."
else
    MachineType="physical machine."
fi
printf "# Machine Type: \t$MachineType\n"
```

Add the MachineType variable to the variables section of the script. And then test this new code.

```
[root@testvm1 student]# ./mymotd
#####################################################################
# MOTD for Sun Jan 14 09:49:29 EST 2018
# HOST NAME:           testvm1
# Machine Type:        VM running under VirtualBox.
```

This is again correct for my test VM. Your results may differ.

---

It it often helpful to know the architecture of the host computer, that is, whether it is 32- or 64-bit. This next experiment adds some code to determine that.

---

## EXPERIMENT 11-7

Add the three lines of code below to determine the architecture of the host as 32 or 64 bits.

```
# Get the host physical architecture
HostArch=`echo $HOSTTYPE | tr [:lower:] [:upper:]`
printf "# Host architecture: \t$HostArch\n"
```

Add HostArch to the variables section and test.

```
[root@testvm1 student]# ./mymotd
#####################################################################
# MOTD for Sun Jan 14 10:43:05 EST 2018
# HOST NAME:           testvm1
# Machine Type:        VM running under VirtualBox.
# Host architecture:   X86_64
```

And this shows that our VM is 64-bit, which is correct. Most hosts today are 64-bit and only a few 32-bit ones are still around, such as my ASUS EeePC. However some of the small, single board computers (SBC) are still 32-bit.

---

Even in a VM the motherboard information is interesting, so let's get that data now. The ability to get this information without taking the computer apart is very useful.

```
                          EXPERIMENT 11-8
```

The following code is added after the host architecture code and uses dmidecode to extract information about the motherboard.

```
########################################################################
# Get the motherboard information                                      #
########################################################################
MotherboardMfr=`dmidecode -t 2 | grep Manufacturer | awk -F: '{print $2}' |
sed -e "s/^ //"`
MotherboardModel=`dmidecode -t 2 | grep Name | awk -F: '{print $2}' |
sed -e "s/^ //"`
printf "# Motherboard Mfr: \t$MotherboardMfr\n"
printf "# Motherboard Model: \t$MotherboardModel\n"
printf "#----------------------------------------------------------------\n"
```

Note that the lines of code that obtain the motherboard information are both wrapped in the listing above. Be sure to enter them on a single line. I also added a line to print a separator in order to set it apart from the next section of data.

Add the two new variables to the variable initialization section.

```
MotherboardMfr=""
MotherboardModel=""
```

Now test the program to verify the results.

```
[root@testvm1 student]# ./mymotd
########################################################################
# MOTD for Sun Jan 14 10:57:05 EST 2018
# HOST NAME:           testvm1
# Machine Type:        VM running under VirtualBox.
# Host architecture:   X86_64
# Motherboard Mfr:     Oracle Corporation
# Motherboard Model:   VirtualBox
#----------------------------------------------------------------
```

This first section of the results is excellent and correct for the virtual machine. It looks nice and is easy to read.

Up to this point we have extracted and printed some general information about the host. Now we want to add a section that will show us some information about the CPU itself. Much of this information is located in the /proc filesystem. Many times it is not available as a single, well-formatted data point, so we need to use our Linux tools to extract what we want and format it appropriately.

---

## EXPERIMENT 11-9

We start obtaining CPU information by getting the CPU model information from the /proc filesystem. These lines of code do that so add them to the end of the program just above the Quit function call.

```
###################################################################
# Get the CPU information                                         #
###################################################################
# Starting with the specific hardware model
CPUModel=`grep "^model name" /proc/cpuinfo | head -n 1 | cut -d : -f 2 |
sed -e "s/^ //"`CPUModel
printf "# CPU Model:\t\t$CPUModel\n"
```

The line that assigns the value to the CPUModel variable is wrapped so be sure to enter in on one line in your program. Add the CPUModel variable to the variables section and test.

```
[root@testvm1 student]# ./mymotd
###################################################################
# MOTD for Sun Jan 14 15:54:24 EST 2018
# HOST NAME:            testvm1
# Machine Type:         VM running under VirtualBox.
# Host architecture:    X86_64
# Motherboard Mfr:      Oracle Corporation
# Motherboard Model:    VirtualBox
#-----------------------------------------------------------------
# CPU Model:            Intel(R) Core(TM) i9-7960X CPU @ 2.80GHz
```

This latest addition to our code produces good information about the CPU installed in our system.

---

Let's locate some additional CPU information, such as the number of CPUs and the packaging info – how many cores per chip – and whether we have hyperthreading.

---

**EXPERIMENT 11-10**

---

This experiment collects some CPU data and then makes some educated determinations of how the CPUs are packaged and whether the CPUs are capable of Hyperthreading.

First, let's add a bunch of new variables to the initialization section.

```
PhysicalChips=0
Siblings=0
HyperThreading="No"
CPUSpeed=""
NumCores=0
Package=0
Arch=""
CPUdata=""
CPUArch=""
```

There is a lot of code here because it is all related and needs to be complete for the test to succeed. Be careful as you enter it. Especially be careful of the lines that are wrapped in the listing below.

```
################################################################################
# Get some CPU details.                                                        #
################################################################################
# Get number of actual physical chips
PhysicalChips=`grep "^physical id" /proc/cpuinfo | sort | uniq | wc | awk
'{print $1}'`
if [ $PhysicalChips -eq 0 ]
then
    let PhysicalChips=1
fi
# Get the total number of cores
CPUs=`cat /proc/cpuinfo | grep "cpu cores" | head -n 1 | cut -d : -f 2 |
sed -e "s/^ //"`

# Do we have HyperThreading
```

```
Siblings=`grep "^siblings" /proc/cpuinfo | head -n 1 | cut -d : -f 2 |
sed -e "s/^ //"`
if [ $Siblings -gt $CPUs ]
then
    # Yes we have HyperThreading
    HyperThreading="Yes"
fi

# Now Cores per CPU
# We are assuming each package has the same number of cores - the next line
is wrapped
NumCores=`grep "^cpu cores" /proc/cpuinfo | sort | uniq | awk -F: '{print $2}' |
sed -e "s/^ //"`
case "$NumCores" in
    1) Package="Single Core";;
    2) Package="Dual Core";;
    4) Package="Quad Core";;
    6) Package="Six Core";;
    8) Package="Eight Core";;
   12) Package="Twelve Core";;
   16) Package="Sixteen Core";;
   18) Package="Eighteen Core";;
   20) Package="Twenty Core";;
   24) Package="Twenty-four Core";;
   26) Package="Twenty-six Core";;
   28) Package="Twenty-eight Core";;
   30) Package="Thirty Core";;
   32) Package="Thirty-two Core";;
    *) Package="Single Core"
       NumCores=1;;
esac

# Get the CPU architecture which can be different from the host architecture
CPUArch=`arch`
# Now lets put some of this together to make printing easy
CPUdata="$PhysicalChips $Package $CPUArch"

# Get the CPU speed - The next line is wrapped
CPUSpeed=`grep "model name" /proc/cpuinfo | sed -e 's/.*\( [0-9]*.[0-9]*[GM]
Hz\)/\1/' -e 's/^ *//g' | uniq`
```

```
# Let's print what we have
printf "# CPU Data:\t\t$CPUdata\n"
printf "# HyperThreading:\t$HyperThreading\n"
printf "#--------------------------------------------------------------------\n"
```

Be sure to check this code over carefully as you enter it. And then we test again.

```
[root@david development]# ./mymotd
######################################################################
# MOTD for Mon Jan 15 15:35:09 EST 2018
# HOST NAME:            david
# Machine Type:         physical machine.
# Host architecture:    X86_64
# Motherboard Mfr:      ASUSTeK COMPUTER INC.
# Motherboard Model:    TUF X299 MARK 2
#-------------------------------------------------------------
# CPU Model:            Intel(R) Core(TM) i9-7960X CPU @ 2.80GHz
# CPU Data:             1 Sixteen Core x86_64
# HyperThreading:       Yes
#-------------------------------------------------------------
```

Our first two sections are complete. The next section that details the system memory is a little easier.

---

## EXPERIMENT 11-11

This experiment adds code to display a few memory statistics. Here again we use resources readily available.

The /proc/meminfo file has the data we need but it is in KB and we want it in GB for the sake of clarity. To do this we add the following procedure to the procedure section of the script. Bash does not have decent math capability, so this code uses the bc calculator command, which has its own unique syntax.

```
######################################################################
# Convert KB to GB                                                   #
######################################################################
kb2gb()
{
```

```
    # Convert KBytes to Giga using 1024
    # first convert the input to MB
    echo "scale=3;$number/1024/1024" | bc
}
```

The following code, which should be added just before the final Quit procedure call at the end of the script, gets the data from the /proc/meminfo file and then converts the numbers to GB. It then prints the results.

```
###############################################################################
# Memory and Swap data                                                       #
###############################################################################
# Get memory size in KB.
number=`grep MemTotal /proc/meminfo | awk '{print $2}'`
# Convert to GB
mem=`kb2gb`
# Get swap size in KB
number=`grep SwapTotal /proc/meminfo | awk '{print $2}'`
# Convert to GB
swap=`kb2gb`

printf "# RAM:\t\t\t$mem GB\n"
printf "# SWAP:\t\t\t$swap GB\n"
printf "#-----------------------------------------------------------------\n"
```

And we need to add the new variables to the variable section.

```
number=0
mem=0
swap=0
```

Now it is once again time to test.

```
[root@david development]# ./mymotd
###############################################################################
# MOTD for Mon Jan 15 21:56:40 EST 2018
# HOST NAME:          david
# Machine Type:       physical machine.
# Host architecture:  X86_64
# Motherboard Mfr:    ASUSTeK COMPUTER INC.
# Motherboard Model:  TUF X299 MARK 2
```

```
#-----------------------------------------------------------------
# CPU Model:            Intel(R) Core(TM) i9-7960X CPU @ 2.80GHz
# CPU Data:             1 Sixteen Core x86_64
# HyperThreading:       Yes
#-----------------------------------------------------------------
# RAM:                  62.586 GB
# SWAP:                 14.902 GB
#-----------------------------------------------------------------
```

On the testvm1 host the results of the test look like this.

```
[root@testvm1 student]# ./mymotd
#################################################################
# MOTD for Mon Jan 15 21:57:32 EST 2018
# HOST NAME:            testvm1
# Machine Type:         VM running under VirtualBox.
# Host architecture:    X86_64
# Motherboard Mfr:      Oracle Corporation
# Motherboard Model:    VirtualBox
#-----------------------------------------------------------------
# CPU Model:            Intel(R) Core(TM) i9-7960X CPU @ 2.80GHz
# CPU Data:             1 Quad Core x86_64
# HyperThreading:       No
#-----------------------------------------------------------------
# RAM:                  3.854 GB
# SWAP:                 7.999 GB
#-----------------------------------------------------------------
```

If you have other hosts on which to test, you should do that to verify that the results are correct for other circumstances.

Although this script is not yet complete based on the set of requirements I created for it at the beginning of this chapter, I think we have gone far enough that you can finish on your own. So I leave the completion of this script as an exercise for you, the SysAdmins of the world.

Just in case you like this code but need some additional guidance or just don't care about finishing it, the completed code for this bash script can be downloaded from: https://github.com/Apress/linux-philo-sysadmins/tree/master/Ch11

Regardless of which method you choose, you should feel free to make any modifications to this code that you like in order to meet your own requirements.

# Fixing a Script

Many times we need to repair existing scripts. I recently had a problem with a script that I had written. Fortunately I was made aware of the issue before any damage was done. As you can see from the mymotd script, I like to provide a moderate number of comments to help me figure things out later. It makes it so much easier if I do not have to determine how the code works every time I need to modify it to either fix it or add new function.

As I mentioned in the "Test in Production" section of this chapter, sometimes fixing a script needs to start with the very basics. In that case I added comments to make the code easier to read and resolved any obvious bugs as I came upon them. Because of the circumstances mentioned earlier, the only environment we had was production. Every time I made even a minor change to the code, I had to test ensure that the change worked as expected and that nothing else that might depend on the altered code had been broken.

In a more recent case, it was my own reasonably well-commented code that did not work quite correctly. In this situation an MP3 file was created on a USB stick with a filename that included the date in MMDDYYYY-X format where X is a sequence number. My program changed the name of the file to be something that included that date as taken directly from the filename but rearranged to YYYYMMDD-X, and then copied the file to the server. If the recording device created two files in a single day, they both had the same date but the files were differentiated by the sequence number. My script was designed to keep them sequential so they would be sorted in the order of their creation.

The problem arose when a file was created and then transferred and then another file was created the same day. It would have the same filename as the first file and overwrite it on the server.

To fix this I decided to use the files' timestamps to create my own in the format YYYYMMDD-HHMMSS and to eliminate the use of the sequence number in the new filenames.

This particular fix was a simple matter of making a single minor change that corrected for an edge condition that I had not previously considered. Testing was easy; just create the edge conditions and run the program while ensuring that it still ran correctly when the edge conditions were not present. I keep a couple of sample MP3 files on hand for testing and just copy them to the USB memory stick.

# Summary

Testing code for a SysAdmin is much like writing it – fast and less than rigorous. I hope that last bit sounds better than "fast and loose." Writing code quickly usually means testing it quickly as well. That does not mean that testing shell scripts needs to be haphazard. "Test early, test often" is a good mantra for making the testing part of the coding. With the application of this tenet, the task of testing shell scripts becomes second nature and an integral part of the act of writing the script in the first place.

I found the mymotd script in this chapter to be a good excuse for rewriting my original version. I wrote the script in 2007 and my better understanding of hardware architecture and reporting in Linux has helped me with this version. My knowledge of Linux tools, whether new or not, has also improved and given me more flexibility to simplify this new script.

Notice that the variable names are all ones that make sense in terms of the task being performed. It is possible to look at the variable name and get an idea of the kind of data it is supposed to contain. This also helps make testing easier.

# Use Commonsense Naming

I have mentioned in several places in this book that typing is not my forte and that the Lazy SysAdmin does everything possible to reduce typing. I take that seriously. This tenet expands on that, but there is much more to it than just reducing the amount of typing I need to do. It is also about the readability of scripts and naming things so that they are more understandable.

One of the original Unix philosophy tenets – although one of the lesser ones – was to always use lowercase and keep names short. An admirable goal but not one so easily met in the world of the SysAdmin. In many respects my own tenet would seem a complete refutation of the original. However, the original was intended for a different audience, and this one is intended for SysAdmins with a different set of needs.

I think the ultimate goal is to create scripts that are readable and easily understood in order to make them easily maintainable. And then to use other, simple scripts and cron jobs to automate running those scripts. Keeping the script names reasonably short also reduces typing when executing those scripts from the command line, but that is mostly irrelevant when starting them from another script or as cron jobs.

## Script and Program Names

Does the program name dbu mean anything to you? Did the program name dd mean anything to you before you became a Linux geek? The answer to both is probably "no." While dd is a common GNU utility, "disk dump," dbu is a shell script of my own creation. The name will still mean nothing to you, but to me it means David's backup. It is easy to type, and once you know what it means the name will stick with you.

If you explore all of the original GNU core utilities, you find that their names are quite short – many of them being two or three letters. This is great but there are thousands of Linux commands overall and only so many meaningful short combinations. One property of any name should be that it has some meaningful connection to the purpose of the program or script.

The name we used for our script in Chapter 11, mymotd, is a little longer but is also is a bit more meaningful than might be the case with a shorter name. We could have used davesmotd, dmotd, mmotd, davesMOTD, dMOTD, or any other relatively meaningful name. The capital letters in some of the names do help make it easier to discern the function of the script, but they do make it just a bit harder to type the names on the command line.

As with my "dbu" program, there is still some room for very short names. For example, there is a very nice program called "mtr" that is an interactive replacement for the old traceroute program. The mtr program maintains an active and continuous traceroute with a dynamic display that shows the number of packets lost at each hop and can show multiple routes for if the packets are being rerouted for some reason. Very interesting and useful.

The mtr program was originally named that because a person named Matt Kimball wrote and maintained it. Therefore, it was "Matt's traceroute." After Matt stopped supporting it, Roger Wolff took over. It is still named mtr but that now stands for "my traceroute."

Naming scripts with very short names can be a challenge because many of the existing short letter combinations are already taken. I always try to do some research when naming a script to ensure it won't cause a problem with an executable already installed on my computer. I usually do a quick check with the `which` command as shown in Experiment 12-1.

---

## EXPERIMENT 12-1

Since we have not copied the mymotd script to any of the standard executable path locations, it should not appear when we use the command below.

```
[root@david ~]# which mymotd
/usr/bin/which: no mymotd in (/usr/lib64/qt-3.3/bin:/usr/local/sbin:/usr/
local/bin:/usr/sbin:/usr/bin:/root/bin)
```

The `which` command displays the paths it searched in its attempt to locate the specified executable file.

Regardless of its state of completion, copy the mymotd script to /usr/local/bin, which is the correct location in the Linux FHS to store locally created executable files. Then run the `which` command again.

```
[root@testvm1 student]# cp mymotd /usr/local/bin
[root@testvm1 student]# which mymotd
/usr/local/bin/mymotd
```

We have determined that there is currently no executable file installed that might cause a problem with the name we have chosen for our file and then we copied our executable to the appropriate location.

Not all conflicts will arise when you first write a new script. After checking the installed programs, I also do a Google search. I try to find any information out there about programs that might have a naming conflict with mine. Longer names are much less likely to conflict, but they don't really need to be too long.

I once had a situation where the problem occurred much later. I was attempting to install a new program using yum, which, like its successor, dnf, is a wrapper around the rpm command. I received an error indicating that one of the files that needed to be installed from the new RPM package was in conflict with a file with the same name from another package.

This was not one of my scripts but another pair of RPMs that were in conflict. I was able to remove the conflict by removing the RPM that was already installed because it was no longer needed.

This type of conflict should be very rare. Even when files have the same names – which is unlikely in the first place – so long as they are located in different directories, they do not conflict during installation. If they are both executables and located in different directories in the $PATH, however, the one located on the first directory listed in $PATH is the one that will be run by the command. To run the other, you would need to use the fully qualified path name to ensure that the correct program is run.

Naming scripts can be a bit tricky with potential conflicts like this. One reason I like to use script names that are a bit longer, say four to eight or ten characters, is to help prevent naming conflicts. I sometimes add an uppercase letter to my script names to help it stand out and help to clarify the name a bit in a long list.

The bottom line here is that the name should be memorable and meaningful – to you as well as well as other SysAdmins, easy to type, and easy to spot in a list. Those are my personal criteria. You may have others and that is perfectly fine. Just remember that other SysAdmins may someday need to work with the hosts on which your scripts are located.

# Variables

Back when I purchased my first IBM PC in 1981, I ordered it with the maximum of 64KB on the motherboard[1] while the cheapest model had only 16K. That was not a lot of space in which to work. BASIC was included with the PC in an on-board ROM and made a good choice for many people learning to program in those days.

Because of the limited space it was important to be frugal with memory usage when writing programs in BASIC. I did not do things to make it look pretty like indent loops and subroutines because each tab or space took up one Byte of memory that might be needed for something important. I kept variable names as short as possible. I typically used single letters or two-character variable names with a letter and a number such as A7. Comments were nonexistent if we wrote fairly large programs because there was not space for them. I did all of this to save memory. but it made my programs very difficult to read.

I wish I had saved some of the really horrible code I have either written myself or that I had to fix that was written by someone else. And there has been a lot of both.

# Naming Variables

I tend to make my script variables long enough to be indicative of their content as you could see in the project in Chapter 11. Those variable names were lengths ranging from fairly short to moderate. All of them were designed to make it easy for myself and future script maintainers to read and understand the code.

The variable names in my scripts tend to reflect their content. Thus, you should be able to deduce that a variable named $CPUArch probably contains information pertaining to the architecture of the CPU. You might not know the exact type of data,

---

[1]It was possible to add more memory to the PC with add-in boards that plugged directly into the system bus. I later added a 256KB memory adapter that I built from parts.

but you should have a general idea what to expect when you view the contents of that variable. You would probably expect to see something like "X86_64" or just "64" for the value of this variable. At least in my scripts, that would be the case.

The thing to keep in mind is that variable names are only typed while writing and maintaining the script. The script can then be run as many times as needed, and I never need to type any of those variable names.

## Make Everything a Variable

This is a pretty common best practice. Even if you need to use "constants" like Pi, or Euler's constant, or constants related to a specific field of endeavor, they should be declared as variables and then the variable used in calculations. Of course, bash itself does only integer arithmetic, but there are other types of variables.

I like to use variables for paths and file names used in my scripts. I also use variables for data that will be printed such as in the mymotd script in the previous chapter. Using variables like $Date, $host, $MachineType, $MotherboardModel, and so on, as we did in that script makes it easier to read and understand the functionality. When I see a statement like the one in Figure 12-1, I understand immediately what the code is supposed to accomplish – even when it is out of context as it is here. The type value we would expect to find assigned to the variable is clear.

```
MotherboardModel=`dmidecode -t 2 | grep Name | awk -F: '{print $2}' | sed -e "s/^
//"`
```

***Figure 12-1.*** *The desired content of the variable is obvious from the variable name*

You should be able to deduce from the variable name a bit about how this code works. Clearly the dmidecode utility is used to obtain information about the motherboard which and that "type" 2 is motherboard information. It also tells us the line of output containing the string, "Name," contains the specific information we are looking for. The rest of the code is to extract the data string containing the model information and clean it up for use by our script.

So let's try this little experiment to illustrate.

---

**EXPERIMENT 12-2**

Enter the following intentionally incorrect command-line program on a single line.

```
[root@david ~]# MotherboardModel=`dmidecode -t 2 | grep Version | awk -F:
'{print $2}' | sed -e "s/^ //"`;echo $MotherboardModel
Rev 1.xx
```

The value of the variable is clearly wrong because the data does not match what would be expected from the name of the variable. This is clearly not the model of the motherboard – it is a revision number.

Now use the following corrected code. Again on a single line.

```
[root@david ~]# MotherboardModel=`dmidecode -t 2 | grep Name | awk -F:
'{print $2}' | sed -e "s/^ //"`;echo $MotherboardModel
TUF X299 MARK 2
```

The result is clearly more appropriate for the variable even if we don't know exactly what the motherboard model is before we run the code.

---

Even if the variables are used only once after they are assigned, it makes sense to do so. I have found on several occasions that in later script maintenance, I added more code that also used that variable. This has saved typing long path names a second or third time in my scripts.

For example, if I have the path name for customer invoices, ~/Documents/business/Customer/invoices in my script, it is easy to set a variable such as $Invoices and use that in my script rather than the full path. This makes it easy to refer to that variable in other places in the script as well. By not having to type the long path name again, I also prevent possible typing errors in the path name, which would lead to errors during execution.

Many times I build up path names from multiple variables because I need that extra flexibility and it also reduces typing. For example, my rsbu backup program uses a new directory every day for a new set of backups. The tree is structured like this.

```
/-
  |
  \-path to backup media
      |
      \Backups
          |
          |--host1
          |    |--2018-01-01
          |    |    \--data
          |    |--2018-01-02
          |    |    \--data
          |    |--2018-01-03
          |    |         \--data
          |    etc
          --host2
          |    |--2018-01-01
          |    |    \--data
          |    |--2018-01-02
          |    |    \--data
          |    |--2018-01-03
          |    |    \--data
          etc etc
```

A new date subdirectory is added for each host, each day. So we need to create a series of variables to use in the code that can generate this directory structure. Experiment 12-3 shows one method for accomplishing this.

---

**EXPERIMENT 12-3**

We do not need to create a script for this experiment. Enter the commands below to begin the setup. These variables, once defined at the command line, remain part of the environment until they are unset using the unset command or set to null.

```
[student@testvm1 ~]$ BasePath="/media/Backup-Drive/Backups"
[student@testvm1 ~]$ BackupDate=`date +%Y-%m-%d`
[student@testvm1 ~]$ YesterdaysDate=`date -d "now-1days" "+%Y-%m-%d"`
```

Now verify the values of the variables we just set.

```
[student@testvm1 ~]$ echo $BasePath;echo $BackupDate;echo
$YesterdaysDate;echo $HOSTNAME
/media/Backup-Drive/Backups
2018-01-22
2018-01-21
testvm1
```

Note that the $HOSTNAME variable is a BASH built-in variable so we do not need to set it. Now set the main backup path for this host. I use this program to back up multiple hosts so I keep the backups for each host in a separate directory. This won't work for remote hosts, but it is a nice shortcut for use in this experiment.

```
[student@testvm1 ~]$ BackupPath="$BasePath/$HOSTNAME/"
[student@testvm1 ~]$ echo $BackupPath
/media/Backup-Drive/Backups/testvm1/
```

All that is left in order to complete the current backup path is to add today's date.

```
[student@testvm1 ~]$ TodaysBackupPath="$BackupPath$BackupDate"
[student@testvm1 ~]$ echo $TodaysBackupPath
/media/Backup-Drive/Backups/testvm1/2018-01-22
```

But since I use rsync and some of its most interesting – and fun – features,[2] I need to generate the path for yesterday's backups as well.

```
[student@testvm1 ~]$ YesterdaysBackupPath="$BackupPath$YesterdaysDate"
[student@testvm1 ~]$ echo $YesterdaysBackupPath
/media/Backup-Drive/Backups/testvm1/2018-01-21
```

I have generated the path for the backup from yesterday so that rsync can simply create hard links from yesterday's backup files to today's directory and only perform a backup on the files that have changed.

I use this series of variables containing elements of the paths I need in various parts of the script in order to generate multiple paths for multiple hosts. A modification to the $BasePath variable can also be used to mount the external hard drives I use for backup.

---

[2]Here is a link to an article I wrote about using rsync for backups: https://opensource.com/ article/17/1/rsync-backup-linux

Even though the variable names are fairly long, they are reasonably easy to type within the script. These names make it easy to understand the function of each variable and how they fit into the whole. The names could undoubtedly be made shorter and still be understandable, but I like them this way.

Of course there are some edge cases that this code does not directly address, but I have more complex code in my script to deal with that. I did not want to cloud the basics with edge cases like what happens when there are no previous backups, and how to deal with the possibility that a previous backup exists but it is not from yesterday. Many of the variables defined in Experiment 12-3 are also used to help deal with those edge cases.

# Procedures

Bash is a command-line language that supports the use of procedures. Procedures in scripts need names just as variables do. The script we created in Chapter 11 contains a few procedures that are named to provide an insight into their function.

For example, the Help() procedure is obviously intended to print help information and the GPL() procedure prints the GPL license statement. The kb2gb() procedure is a bit more obscure, but with only a little consideration it should be clear that it converts Kilobytes to Gigabytes.

# Hosts

Yes, hosts – computers on a network – need naming. Most organizations have some sort of convention for naming hosts. Most of the SysAdmins I know have established some sort of conventions even if their organization has not imposed one.

One place I worked used the major Greek and Roman gods to name their Linux servers while their Unix and Linux workstations received the names of lesser gods and mythological personages. Other places have used names from *Star Trek* or *Star Wars* for their hosts.

Most SysAdmins have home networks and we all have some sort of naming convention that we use. Whether based on gaming, mythological gods and characters, kids and grandkids, birds, pets, ships, movies, states, minerals, subatomic particles, chemicals, the names of scientists, or whatever, I have seen many different conventions used. Ben Cotton, my technical reviewer, uses the town names of places where he has been storm chasing.

I use the names of Essex class aircraft carriers for most of the hosts in my home network as a tribute to my father who was on one of them, the Bunker Hill, in the Pacific during WWII. For a two-word name like that, I just run the words together to create "bunkerhill." By convention, host names are always in lowercase. A little testing will reveal that the Internet DNS system ignores case when performing lookups, but I do like to go with convention for things like this.

# Organizational Naming

Many organizations have well-defined naming conventions while others leave those details up to the System Administrators.

A couple of the organizations I have worked for had conventions for naming hosts, other network nodes, programs, and scripts. I think this is a bit overkill, but it is better to have an extensive and well-documented convention than none at all.

Most of the places I have worked had naming conventions for network hosts and nodes, but most of the lower-level naming such as scripts was left to the SysAdmins. This is my preferred situation. Most organizations do not need to deal in such detail with naming conventions.

Whatever conventions you have at the SysAdmin level should be well documented.

# Summary

As with other tenets of the Linux Philosophy for System Administrators, there is not one particular "right" way to do things when creating names for files, procedures, scripts, variables, and anything else. It really is about what works best for you. You should feel no pressure to name things in any particular way other than what makes sense and is meaningful to you.

Common sense in naming is the real key here. The main criteria I use is, "will this name be meaningful to me or another SysAdmin in a few years when the script needs to be maintained?"

The use of common sense by SysAdmins when naming things contributes to our objective of being the Lazy SysAdmin. Code that is easy to read takes far less time to maintain than code that is not. Having to maintain poorly written code that is unintelligible until it has been completely rewritten sucks up huge amounts of time and effort that would be better spent elsewhere.

# CHAPTER 13

# Store Data in Open Formats

The reason we use computers is to manipulate data. It used to be called "Data Processing" for a reason and that was an accurate description. We still process data although it may be in the form of video and audio streams, network and wireless streams, word processing data, spreadsheets, images, and more. It is all still just data.

We work with and manipulate text data streams with the tools we have available to us in Linux. That data usually needs to be stored, and when there is a need to store data, it is always better to store it in open file formats than closed ones.

Although many user application programs store data in ASCII formats, including simple flat ASCII and XML, this chapter is about configuration data and scripts that relate directly to Linux. The files we will consider in this chapter are about system configuration.

## Closed Is Impenetrable

Way back before the Registry[1] was introduced with Windows 3.1, most utilities and applications stored their configuration data in .ini files. These .ini files were stored as ASCII text and were easy to access, read, and even to modify. All it took was a simple text editor to make changes to these .ini configuration files.

The registry changed all that by storing configuration data in a single, large, and impenetrable binary data file. Although individual programs could store configuration data in .ini files, the Registry was touted as a way to centralize control over program configuration, and its binary format was allegedly faster to parse than ASCII text files.

---

[1]Wikipedia, Windows Registry, https://en.wikipedia.org/wiki/Windows_Registry

© David Both 2018
D. Both, *The Linux Philosophy for SysAdmins*, https://doi.org/10.1007/978-1-4842-3730-4_13

As System Administrators we have need to use many different types of data. Binary formats are by their very nature obscure and require special tools and knowledge to manipulate. There is a plethora of tools available that provide registry viewing and editing capability. These tools range from so-called freeware to expensive commercial programs. The necessity to use special tools that are themselves closed in order to manage a computer is a further step into impenetrability.

Part of the problem with all this is that the writers of these tools need to have information about the contents of registry entries that are being viewed or edited. Without that inside knowledge from the vendors of the proprietary software these tools are also useless. And one reason that proprietary software stores configuration data in a binary and proprietary format is to hide things from users.

This all stems from the closed and proprietary philosophy adhered to by these vendors. It appears on the surface to be about protecting the users from doing "stupid things," but it is also a good way to obscure information.

I did try to locate a binary format Linux system configuration file in /etc but was unable to. Not one of the hundreds of configuration files in that directory was in a binary format. That is a really good thing, but it leaves me without a sample of a binary configuration file that I can use to show you what one is like.

One of the issues with binary formats is that there would have been no reason to create the many powerful tools we have in Linux. None of the data streams that could be generated from binary format files would be usable for tools like grep, awk, sed, cat, vim, emacs, or any of the hundreds of other text-based tools we take for granted every day while we administer the systems for which we are responsible.

# Open Is Knowable

"Open source" is about the code and making the source code available to any and all who want to view or modify it. "Open data[2]" is about the openness of the data itself.

The term open data does not mean just having access to the data itself, it also means that the data can be viewed, used in some manner, and shared with others. The exact manner in which those goals are achieved may be subject to some sort of attribution and open licensing. As with open source software, such licensing is intended to ensure the continued open availability of the data and not to restrict it any manner.

---

[2]Wikipedia, Open Data, https://en.wikipedia.org/wiki/Open_data

Open data is knowable. That means that access to it is unfettered. Truly open data can be read freely and understood without the need for further interpretation or decryption. In the SysAdmin world, open means that the data we use to configure, monitor, and manage our Linux hosts is easy to find, read, and modify when necessary. It is stored in formats that permit that ease of access, such as ASCII text. When a system is open the data and software can all be managed by open tools – tools that work with ASCII text.

# Flat ASCII Text

Flat text files are open and knowable. They are easy to read by both programs and SysAdmins so it is easy to see when things are working – or not. Most Linux configuration files are simple flat ASCII text files, which make them easy to view and modify with the simple Linux text manipulation tools that are already at our disposal.

So we can use cat and less to view the Linux configuration files, and grep to extract and view lines containing specified strings. We can use vi, vim, emacs, or any other text editor to modify configuration files that are ASCII text format.

In one of my jobs – the one where we used Perl CGI scripts to manage the email system – we used flat text files to store all of our data. This data included departmental information such as who was authorized to access the data for that department. It also contained the ID and login information for the email users for each department.

We wrote some Perl programs to manage access to this data, both for us as the overall email SysAdmins, as well as for the departmental administrators. The data was still flat ASCII text files, so we could use basic Linux command-line tools to access and modify the data, especially when making mass changes to the files. At the same time we were also able to use our web-based Perl CGI scripts to work with individual personnel and departmental records.

We did think about using MySQL for record management but we decided that ACII files made more sense for their ease of access. One of our SysAdmins wrote a series of Perl scripts in about a week that allowed us to use SQL-like function calls from within the Perl scripts so we had the best of both worlds.

# System Configuration Files

Most of the system-wide configuration files are located in the /etc directory and its subdirectories. The files in /etc provide configuration data for many of the system services and servers such as email (SMTP, POP, IMAP), web (HTTP), time (NTP or chrony), SSH, network adapters and routing, the GRUB boot loader, display screen, and printer configuration, and much more.

You can also find configuration files that provide system-wide configuration that affects all users, such as /etc/bashrc. The /etc/bashrc file provides initial setup and configuration for all users when they open a bash shell. Figure 13-1 shows the content of the /etc/bashrc file on my Fedora VM.

```
# /etc/bashrc

# System wide functions and aliases
# Environment stuff goes in /etc/profile

# It's NOT a good idea to change this file unless you know what you
# are doing. It's much better to create a custom.sh shell script in
# /etc/profile.d/ to make custom changes to your environment, as this
# will prevent the need for merging in future updates.

# Prevent doublesourcing
if [ -z "$BASHRCSOURCED" ]; then
  BASHRCSOURCED="Y"

  # are we an interactive shell?
  if [ "$PS1" ]; then
    if [ -z "$PROMPT_COMMAND" ]; then
      case $TERM in
      xterm*|vte*)
        if [ -e /etc/sysconfig/bash-prompt-xterm ]; then
            PROMPT_COMMAND=/etc/sysconfig/bash-prompt-xterm
        elif [ "${VTE_VERSION:-0}" -ge 3405 ]; then
            PROMPT_COMMAND="__vte_prompt_command"
        else
            PROMPT_COMMAND='printf "\033]0;%s@%s:%s\007" "${USER}"
"${HOSTNAME%%.*}" "${PWD/#$HOME/\~}"'
        fi
        ;;
      screen*)
```

*Figure 13-1.* *The /etc/bashrc file provides configuration for all bash shell sessions when they are opened*

```
        if [ -e /etc/sysconfig/bash-prompt-screen ]; then
            PROMPT_COMMAND=/etc/sysconfig/bash-prompt-screen
        else
            PROMPT_COMMAND='printf "\033k%s@%s:%s\033\\" "${USER}"
"${HOSTNAME%%.*}" "${PWD/#$HOME/\~}"'
        fi
        ;;
    *)
        [ -e /etc/sysconfig/bash-prompt-default ] &&
PROMPT_COMMAND=/etc/sysconfig/bash-prompt-default
        ;;
    esac
  fi
  # Turn on parallel history
  shopt -s histappend
  history -a
  # Turn on checkwinsize
  shopt -s checkwinsize
  [ "$PS1" = "\\s-\\v\\\$ " ] && PS1="[\u@\h \W]\\$ "
  # You might want to have e.g. tty in prompt (e.g. more virtual machines)
  # and console windows
  # If you want to do so, just add e.g.
  # if [ "$PS1" ]; then
  #   PS1="[\u@\h:\l \W]\\$ "
  # fi
  # to your custom modification shell script in /etc/profile.d/ directory
  fi

if ! shopt -q login_shell ; then # We're not a login shell
  # Need to redefine pathmunge, it gets undefined at the end of /etc/profile
  pathmunge () {
      case ":${PATH}:" in
          *:"$1":*)
              ;;
          *)
              if [ "$2" = "after" ] ; then
                  PATH=$PATH:$1
              else
                  PATH=$1:$PATH
              fi
      esac
  }

  # By default, we want umask to get set. This sets it for non-login shell.
  # Current threshold for system reserved uid/gids is 200
  # You could check uidgid reservation validity in
  # /usr/share/doc/setup-*/uidgid file
  if [ $UID -gt 199 ] && [ "`id -gn`" = "`id -un`" ]; then
     umask 002
  else
     umask 022
  fi
```

*Figure 13-1.*  (*continued*)

```
SHELL=/bin/bash
# Only display echos from profile.d scripts if we are no login shell
# and interactive - otherwise just process them to set envvars
for i in /etc/profile.d/*.sh; do
    if [ -r "$i" ]; then
        if [ "$PS1" ]; then
            . "$i"
        else
            . "$i" >/dev/null
        fi
    fi
done

    unset i
    unset -f pathmunge
  fi

fi
# vim:ts=4:sw=4
```

***Figure 13-1.*** (*continued*)

Relax – we are not going to examine every line of the /etc/bashrc file in Figure 13-1. However, there are a few things that we should observe in this file.

First, just look at all of the comments. This file is meant to be read by users. We SysAdmins are, after all, advanced users. One thing I like about Red Hat-based distributions is that most of the configuration files and scripts are well commented.

One of the functions of this script is to set the shell command prompt. The script determines whether the shell is a standard xterm or vte terminal session, or if it is in a screen session. It sets the prompt string differently depending upon that condition. It also uses external files such as /etc/sysconfig/bash-prompt-xterm, which contains the prompt configuration in a file and location easily managed by the SysAdmin.

Up near the top of the file is a series of comments that briefly describe the function of the script along with an admonishment not to change this particular file. The comments also tell you where your own modifications should go. We will look at that a little further on.

Notice how the indents make the structure of this script fragment easier to read than if everything were jammed up against the left margin.

Did you catch that as we went by? This configuration file is an executable program. It is a bash script that contains program logic that can determine which execution path to take depending upon outside conditions. This script is not complete in itself; it is actually a fragment that can be sourced – imported – into other scripts as necessary.

Sourcing is a bash shell method for including the content of other bash scripts or fragments into a script. This allows the contents of the fragment being sourced to be used by multiple scripts. You can think of it like function libraries used by compiled programs. The sourced file is loaded into the calling script at the location of the source command. It is then immediately executed.

Sourcing can be accomplished by using the source command. The period (.) is an alias for the source command. This is illustrated in Figure 13-2, which is a fragment of the code in Figure 13-1.

```
# Only display echos from profile.d scripts if we are no login shell
# and interactive - otherwise just process them to set envvars
for i in /etc/profile.d/*.sh; do
    if [ -r "$i" ]; then
        if [ "$PS1" ]; then
            . "$i"
        else
            . "$i" >/dev/null
        fi
    fi
done
```

*Figure 13-2.*  *This code fragment sources the \*.sh files located /etc/profile.d. Other files in that directory are ignored*

The lines highlighted in Figure 13-2 source the code from all of the *.sh files in /etc/profile.d into this code fragment.

So how does the program fragment in Figure 13-1 get executed? Where is the code or trigger that imports – sources – this code into it so it can be executed. Good questions. The /etc/profile script in Figure 13-3 sources the /etc/bashrc file.

```
# /etc/profile

# System wide environment and startup programs, for login setup
# Functions and aliases go in /etc/bashrc

# It's NOT a good idea to change this file unless you know what you
# are doing. It's much better to create a custom.sh shell script in
# /etc/profile.d/ to make custom changes to your environment, as this
# will prevent the need for merging in future updates.
```

*Figure 13-3.*  *The /etc/profile script sets the global environment for all shells on the system when they are launched. It also sources the bash script fragments in /etc/profile.d and /etc/bashrc.*

263

```
pathmunge () {
    case ":${PATH}:" in
        *:"$1":*)
            ;;
        *)
            if [ "$2" = "after" ] ; then
                PATH=$PATH:$1
            else
                PATH=$1:$PATH
            fi
    esac
}


if [ -x /usr/bin/id ]; then
    if [ -z "$EUID" ]; then
        # ksh workaround
        EUID=`id -u`
        UID=`id -ru`
    fi
    USER="`id -un`"
    LOGNAME=$USER
    MAIL="/var/spool/mail/$USER"
fi

# Path manipulation
if [ "$EUID" = "0" ]; then
    pathmunge /usr/sbin
    pathmunge /usr/local/sbin
else
    pathmunge /usr/local/sbin after
    pathmunge /usr/sbin after
fi

HOSTNAME=`/usr/bin/hostname 2>/dev/null`
HISTSIZE=1000
if [ "$HISTCONTROL" = "ignorespace" ] ; then
    export HISTCONTROL=ignoreboth
else
    export HISTCONTROL=ignoredups
fi

export PATH USER LOGNAME MAIL HOSTNAME HISTSIZE HISTCONTROL

# By default, we want umask to get set. This sets it for login shell
# Current threshold for system reserved uid/gids is 200
# You could check uidgid reservation validity in
# /usr/share/doc/setup-*/uidgid file
if [ $UID -gt 199 ] && [ "`id -gn`" = "`id -un`" ]; then
    umask 002
```

***Figure 13-3.*** (*continued*)

```
else
    umask 022
fi

for i in /etc/profile.d/*.sh ; do
    if [ -r "$i" ]; then
        if [ "${-#*i}" != "$-" ]; then
            . "$i"
        else
            . "$i" >/dev/null
        fi
    fi
done

unset i
unset -f pathmunge

if [ -n "${BASH_VERSION-}" ] ; then
        if [ -f /etc/bashrc ] ; then
                # Bash login shells run only /etc/profile
                # Bash non-login shells run only /etc/bashrc
                # Check for double sourcing is done in /etc/bashrc.
                . /etc/bashrc
        fi
fi
```

***Figure 13-3.*** (*continued*)

The /etc/profile file is also a script fragment. We could spend some time here to locate the manner in which /etc/profile is launched, but that would take us in the wrong direction for what we are trying to accomplish here. Suffice it to say that when called from a bash itself, it is invoked as a login shell, it reads /etc/profile first (if it exists) and then ~/.bash_profile, ~/.bash_login, and ~/.profile, in that order (if they exist[3]).

# Global Bash Configuration

Now, let's make some global configuration changes to bash.

The /etc/bashrc file mentions the /etc/profile.d directory. Let's look at that directory and its files in Experiment 13-1. While we are at it, we will add some global bash configuration of our own.

---

[3]See the bash man page for this and much more detail.

```
┌─────────────────────────────────────────────────────────────────┐
│                       EXPERIMENT 13-1                            │
└─────────────────────────────────────────────────────────────────┘
```

This experiment should be performed as root. Our objective is to make some additions to the global configuration for the bash shell.

Make /etc/profile.d the PWD and list the contents.

```
[root@testvm1 ~]# cd /etc/profile.d/ ; ls -l
total 100
-rw-r--r--. 1 root root  664 Jul 25  2017 bash_completion.sh
-rw-r--r--. 1 root root  196 Aug  3 04:18 colorgrep.csh
-rw-r--r--. 1 root root  201 Aug  3 04:18 colorgrep.sh
-rw-r--r--. 1 root root 1741 Nov 10 12:53 colorls.csh
-rw-r--r--. 1 root root 1606 Nov 10 12:53 colorls.sh
-rw-r--r--. 1 root root   69 Aug  4 19:53 colorsysstat.csh
-rw-r--r--. 1 root root   56 Aug  4 19:53 colorsysstat.sh
-rw-r--r--. 1 root root  162 Aug  5 02:00 colorxzgrep.csh
-rw-r--r--. 1 root root  183 Aug  5 02:00 colorxzgrep.sh
-rw-r--r--. 1 root root  216 Aug  3 04:57 colorzgrep.csh
-rw-r--r--. 1 root root  220 Aug  3 04:57 colorzgrep.sh
-rwxr-xr-x. 1 root root  249 Sep 21 03:40 kde.csh
-rwxr-xr-x. 1 root root  288 Sep 21 03:40 kde.sh
-rw-r--r--. 1 root root 1706 Jan  2 10:36 lang.csh
-rw-r--r--. 1 root root 2703 Jan  2 10:36 lang.sh
-rw-r--r--. 1 root root  500 Aug  3 11:02 less.csh
-rw-r--r--. 1 root root  253 Aug  3 11:02 less.sh
-rwxr-xr-x. 1 root root   49 Aug  3 21:06 mc.csh
-rwxr-xr-x. 1 root root  153 Aug  3 21:06 mc.sh
-rw-r--r--. 1 root root  106 Jan  2 07:21 vim.csh
-rw-r--r--. 1 root root  248 Jan  2 07:21 vim.sh
-rw-r--r--. 1 root root 2092 Nov  2 10:21 vte.sh
-rw-r--r--. 1 root root  120 Aug  4 23:29 which2.csh
-rw-r--r--. 1 root root  157 Aug  4 23:29 which2.sh
```

All of the files with *.sh extensions are executed by the code in /etc/bashrc or .etc/profile. The ones with other extensions are not executed. We will make our additions to the bash configuration by creating a new file in this directory.

Use your favorite editor to create a new file named "mybash.sh" in this directory. Add the following content to the file.

```
################################################################
# The following are global changes to BASH configuration       #
################################################################
alias lsn='ls --color=no'
alias vim='vim -c "colorscheme desert" '
TestVariable="Hello World"
set -o vi
```

Before we test this, let's ensure that the aliases are not already there and that the TestVariable is null.

```
[root@testvm1 profile.d]# alias
alias cp='cp -i'
alias egrep='egrep --color=auto'
alias fgrep='fgrep --color=auto'
alias grep='grep --color=auto'
alias l.='ls -d .* --color=auto'
alias ll='ls -l --color=auto'
alias ls='ls --color=auto'
alias mc='. /usr/libexec/mc/mc-wrapper.sh'
alias mv='mv -i'
alias rm='rm -i'
alias which='(alias; declare -f) | /usr/bin/which --tty-only --read-alias --
read-functions --show-tilde --show-dot'
alias xzegrep='xzegrep --color=auto'
alias xzfgrep='xzfgrep --color=auto'
alias xzgrep='xzgrep --color=auto'
alias zegrep='zegrep --color=auto'
alias zfgrep='zfgrep --color=auto'
alias zgrep='zgrep --color=auto'
[root@testvm1 profile.d]# echo $TestVariable

[root@testvm1 profile.d]#
```

Now test the results. This change will not affect bash sessions that are already open. New sessions will reflect the changes. So open a new terminal session. As the student user, run the following commands to verify the results.

```
[root@testvm1 profile.d]# echo $TestVariable
Hello World
[root@testvm1 profile.d]# alias
alias cp='cp -i'
alias egrep='egrep --color=auto'
alias fgrep='fgrep --color=auto'
alias grep='grep --color=auto'
alias l.='ls -d .* --color=auto'
alias ll='ls -l --color=auto'
alias ls='ls --color=auto'
alias lsn='ls --color=no'
alias mc='. /usr/libexec/mc/mc-wrapper.sh'
alias mv='mv -i'
alias rm='rm -i'
alias vim='vim -c "colorscheme desert" '
alias which='(alias; declare -f) | /usr/bin/which --tty-only --read-alias --
read-functions --show-tilde --show-dot'
alias xzegrep='xzegrep --color=auto'
alias xzfgrep='xzfgrep --color=auto'
alias xzgrep='xzgrep --color=auto'
alias zegrep='zegrep --color=auto'
alias zfgrep='zfgrep --color=auto'
alias zgrep='zgrep --color=auto
```

It is easy to make changes to ASCII files as this experiment shows. Notice that a reboot was not required to make these changes take effect – they were in effect immediately for new bash terminal sessions.

# User Configuration Files

Let's look at the so-called hidden files in your own home directory – those whose names begin with a period (.). These are user-specific configuration files that you can change to meet your own needs and preferences. Let's look at the .bashrc file, which is the configuration file in which individual users can set their own bash configuration such as aliases, functions, and environment variables that are unique to them.

```
┌─────────────────────────────────────────────────────────────────────┐
│                        EXPERIMENT 13-2                               │
└─────────────────────────────────────────────────────────────────────┘
```

Perform this Experiment as the student user.

The .bashrc file is short so we can view it with cat. Let's be sure we are in the home directory for the student user and then display the file.

```
[student@testvm1 ~]$ cd ; cat .bashrc
# .bashrc

# Source global definitions
if [ -f /etc/bashrc ]; then
        . /etc/bashrc
fi

# Uncomment the following line if you don't like systemctl's auto-paging
feature:
# export SYSTEMD_PAGER=

# User specific aliases and functions
```

This file is well commented also and even tells us where to add our own configuration. So let's add something innocuous that will allow us to test this local configuration. Use your favorite editor to add the following line to the end of the file.

```
StudentVariable="This is a local variable."
```

View the variable.

```
[student@testvm1 ~]$ echo $StudentVariable

[student@testvm1 ~]$
```

The variable has not been added to the environment. It will now be part of the environment for bash terminal sessions opened from now on. It can be added to existing bash terminal sessions by sourcing the .bashrc file like this.

```
[student@testvm1 ~]$ . .bashrc
[student@testvm1 ~]$ echo $StudentVariable
This is a local variable.
```

These are trivial examples, but they should give you some idea of how flexible having open format configuration files can be. It is easy to follow the logic of the files and easy to modify them when needed. Although each distribution varies in how it adds comments to these files, all of the ones I have used have enough information in the comments to enable me to figure out the appropriate location for me to alter the configuration. They also contain enough information to allow me to follow the logic. That doesn't mean I don't have to work a bit to understand it all, but I can do it if I need to or am just curious.

Be aware that the local user bash configuration overrides the global configuration. So if a user has the knowledge and wants to alter a global configuration parameter for themselves, they can do that by setting it in the ~/.bashrc file.

# ASCII Rocks

Now we can see how the openness created by using ASCII text files for configuration allows us to explore and understand many of the processes of our Linux operating system. ASCII is the go-to format for configuration files and for shell scripts.

Many system-level executables are also bash scripts that set configurations and launch the binaries. Let's check out the /bin directory to verify this.

---

**EXPERIMENT 13-3**

---

Perform this experiment as the root user.

Make /bin the PWD and count the number of files just to see how many executables there are altogether.

```
[root@testvm1 ~]# cd /bin/ ; ls | wc -l
2605
```

Let's figure out how many are ASCII text files.

```
[root@testvm1 bin]# for I in `ls`;do file $I;done | grep ASCII | wc -l
355
```

Over 13% of the executable files in /bin are ASCII shell scripts. Now view the list of files that are ASCII scripts. The specific results from your host will almost certainly differ from mine.

```
[root@testvm1 bin]# for I in `ls`;do file $I;done | grep ASCII | less
```

I won't list those files here, but you should look through them a bit just to see what is there.

Now let's look at one of these scripts. I chose the ps2ascii script, which is used as a wrapper around the ghostscript program.

---

**Note**   If the host you are using does not have the ps2ascii program installed, you can either install it or choose a different ASCII file to explore for the rest of this experiment.

---

```
[root@testvm1 bin]# cat ps2ascii
#!/bin/sh
# Extract ASCII text from a PostScript file.  Usage:
#       ps2ascii [infile.ps [outfile.txt]]
# If outfile is omitted, output goes to stdout.
# If both infile and outfile are omitted, ps2ascii acts as a filter,
# reading from stdin and writing on stdout.

# This definition is changed on install to match the
# executable name set in the makefile
GS_EXECUTABLE=gs

trap "rm -f _temp_.err _temp_.out" 0 1 2 15

OPTIONS="-q -dSAFER -sDEVICE=txtwrite"
if ( test $# -eq 0 ) then
    $GS_EXECUTABLE $OPTIONS -o - -
elif ( test $# -eq 1 ) then
    $GS_EXECUTABLE $OPTIONS -o - "$1"
else
    $GS_EXECUTABLE $OPTIONS -o "$2" "$1"
fi
```

The ghostscript program converts Postscript and PDF files to ASCII text files by extracting the text out of the originals. This wrapper has comments that tell us what the program does. It sets some variables and then runs the program with options for different conditions.

Scripts like ps2ascii allow a great deal of flexibility when launching programs. They make life easier for users because the scripts can manage the task of setting up options and arguments that are passed to the main program.

# Final Thoughts

Open data in Linux enables us as SysAdmins to explore everything in order to satisfy our curiosity about how Linux works. The use of ASCII text files for scripting and configuration files allows us access to the inner workings of the environment in which we work every day.

We were able to use that openness to trace our way through some related bash configuration programs and files. We discovered how to make global and local changes. We added some configuration of our own so that bash is now configured more to our own liking.

And, if we want or need to, we can download the source code used to compile the executable code for the kernel and all of the open source programs and utilities available with our Linux distribution. I have done that on a couple of occasions because I wanted to know more. You can, too, if your curiosity takes you there.

All of this is only possible in an open operating system.

# CHAPTER 14

# Use Separate filesystems for Data

There is a lot to this particular tenet, and it requires understanding the nature of Linux filesystems and mount points. If you skipped Chapter 6, "Use the Linux FHS," you should go back and read it now.

---

**Note**   The primary meaning for the term "filesystem" in this chapter is a segment of the directory tree that is located on a separate partition or logical volume that must be mounted on a specified mount point of the root filesystem to enable access to it. We also use the term to describe the structure of the metadata on the partition or volume such as, EXT4, XFS, or other structure. These different usages should be clear from their context.

---

## Why We Need Separate filesystems

There are at least three excellent reasons for maintaining separate filesystems on our Linux hosts. First, when hard drives crash, we may lose some or all of the data on a damaged filesystem, but, as we will see, data on other filesystems on the crashed hard drive may still be salvageable.

Second, despite having access to huge amounts of hard drive space, it is possible to fill up a filesystem. When that happens, separate filesystems can minimize the immediate effects and make recovery easier.

© David Both 2018
D. Both, *The Linux Philosophy for SysAdmins*, https://doi.org/10.1007/978-1-4842-3730-4_14

Third, upgrades can be made easier when certain filesystems such as /home are located on separate filesystems. This makes it easy to upgrade without needing to restore that data from a backup.

I have frequently encountered all three of these situations in my career. In some instances, there was only a single partition and so recovery was quite difficult. Recovery from these situations was always much easier and faster when the host was configured with separate filesystems.

Keeping data of all types safe is part of the SysAdmin's job. Using separate filesystems for storing that data can help us accomplish that. This practice can also help us achieve our objective to be a Lazy Admin. Backups do allow us to recover most of the data that would otherwise be lost in a crash scenario, but using separate filesystem may allow us to recover all of the data up to the moment of a crash. Restoring from backups takes much longer.

# Hard Drive Crashes

Has your computer hard drive ever crashed leaving your Linux computer unable to boot; with all of your data on the on the crashed hard drive; with no recent backups? Most of us have. And our friends, coworkers, or customers have all experienced this as well.

Having separate filesystems makes it possible in some – but not all – hard drive crashes to recover data from potentially untouched filesystems. When a single filesystem is used for the entire directory tree, it is far more likely that any type of hard drive crash will result in the loss of all data.

Unfortunately there are hard drive failure modes that can prevent the drive from working at all and all of the data on the drive will be lost.

# Full filesystems

Despite having huge amounts of hard drive space available to us, filesystems can fill up. Runaway programs can very quickly fill up a filesystem. If there is only a single filesystem, it is likely that the host will crash and much valuable data will be lost.

I have seen filesystems fill up in moments. In a host with a single filesystem the results can be catastrophic. The specific symptoms may vary but can range from users not being able to create new files, save modified ones, or log in to the desktop, to a host that is completely unresponsive and not even accessible remotely via SSH. In some cases the only way to regain control is to power the system down and boot to a recovery mode. Then it is possible to locate and delete the file or files filling the disk and to try and understand what caused that to happen. The worst case I encountered was testing a VM for this book and the VM would not terminate.

In a host that is configured with separate filesystems, any effects from filling one filesystem will be minimized and the symptoms will likely be less damaging. Recovery from the condition will usually be faster and easier.

# Laptop Lament

This happened today.

Today – yes, really, today as I write this on December 26, 2017 – a friend of mine sent me a text to let me know that the laptop computer I have been supporting for her would not boot.

A few years ago my friend, Cyndi, who is also my Yoga instructor, was becoming unhappy because her computer was constantly slowing down due to malware infestations. She asked me to help and I agreed. I told her about Linux, and she decided to try it.

Over the years, I have helped Cyndi keep her computer running with hardware repairs, software updates, and upgrades to newer releases of Fedora, which is what I started her out with. She always calls me first when she has a computer problem that she cannot figure out on her own. Today was no exception.

The first text came as I was working on Chapter 8 of this book. It said that her computer would not boot and it was printing a repeating series of messages on the screen. After a couple text exchanges I determined that I should look at the laptop and she brought it to my home office. Based on the messages that showed a long series of I/O errors on /dev/sda, I determined that the hard drive was failing. I also told her that I was not sure I could salvage the data from the hard drive but would try.

At this point I checked her external USB backup drive and determined that the latest backups were several months old. That part is my fault and I have since fixed it. We discussed the situation and she told me to do what I could. After she left, I removed the 320GB hard drive from the laptop and inserted it in one of the slots in my hard drive docking station for exploration.

Here is what I already knew. When I installed Linux on the laptop, I used separate filesystems for /usr, /var, /tmp, /swap, and /home, like I always do when I install Linux. That meant that the /home filesystem was on a different logical volume than the root (/) filesystem. Because the problem was during the startup sequence – technically after boot and during startup while systemd was starting various services – there was a good possibility that the other logical volumes were unaffected, including the volume on which I had installed her home directory, /home.

After the hard drive spun up, I used the lvscan tool to locate all of the logical volumes on my main workstation. The results included the logical volumes on the defective hard drive as shown in Figure 14-1.

```
[root@david ~]# lvscan
  ACTIVE                  '/dev/fedora_mobilemantra/home' [<48.83 GiB] inherit
  ACTIVE                  '/dev/fedora_mobilemantra/root' [<29.30 GiB] inherit
  ACTIVE                  '/dev/fedora_mobilemantra/tmp' [19.53 GiB] inherit
  ACTIVE                  '/dev/fedora_mobilemantra/var' [19.53 GiB] inherit
  ACTIVE                  '/dev/fedora_mobilemantra/usr' [<34.18 GiB] inherit
  ACTIVE                  '/dev/fedora_mobilemantra/swap' [7.81 GiB] inherit
  ACTIVE                  '/dev/vg_david2/home' [50.00 GiB] inherit
  ACTIVE                  '/dev/vg_david2/stuff' [130.00 GiB] inherit
  ACTIVE                  '/dev/vg_david2/Virtual' [590.00 GiB] inherit
  ACTIVE                  '/dev/vg_david2/Pictures' [75.00 GiB] inherit
  ACTIVE                  '/dev/david1/root' [9.31 GiB] inherit
  ACTIVE                  '/dev/david1/tmp' [<28.63 GiB] inherit
  ACTIVE                  '/dev/david1/var' [<18.63 GiB] inherit
  ACTIVE                  '/dev/david1/usr' [<46.57 GiB] inherit
  ACTIVE                  '/dev/david1/swap' [14.90 GiB] inherit
  ACTIVE                  '/dev/vg_Backups/Backups' [3.63 TiB] inherit
```

*Figure 14-1.  lvscan displays the logical volumes including those on the defective hard drive*

The results from the lvscan command also lists the device files assigned to the logical volumes on the laptop hard drive. These device files were created by udev[1] as soon as the hard drive was up to speed and could be read. As I mentioned in Chapter 5, "Everything Is a File," udev is responsible for detecting when new devices are plugged into the system, and creating device files for them in /dev.

---

[1]Unnikrishnan A, Linux.com, *Udev: Introduction to Device Management In Modern Linux System*, https://www.linux.com/news/udev-introduction-device-management-modern-linux-system

Among the listed logical volumes is /dev/fedora_mobilemantra/home, which is the home directory for my friend's hard drive. At this point I knew all I needed in order to mount the home directory on /mnt on my workstation. I did that and started exploring the home directory. Everything looked good and I was able to read several of the files without a problem.

---

**Note**    I was fortunate that the hard drive had not failed catastrophically. In this case the errors were apparently bad sectors on the / (root) partition that left the other partitions intact so they could be recovered.

---

The simplest way to both create a backup of the home directory and discover if any of the many files located there have errors is to use the tar command. No errors occurred during the creation of the tarball so I was able to retrieve all of the data from the home directory.

Cyndi was very happy when I called her with this news of the continued digital existence of her data.

I used the dd command, as shown in Figure 14-2, to perform a quick test of the entire hard drive. An I/O error occurred after reading only 115GB out of a total of 320GB. I could have continued to focus in on the location of the error, but it is enough to know at this time that the errors caused problems with startup, which indicates they are located in the / (root) filesystem.

```
[root@david ~]# dd if=/dev/sdi of=/dev/null
dd: error reading '/dev/sdi': Input/output error
224078480+0 records in
224078480+0 records out
114728181760 bytes (115 GB, 107 GiB) copied, 1551.07 s, 74.0 MB/s
```

***Figure 14-2.*** *Using the dd command to test the hard drive. This also shows the I/O error that occurred*

Sending the "outfile" data to /dev/null prevents it from being displayed in the terminal session as STDOUT. Displaying STDOUT to the terminal also significantly slows down the entire process. However any STDERR messages indicating I/O errors will still display on the terminal. Neither the hard drive nor any of its partitions were mounted while running this command.

I ordered a new hard drive for her laptop and installed that. I then installed Fedora 27, the most current release at this time, and restored the saved data to her home directory. Everything worked fine and all her data proved to be intact.

This story is a perfect illustration of one reason to use separate filesystems for data. It also shows quite nicely that understanding the Linux Filesystem Hierarchical Structure can be important to us as SysAdmins. It shows an appropriate use for the /mnt mount point and the /dev/null device. It is also a nice example of the fact that everything is a file and the device special files in /dev can be used with simple tools.

## Data Security

This tenet is about data security as much as anything else. In this context, I mean security in the sense of maintaining the continued existence and integrity of the data. Today's hard drives are huge, with some running into multiple terabytes. And hard drives are one of the most common devices to fail in a computer, along with others that have mechanical moving parts such as fans. So the larger the hard drive is, the more data that could be lost when it fails.

Of course one part of securing your data is to make backups. Another very important part is ensuring that the data – the actual data like documents, project files, financial files, graphics, video, audio, user configuration files, and more, is as safe from the results of corruption as possible. Because backup systems fail, too.

According to the Linux Filesystem Hierarchical Standard, "Disk errors that corrupt data on the root filesystem are a greater problem than errors on any other partition. A small root filesystem is less prone to corruption as the result of a system crash.[2]" The reasoning behind this is that in most systems the greatest number of disk writes takes place in the root partition so it is most likely to be corrupted by a problem. This seems to be the case in the previous example.

---

[2]LSB Work group - The Linux Foundation, *Filesystem Hierarchical Standard V3.0*, 3, https://refspecs.linuxfoundation.org/FHS_3.0/fhs-3.0.pdf

The corollary to that is that directories that are part of the root filesystem are more likely to suffer from the side effects of those system crashes than directories that are not. This is demonstrably the case because I was unable to mount the root filesystem so could not recover any of the files on it. I was able to mount the /home filesystem.

And that leads us to the conclusion that maintaining separate filesystems for directory trees that contain user data is a good idea. It also reinforces the statement in the above quote that the root filesystem should be as small as reasonably possible. The amount of used space in the root filesystem of my primary workstation is only 444MB, which is not a lot. Nevertheless, I do recommend, considering the huge size of current hard drives, that the root filesystem be allocated about 5GB of disk space to allow for unexpected occurrences.

# Recommendations

There are some specific parts of the Linux directory tree that I recommend being placed on separate filesystems. Sometimes I even recommend placing them on a separate hard drive to further ensure their safety and to facilitate recovery because the data on the filesystems maintained on a separate drive would not need to be restored from backup if the drive containing the root filesystem needs to be replaced.

All that is required to mount the preexisting filesystems as part of the reinstalled directory tree is to add appropriate entries in the /etc/fstab file. This enables them to be mounted when the system is rebooted after the installation of the operating system in a new drive. Configuring this can be accomplished during the Linux installation using a "custom" disk configuration. The details of that procedure are outside the scope of this book.

Current Red Hat-based installations like Fedora and CentOS use a default disk configuration that can be far from ideal. CentOS 7 puts everything in the root (/) partition except for /boot and a separate volume for swap.

Fedora 27 puts 1GB in /boot, 50GB in /root, a few GB in swap – the actual amount depends upon the amount of RAM in the system, and all the rest is placed in /home. On my test VM this is 195GB. That is really way too much for my needs on most of the systems I use. I have found with a good deal of experimentation that the actual numbers vary depending upon the size of the hard drive. But the result is still the same.

Those defaults can result in suboptimal disk usage and lead to problems later in the life of the host. Even though /home is a separate filesystem on its own logical volume in these default installations, its size is far too large for many environments. For example, the home directory on my main workstation has only about 30GB of data including this book and lots of photos, all going back over 20 years. There are others filesystems that need to be considered as well.

Three of the main branches of the Linux filesystem hierarchy are specifically designed to be located on separate partitions or volumes as a separate filesystem.[3] This is possible because conforming to the Linux FHS makes it so. These three branches are /usr, /opt, and /var. I have also found other branches that work well as separate filesystems, /home, /tmp, and /opt.

Let's look at the branches of the directory tree that I recommend as being separate filesystems. All of these filesystems can be placed on one or more hard drives separate from the drive that contains the root filesystem. This helps to ensure the overall survivability of those directory branches that are not located on the failing drive.

You can refer back to Table 6-1 for a brief description of these branches of the Linux FHS, or you can refer to the *Filesystem Hierarchical Standard V3.0*[4].

## /boot

The /boot directory tree is an interesting one because it cannot be part of a logical volume configuration. It must be a separate disk partition with a Linux EXT2, EXT3, EXT4, VFAT, or XFS filesystem. These are the only filesystems supported by current versions of the Fedora and CentOS6 and CentOS7 installation program, Anaconda.

Because most modern distributions use logical volume management, this directory must be a separate filesystem. If this is the case, you won't have a choice. However if you do not use logical volume management and use filesystems such as EXT4 that are directly created on the raw partitions, you could make /boot part of the root (/) filesystem.

I recommend that /boot always be a separate filesystem even if logical volumes are not used for other filesystems on the host.

---

[3]Ibid., 3.
[4]Ibid.

# /home

Clearly /home should be a separate filesystem. The experience I discussed above, as well as others like it over the years, have made it abundantly clear to me that /home should always be a separate filesystem from the rest of the directory tree. The default filesystem configurations of the distributions with which I am familiar make it clear that this is a best practice aside from any size issues.

When upgrading from one version of Fedora to the next, for example, having my data, especially /home on a separate filesystem has made release level upgrading easy even when I choose not to use the provided upgrade tools and simply install a new release of Fedora over an old one. This requires the same procedure as recovery from root filesystem corruption; it would be necessary to perform a custom configuration of the filesystem and choose to keep the existing home directory without formatting it.

/home is also one of the filesystems I recommend be placed on a hard drive separate from the one on which the operating system is located. This helps to ensure that the data on /home is safe if the primary drive fails. It also improved performance by spreading disk access over more than one hard drive so that the operating system does not have to wait for user data access and vice-versa.

Although the FHS specifies /home as the "home" directory, it also recognizes that the location of the home directories in the directory tree has typically been subject to the standards of the organizations and the discretion of the SysAdmins managing the systems. I have encountered /var/home, /opt/home, /homedirs, and others. I like to follow the standard in this.

Having the home directory as a separate filesystem enables it to be moved to a different mount point if the need arises. Other things may need to be changes as well in order to make this work, such as default paths.

The root user's home directory is /root and this directory should remain part of the root filesystem. The reason for this is to ensure that the tools and files that we store in the root home directory for convenience will still be available in recovery modes and runlevels that don't mount the other filesystems.

Many non-login accounts related to system services also have home directories in other locations. The specific location varies by service but is generally a directory that is part of the service itself.

# /usr

The /usr branch contains nonessential commands, that is, user commands and not system administration commands that would be required during boot and startup or when running in recovery mode.

Although the preceding statement is that found in the FHS documentation, it is no longer strictly true in practice on Fedora and CentOS 7. In efforts to simplify the filesystem hierarchy, these distributions are using symbolic links to mount points in /usr for /bin, /sbin, /lib, and /lib64. The /bin directory is a symlink to /usr/bin, /sbin is a symlink to /usr/sbin, /lib is a symlink to /usr/lib, and /lib64 is a symlink to /usr/lib64.

The files required for boot are now part of the Linux initial RAM filesystem, initramfs.[5] So the directories that are now symlinks no longer need to be available at boot time.

I typically make /usr a separate filesystem as much to prevent problems with it being part of the root filesystem as to ensure the security of the data here. Most user-level commands and libraries are located here. This is considered to be a directory tree with static files – ones that typically do not change in the course of the host's operation.

One of the reasons this tree is called the "secondary hierarchy" is that in many ways it has a structure similar to the main tree starting with the root directory. There is one subdirectory tree that is for local files, /usr/local.

The /usr/local directory tree contains subdirectories etc, bin, sbin, include, lib, lib64, share, and more. The purpose of the /usr/local tree is to be a place where local programs and configuration files can be stored.

This is where I place all of my locally written scripts and any configuration files they require. The scripts themselves are located in /usr/local/bin and the configuration files are placed in /usr/local/etc. Documentation such as man pages written for these scripts would be located in /usr/local/share.

Another option would be to make /usr part of the root filesystem but to make /usr/local a separate filesystem. I only back up /usr/local anyway and since I never do a bare metal recovery of the entire system, this makes some sense. If I have an issue with the operating system or the hard drive on which it is installed, that would require a complete reinstallation, everything except for the /usr/local tree is re-created during the installation.

---

[5]Wikipedia, *initial ramdisk*, https://en.wikipedia.org/wiki/Initial_ramdisk

It is also possible for both /usr and /usr/local to be separate filesystems. The /usr filesystem would be mounted on the /usr mount point and then the local branch would be mounted on the /usr/local mount point.

The /user tree is explicitly not for large programs such as commercial software or large open source applications. It is for small to moderately sized locally coded programs to meet the needs of SysAdmins or local regular users.

Large software applications should be installed in another location. The /opt directory tree is recommended.

# /opt

Large programs should be installed in the /opt directory tree. This directory should be created as a separate filesystem so that it can be easily expanded in size if that should become necessary.

The /opt branch supports a complete hierarchy of subdirectories for multiple vendors to install their software as well as a complete set of directories reserved for local SysAdmin use, /opt/bin, /opt/doc, /opt/include, /opt/info, /opt/lib, and /opt/man.[6]

# /var

The /var branch of the Linux filesystem hierarchy is an interesting combination of – well, stuff. It is intended to contain "variable" data – data that can change, but that is not configuration data. Because the data in /var is not needed by the operating system in any type of recovery or maintenance mode, or during the initial boot-up sequence, it can be safely created as a separate filesystem.

The data located in /var is user data and databases. We find many different types of data in /var. For example /www would contain the files required for a web site if the host were a web server. In fact, I have multiple sites running on my web server and they each have a directory of their own such as, /var/wwwboth, /var/wwwlinuxdatabook, and so on. This makes it easy to determine which directory branch contains the data for each web site. The only configuration needed to accomplish this is in the web site configuration files. I use the Apache web server so that would be /etc/httpd/conf/httpd. conf.

---

[6]Ibid., 13.

MariaDB – a fork of MySQL – maintains its databases in /var/lib/mysql. SendMail stores user inboxes in /var/spool/mail. BIND provides name services with the databases located in /var/named. And there is much more data stored there as well.

# /tmp

The /tmp directory is a place where users and services can store files temporarily. Think of /tmp a place where data of any type can be stored by any user or process – temporarily. There is a strong likelihood that files stored in /tmp will be deleted, usually at the next boot.

I use /tmp for downloading large files such as ISO images like the installation images for various distributions. These can be quite large and, along with files created by various system processes can fill a small /tmp filesystem. Because of this I like to make my /tmp filesystem very large, usually 10GB or more. For my main workstation I currently have 30GB allocated to /tmp. In these days of multi-terabyte hard drives 30GB is a very reasonable size.

If the /tmp filesystem does fill up, strange things can happen. I mentioned in Chapter 6, "Use the Linux FHS," the problems that occurred when I managed to fill up the /tmp filesystem. GUI desktop logins failed because the desktop could not create new files in /tmp, but the console and remote SSH logins continued to work.

However, the problem would be worse if /tmp were part of the root filesystem. In that case, many other symptoms would be likely as various additional services were unable to find sufficient disk space in which to work.

# The Other Branches

All of the other branches of the Linux filesystem hierarchy must be an atomic part of the root filesystem. They cannot be created as separate filesystems and mounted to the directory tree at the appropriate mount point. The programs and data stored in these other branches of the directory tree are required to be available during early stages of boot and when running in low-level recovery or maintenance modes.

# Starting with Separate filesystems

The best time to set up separate filesystems for one or more components of the Linux filesystem hierarchy is when the operating system is first installed. Most Linux installers, such as Red Hat's Anaconda, provide the ability to do a custom disk configuration during the installation. At this time you can specify separate logical volumes to contain one or more of the filesystems we have discussed in this chapter that are capable of being mounted separately.

The installers – at least the ones with which I am familiar – also have the ability to recognize existing partitions, volumes, and filesystems and display identifying information about them. This makes it easy to reinstall Linux after the hard drive containing the OS crashes and needs to be replaced. It also enables easy release upgrades – from Fedora 27 to Fedora 28, for example – when a complete reinstallation is desirable. The OS can be installed and the root filesystem can be reformatted without touching the /home, /usr, and /var filesystems. This would keep intact all of my personal data, email inbox, and my web site data, for example.

# Adding Separate filesystems Later

It is not particularly difficult to convert one or more of the directories discussed here to a separate filesystem to a system well after the original installation. It just requires some foresight and planning.

The basic process is simple. In fact there are multiple ways to do this. Here is what one process would look like for the /home directory. This procedure assumes that /home is not currently on a separate filesystem from the root filesystem.

1.   Install a new hard drive, if necessary.

2.   Create a partition or logical volume on the drive.

3.   Add a filesystem label to the new partition or volume. This makes the new filesystem easily identifiable when it is not mounted and allows mounting by label.

4.   Back up the data in the current home directory. If there is room, store the backup in /tmp. This is one good reason to make /tmp large.

5.  Delete the data from the current /home directory. This step frees up that space that would not be accessible after the new filesystem is mounted at /home on the main trunk of the filesystem hierarchy.

6.  Add an entry in /etc/fstab that specifies the mount for the new filesystem on /home.

7.  Mount the new volume on /home.

8.  Restore the data to /home.

9.  Test and verify that all data was correctly restored.

Let's do a version of this in Experiment 14-1.

---

**EXPERIMENT 14-1**

This experiment should be performed as root. After making a backup of the existing /home directory, we will delete the existing partition on the USB device and create a Linux partition, format the new partition as EXT4, mount is as /home, then restore the backed-up data.

---

**Note**   Unexpected results may occur if you do not log out of all of the student user sessions.

If you are logged in as the student user, log out of all student login sessions.

---

**Warning!**   This experiment may cause loss of data in your home directory. You should only perform this experiment on a virtual machine or host that is intended for training and is not in use for production.

---

We will use the USB drive as the location of our new home drive. If the USB device is already inserted in your system, unmount it and remove it.

---

**Warning!**   This experiment will destroy all of the existing data on the USB device. Ensure you are using the one designated for these experiments before you continue.

---

Insert the USB drive in a USB port. Do not mount it. Use dmesg to determine the device special file assigned to the device. In my VM this is /dev/sdb.

We will use fdisk to delete the existing partition and create a new Linus partition. Use fdisk to view the existing partition.

```
[root@testvm1 ~]# fdisk /dev/sdb

Welcome to fdisk (util-linux 2.30.2).
Changes will remain in memory only, until you decide to write them.
Be careful before using the write command.

Command (m for help): p
Disk /dev/sdb: 62.5 MiB, 65536000 bytes, 128000 sectors
Units: sectors of 1 * 512 = 512 bytes
Sector size (logical/physical): 512 bytes / 512 bytes
I/O size (minimum/optimal): 512 bytes / 512 bytes
Disklabel type: dos
Disk identifier: 0x73696420

Device     Boot Start     End Sectors  Size Id Type
/dev/sdb1        2048 127999  125952 61.5M  c W95 FAT32 (LBA)

Command (m for help):
```

Notice that the existing partition is probably a FAT32 (VFAT) one. We want to use EXT4 for our /home filesystem. Delete the existing partition, and then print the results to verify that the partition has been deleted.

```
Command (m for help): d
Selected partition 1
Partition 1 has been deleted.

Command (m for help): p
Disk /dev/sdb: 62.5 MiB, 65536000 bytes, 128000 sectors
Units: sectors of 1 * 512 = 512 bytes
Sector size (logical/physical): 512 bytes / 512 bytes
I/O size (minimum/optimal): 512 bytes / 512 bytes
Disklabel type: dos
Disk identifier: 0x73696420
```

Create the new partition using all of the space on the device. Take the defaults for partition type and number. Answer yes when asked if you want to remove the VFAT signature. Then take the defaults for starting and ending sectors.

```
Command (m for help): n
Partition type
   p   primary (0 primary, 0 extended, 4 free)
   e   extended (container for logical partitions)
Select (default p):

Using default response p.
Partition number (1-4, default 1):
First sector (2048-127999, default 2048):
Last sector, +sectors or +size{K,M,G,T,P} (2048-127999, default 127999):

Created a new partition 1 of type 'Linux' and of size 61.5 MiB.
Partition #1 contains a vfat signature.

Do you want to remove the signature? [Y]es/[N]o: y

The signature will be removed by a write command.
```

Verify that the new partition is a Linux type 83 partition.

```
Command (m for help): p
Disk /dev/sdb: 62.5 MiB, 65536000 bytes, 128000 sectors
Units: sectors of 1 * 512 = 512 bytes
Sector size (logical/physical): 512 bytes / 512 bytes
I/O size (minimum/optimal): 512 bytes / 512 bytes
Disklabel type: dos
Disk identifier: 0x73696420
```

```
Device       Boot Start    End Sectors  Size Id Type
/dev/sdb1         2048 127999  125952 61.5M 83 Linux
```

Filesystem/RAID signature on partition 1 will be wiped.

Command (m for help):

Now write the new partition table to the USB device.

```
Command (m for help): w
The partition table has been altered.
Calling ioctl() to re-read partition table.
Syncing disks

[root@testvm1 ~]#
```

Create an EXT4 filesystem. Notice that we are adding the filesystem to the sdb1 partition, not the disk itself, sdb. On a small device, this will not take long.

```
[root@testvm1 ~]# mkfs -t ext4 /dev/sdb1
mke2fs 1.43.5 (04-Aug-2017)
Creating filesystem with 62976 1k blocks and 15744 inodes
Filesystem UUID: 915c4857-cc81-4637-80ac-5e69d40329df
Superblock backups stored on blocks:
        8193, 24577, 40961, 57345

Allocating group tables: done
Writing inode tables: done
Creating journal (4096 blocks): done
Writing superblocks and filesystem accounting information: done
```

Create a label for the partition and then verify that it was created.

```
[root@testvm1 ~]# e2label /dev/sdb1 home
[root@testvm1 ~]# e2label /dev/sdb1
home
[root@testvm1 ~]#
```

It is time to back up the current home directory. Since the host on which you are performing these experiments is designated for training, there should not be very much to back up so this should not take long. We will create a simple tarball as our backup.

```
[root@testvm1 ~]# tar -cvf /tmp/home.tar /home
```

Now we need to be a little careful. We will not add an entry to /etc/fstab for this experiment. And we will not delete any of the current content of /home.

---

**Tip**   Mounting the home filesystem located on the USB device on the /home mount point does not delete or damage the existing data in the current home directory. The new filesystem is mounted over the existing data, which can no longer be accessed. After the home filesystem on the USB device is unmounted, the original home directory and its data will again be accessible.

---

Now let's mount the newly created home filesystem on /home. We will use the device special file to explicitly specify the device we want to mount. This prevents any potential conflict with any other home filesystem that might have the label of "home." We also take a quick look at the contents that should be empty except for the lost+found directory.

```
[root@testvm1 ~]# mount /dev/sdb1 /home ; ls -lR /home
/home:
total 12
drwx------. 2 root root 12288 Feb  2 14:49 lost+found

/home/lost+found:
total 0
[root@testvm1 ~]#
```

Remember that the original data in /home is still there, it is just masked by the empty filesystem that is mounted on the /home mount point.

Now we can restore the backup data to the home directory. When extracting data from a tarball, it is always restored into the current directory. So if we want to restore /home, we need to make the root directory (/) the PWD before performing the extraction, which we do in the following command.

```
[root@testvm1 ~]# cd / ; tar -xf /tmp/home.tar
[root@testvm1 /]#
```

Let's verify that the extraction worked properly.

```
[root@testvm1 /]# ls -l /home
total 16
drwx------. 2 root    root    12288 Jan 15 10:04 lost+found
drwx------. 6 student student  1024 Jan 31 09:03 student
[root@testvm1 /]# ls -l /home/student/
total 37
-rw-rw-r--. 1 student student   84 Jan 27 15:28 error.txt
-rw-rw-r--. 1 student student   15 Jan 27 11:41 file0.txt
-rw-rw-r--. 1 student student   15 Jan 27 11:41 file1.txt
-rw-rw-r--. 1 student student   15 Jan 27 11:41 file2.txt
-rw-rw-r--. 1 student student   15 Jan 27 11:41 file3.txt
-rw-rw-r--. 1 student student   15 Jan 27 11:41 file4.txt
-rw-rw-r--. 1 student student   15 Jan 27 11:41 file5.txt
-rw-rw-r--. 1 student student   15 Jan 27 11:41 file6.txt
-rw-rw-r--. 1 student student   15 Jan 27 11:41 file7.txt
-rw-rw-r--. 1 student student   15 Jan 27 11:41 file8.txt
-rw-rw-r--. 1 student student   15 Jan 27 11:41 file9.txt
-rw-rw-r--. 1 student student   60 Jan 27 15:28 good.txt
-rwxr-xr--. 1 student student 9830 Jan 30 09:28 script.template.sh
-rw-rw-r--. 1 student student   42 Jan 27 15:16 test1.txt
```

You can also do this.

```
[root@testvm1 /]# df -h /home
Filesystem      Size  Used Avail Use% Mounted on
/dev/sdb1        56M   36M   16M  70% /home
```

Note the small amount of available space that is due to the very small size of the USB device I am using.

At this point the new /home filesystem is in use for the user student. Log back in as the student user and verify that everything works as it should. Then log out as the student user.

Now we need to unmount the /home filesystem.

```
[root@testvm1 /]# umount /home
```

It is now safe to remove the USB device from the host. The original home directory is now unmasked and is in use.

# Final Thoughts

Separate filesystems make our jobs as SysAdmins easier. Maintaining parts of the directory tree in separate filesystems, we provide more flexibility in the case of drive crashes, enable flexibility in moving filesystems to different mount points, and make it easier to perform complete operating system reinstallations when they are needed. It also improves the survivability of other parts of the directory structure in case one hard drive crashes.

It did take me a while to figure out what a good idea this is, but since that time I have always maintained separate filesystems for the directories discussed here. That has saved my data more than once.

# Make Programs Portable

Portable programs make life much easier for the lazy SysAdmin. Portability is an important consideration because it allows programs to be used on a wide range of operating system and hardware platforms. Using interpretive languages such as bash and Perl that can run on many types of systems can save loads of work.

Programs written in compiled languages such as C must be recompiled at the very least when porting from one platform to another. In many cases, platform-specific code must be maintained in the sources in order to support the different hardware platforms that the binaries are expected to run on. This generates a lot of extra work, both writing and testing the programs.

Perl, bash, and many other scripting languages are available in most environments. With very few exceptions programs, written in Perl, bash, Python, PHP, and other languages can run unchanged on many different platforms.

## Intel PC to Mainframe

At one place I worked I was responsible for one Intel host that ran Linux and a fairly large Apache web site with an internally built database engine. We wrote a large number of Perl and bash programs that were used as CGI to generate web pages based on the data retrieved from the database. Even the database software was written in Perl by one of our SysAdmins.

As part of our disaster recovery plan, all of the mainframe and Unix programs that we were running – our entire inventory of software – was supposed to be migrated to a recovery service with a location in Philadelphia. The service did not provide Intel-based computers, so our web site could not be directly supported with identical hardware.

However, part of the hardware we had at my organization, and which was also replicated at the disaster recovery site, was an IBM Z series mainframe that could support a large number of Red Hat instances. We decided it would be wise to test our

© David Both 2018
D. Both, *The Linux Philosophy for SysAdmins*, https://doi.org/10.1007/978-1-4842-3730-4_15

software and see if it could be migrated to an IBM Z series box. We were hoping that we would not need to make too many changes to make it work. I was provided with access to a dedicated Red Hat instance on the Z series mainframe and told to report my results.

I started by identifying the software and related data that would have to be moved. This was easy because we used standard directory locations for files and data as defined by the Linux Filesystem Hierarchical Standard.

It took less than five minutes to create a tarball of the files we needed to transfer, and a few seconds to scp (secure copy) the tarball to the mainframe. I extracted the files from the tarball, started the various servers using a startup shell program, "automate everything," and started testing. Everything worked flawlessly. Total time from start to finish to transfer and up and running – except the testing itself – twelve minutes.

This was in part due to the fact that our database was in fact a flat ASCII text file, in accordance with the tenet in Chapter 13: "Store data in open format files." No magical incantations were required to modify it, convert from one binary format to another, or ASCII to EBCDIC, or export it from one system and import it on another. It just worked.

But this easy migration was also made possible by the fact that we used Perl and bash, which made for portable programs.

# Architectures

Linux runs on a number of architectures. Actually, quite a lot of hardware architectures.[1] Wikipedia maintains a long list of hardware architectures supported by Linux, but here are just a few.

Of course Linux supports Intel and AMD.

It also supports 32- and 64-bit ARM architectures that are found in practically every mobile phone on the planet and devices such as the Raspberry Pi.[2] Most mobile phones use a form of Linux called Android.

Freescale (formerly Motorola) 68K architecture; Texas Instruments 320 family, Qualcomm Hexagon; Hewlett Packard's PA-RISC; IBM's S390 and Z series; MIPS; IBM's Power, PowerPC, SPARC, and many more.

---

[1]Wikipedia, *List of Linux-supported computer architectures*, https://en.wikipedia.org/wiki/List_of_Linux-supported_computer_architectures
[2]Raspberry Pi Foundation, https://www.raspberrypi.org/

Each of these architectures is different at the hardware instruction set[3] level. Each architecture needs different compilers, or at least a compiler that is capable of supporting their respective instruction sets. This in turn means that any programs using a compiled language for any of these many architectures must be recompiled when migrated from one to another. This is a form of portability despite the fact that the programs need to be recompiled.

The sense that I mean in this chapter is that programs should just work when moved from one architecture to another. No recompiling or rewriting should be required. Only shell and other interpretive scripting languages can do that.

# Portability Restrictions

When I first heard the term portable in connection with software, it was in the sense of making a copy of a program that could be moved from one computer to another of the same architecture and operating system and run it there. Searching Google results in a large number of hits that all relate to moving software from one Windows computer to another using various techniques including things like running the program from a USB drive that can be inserted into any computer. Other techniques were described a little less clearly.

## Licensing

Other results referred to simply installing programs on more than one hard drive. Vendors can attempt to prevent this for various reasons, and in some cases it is quite illegal. End user license agreements (EULA) may explicitly state that you have the right to install and use a program on only one computer. More lenient ones may allow you to install it on multiple computers – with some specified limit – but to only use it on one computer at a time.

I do not intend to become embroiled in a discussion about licensing agreements. But true portability is affected by licensing, so some consideration of it is necessary. Sometimes technology is not the restrictive factor in portability.

## Technology

However, sometimes technology is the limiting factor in software is portability.

---

[3]Free On-Line Dictionary of Computing, *Instruction Set*, http://foldoc.org/instruction+set

## Compilers and Code

We have already looked at portability with respect to supported platforms. For compiled programs, this means that compilers must be available to create binaries compatible with the supported platforms. We have already seen that Linux is supported on a wide range of hardware platforms so there are clearly compilers that support those platforms.

We can say that there is a certain level of compatibility with these platforms, and that code will be semi-portable between them. That basically means that the code can be placed in a single code base, if desired, but that considerations need to be made within the code in order to support targeted platforms. These differences are due to the inherent differences in the hardware instruction sets of each platform.

The good news is that the GNU Compiler Collection[4] (GCC) used by Linux contains compilers for the C, C++, Objective C, Fortran, Java, and Ada programming languages. GCC can run on more than sixty operating system platforms including Linux, DOS, Windows, many Unix variants, MIPS, NeXT, and a bunch I never heard of before finding the *GCC Definition* referenced in footnote 4. We can also see in that document that GCC supports a wide range of processors for which it can compile binary code.

This all means that we have some level of portability in the compiled binary world. The drawback is that code compiled for one hardware platform will not run on a different hardware platform so it must be recompiled. Sometimes significant changes must be made to the code in order to get it to compile. This takes a lot of effort and most developers won't bother with trying to make their code compile on all or even most of the hardware platforms that they could. They usually pick one or two that together have the most potential customers and don't go beyond that.

If that source code is open source, then some programmer with a need or desire to make this code run on one of the less common hardware platforms can do that. If they do, it will certainly take a good bit of work and knowledge to make it happen.

This is definitely not the appropriate choice for us lazy admins. Let's make our code much more portable right from the start and eliminate most of this extra work. Compiled code rates low on my portability scale because of the amount of work required to move it from one platform to another. It can be done, but I don't want to do it myself.

---

[4]The Linux Information Project, *GCC Definition*, http://www.linfo.org/gcc.html

# LibreOffice

LibreOffice[5] is a good example of compiled code that is portable. I use LibreOffice extensively for various projects, including writing this book. LibreOffice is available for many operating system platforms including Linux, various Windows releases, Mac OS, and Android. There is even a "Portable"[6] version packaged using PortableApps. com.[7] This packaging enables the application to be used from one's own USB stick, for example, on any Windows computer.

So LibreOffice is portable in multiple senses. It is also open source so that you can download the source code from the LibreOffice web site and modify it to suit your own needs. Most of us would never do that, but the code is available so we can view it or change it if we need or want to. LibreOffice is distributed under the Mozilla Public License Version 2.0.[8]

# Shell Scripts

Here we are, back at shell scripts. Why? Because the vast majority of shell scripts work on any hardware platform under Linux. In most cases, they will also work on other Unix and Unix-like operating systems.

> *The shell is actually a programming language: it has variables, loops, decision-making, and so on.*
>
> —The Unix Programming Environment[9]

This statement applies to every shell I have ever used. In previous chapters you have already seen how short shell programs can be written directly at the command line in order to facilitate the rapid solution to a problem. We have also covered creating executable files in which to store these ad hoc programs so they will be available in the future and for other SysAdmins who might need the same solution.

---

[5]LibreOffice, Home page, https://www.libreoffice.org/

[6]LibreOffice, Portable Versions, https://www.libreoffice.org/download/portable-versions/

[7]PortableApps.com, Home page, https://portableapps.com/

[8]LibreOffice, Licenses, https://www.libreoffice.org/about-us/licenses/

[9]Kernighan, Brian W.; Pike, Rob (1984), "3. Using the Shell," *The UNIX Programming Environment,* Prentice Hall, Inc., ISBN 0-13-937699-2, 94

I prefer to use bash because it is the default shell for all Linux distributions, and it is available for Unix as well. Other shells are also widespread, like ksh, csh, tcsh, and zsh, but they may need to be installed because they may not be by default.

The fact that the bash shell is nearly 100% compliant[10] with the Portable Operating System Interface (POSIX[11]) standard means that you can expect bash shell scripts that run on one operating system and hardware platform to also run on all others on which bash is supported. That does not mean that you might not run into some issues. For example, the mymotd script that we wrote in Chapter 11 looks for some specific hardware data that might not be available or might be available but in a different manner than our script assumes. The script will run, but you might encounter some anomalous results.

# Portability with Windows

So far, we have concentrated on compatibility within Linux and Unix operating systems. But what about Windows? Although this book and the Linux Philosophy for SysAdmins is about the Linux environment, this chapter would not be complete if we did not look, however briefly, at Windows, too.

As discussed above, it is possible to create source code that can be compiled on Linux, various versions of Unix, Windows, and other operating systems. It takes a lot of work to do this, but it can and has been done. The real question is how we can run our shell scripts on both Linux and Windows.

There are a couple ways to provide script portability between Linux and Windows.

## Cygwin

Cygwin is a free open source product that can be downloaded and installed on your Windows computer. Cygwin supports Windows Vista and later and installs a very flexible Linux environment and a nearly complete set of programs, utilities, and desktop environments that have been ported from Linux and the GNU Utilities.

It is possible to use Cygwin to install bash, tcsh, other shells, the KDE and other Linux desktops, and many Linux utilities that we SysAdmins have become accustomed to. Not only is it possible to have a Linux experience on Windows, but also our bash and

---

[10]Newham and Rosenblatt, *Learning the Bash Shell* (O'Reilly 1998), ISBN 1-56592-347-2, 248.

[11]Wikipedia, *POSIX*, https://en.wikipedia.org/wiki/POSIX

other scripts are now portable to Windows. The Cygwin environment even extends to imposing the /dev directory and the usual device special files that we expect to find on any Linux host.

This portability does have its limits, though. For example, hardware and operating system specific functions may not work correctly. Therefore, it may be necessary to add some code to shell scripts to determine the operating system environment and act accordingly to allow for the differences. This is nothing new and has been done between different Linux distributions and between Linux and various versions of Unix. Adding a little bit of additional code to a script to allow it to run on multiple operating systems is a very easy way to ensure a higher level of portability.

In other cases, bash scripts may port in the sense that they will run, but it would make no sense to so-so. For example, the post-installation script I have written to handle all of tasks that the Fedora Linux installation does not would run but it would generate many errors.

I have spent a little time to install and learn a bit about Cygwin, but I don't normally use Windows except for a few tests like this. The Cygwin bash shell is familiar and offers a good opportunity to use Linux commands and scripts that are not operating-system dependent.

## PowerShell

Microsoft released the first version of their PowerShell[12] in 2006. In January of 2018, they made PowerShell available under the MIT license.[13] The code itself is now available for many platforms, including Linux. PowerShell is an object oriented scripting language and shell that is – among other things – intended to provide script portability between the Windows and Linux platforms.

I have not used PowerShell although I have played with it just a bit to see what it is about. It is very different from any of the Linux and Unix shells I have used. I suspect if I spent some time with it, I could learn to use it as well as I use the bash shell. With all I still have to learn about Linux, I am probably not going to use PowerShell myself. However, if you need script portability between Linux and Windows operating systems, you should definitely check it out.

---

[12]Opensource.com, February 6, 2018, *Power(Shell) to the people*, https://opensource.com/article/18/2/powershell-people

[13]Linux Foundation, *MIT License*, https://spdx.org/licenses/MIT

## Windows Subsystem for Linux

The Windows Subsystem for Linux[14] (WSL) allows Linux ELF binaries to run on an X64 version of Windows 10 hosts. This compatibility layer enables Windows users to install and run a number of different Linux distributions from the Windows store.

WSL has its limits, but it provides another option for users needing cross-platform compatibility.

# The Internet and Portability

We have been looking at shell scripts in terms of running them from the command line. What happens when we use other programs to run our scripts? For example, one method for making our scripts portable is to run them as CGI programs on a web server and deliver the results to the requesting web browser.

The advantage of this approach to portability is that the user needs no special tools, virtual machines, or compatibility layers. There is no need to download and install software on the client, the user's host. The script is run and the work is done on the web server. Only a stream of data that is used by a browser to generate and display a page containing the information that resulted from the work done by the web server is sent to the requesting client.

Let's take a quick look at creating scripts for this type of environment.

# Creating Web Pages

Back in the stone age of the Internet when I first created my first business web site, life was good. I installed the Apache HTTP server and created a few simple HTML pages that stated a few important things about my business and provided information like an overview of my product and how to contact me. It was a static web site because the content seldom changed. Maintenance was simple because of the unchanging nature of my site.

---

[14]Microsoft, *The Windows Subsystem for Linux*, https://docs.microsoft.com/en-us/windows/ wsl/about

# Static Content

Static content is easy and still common. Let's take a quick look at a couple of sample static web pages. You don't need a working web site to perform these little experiments. Just place the files in your home directory and open them with your browser. You will see exactly what you would if the file were served to your browser via a web server.

The sole function of a web server is to send the text data to create a web page from the server to the browser. In the experiments in this chapter we will simply create the text data streams as files in your /home/~ directory.

The first thing we need on a static web site is the index.html file, which is usually located in the /var/www/html directory. This file can be as simple as a text phrase such as "Hello world" without any HTML markup at all. This would simply display the text string without any formatting.

---

**EXPERIMENT 15-1**

---

All of the experiments in this chapter can be performed as the student user.

Create index.html in your home directory and add the text "Hello world" without the quotes or any HTML markup as it's only content.

Open the index.html in your browser with the following URL.

```
file:///home/<yourhomedirectory>/index.html
```

The results are pretty unimpressive. Just a bit of text on your browser window.

---

So HTML markup is not required, but if you had a large amount of text that needed formatting, the results of a web page with no HTML coding would be incomprehensible with everything running together.

So the next step is to make the content more readable by using a bit of HTML coding to provide some formatting.

---

**EXPERIMENT 15-2**

The following data creates a page with the absolute minimum markup required for a static web page with HTML. Add the H1 markup to the text in your index.html file.

```
<h1>Hello World</h1>
```

Now view index.html and see the difference.

Of course you can put a lot of additional HTML around the actual content line to make a more complete and standard web page. That more complete version as shown below will still display the same results in the browser. It also forms the basis for a more standardized web site. Go ahead and use this content for your index.html file and display it in your browser.

```
<!DOCTYPE HTML PUBLIC "-//w3c//DD HTML 4.0//EN">
<html>
<head>
<title>My Web Page</title>
</head>
<body>
<h1>Hello World</h1>
</body>
</html>
```

The results using the more complex form do not change much, but it makes for a complete HTML coded web page. The one thing the above HTML code does change is that we now have a title, "My Web Page," which appears in the browser tab or title bar.

---

I built a couple of static web sites using these techniques, but my life was about to change.

# Dynamic Web Pages for a New Job

I once took a new job in which my primary task was to create and maintain the CGI (Common Gateway Interface) code for a very dynamic web site. In this context, dynamic means that the HTML needed to produce the web page on a browser was generated from data that could be different every time the page was accessed. This includes input from the user on a web form that is used to look up data in a database. The resulting data is surrounded by appropriate HTML and displayed on the requesting browser. But it does not need to be that complex.

Using CGI scripts for a web site allows you to create simple or complex interactive programs that can be run to provide a dynamic web page that can change based on input, calculations, current conditions in the server, and so on. There are many languages that can be used for CGI scripts. We will look at two of them, Perl and BASH. Other popular CGI languages are PHP and Python.

This chapter does not cover installation and setup of Apache or any other web server. If you have access to a web server that you can experiment with, you can directly view the results as they would appear in a browser. Otherwise, you can still run the programs from the command line and view the HTML that would be created. You can also redirect that HTML output to a file and then display the resulting file in your browser.

## Using Perl

Perl is a very popular language for CGI scripts. Its strength is that it is a very powerful language for the manipulation of text.

To get CGI scripts to execute, you need the following line in the in httpd.conf for the web site you are using.

```
ScriptAlias /cgi-bin/ "/var/www/cgi-bin/"
```

This tells the web server where your executable CGI files are located. For this experiment, let's not worry about the server side of things. We can still do everything we need without a web server.

---

### EXPERIMENT 15-3

Create a new file, index.cgi, and add the following Perl code to it. This file should also be located in your home directory for this experiment.

```
#!/usr/bin/perl
print "Content-type: text/html\n\n";
print "<html><body>\n";
print "<h1>Hello World</h1>\n";
print "Using Perl<p>\n";
print "</body></html>\n";
```

Set the permissions on index.cgi to 755 because it must be executable.

```
[student@testvm1 ~]$ chmod 755 index.cgi
```

Run this program from the command line and view the results. It should display the HTML code it will generate.

```
[student@testvm1 ~]$ ./index.cgi
Content-type: text/html

<html><body>
<h1>Hello World</h1>
Using Perl<p>
</body></html>
[student@testvm1 ~]$
```

We now have a Perl program that can generate HTML for viewing in a web browser.

When using a web server, you would set the ownership of the file to apache.apache. The file would also be located in /var/www/cgi-bin.

Now view the index.cgi in your browser. All you get from this is the contents of the file. Browsers really need to have this delivered as CGI content. It does not really know how to do that unless the server tells it that the directory in which the program is located is specified as shown above in httpd.conf. But you get the idea.

To see what this would look like in your browser, run the program again and redirect the output to a new file, test1.html.

```
[student@testvm1 ~]$ ./index.cgi > test1.html
[student@testvm1 ~]$ cat test1.html
Content-type: text/html

<html><body>
<h1>Hello World</h1>
Using Perl<p>
</body></html>
[student@testvm1 ~]$
```

Now use your browser to view the file you just created that contains the generated content. You should see a nicely formatted web page.

The CGI program in Experiment 15-3 still generates static content because it always displays the same output. In Experiment 15-4 we use the Perl "system" command to execute the Linux command following it in a system shell. The result is returned to the program. In this case we simply grep the current RAM usage out of the results from the free command.

---

**EXPERIMENT 15-4**

Add the following line to your index.cgi program.

```
system "free | grep Mem\n";
```

Your program should now look like this.

```
#!/usr/bin/perl
print "Content-type: text/html\n\n";
print "<html><body>\n";
print "<h1>Hello World</h1>\n";
print "Using Perl<p>\n";
system "free | grep Mem\n";
print "</body></html>\n";
```

Run the program two or three times from the command line to see that the free command returns different numbers almost every time.

```
[student@testvm1 ~]$ ./index.cgi
Content-type: text/html

<html><body>
<h1>Hello World</h1>
Using Perl<p>
Mem:       4042112     300892     637628        1040     3103592     3396832
</body></html>
[student@testvm1 ~]$ ./index.cgi
Content-type: text/html

<html><body>
<h1>Hello World</h1>
Using Perl<p>
Mem:       4042112     300712     637784        1040     3103616     3396996
```

```
</body></html>
[student@testvm1 ~]$ ./index.cgi
Content-type: text/html

<html><body>
<h1>Hello World</h1>
Using Perl<p>
Mem:        4042112      300960      637528      1040    3103624    3396756
</body></html>
[student@testvm1 ~]$
```

Run the program again and redirect the output to the results file.

```
[student@testvm1 ~]$ ./index.cgi > test1.html
```

Reload the ~/test1.html file in your browser. You should see the additional line that displays the system memory statistics. Run the program while redirecting the output to this file and refresh the browser a couple of more times and notice that the memory usage should change occasionally.

## Using BASH

Bash is probably the simplest language of all for use in CGI scripts. Its primary strengths for CGI programming are that it has direct access to all of the standard GNU utilities and system programs and that SysAdmins should be familiar with it.

---

### EXPERIMENT 15-5

---

Rename the existing index.cgi to Perl.index.cgi and create a new index.cgi with the following content.

```
#!/bin/bash
echo "Content-type: text/html"
echo ""
echo '<html>'
echo '<head>'
echo '<meta http-equiv="Content-Type" content="text/html; charset=UTF-8">'
echo '<title>Hello World</title>'
echo '</head>'
```

```
echo '<body>'
echo '<h1>Hello World</h1><p>'
echo 'Using BASH<p>'
free | grep Mem
echo '</body>'
echo '</html>'
exit 0
```

Remember to set the permissions to executable. Run this program from the command line and view the output.

```
[student@testvm1 ~]$ chmod 755 index.cgi
[student@testvm1 ~]$ ./index.cgi
Content-type: text/html

<html>
<head>
<meta http-equiv="Content-Type" content="text/html; charset=UTF-8">
<title>Hello World</title>
</head>
<body>
Hello World</h1><p>
Using BASH<p>
Mem:      4042112      290076      647716         1040      3104320      3407516
</body>
</html>
```

Run this program again and redirect the output to the temporary results file you created before. Then refresh the browser to view what it looks like displayed as a web page. The results should be the same with the exception that some of the memory numbers will be a bit different.

# CGI – Open and Portable

You can see from these experiments that it is easy to create open and portable CGI programs that can be used to generate a wide range of dynamic web pages. These are trivial examples but you should now see some of the possibilities.

Although the most common way we think about scripts is in terms of running them from the command line, they can also be used with other software to perform some very interesting tasks. CGI scripts written in common languages are a fine example of this.

Because the languages used to create our CGI programs are supported on many operating systems, these programs are portable. You may need to install bash on a Windows web server, but that too is possible. Other languages like Python and PHP, for example, can also be used to generate dynamic web pages and, along with Perl, are easily available on most platforms, both operating system and hardware.

# WordPress

WordPress[15] is a powerful open source program that allows creation and management of web pages. It is a great example of writing a complete program in a scripting language to generate and deliver web-based dynamic content. WordPress itself is just the code that generates web pages; a web server such as the Apache HTTP server is still required to deliver the data from the server to the client web browser.

WordPress is written in PHP so is easily portable to any platform that runs PHP.[16] PHP is a programming language especially well-suited to writing dynamic web pages. I sometimes forgot to install PHP because it is not always installed by default. I added the PHP installation to my post-installation script so it will always be there. But if you have trouble running WordPress, check to ensure PHP is installed.

WordPress is extremely flexible because it uses themes to generate the look and feel of a web site. By changing themes it is possible to change how a web site looks in a few seconds with a few mouse clicks. I use WordPress on all of my web sites because it is so easy and flexible. I have even taught nontechnical people how to use the word processing-like interface to create new web pages and posts.

Although many aspects of WordPress themes can be altered through its own web-based administration interface, some things require working directly with the CSS style sheets that, along with theme specific PHP code, define the look and feel of each theme. It is possible to work with the CSS through the WordPress interface, but I find using Vi or Vim in a terminal session works best for me.

Before I modify anything, however, I always make a new copy and leave the original intact. I usually rename the copy to something like, "my-wordpress-theme" to differentiate it from the original. Then I use the WordPress admin interface to switch to my new theme. Now I can modify the new theme and not need to be concerned that updates to the original theme will wipe out my changes.

---

[15]WordPress, Home page, `https://wordpress.org/`
[16]Wikipedia, PHP, `https://en.wikipedia.org/wiki/PHP`

Of course I can modify the CSS to change things like colors and fonts. I can also modify the PHP code for the themes, as well, in order to change the page structure a bit. I have done this on a few occasions when the theme needed a bit of tweaking. I have also modified the PHP code for a theme when installing some of the many plug-ins available for WordPress.

The only reason that all of this is possible – in terms of both portability and the ability to change anything about it – is that WordPress and the themes available for it are all open and accessible. The files that make up this application are all stored as ASCII text files. And it is open source, which means that the GPLv2[17] license under which WordPress is distributed allows all of this.

# Final Thoughts

I was going to try to define portability in this chapter. As I progressed in my writing, however, I began to realize that portability is a range of values and not just a binary response – yes, it is portable or no, it is not portable. And portable as they are, shell scripts still may need to be tweaked in order to produce the desired results when run on different operating system and hardware platforms.

Portability is a key ingredient in reducing our workload. Writing code that is portable – or at least as portable as possible – is an excellent method for only needing to do a job once. Why write code for several different platforms when it can be done once to run on all of those platforms with shell scripts?

Command-line scripts are where we spend most of our time as SysAdmins and making these portable is important. Fortunately most shell scripts, especially those written in bash, are high on the portability scale. Writing portable CGI code for web sites we manage is another good step, where it is applicable.

More time saving comes from using open source code that is portable and has been tested and created for many environments. We looked at WordPress as one example of this. Just because we can write our own amazing CGI scripts to drive a web site does not mean that it is efficient to do so. WordPress is already written, it is open source, and it does a great job. And if you don't like WordPress there are many other options available as well.

Portability rocks!

---

[17]Free Software Foundation, Free Software Licensing Resources, `https://www.fsf.org/licensing/education`

## Final Thoughts

# CHAPTER 16

# Use Open Source Software

This tenet may not mean exactly what you think it does. Most times we think of open source software as something like the Linux kernel, LibreOffice, or any of the thousands of open source software packages that make up our favorite distribution. In the context of system administration, open source means the scripts that we write to automate our work.

> *Open source software is software with source code that anyone can inspect, modify, and enhance.*[1]

— Opensource.com

The web page from which the quote above was taken contains a well-written discussion of open source software, including some of the advantages of open source. I suggest you read that article and consider how it applies to the code we write – our scripts. The implications are there if we look for them. This chapter will hopefully help you to achieve some insight just as writing it enlightened me.

## Definition of Open Source

The official definition of open source is quite terse. The annotated version of the open source definition[2] at opensource.org contains ten sections that explicitly and succinctly define the conditions that must be met for software to be considered truly open source.

---

[1]Opensource.com, *What is open source?*, https://opensource.com/resources/ what-open-source

[2]opensource.org, *The Open Source Definition (Annotated)*, https://opensource.org/ osd-annotated

311

This definition is important to the *Linux Philosophy for SysAdmins*, so I include the text of that annotated definition here. You do not have to read this definition, but I suggest you do so in order to gain a more complete understanding of what the term open source really means.

---

**Note**    The Open Source Definition is not a license. It describes the conditions that any license must meet in order to be considered an open source license.

---

# The Open Source Definition (Annotated)

Version 1.9

The indented, italicized sections below appear as annotations to the Open Source Definition (OSD) and are not a part of the OSD. A plain version of the OSD without annotations can be found here.

## Introduction

Open source doesn't just mean access to the source code. The distribution terms of open-source software must comply with the following criteria:

## 1. Free Redistribution

The license shall not restrict any party from selling or giving away the software as a component of an aggregate software distribution containing programs from several different sources. The license shall not require a royalty or other fee for such sale.

*Rationale: By constraining the license to require free redistribution, we eliminate the temptation for licensors to throw away many long-term gains to make short-term gains. If we didn't do this, there would be lots of pressure for cooperators to defect.*

## 2. Source Code

The program must include source code, and must allow distribution in source code as well as compiled form. Where some form of a product is not distributed with source code, there must be a well-publicized means of obtaining the source code for no more than a reasonable reproduction cost, preferably downloading via the Internet without charge. The source code must be the preferred form in which a programmer would modify the program. Deliberately obfuscated source code is not allowed. Intermediate forms such as the output of a preprocessor or translator are not allowed.

*Rationale: We require access to un-obfuscated source code because you can't evolve programs without modifying them. Since our purpose is to make evolution easy, we require that modification be made easy.*

## 3. Derived Works

The license must allow modifications and derived works, and must allow them to be distributed under the same terms as the license of the original software.

*Rationale: The mere ability to read source isn't enough to support independent peer review and rapid evolutionary selection. For rapid evolution to happen, people need to be able to experiment with and redistribute modifications.*

## 4. Integrity of The Author's Source Code

The license may restrict source-code from being distributed in modified form *only* if the license allows the distribution of "patch files" with the source code for the purpose of modifying the program at build time. The license must explicitly permit distribution of software built from modified source code. The license may require derived works to carry a different name or version number from the original software.

*Rationale: Encouraging lots of improvement is a good thing, but users have a right to know who is responsible for the software they are using. Authors and maintainers have reciprocal right to know what they're being asked to support and protect their reputations.*

*Accordingly, an open-source license must guarantee that source be readily available, but may require that it be distributed as pristine base sources plus patches. In this way, "unofficial" changes can be made available but readily distinguished from the base source.*

## 5. No Discrimination Against Persons or Groups

The license must not discriminate against any person or group of persons.

*Rationale: In order to get the maximum benefit from the process, the maximum diversity of persons and groups should be equally eligible to contribute to open sources. Therefore we forbid any open-source license from locking anybody out of the process.*

*Some countries, including the United States, have export restrictions for certain types of software. An OSD-conformant license may warn licensees of applicable restrictions and remind them that they are obliged to obey the law; however, it may not incorporate such restrictions itself.*

## 6. No Discrimination Against Fields of Endeavor

The license must not restrict anyone from making use of the program in a specific field of endeavor. For example, it may not restrict the program from being used in a business, or from being used for genetic research.

*Rationale: The major intention of this clause is to prohibit license traps that prevent open source from being used commercially. We want commercial users to join our community, not feel excluded from it.*

## 7. Distribution of License

The rights attached to the program must apply to all to whom the program is redistributed without the need for execution of an additional license by those parties.

*Rationale: This clause is intended to forbid closing up software by indirect means such as requiring a non-disclosure agreement.*

## 8. License Must Not Be Specific to a Product

The rights attached to the program must not depend on the program's being part of a particular software distribution. If the program is extracted from that distribution and used or distributed within the terms of the program's license, all parties to whom the program is redistributed should have the same rights as those that are granted in conjunction with the original software distribution.

*Rationale: This clause forecloses yet another class of license traps.*

## 9. License Must Not Restrict Other Software

The license must not place restrictions on other software that is distributed along with the licensed software. For example, the license must not insist that all other programs distributed on the same medium must be open-source software.

*Rationale: Distributors of open-source software have the right to make their own choices about their own software.*

*Yes, the GPL v2 and v3 are conformant with this requirement. Software linked with GPLed libraries only inherits the GPL if it forms a single work, not any software with which they are merely distributed.*

## 10. License Must Be Technology-Neutral

No provision of the license may be predicated on any individual technology or style of interface.

*Rationale: This provision is aimed specifically at licenses which require an explicit gesture of assent in order to establish a contract between licensor and licensee. Provisions mandating so-called "click-wrap" may conflict with important methods of software distribution such as FTP download, CD-ROM anthologies, and web mirroring; such provisions may also hinder code re-use. Conformant licenses must allow for the possibility that (a) redistribution of the software will take place over non-Web channels that do not support click-wrapping of the download, and that (b) the covered code (or re-used portions of covered code) may run in a non-GUI environment that cannot support popup dialogues.*

The Open Source Definition was originally derived from the Debian Free Software Guidelines (DFSG).

Opensource.org site content is licensed under a Creative Commons Attribution 4.0 International License

# Why This Is Important

The definition of open source is important to us as SysAdmins for several reasons. First, this definition provides us with a framework for evaluating the many licenses that are out there. Some of them are truly open source licenses while others only feign being open source.

True open source licenses allow us to easily and legally find, download, and use code that is open sourced. Without the assurance that the code we use is open sourced, we would be unable to use huge amounts of existing code that already meets many of the needs we have. Code that is distributed under any of the licenses recognized to be open source is free of any encumbrances. Understanding the requirements for true open source licensing allows us to ensure that the code we are using is properly licensed. Properly licensed open source code is freely available, and we can use it on as many computers as we like and copy it to give to others. There are no restrictions on how we can use or share it. There are a number of good yet different open source licenses.

The Open Source Initiative is the recognized authority for approving open source licenses. Their web site has a current list of approved open source licenses.[3] We should apply one of these approved licenses when we make our code open source. We should also ensure that the software we obtain from others for our own use is distributed under one of these approved licenses.

# Coining the Term

I enjoy learning about the history of Unix, Linux, and open source and so I think it important to acknowledge that Christine Peterson[4] coined the term "open source." In February of 1998, Peterson was in a series of meetings with Eric S. Raymond, Jon "maddog" Hall, and many other leaders to discuss licensing Netscape as free software. A number of people, especially Peterson, did not think that "free software" properly defined what they were trying to accomplish.

She came up with the term "open source" and approached some of the other attendees with the idea. In a meeting on February 5, some of the attendees started using "open source" to describe software that was free of restrictions and for which the source code was readily available. This story is really hers to tell so please read her article[5] at Opensource.com. In a comment at the end of the article on Opensource. com, Eric Raymond validates and supports Peterson's account of the birth of this now ubiquitous term.

# Licensing Our Own Code

One of the best ways I know to give back to the open source community that provides us with all of these incredible programs like the GNU Utilities, the Linux kernel, LibreOffice, WordPress, and thousands more, is to open source our own programs and scripts with an appropriate license.

---

[3]Open Source Initiative, *Licenses*, `https://opensource.org/licenses`
[4]Wikipedia, *Christine Peterson*, `https://en.wikipedia.org/wiki/Christine_Peterson`
[5]Peterson, Christine, Opensource.com, *How I coined the term 'open source,'* `https://opensource.com/article/18/2/coining-term-open-source-software`

Just because we write a program and we believe in open source and agree that our programs should be open source code, does not make it so. As SysAdmins we do write a lot of code, but how many of us ever consider the issue of licensing our own code? We must make the choice and explicitly state that the code is open source and under which license it is being distributed. Without this critical step, the code we create is subject to becoming fettered with proprietary licenses so that the community cannot take advantage of our work.

Remember the bash shell template we created back in Chapter 10? We included the GPL V2 license header statement as comments in the code, and we even provided a command-line option that would print the license header on the terminal. When distributing code, I also recommend that we make it practice to include a text copy of the entire license with the code.

I find it very interesting that in all of the books I have read and all of the classes I have attended, not once did any of them tell me to be sure to license any code I wrote in my tasks as a SysAdmin. All of these sources completely ignored the fact that SysAdmins write code, too. Even in the conference sessions on licensing that I have attended, the focus was on application code, kernel code, or even GNU-type utilities. None of the presentations even so much as hinted at the fact that we SysAdmins write huge amounts of code to automate our work or that we should even consider licensing it in any way. Perhaps you have had a different experience, but this has been mine. At the very least, this frustrates me; at the most it angers me.

We devalue our code when we neglect to license it. Most of us SysAdmins don't even think about licensing, but it is important if we want our code to be available to the entire community. This is neither about credit nor is it about money. This is about ensuring that our code is now and always will be available to others in the best sense of free and open source.

Eric Raymond writes that in the early days of computer programming and especially in the early life of Unix, sharing code was a way of life.[6] In the beginning this was simply reusing existing code. With the advent of Linux and the open source licensing, this became much easier. It feeds the needs of System Administrators to be able to legally share and reuse open source code.

---

[6]Raymond, Eric S., *The Art of Unix Programming*, Addison-Wesley (2004), 380, ISBN 0-13-13-142901-9.

Raymond states, "Software developers want their code to be transparent, Furthermore they don't want to lose their toolkits and their expertise when they change jobs. They get tired of being victims, fed up with being frustrated by blunt tools and intellectual-property fences and having to repeatedly reinvent the wheel."[7] This statement also applies to SysAdmins.

This leads us to the problems associated with organizational code sharing and open source.

# Organizational Code Sharing

As SysAdmins our natural inclination is to share code. We like to help people, which is why we are SysAdmins in the first place. Yes, some of us just prefer computers to people but we all like to share our code.

Many organizations have no idea how to share code or the advantages of doing so. Others have figured this out and some even pay employees to write open source code.

## Silos Suck

Having worked at a good number of different organizations as a SysAdmin, I have found that many suck at sharing code both externally and internally. Most of the places I have worked at have never even thought about sharing code internally let alone externally. Every development project was isolated from every other one. Departments were like silos, tall and narrow with lots of silage inside, self-enclosed fiefdoms eschewing contact with the outside world. In many ways they acted like rivals instead of teams working for the same organization.

I always found it difficult to obtain code from other departments in these organizations. The PHBs of other internal organizations always seemed to think that we were in some sort of competition with them and that sharing code was a zero sum game in which the one sharing the code was the loser. At the very least it took weeks of discussion and sometimes some sort of written legal forms that included a non-disclosure agreement. I am not talking about two departments writing commercial code that might overlap or compete in some way in the external marketplace; I am talking about two internal lab organizations, for example, that perform essentially the same tasks every day. Sharing code would have made so much sense, saved so much work, and been so easy to do.

---

[7]Ibid.

In some cases it was just easier to write our own code than it was to struggle through the bureaucratic nonsense to obtain code we already knew would solve a problem for us. What a waste of time!

## Open Organizations and Code Sharing

That type of internal organization that results in uncommunicative silos needs to be replaced by an open organization[8] that will encourage code sharing at least internally. Jim Whitehurst, CEO of Red Hat, has written a book, *The Open Organization*,[9] which discusses the advantages and qualities of the open organization and how to make the transition. Whitehurst has also written a very interesting article, "Appreciating the full power of open,"[10] for Opensource.com in which he discusses the concept of sharing, "Sharing something often increases its value, because sharing allows more and more smart, creative people to get their hands on it. The value actually increases as you remove restrictions to sharing—if you share as much as you can with as many people as you can. That means sharing your instructions, your recipe, your source code, and opening it up to everyone, not limiting access to certain persons, groups, or 'fields of endeavor,' as the Open Source Initiative[11] puts it."

In 2005, Karl Fogel wrote an interesting book, *Producing Open Source Software – How to Run a Successful Free Software Project*,[12] and followed up with a second edition in 2017. Fogel covers in detail the techniques, technology, legal issues, and the social and political infrastructure of creating open source software. This is an interesting book that details many practical aspects of creating software that is truly open source. It discusses the advantages of sharing code internally as well as externally using open source licensing.

---

[8]Opensource.com, *What is The Open Organization*, https://opensource.com/open-organization/resources/what-open-organization

[9]Whitehurst, Jim, *The Open Organization*, Harvard Business Review Press (June 2, 2015), ISBN 978-1625275271

[10]Opensource.com, *Appreciating the full power of open,* https://opensource.com/open-organization/16/5/appreciating-full-power-open

[11]See the *Annotated Open Source Definition* in this chapter.

[12]Fogel, Kark, *Producing Open Source Software*, https://producingoss.com/en/index.html

Some organizations pay their employees to write open source code. For example, many companies pay some of their employees to write code for the kernel, which ultimately, if approved by Linus Torvalds, will be shared with programmers throughout the world. This is not always purely altruistic because many companies that do this wish to make the kernel work better for their own software. In many cases this new or revised code will make Linux work better for everyone and Torvalds may accept it into the kernel source code tree.

Many open source projects besides the kernel are supported by organizations that understand the value proposition of supporting open source software both monetarily and with code.

## Things to Avoid

This chapter is about using open source software but that means that we also need to distinguish true open source software from that which has hidden restrictions or simply does not comply with the licensing under which they claim their software is distributed. It is a sad thing that we need to discuss companies that falsely claim their software to be open source.

This is one of the reasons I have included the Open Source Definition in this chapter. Understanding the objectives of open source can help you to understand when a license does not meet the requirements. But there are other things to beware of also.

If a software vendor states that their software is open source, then the source code should be easily available for download from the Internet. In some cases I have been interested in software and in viewing the web site found no indication that the source code was available. In those cases, no one responded to my queries about that issue.

If in order to download some software, you are required to provide your name, email address, and other identifying information, the software is definitely not from a reputable company even if they claim to use an open source license. I have seen many alleged "free white paper" downloads that would actually interest me if they did not require "registration" of some sort. I recommend giving these companies a wide berth. They are probably using the false or misleading promise of open source software to build a spammer's list of email addresses.

# Code Availability

It is one thing to license code with an open source license; it is quite another to actually make it available to others. The definition of open source code that I quoted at the beginning of this chapter implies that our code must be made available is some way so that anyone who has the inclination can download and view the source code. And in just the previous section of this chapter, I mention that requirements such as filling out a registration form are indicative that the code is being illegally restricted if it is truly distributed under an open source license.

How do we make our code freely available under an open source license? There are a number of good ways to share our code. Let's look at some.

# How Do I Share My Code?

Now that our code can be distributed under an approved open source license, how do we actually distribute it and make it available to others? Note that the open source definition at the beginning of this chapter does not specify how the open source software should be delivered.

Nothing I have ever read defines an approved mechanism for distributing open source software. The licenses I have read as well as the legal opinions I have read that refer to distribution of open source software are all about making the source code available along with the executables. For scripts the executable *is* the source.

Sharing our open source code can be trivially easy. For me it started when I installed some of the scripts I had written to ease my tasks of system management on the computers I built or repaired for customers and friends. I then started putting a few of my scripts onto USB thumb drives so I could give them to people. Not that I did any of that very much. I had a few customers and not a lot of folks are interested in a few bash scripts. More people were interested in a live DVD or USB drive of Fedora than my scripts.

The next step is to make the scripts available for download from the Internet and I have done this with mine. In order to make these scripts more widely available, I have posted them on my technical web site, The DataBook for Linux,[13] at http://www.linux-databook.info/?page_id=5245. You can download them and use them as you see fit within the terms of the licenses. The code is all distributed under the GPL V2 and the PDF documents are published under a Creative Commons Attribution-ShareAlike license.

---

[13]Both, David, *The DataBook for Linux*, http://www.linux-databook.info

It is also appropriate to use developer collaboration sites such as SourceForge[14] and GitHub.[15] These sites allow others to easily download a copy of your code in order to participate in development. They provide version management and allow you as the primary developer to merge only that code which you deem appropriate.

I used SourceForge on one of my projects for a while, but that project is long dead and has been superseded by another. One of the advantages of sites like SourceForge and GitHub are that they make it easy for others to take over a project when the current lead developer decides to move on. That is what happened with the project I became the lead on. I took it over from another developer who needed to spend his time on other projects.

# Code Sharing Considerations

There are a couple of important things to consider about sharing your code. I will touch on them only briefly here. The important thing is that you are aware of them and can get more information of you need it.

## Confidentiality

Confidentiality is a concern for many and rightly so. Data or code that is intended to be confidential may be exposed in open source software.

Of course hiding the code that is allegedly confidential or a trade secret makes the program as a whole proprietary. If you remove the guts of your code from a program and hide it, then the entire program is useless from an open source standpoint. To be truly open source you have to go all the way. All the code is open or it is not.

Data is another beast altogether. Eric Raymond's Rule of Separation[16] discusses the separation of policy from implementation. This means that the user interface for a program, which is where policy is implemented, should be separate from the parts of the program that implement the mechanics. This makes it possible to use a text mode or GUI interface and to alter those interfaces without changing the underlying logic of the program.

We can also apply this rule of separation to the data used by a program. Data should never be stored as part of the program although I have seen that done. I have made that mistake myself.

---

[14]https://sourceforge.net/

[15]https://github.com/

[16]Raymond, *The Art of Unix Programming*, 15–16.

The data used by a program must be separate from the program code as a matter of good programming form. This ensures that the data itself is easily altered when the externals that the data refer to change. Even with scripts, configuration data should be maintained separately from the code that makes up the program's logic. Using separate configuration files makes it possible for a non-sophisticated user to make changes without worry of damaging the code itself.

The separation of data from the program also means that it is not necessary to distribute any data that might be confidential with the code itself.

## Providing Support

What happens when I distribute my code and someone finds a bug? Am I obligated to fix it? Is it necessary for me to answer questions from the people who use my software?

The answer to these questions is "no." We are not under any obligation to support the open source code we make available. Why? Because the open source licenses – at least the GPL V2[17] that I use – specifically state that there is no warranty.

> 11. BECAUSE THE PROGRAM IS LICENSED FREE OF CHARGE, THERE IS NO WARRANTY FOR THE PROGRAM, TO THE EXTENT PERMITTED BY APPLICABLE LAW. EXCEPT WHEN OTHERWISE STATED IN WRITING THE COPYRIGHT HOLDERS AND/OR OTHER PARTIES PROVIDE THE PROGRAM "AS IS" WITHOUT WARRANTY OF ANY KIND, EITHER EXPRESSED OR IMPLIED, INCLUDING, BUT NOT LIMITED TO, THE IMPLIED WARRANTIES OF MERCHANTABILITY AND FITNESS FOR A PARTICULAR PURPOSE. THE ENTIRE RISK AS TO THE QUALITY AND PERFORMANCE OF THE PROGRAM IS WITH YOU. SHOULD THE PROGRAM PROVE DEFECTIVE, YOU ASSUME THE COST OF ALL NECESSARY SERVICING, REPAIR OR CORRECTION.

*Figure 16-1.* *The GPL V3 under which I make my scripts available contains this clause that makes it clear that the code has no warranty whether implied or explicit (The original is in uppercase.)*

---

[17]Open Source Initiative, Licenses – GPL V2, `https://opensource.org/licenses/GPL-2.0`, Section 11.

If you read the various approved licenses at opensource.org you will find they all have similar wording. However, despite the statements in the licenses, most of us want our code to work for anyone who obtains it – as well as ourselves. So we fix any problems that arise because it will work better for our users as well as for us.

Companies such as Red Hat, and organizations like The Document Foundation,[18] the entity responsible for the LibreOffice suite of office programs, all have support structures, bug and problem reporting procedures, and volunteers to assist with usage problems and to provide guidance and support.

# Parting Thoughts

Using the open source software created by others is important but I am not suggesting that we completely forgo the use of proprietary software when it meets a need that cannot otherwise be met. By this I mean that we consider proprietary software after extensive Google searches have failed to locate appropriate open source software, and then exploring the possibility of writing a script to perform the task in question.

If you choose to write a script to solve the problem, open source your own code. Make it available for others because if you need to perform this task, others also need to do so. You will be saving others the work you invested in creating the script.

Stay away from the trap of always writing your own code when something is already available. We could write our own web-based content management or blogging software, but there is already plenty of software that does that. WordPress, Drupal, Joomla, Plone, OpenCms, Mambo, and many more are already available and it will take far less work that writing your own. Write a plug-in for whichever one you choose if some bit you need is not already available.

Use open source software written by others when you can; the rest of the time write open source software that others can use.

---

[18]The Document Foundation, https://www.documentfoundation.org/

# PART IV

# Becoming Zen

Part 4 of this book takes us from the everyday practical aspects of being a SysAdmin to the more esoteric world of the Zen. We look at various aspects of the *Linux Philosophy for SysAdmins* that are about making our own choices, doing things in ways that make sense to us, dealing with and respecting all of those we work with including the PHBs, and giving back to the community.

You will find only a couple of experiments in this part of the book. However, you will find some advice and suggestions that I usually try to impart to students and new SysAdmins – those for whom I have been a mentor.

Enter and become Zen with me.

PART IV

Becoming Zen

# CHAPTER 17

# Strive for Elegance

Elegance is one of those things that can be difficult to define. I know it when I see it, but putting what I see into a terse definition is a challenge. Using the Linux `dict` command, Wordnet provides one definition of elegance as, "a quality of neatness and ingenious simplicity in the solution of a problem (especially in science or mathematics); 'the simplicity and elegance of his invention.'"

In the context of this book, I think that elegance is a state of beauty and simplicity in the design and working of both hardware and software. When a design is elegant, software and hardware work better and are more efficient. The user is aided by simple, efficient, and understandable tools.

Creating elegance in a technological environment is hard. It is also necessary. Elegant solutions produce elegant results and are easy to maintain and fix. Elegance does not happen by accident; you must work for it.

The quality of simplicity is a large part of technical elegance. So large, in fact that it deserves a chapter of its own, Chapter 18, "Find the Simplicity," but we do not ignore it here. This chapter discusses what it means for hardware and software to be elegant.

## Hardware Elegance

Yes, hardware can be elegant – even beautiful, pleasing to the eye. Hardware that is well designed is more reliable as well. Elegant hardware solutions improve reliability.

Many of us SysAdmins have responsibility for hardware as well as software. This is especially true of those of us who work in smaller organizations, but it can also be true in larger environments as well. In my five-year stint at Cisco, the SysAdmin part of my job required me to rack and cable new servers, identify and fix hardware problems, help design rack layouts and power requirements, and more hardware related tasks.

Understanding hardware elegance is just as important as understanding software and operating system elegance.

© David Both 2018
D. Both, *The Linux Philosophy for SysAdmins*, https://doi.org/10.1007/978-1-4842-3730-4_17

# The PCB

A Google search for "pcb[1] reliability" reveals many articles and papers on PCB design and reliability. One article by Darvin Edwards, "PCB Design and Its Impact on Device Reliability,"[2] discusses four broad areas of PCB design that affect reliability. One factor Edwards discusses is that of thermomechanical reliability. Repeated power cycling causes rapid thermal changes, which in turn causes expansion and contraction of the components, traces (electrical conductors), and solder joints. Over time these repeated thermal stress cycles can cause various types of failures on the PCB.

In one of my technical drafting classes in college, one of my assignments was to create a set of drawings for a printed circuit board. The layout was already provided, and all I really needed to do was to redraw it using some new technique we had just been taught.

As I looked at the component layout in the drawing and the traces, and land patterns – places where components are soldered on the PCB, I had a bit of insight. One of the things we had also learned in class was that each solder joint is a potential point of failure and each jumper used – short lengths of wire used to "jump" over other traces – on a PCB added two points of failure, one for each solder joint. There were two jumpers on this board and I decided to see if I could alter the design to eliminate them. I was able to reroute a couple of the traces to different locations and eliminate the jumpers. I showed this to the instructor, and his response was that it was a more elegant solution. He gave me a good grade on that project.

# Motherboards

Hardware elegance can mean the simple and well laid-out design of a motherboard, which is a fairly large PCB. As previously discussed, good motherboard design can improve reliability.

In my opinion a well laid-out motherboard, one that looks good with sleek lines of the conductors and land patterns (mounting pads to which components are soldered) on the surface is elegant. A motherboard with well-placed components that do not interfere with each other or with additional components that might be added later such as powerful but long video adapters, a CPU socket that is placed on the motherboard so that RAM memory

---

[1]Printed Circuit Board

[2]Edwards, Darvin, Electronic Design, *PCB Design and Its Impact on Device Reliability*, `http://www.electronicdesign.com/boards/pcb-design-and-its-impact-device-reliability`

and other motherboard components do not interfere with adding high-capacity air cooling fans or liquid cooling equipment – that is elegant design. Frankly, I have always appreciated the look of a well-designed motherboard. These motherboards are truly works of art.

## Computers

A well-designed computer is elegant. This includes a case that is designed with easy access to the internal components and that provides for plenty of unrestricted airflow, lots of locations to mount fans and liquid cooling radiators, and plenty of options for easy cable routing.

This is not about lots of LED lighting on the motherboard, fans, LED strips, and fancy lighting controllers. Such things are for show and fun. The latest motherboard I purchased for my main workstation is an ASUS TUF X299 that met all of the requirements I had for this workstation. It was also the only one that met all of my needs. It also just happens to have a string of LEDs along the back edge that produce a simple light show of scrolling colors. I have not turned them off in BIOS because they are a bit of fun, but I would not go out of my way to add LED shows to my set of requirements.

A computer is elegant when the external power and hard drive activity LEDs are easily visible and a decent brightness so they can be seen in all lighting conditions. The power and reset switches are also easily accessible but not obtrusive so that they might be accidentally bumped and cause the computer to reset or power off.

I could go on, but you get the idea.

## Data Centers

Hardware elegance also means a well-planned and constructed computer room or data center. Rack enclosures are laid out in such a way that multiple power sources can reach them with ease and access to both front and rear are unimpeded. The cabling is neat and orderly - unlike that in Figure 17-1 which is a mess; it is cut to length and flows without kinks or tangles through the cable channels and trays throughout the computer room.

***Figure 17-1.*** *It may get the job done, but this cabling job is definitely not elegant. Creative Commons CC0*

Uninterruptible power supplies should be used to maintain power to all devices until a generator can be brought online and power switched over to that for long-term stability in the event of power failures. Power and grounding leads themselves should be routed for safety as well as ease of access.

# Power and Grounding

It is hard to imagine that power and grounding feeds to a computer should have a term like "elegance" applied to them. but here is something to consider about that.

In about 1976 I was working for IBM as a Customer Engineer in Lima, Ohio. In addition to fixing broken computers and installing new ones, one of my duties was to assist customers in planning for the installation of new computers. This included planning for appropriate power and grounding. In this particular instance, I had a long discussion with my customer about the requirements for power and a good ground. Good grounding is essential for the proper electronic operation and stability of computers.

So what constitutes a good ground? It is a large gauge wire with green insulation (green wire ground) that runs from the device being protected, the computer, to a copper stake that is embedded at least 10 feet deep into moist earth. The green wire ground must not have any other grounding wires connected to it, and it must not be connected to any grounding or neutral buses in any of the power distribution boxes through which it passes. Note that this is IBM's definition for the integrity of the logical operation of the computer as well as for human safety.

After our discussion, the customer said that they had an old well on the grounds that was lined with copper and that was at least 80 feet deep with over 60 feet of water in it. This was a great ground, and I agreed that bonding the green wire ground from the computer to the well casing was appropriate grounding. Using this preexisting and amazingly good ground point was an elegant solution.

After the installation we had nothing but problems. These were seemingly random but frequent problems that one day would be indicative of memory failures, the next day a disk problem, the next day a processor problem, and so on. We replaced memory, CPU boards, and pretty much everything we could think of over a period of about two weeks, and the customer was understandably getting upset.

I was by now fairly certain that this was a grounding problem. I discussed the ground with the plant electrician and he said that he had run the ground wire just as we had discussed. But I had to see for myself to be sure.

I got out my oscilloscope and used an induction clamp on the ground wire so that I could see any electrical noise on the ground line. As I got this all hooked up, the vice president of IT came by and I told him what I was doing. He was a bit skeptical, to say the least.

Just as we were finished with our discussion, we both heard an electrical motor start up and a large burst of electrical noise showed up on the scope. A moment later, someone ran out of the computer room and yelled that the computer was down. I could not have asked for a better audience to this than the disgruntled vice president. Especially since the motor we had heard starting up was the compressor motor on the large soft drink machine that we were standing next to.

We had the electrician begin removing the front panels to all of the electrical distribution boxes in order to see and verify the integrity of the green wire ground. In the first box we looked at, I immediately saw the problem. There was a big, ugly, nasty looking, very old wire that had been grafted onto our once-pristine green wire ground.

About this time someone came into the little room in which we had been standing during all of this and ran a few letters through the postage machine. The resultant noise on the ground wire said it all because both of these devices were plugged into the same power outlet. We had the electrician clip that ugly, old ground wire off of my nice new, clean green wire ground and the customer never had another problem caused by grounding issues.

Sometimes elegance is a pristine green wire ground.

## Software Elegance

Here I am, back to talking specifically about shell scripts, which is the type of coding that SysAdmins typically do. It would be very unusual for a SysAdmin to write code in a language such as C, which requires much more development effort and needs to be compiled. This is a poor use of time for a SysAdmin.

There are many opinions on software elegance. What makes software elegant, and what does "elegant" even mean in the software world? Here are some of my opinions with a bit of explanation for each.

In general, elegance is code that looks good, even pretty, and follows the tenets outlined in this book. In my opinion, software is elegant when you use these guidelines. This is my list of characteristics, and I am willing to bet that other SysAdmins have their own ideas about what constitutes software elegance. In any event these are not hard and fast rules – just guidelines. The most important aspect of any software is that it should perform the task you wrote it to do. Using these guidelines makes it easier for others – and you – to understand what you did and maintain the code you wrote.

1.   **Use consistent indenting** - Code should be consistent in the indenting of procedures and flow control structures. This helps to make it easier to visualize the structure of the program and the flow of execution under various circumstances.

    I know that some developers use tabs for indentation and others spaces. The number of tabs or spaces people use vary as well. That is mostly irrelevant so long as the code can be easily read by anyone who did not write it – and by those who did write it as well.

2.   **Design with a clear layout** - Code should be well laid out and sequenced so that it is easy to see the flow of execution under various conditions.

    The most efficient code is that which executes in a straight-through fashion and which does not jump around or have unnecessary flow control structure that slow it down.

    There are good reasons for using procedures, such as to prevent replication of the same code in multiple places. However, the main body of the program should flow in a straightforward fashion where possible.

3.   **Use STDIO** - We have already seen that STDIO is a powerful enabler; it allows us to chain many small programs together in order to perform complex tasks that no single program can do.

    A program with a captive user interface (CUI) such as a menu, does not provide for STDIO. Such a program is limited to a stand-alone existence and cannot work as a within a data stream.

Captive user interfaces should be avoided because they are so limiting and do not play well with the command-line pipes and redirection.

The fdisk program is one example of a useful and powerful utility that uses a menu interface. The problem with this is that fdisk cannot be used in scripts. Someone wrote a separate program for performing fdisk functions from within scripts. The current tool for this is sfdisk.

4. **Add meaningful comments** - The program is well commented with meaningful information. This helps to make the purpose of the code clear for maintainers and to ensure that problems can be located and fixed quickly.

5. **Each program should do one thing well** - This guideline has long been a tenet of the Unix and the Linux Philosophies and has resulted in the Core Utilities, and other core utilities that are small, targeted to a single task and that perform that task well. This results in powerful and flexible command-line programs that can be combined into pipelines to perform complex tasks that a single program cannot.

One side effect of this is that programs that do one thing tend to be small. This makes them easy to understand and modify when necessary.

The corollary to this tenet is that adding more features to these small programs is not usually a good idea. The need for a so-called "new feature" should really be seen as the need for a new program that should also follow these guidelines. Most new features, when patched onto existing programs, simply create code bloat and make the programs harder to use and maintain.

6. **Silence is golden** - Linux command-line tools usually do not display a message to the SysAdmin that all has gone well. This keeps undesired messages from entering the STDOUT data stream feeding a pipeline and causing confusion for later programs.

7.  **Always use the least amount of code necessary** - The minimum amount of code necessary to perform the desired task is used. Everything else is cruft and should be eliminated. This is the crux of simplicity and the opposite of complexity.

    Some programmers like to show off with a twisty maze of complex code that is impossible to determine the entrances and exits. This type of code is poor practice and is subject to bugs.

    On the other extreme, there is a game, a competition, really, called "code golf."[3] The objective is to implement a specified algorithm with the smallest possible resultant executable binary. This is most definitely *not* what we are doing in this particular guideline. Competitions such as this are fine so long as they are not carried over into the actual practice of system administration. In the context of the SysAdmin, using the least amount of code necessary means to also meet as many as possible of the rest of these guidelines. Code golf does not because it ignores everything else in the pursuit of minimization.

8.  **The output is easy to read and understand** - When any output is necessary at all, it should be easily interpreted by the user. For many programs, the output is their reason for being.

    Output that is cluttered with messages and other information that have little or nothing to do with the purpose of the program obfuscates the important data. The actual structure of the output is irrelevant so long as it serves the intended purpose with clarity.

9.  **Use meaningful variable names** - I like to use meaningful variable names in my command line and shell programming. Random variable names or names like $X have little meaning to whoever needs to debug code a couple years down the road; that includes the person who originally wrote the code.

---

[3]Wikipedia, *Code Golf,* https://en.wikipedia.org/wiki/Code_golf

Names like $AccountTotal and $NumberOfUsers are far more meaningful than $A1, $B3, for example. They make it much easier to read the code. They also serve as a good starting place for the tenet "Document everything," in Chapter 20. Well-named variables tell program maintainers what to expect in terms of how the variable fits into the logic of the program as well as the kinds of values to expect when debugging the program.

Going back to the Perl programs that I was tasked with cleaning up, the variable names were so random that it turned out several of those variable names pointed to the same thing. I renamed all of the variables in the program and then was able to substitute a single variable name for those other different names for the same variable. Just that little step made a big leap forward in cleaning up that particular program.

10. **Follow Eric S. Raymond's 17 Unix Rules**[4] - These are 17 rules that should be read and understood by all developers including SysAdmins. Raymond expounded at length on these rules in his book, *The Art of Unix Programming*.[5] Wikipedia has a nice summary of these rules (see footnote 3).

    If you think an important guideline is absent from my list, it is probably in Raymond's list of rules. Be sure to read these rules because they apply to SysAdmins as well as developers.

11. **Test everything** - Is this not blindingly obvious?! Apparently not, because I have encountered plenty of software that has clearly not been well tested.

    My job at Cisco was twofold. Part of the time I was assistant to the lab manager where the testing department's tests were run. The rest of the time I was one of the testers, assigned to test Linux powered appliances.

---

[4]Wikipedia, *The Unix Philosophy*, Section: *Eric Raymond's 17 Unix Rules*, https://en.wikipedia.
org/wiki/Unix_philosophy#Eric_Raymond%E2%80%99s_17_Unix_Rules
[5]Raymond, Eric S., *The Art of Unix Programming*, http://www.catb.org/~esr/writings/taoup/
html/

Testing is not just running a series of test programs to verify that the software under test could perform its design tasks – it is also ensuring that the software does not fail when it encounters unexpected input. One of the most common vulnerabilities that hackers use to obtain unauthorized access to computers and other devices that are run by software is the inability of the software to handle unexpected input.

Other testing that I did was to simply peruse the documentation and the code to determine whether the code met the specifications outlined in the documentation. If it did not, I had to fail it, or the development team would have to obtain an exception, which was rare.

Part of what I did while reviewing both the code and the documentation was to ensure that the design of the code supported the Linux Philosophy and well-documented standards such as the filesystem Hierarchical Standard, and standards created to ensure consistency of usage among all Linux distributions.

12. **Clean out the cruft** - Cruft is all of the old code in a program that is never used. Many programs evolve over time and sometimes code that was once useful is no longer needed. As I fix my own scripts or add new features or options, I sometimes find myself with code and variables that are no longer used and which need to be cleaned out.

Following these guidelines will help ensure that the code you write remains easy to read and modify. It will look good and it will run well. It will be elegant.

# Fixing My Web Site

By now you already know that I use WordPress for hosting my own web sites and others as well. I use it because it is free, open source software that performs its task well and provides great flexibility. However, things do go wrong. You can count on it. In this particular case, I have encountered the problem twice on different web sites and have now fixed it twice.

The symptom of this problem was perplexing until I determined the source. Things looked normal on the blog page, which is the home page for my both.org web site. The problem was only visible when I tried to display any of the static pages I have for this web site.

The static pages displayed the theme elements such as the top banner and the web site name. Each page showed the correct title for that page, but none of the content. It was a page without content. I tried changing themes to no avail – that meant the problem was not with the theme itself. I installed another instance of WordPress and pointed it to the existing MySQL database for the both.org web site. The symptom did not change or go away.

The only place left to check was the MySQL database. It is too bad that I forgot about the mysqlcheck tool; I might have easily fixed the problem that way. It is a good thing I forgot about the mysqlcheck tool because I learned a lot more than I would have otherwise.

This problem was really quite simple to fix. I copied the MySQL database files for that web site from my daily backup to the /var/lib/mysql/wordpress directory and restarted MySQL.

WordPress can use a different MySQL database for each web site or a single MySQL database with different tables for each web site. The tables for each web site have different prefixes for the table names. This prefix is defined in the WordPress wp-config. php file for each site.

I located the correct set of database files in /var/lib/mysql/wordpress directory and saved them to another location just in case. I then went to one of my backups that was a couple days old since I was unsure exactly when this problem had begun. I copied the backup files to the /var/lib/mysql/wordpress directory and restarted MySQL. Everything worked fine at this point. I may not have needed the MySQL restart, but I figured I might as well get a clean restart to flush anything that might be in a cache somewhere.

The only way this could work is that both WordPress and MySQL are open so that I was able to view the code for WordPress and the configuration and data files for both WordPress and MySQL. I could have downloaded the source for MySQL but did not need to. I didn't really need to do that for WordPress either but because it is written in PHP it is wide open.

The data files for MySQL are stored in the Linux FHS defined location, /var, which is for – database files! I was able to find them, determine which files were for my web site, and easily replace them with earlier backups.

Another contributing factor is that the backup script that I wrote creates backups that store files in their normal format and directory structure. It does not compress them into tarballs, zip files, or – even worse – some proprietary backup format. I can access my files with command-line tools like cd and cp; the Midnight Commander (mc) text mode file manager; or a GUI file manager such as Krusader, Dolphin, or others. When I find the backup files I want, I can simply copy them to the desired location to replace the damaged ones.

It is also possible to use the `mysqldump` command to export the data to a file that is a script of SQL commands that will rebuild the database. I have tried this in the past and found that it works quite well. Either method would work just as well, but I like my own method better.

The elegance of WordPress, MySQL, and my backup solution, when taken together, result in an easy resolution to the problem at hand. One of the things I learned from fixing this problem is that fancy backup solutions are not necessary for a MySQL database.

# Removing Cruft

Creating elegance is hard work. Maintaining it can be even more difficult. Cruft is superfluous programs and code within programs, old data files, and directories with files left over from programs that have been removed.

Cleaning out cruft is an important part of our job as SysAdmins. Among the things we can search for cruft are old or unused software, old code in our own scripts, and old configuration and data files. Fortunately we have some tools that can assist us in this task.

# Old or Unused Programs

I just removed some programs I don't use. I was using the KDE Application Launcher and noticed that several of the Calligra office suite programs were in the list. I never use Calligra preferring LibreOffice. It had been installed by default with Fedora and I did us it several months ago for a test. Because I will never use it for my productive work, I decided to delete it.

But how do we actively search for unused programs? There is a way to find what are called orphans – programs that are not required by any other program. There are usually very few of these so it cannot hurt to use the tools we have to try to find them. For this task we use the rpmorphan utility to list RPM packages that are not dependencies for any other packages installed on the host.

---

**EXPERIMENT 17-1**

---

Install the rpmorphan package if it is not already.

`[root@testvm1 ~]` **dnf -y install rpmorphan**

List the orphaned packages.

```
[root@testvm1 ~]# rpmorphan
liberation-sans-fonts
liberation-serif-fonts
libertas-usb8388-firmware
libkolab
libsss_autofs
libsss_sudo
libyui-mga-gtk
libyui-mga-qt
libyui-qt-graph
[root@testvm1 ~]#
```

Your list of orphaned packages will be different from mine. Some of these "orphaned" packages on my test VM may be OK to delete, but I really do want the extra fonts. I also cannot say whether the other packages can be safely removed without a good bit of research, but I did look at the libkolab package and it looks like it can be safely removed from my VM host. Remove it if it is installed and then reinstall, or install it if it is not already, so we can see another option.

`[root@testvm1 ~]#` **dnf -y remove libkolab ; dnf -y install libkolab**

Let's use the time functions of rpmorphan to identify the newest package. First let's look at orphans installed more than one day ago.

```
[root@testvm1 ~]# rpmorphan -install-time +1
liberation-sans-fonts
liberation-serif-fonts
libertas-usb8388-firmware
libsss_autofs
libsss_sudo
libyui-mga-gtk
libyui-mga-qt
libyui-qt-graph
```

Note that libkolab is not in this list. Now find the orphans that were installed less than one day ago.

```
[root@testvm1 ~]# rpmorphan -install-time -1
libkolab
```

The only orphan we see is libkolab. If other packages had been installed in the past day, they would also have been found and could be removed.

---

The rpmorphan tool has many interesting options that enable us to do things like locate those orphaned packages older than a certain date. It can also find packages newer than a certain date. This latter option allows us to remove packages that may have been added for testing purposes.

Read the rpmorphan man page to understand more about some of the interesting options. You will see that it also has a GUI option, but I prefer the command-line interface. This program illustrates an important consideration that many programmers like to follow. It is really related to Eric Raymond's Rule of Separation.[6] In this case the programmers have separated the logic and functional aspects of the program from the user interfaces. This separation of logic from the user interface allowed them to create a command-line interface and two graphical interfaces, one based on tk and the other on curses.

---

[6]Raymond, Eric S., *The Art of Unix Programming*, Section *The Rule of Separation*, http://www.catb.org/~esr/writings/taoup/html/ch01s06.html#id2877777

**Caution**!    Don't remove orphan packages indiscriminately. This may result in removing needed packages. Just because they are orphans does not mean they are not needed. Be judicious when removing orphan packages. The rpmorphan tool simply allows us to identify packages that should be investigated further so that we may make a determination of whether they are truly safe to remove.

The deborphan tool can be used for Debian distributions. In fact, rpmorphan is based on deborphan. The rpmorphan tool only locates the orphans, it does not remove them. If you do decide to remove any orphan packages, you would use a package manager such as yum or dnf.

These tools cannot uncover all of the packages we might wish to remove from our systems. Finding orphans is one thing but many packages that do not show up as orphans might also be removed. For example, the Calligra office suite I mentioned earlier in this chapter does not show up as an orphan and neither does LibreOffice or many other user-level applications. Sometimes the most disk space can be recovered by removing these large programs.

You can use the Application Launcher for your desktop to locate user-level packages that you never use. This can also help you find some GUI administration tools you never use.

**Caution**!    Never attempt to remove packages using the -y option for your package manager. This may result in removing many packages that you would not want to remove. When your package manager displays the list of packages that it will remove if you respond with "y," be sure to inspect the list carefully. You can choose "y" or "n" after checking the list. This is much safer.

If you do decide to remove the packages you find, be careful that you will not remove other software that is needed. I always use the package removal command without the -y option that would remove without stopping to ask all packages dependent upon the one I am removing as well as the packages that the one I am removing is dependent upon. Be sure to check the list of packages that your package manager is preparing to remove and respond "no" if there are any packages you think should not be removed.

I once tried to remove a single package I thought I did not need. The list of packages that would have also been removed as dependencies ran into the hundreds and would have completely removed the KDE desktop from my system. That was definitely not what I wanted to do.

# Old Code in Scripts

Finding cruft code in scripts is also a task that should be undertaken at least occasionally by SysAdmins. Getting rid of unused code and locating syntax errors can be challenging, but there are some tools we have to help us.

The shellcheck utility is like lint[7] for C and other languages. It scans scripts written for bash and bash-like shells, sh, dash, and ksh, for cruft and syntactical improvements that can be made. It is, as always, your choice as to whether you make the suggested changes or not.

Let's look at how this tool works.

---

**EXPERIMENT 17-2**

Let us start by installing the ShellCheck package – yes, with the uppercase letters as shown.

[root@testvm1 student]# **dnf -y install ShellCheck**

Now let's check the shell script template using shellcheck.

[student@testvm1 ~]$ **shellcheck script.template.sh | less**

I received a number of SC2086 errors like this one.

In script.template.sh line 92:
   if [ $verbose = 1 ]
        ^-- SC2086: Double quote to prevent globbing and word splitting.

The shellcheck utility tool is a bit overzealous about wanting us to place double quotes around our variables. There are some edge cases[8] when this may be an issue, but I have never encountered them myself. So, after checking to ensure that we do not have one of those edge cases, we can exclude these errors as in this next command.

---

[7]Wikipedia, *Lint*, https://en.wikipedia.org/wiki/Lint_(software)

[8]GitHub, shellcheck, *Double quote to prevent globbing and word splitting*, https://github.com/koalaman/shellcheck/wiki/SC2086

```
[student@testvm1 ~]$ shellcheck --exclude SC2086 script.template.sh

In script.template.sh line 152:
RC=0
^-- SC2034: RC appears unused. Verify it or export it.

In script.template.sh line 153:
Test=0
^-- SC2034: Test appears unused. Verify it or export it.

In script.template.sh line 160:
if [ `id -u` != 0 ]
     ^-- SC2046: Quote this to prevent word splitting.
     ^-- SC2006: Use $(..) instead of legacy `..`.
```

Now it is easier to see a couple of unused variables that could be removed from the code. We also see some syntactical recommendations for one of the if statements.

Now you can see a few issues that have been highlighted by shellcheck. Make whatever changes you want to make using this information.

Beyond anything that shellcheck can tell you about syntax, orphan variables, and other things, sometimes you just need to look through the code. For example, one type of cruft that shellcheck does not find is superfluous procedures that are not called from anywhere in the script. These can also be removed if they are not required.

Do you see an unused procedure in the script template? There is one, SelectPkgMgr(), that is not used in the template and shellcheck did not find that it was superfluous.

# Old Files

Sometimes old software is removed when it is no longer needed. In many cases, the package removal procedures leave behind their user-level configuration files. These are usually the hidden "dot" files that we find in our home directories.

The good thing about these left-over configuration files is that if that software package is ever reinstalled we will not have lost our personal configuration. The bad thing is that, over a long period of time, a large number of these files can accumulate.

For example, the personal configuration files for Calligra, which I recently removed are still located in my home directory.

Old data files also are left on our hard drives long past any usefulness they might have had. This is usually because we seldom take the time to assess all of the files we have in order to determine whether they can be deleted, archived, or retained. One easy way to find old files is to use the find command to determine the last time files were accessed.

---
**EXPERIMENT 17-3**

---

First let's make a couple of files old. We do that with the touch command. With no arguments, touch sets atime, mtime, and ctime all to the current system time. First let's use the stat command to look at the attributes of one of the files you created in an earlier experiment, file0. txt. If you do not have this file, create it now.

```
[student@testvm1 ~]$ stat file0.txt
  File: file0.txt
  Size: 15             Blocks: 8         IO Block: 4096    regular file
Device: fd03h/64771d    Inode: 393236      Links: 1
Access: (0664/-rw-rw-r--) Uid: ( 1001/ student)  Gid: ( 1001/ student)
Context: system_u:object_r:user_home_t:s0
Access: 2018-02-02 15:39:56.415630341 -0500
Modify: 2018-01-27 11:41:36.056367865 -0500
Change: 2018-01-28 12:15:03.176000000 -0500
 Birth: -
```

This shows the current Access, Modify, and Change times – atime, mtime, and ctime – of the file. They may be identical but probably are not unless you just now created the file. Now touch the file using no options to set these three attributes to the current time. Then check the times again.

```
[student@testvm1 ~]$ touch file0.txt
[student@testvm1 ~]$ stat file0.txt
  File: file0.txt
  Size: 15             Blocks: 8         IO Block: 4096    regular file
Device: fd03h/64771d    Inode: 393236      Links: 1
Access: (0664/-rw-rw-r--) Uid: ( 1001/ student)  Gid: ( 1001/ student)
Context: system_u:object_r:user_home_t:s0
Access: 2018-02-23 10:28:25.794938943 -0500
Modify: 2018-02-23 10:28:25.794938943 -0500
Change: 2018-02-23 10:28:25.794938943 -0500
 Birth: -
[student@testvm1 ~]$
```

Notice that all three times are now identical. Here we use touch to set the atime – the last time the file was accessed – much earlier. The -a option in the command below tells the touch command to only set the atime. The -t option uses the following timestamp to set the date and time to 16:45:23 on July 15 of 2013.

```
[student@testvm1 ~]$ touch -a -t 1307151645.23 file0.txt
[student@testvm1 ~]$ stat file0.txt
  File: file0.txt
  Size: 15           Blocks: 8          IO Block: 4096    regular file
Device: fd03h/64771d    Inode: 393236        Links: 1
Access: (0664/-rw-rw-r--) Uid: ( 1001/ student)  Gid: ( 1001/ student)
Context: system_u:object_r:user_home_t:s0
Access: 2013-07-15 16:45:23.000000000 -0400
Modify: 2018-02-23 10:28:25.794938943 -0500
Change: 2018-02-23 10:48:13.781669926 -0500
 Birth: -
```

Note that the ctime was also changed. The ctime is the last time the file iNode was changed and that occurred when we set the atime.

So far all we have done is set the conditions for our experiment. Now we can use the find command to look for old files based on their atime. Use the find command as shown below to look for files that are more than two years old. The atime option on the find command uses age in days – actually 24-hour periods that start with "now." Therefore we need to use 365*2 = 730 days as our time period. We set the atime to more than five years ago so the test file should show up in this test.

```
[student@testvm1 ~]$ find . -atime +730
./file0.txt
```

The file0.txt file is displayed as expected. You can also show files that have been accessed more recently than 730 days. Pipe the results through the sort utility to make it easier to see that file0.txt is not among the ones listed.

```
[student@testvm1 ~]$ find . -atime -730 | sort
.
./.bash_history
./.bash_logout
./.bash_profile
./.bashrc
```

```
./.cache
./.cache/mc
./.cache/mc/Tree
./.config
./.config/mc
./.config/mc/ini
./error.txt
./file1.txt
./file2.txt
./file3.txt
./file4.txt
./file5.txt
./file6.txt
./file7.txt
./file8.txt
./file9.txt
./good.txt
./index.cgi
./.lesshst
./.local
./.local/share
./.local/share/mc
./.local/share/mc/history
./.mozilla
./.mozilla/extensions
./.mozilla/plugins
./mymotd
./perl.index.cgi
./script.template.sh
./test1.html
./test1.txt
./.viminfo
```

The `find` command can locate files based on size, permissions, name, and other criteria. However, all it can do is locate files that might be worthwhile to investigate further. That investigation is the only way to know with any degree of certainty what should be done with the files that were found. That usually means investigating the content, but sometimes it is possible to determine the disposition from the name or location of the file.

One potential issue with using the find command is files that have been recently restored from a backup in a manner that did not preserve their attributes. This can make old files look newer than they really are and prevent easy identification of the oldest files. In cases like this it is, once again, necessary to use basic tools such as the ls command or your favorite file manager to search through files, open them to check their content, and delete them if they are no longer needed.

Another criteria that can be used to locate files that might be archived or deleted is by size. There are two ways to do this. We can use the find command or the du command. The find command gives us a bit more control over the results because we can combine the parameters and do fun things like find all files that are larger than 15MB, were last accessed more than five years ago, and which belong to a specific user. In this next experiment we will first look at the du command then the find command.

---

### EXPERIMENT 17-4

Perform this experiment as the student user.

Once again we need to do a little bit of setup in order to make this experiment a bit more interesting than it is with only a few small files in the home directory of the student user. First we will create the ~/Documents directory if it does not exist, and then we will add some files of increasing sizes to it.

```
[student@testvm1 ~]$ mkdir Documents
```

The next command should be entered on a single line. It creates 100 files with increasing amounts of data in the ~/Documents directory.

```
[student@testvm1 ~]$ count=0;while [ $count -lt 100000 ]; do
count=$((count+1000)); echo $count;dd if=/dev/urandom of=~/Documents/file-
$count.txt bs=256 count=$count ;done
```

Make ~/Documents the PWD and list the contents. I only show the first 20 files files here for the sake of brevity. If you like, you can eliminate the head utility program so you can see them all.

```
[student@testvm1 Documents]$ ls -l | head -20
total 1262600
-rw-rw-r--. 1 student student 25600000 Feb 23 15:32 file-100000.txt
-rw-rw-r--. 1 student student 2560000 Feb 23 15:31 file-10000.txt
-rw-rw-r--. 1 student student  256000 Feb 23 15:31 file-1000.txt
-rw-rw-r--. 1 student student 2816000 Feb 23 15:31 file-11000.txt
```

```
-rw-rw-r--. 1 student student  3072000 Feb 23 15:31 file-12000.txt
-rw-rw-r--. 1 student student  3328000 Feb 23 15:31 file-13000.txt
-rw-rw-r--. 1 student student  3584000 Feb 23 15:31 file-14000.txt
-rw-rw-r--. 1 student student  3840000 Feb 23 15:31 file-15000.txt
-rw-rw-r--. 1 student student  4096000 Feb 23 15:31 file-16000.txt
-rw-rw-r--. 1 student student  4352000 Feb 23 15:31 file-17000.txt
-rw-rw-r--. 1 student student  4608000 Feb 23 15:31 file-18000.txt
-rw-rw-r--. 1 student student  4864000 Feb 23 15:31 file-19000.txt
-rw-rw-r--. 1 student student  5120000 Feb 23 15:31 file-20000.txt
-rw-rw-r--. 1 student student   512000 Feb 23 15:31 file-2000.txt
-rw-rw-r--. 1 student student  5376000 Feb 23 15:31 file-21000.txt
-rw-rw-r--. 1 student student  5632000 Feb 23 15:31 file-22000.txt
-rw-rw-r--. 1 student student  5888000 Feb 23 15:31 file-23000.txt
-rw-rw-r--. 1 student student  6144000 Feb 23 15:31 file-24000.txt
-rw-rw-r--. 1 student student  6400000 Feb 23 15:31 file-25000.txt
```

The du -a command simply lists files and their sizes as well as the cumulative size of all the files in each directory. We can use this to easily and quickly find the largest files and the directories that contain the largest amount of data. We run the results through the sort utility to get a numerically sorted listing with the largest files and directories at the end. In this case I only show the last 20 items in the list.

```
[student@testvm1 ~]$ du . -a | sort -n | tail -20
20752    ./Documents/file-83000.txt
21000    ./Documents/file-84000.txt
21252    ./Documents/file-85000.txt
21500    ./Documents/file-86000.txt
21752    ./Documents/file-87000.txt
22000    ./Documents/file-88000.txt
22252    ./Documents/file-89000.txt
22500    ./Documents/file-90000.txt
22752    ./Documents/file-91000.txt
23000    ./Documents/file-92000.txt
23252    ./Documents/file-93000.txt
23500    ./Documents/file-94000.txt
23752    ./Documents/file-95000.txt
24000    ./Documents/file-96000.txt
24252    ./Documents/file-97000.txt
24500    ./Documents/file-98000.txt
```

```
24752    ./Documents/file-99000.txt
25000    ./Documents/file-100000.txt
1262604 ./Documents
1262780 .
```

The results are in Kilobytes. Note that the directories sort out near the bottom because of the files they contain. It can be difficult to separate the directories from the files when using du.

The find command can be a little more specific. Let's find all files that are larger than 20MB.

```
[student@testvm1 ~]$ find . -size +20M
./Documents/file-93000.txt
./Documents/file-94000.txt
./Documents/file-90000.txt
./Documents/file-92000.txt
./Documents/file-89000.txt
./Documents/file-88000.txt
./Documents/file-91000.txt
./Documents/file-98000.txt
./Documents/file-84000.txt
./Documents/file-85000.txt
./Documents/file-83000.txt
./Documents/file-97000.txt
./Documents/file-100000.txt
./Documents/file-96000.txt
./Documents/file-95000.txt
./Documents/file-82000.txt
./Documents/file-87000.txt
./Documents/file-86000.txt
./Documents/file-99000.txt
[student@testvm1 ~]$
```

Notice that the find command does not list the file sizes. We can add a bit of code to the find command to make that happen.

```
[student@testvm1 ~]$ find . -size +20M -exec ls -l {} \;
-rw-rw-r--. 1 student student 23808000 Feb 23 15:32 ./Documents/file-93000.txt
-rw-rw-r--. 1 student student 24064000 Feb 23 15:32 ./Documents/file-94000.txt
-rw-rw-r--. 1 student student 23040000 Feb 23 15:32 ./Documents/file-90000.txt
-rw-rw-r--. 1 student student 23552000 Feb 23 15:32 ./Documents/file-92000.txt
```

```
-rw-rw-r--. 1 student student 22784000 Feb 23 15:32 ./Documents/file-89000.txt
-rw-rw-r--. 1 student student 22528000 Feb 23 15:32 ./Documents/file-88000.txt
-rw-rw-r--. 1 student student 23296000 Feb 23 15:32 ./Documents/file-91000.txt
-rw-rw-r--. 1 student student 25088000 Feb 23 15:32 ./Documents/file-98000.txt
-rw-rw-r--. 1 student student 21504000 Feb 23 15:32 ./Documents/file-84000.txt
-rw-rw-r--. 1 student student 21760000 Feb 23 15:32 ./Documents/file-85000.txt
-rw-rw-r--. 1 student student 21248000 Feb 23 15:32 ./Documents/file-83000.txt
-rw-rw-r--. 1 student student 24832000 Feb 23 15:32 ./Documents/file-97000.txt
-rw-rw-r--. 1 student student 25600000 Feb 23 15:32 ./Documents/file-100000.txt
-rw-rw-r--. 1 student student 24576000 Feb 23 15:32 ./Documents/file-96000.txt
-rw-rw-r--. 1 student student 24320000 Feb 23 15:32 ./Documents/file-95000.txt
-rw-rw-r--. 1 student student 20992000 Feb 23 15:32 ./Documents/file-82000.txt
-rw-rw-r--. 1 student student 22272000 Feb 23 15:32 ./Documents/file-87000.txt
-rw-rw-r--. 1 student student 22016000 Feb 23 15:32 ./Documents/file-86000.txt
-rw-rw-r--. 1 student student 25344000 Feb 23 15:32 ./Documents/file-99000.txt
[student@testvm1 ~]$
```

We now have a listing of the largest files in our home directory. In this case they are all in the ~/Documents directory.

---

Once again we have tools that can help us identify the largest files in our home directory. It still requires some judgment to decide which, if any, of these files can be deleted or archived.

# A Final Word

It is not always possible to do everything discussed in this chapter and the references to which I have pointed you. It would be great if we could but in real life we cannot always do so. Our scripts will never be completely free of cruft, and they will never reach the highest levels of elegance.

The title of the chapter should hint at that. Elegance is something to strive for but we will probably never achieve the pinnacle in which all cruft has been removed, all code made as efficient as possible, added the exact number of perfect comments that are clear and concise to our code, and all of the programming rules and suggestions followed.

This is not possible for a number of reasons. The two I run into most frequently are that the PHBs don't care and won't allow us the time, and that some of these guidelines are – at least to some extent – in conflict.

We do have some tools available to assist with locating cruft in scripts and as files on hard drives. Although these tools can be helpful, they are imperfect and can only do so much. It is really up to us as SysAdmins to search out cruft in our code and directories; sometimes this means manually looking through things to see what is there that can be eliminated. This is time consuming and I dislike doing it, but it does need to be done.

Using these tools to locate the largest and oldest files in our home directories – or those of the other non-root users – on our systems can be the first step in cleaning out the cruft. It gives us a starting point where we can get the best results for the least amount of effort. After deleting the largest and oldest files, it becomes less effective to continue to look for smaller and newer files to delete or move to archival storage.

# CHAPTER 18

# Find the Simplicity

*UNIX is basically a simple operating system, but you have to be a genius to understand the simplicity.*[1]

— Dennis Ritchie

I would never deign to disagree with one of the creators of Unix. However, my own perspective has evolved since I began using Unix and Linux. The tenets of the Linux Philosophy helped me to solidify my understanding of the truth that Linux is simple and that the simplicity is illuminated by the philosophy.

Many of the tenets in this book intersect and reinforce each other. I have no doubt that you have begun to see that for yourself. In Chapter 17, I discussed elegance but one thing I did not list there is simplicity, although it was mentioned in passing there and in many other places in this book. I believe that the concept of simplicity deserves its own chapter in the *Linux Philosophy for System Administrators*.

In this chapter we search for the simplicity of Linux.

## Complexity in Numbers

Yes, GNU/Linux is complex on the surface. One book I know of, *Linux in a Nutshell*,[2] contains a list of 372 Linux commands. Yes, I counted them. Another book, my favorite for beginners, *A Practical Guide to Linux, Commands, Editors, and Shell Programming*,[3] covers "... 98 utilities ...".

---

[1]azquotes.com, `http://www.azquotes.com/quote/246027?ref=unix`

[2]Siever, Figgins, Love & Robbins, *Linux in a Nutshell 6th Edition* (O'Reilly, 2009), ISBN 978-0-596-15448-6 .

[3]Sobell, *A Practical Guide to Linux, Commands, Editors, and Shell Programming, 3rd Edition* (Prentice Hall, 2013), ISBN 978-0-13-308504-4.

© David Both 2018
D. Both, *The Linux Philosophy for SysAdmins*, https://doi.org/10.1007/978-1-4842-3730-4_18

But those numbers are trivial compared to another number I came up with. Experiment 1 illustrates a method for estimating the total number of commands on your Linux computer. Most of the executable files that are command-line commands are located in the /usr/bin directory, so counting the number of files in that directory gives a pretty good estimate.

---

**EXPERIMENT 18-1**

---

Perform this experiment as the student user. Determine how many executables are located in /usr/bin.

```
[student@testvm1 ~]$ ls  /usr/bin | wc -w
2635
```

Yup – that is a lot of commands. Of course the number you see will be different. Ben Cotton, my technical reviewer, informed me that he has 1,992 files in /usr/bin on his laptop. You can see there will be a range depending upon which distribution you have and which packages have been installed.

---

The test VM that I am using to create and test these experiments is a pretty basic installation with the KDE and MATE desktops and a few applications like LibreOffice. That VM has 2,633 executable Linux files, most of which are CLI commands. Those numbers seem overwhelming to someone just learning Linux. They did to me when I was just starting as a baby SysAdmin.

When I was just beginning to learn Linux, back around 1996 or 1997, I picked up a couple of books about Linux – not that there were that many available back then – and discovered what seemed to me at the time an unimaginable number of commands. I thought it would be impossible for me to learn all of those commands.

I cringe when I see articles with titles like "77 Linux commands and utilities you'll actually use,"[4] and "50 Most Frequently Used UNIX / Linux Commands (With Examples)."[5] These titles imply that there are sets of commands that you must memorize, or that knowing large numbers of commands is important.

---

[4]TechTarget.com, http://searchdatacenter.techtarget.com/tutorial/
77-Linux-commands-and-utilities-youll-actually-use
[5]The Geek Stuff, http://www.thegeekstuff.com/2010/11/50-linux-commands/
?utm_source=feedburner

I do read many of these articles, but I am usually looking for new and interesting commands: commands that might help me resolve a problem or simplify a command-line program.

# Simplicity in Basics

Although my mother thinks I am a genius, I really am not. But I am persistent. I never tried to learn all of those Linux commands, regardless of what numbers you might come up with as the total for "all."

I just started by learning the commands I needed at any given moment for whatever project was at hand. I started to learn more commands because I took on personal projects and ones for work that stretched my knowledge to the limit and forced me to find commands previously unknown to me in order to complete those projects. My repertoire of commands grew over time, and I became more proficient at the application of those commands in resolving problems. I began finding jobs that payed me more and more money to play with Linux, my favorite toy.

As I learned about piping and redirection, about Standard Streams and Standard I/O, as I read about the Unix Philosophy and then the Linux Philosophy, I started to understand how and why the command line made Linux and the Core Utilities so powerful. I learned about the elegance of writing command-line programs that manipulated data streams in amazing ways.

I also discovered that some commands are, if not completely obsolete, then seldom used and only in unusual circumstances. For this reason alone, it does not make sense to find a list of Linux commands and memorize them. It is not an efficient use of your time as a SysAdmin to learn many commands that may never be needed.

The simplicity here is to learn what you need to do the task at hand. There will be plenty of tasks in the future that will require you to learn other commands. There are always methods for discovering and learning those commands when you need them. I have found that discovering and learning new commands as the need arose works very well for me. Almost any new project, including writing this book, leads to finding new commands to learn.

# The Never-Ending Process of Simplification

However – just because a solution works does not mean that you should stop looking for better ways. One of the common traits of the SysAdmin is that we are always looking for better ways of doing what we already do. Sometimes I find a command previously unknown to me, and I realize that it is a much better fit than one or two or more that I am already using to accomplish that task.

In one program I wrote over a decade ago, I used a series of commands in a pipeline starting with `dmidecode` to ascertain whether the hardware architecture of a system is 32-bit or 64-bit. It was cumbersome but mostly worked. I later discovered a Linux command, `arch`, that does what it took several commands to do the old way. I made the change in my script; the results have not changed but the program is simpler, more efficient, and more elegant.

Simplicity is not about performance or efficiency – at least not directly – it is more about elegance. Through simplification, my programs become more efficient and performance improves. This is elegance.

Simplicity is a never-ending process. It never stops because I am always learning new things and new ways to apply the things I already know.

# Simple Programs Do One Thing

Most of us who work directly with computers really like to have fun. And early computer programmers were no exception. They wrote plenty of programs that allowed us all to have some serious fun. We geeks just want to have fun, too!

Back in about 1970, I was one of the night computer operators for a small company in Toledo, Ohio. After all the real work was done, we would have some fun on the IBM 1401 mainframe. We would play games like tic-tac-toe, or print off pages of ASCII art that should not be reproduced here. Tic-tac-toe was fun, but it was interesting and challenging to play on that old computer. The computer would always take the first move as "X" and print out the resulting 3x3 matrix on one sheet of computer paper. The human player had to turn on one of the front panel sense-switches to indicate the number of the square in which they wanted to place the "O" and then press a button to tell the computer to continue to run the program. Those were the good old days.

The early Unix programmers gave us fun things like adventure, fortune, and cowsay. The last two can be used to illustrate a bit about simplicity. This simplicity is because both programs are designed to do exactly one thing. The fortune program prints a random fortune to STDOUT, and cowsay takes text strings from STDIN and displays them in the speech balloon of a cartoon cow.

Use your package manager to install both fortune and cowsay because it is not likely that they are already on your computer. On current versions of Fedora, they are "fortune-mod" and "cowsay." For earlier versions of Fedora and other distros, you might need to use "fortune" as the package name.

---

**EXPERIMENT 18-2**

Install fortune-mod and cowsay just in case they are not already. Do this part of the experiment as root.

```
[root@testvm1 ~]# dnf -y install fortune-mod cowsay
```

The rest of this experiment should be performed as the student user. Now run the fortune command a few times to see the results.

```
[student@testvm1 ~]$ fortune
Vulcans believe peace should not depend on force.
-- Amanda, "Journey to Babel", stardate 3842.3
```

I admit it took me several tries before this particular result was displayed. If you want to check, there may now be one or two more files in /usr/bin.

---

It's fine – just go ahead and play with the fortune program for a while.

Done? Then let's proceed to have fun with cowsay. The cowsay program requires a text string as input, so do something like is shown in Experiment 18-3. cowsay takes the text string and places it in the cow's speech balloon. Seems silly but it can get to be addictive. Just be careful about who is looking over your shoulder when you use it.

---

**EXPERIMENT 18-3**

---

Let's try the cowsay program by itself.

```
[root@testvm1 ~]# cowsay hello world!
 _____
< hello world! >
 --------------
        \   ^__^
         \  (oo)_____
            (__)\       )\/\
                ||----w |
                ||     ||
```

It's OK to play with this one for a while, too. I can see that someone might use cowsay instead of echo in a shell program to print messages, but cowsay does not maintain things like the columnar formatting of the original message texts; it just mashes everything together.

We have two small programs that each do exactly one thing. Let's put them together and take advantage of the fact that the cowsay program takes input on STDIN. Experiment 18-4 shows how to do that and the result. Here again, I have to admit to running the programs a few times to get this result, but it is the true output from one of those runs.

---

**EXPERIMENT 18-4**

---

Pipe the output from fortune through cowsay.

```
[student@testvm1 ~]$ fortune | cowsay
 _____
/ But I have a holy crusade. I dislike    \
| waste. I dislike over-engineering. I    |
| absolutely detest the "because we can"  |
| mentality. I think small is beautiful,  |
| and the guildeline should always be     |
| that performance and size are more      |
| important than features.                |
|                                         |
\ - Linus Torvalds on linux-kernel        /
 -----------------------------------------
```

```
    \    ^__^
     \   (oo)_____
        (__)\       )\/\
         ||----w |
         ||       ||
```

Combine two simple programs that are each small and where each does one thing, to create something more complex. It also took me a while to get this result. The misspelling was in the original.

Both fortune and cowsay have simple interfaces, they both perform a single task, they do it well, and they use STDIO. They both have a few command-line options that can be used to modify their behavior just a little, but once you use them together as shown in Experiment 18-4, there is not really much else to learn about them. If you want to explore their few command-line options, you can look up their man pages.

# Simple Programs Are Small

Just to see how small these two programs are, run the command in Experiment 18-5 to find that information. Neither one is very big. Small programs are easy to understand and to maintain.

---

**EXPERIMENT 18-5**

---

This command lets us find the sizes for the cowsay and fortune programs.

```
[student@testvm1 ~]$ ls -l `which cowsay` `which fortune`
-rwxr-xr-x 1 root root  4460 Nov 20 11:20 /usr/bin/cowsay
-rwxr-xr-x 1 root root 28576 Aug  2 19:54 /usr/bin/fortune
```

---

The fact that these programs are small is due to the fact that they each do exactly one thing. Adding more functions to either one of these programs would significantly increase their size and make them harder to maintain. Besides – what would be the point? These two programs are perfect as they are because they both meet the requirements set for them.

Now think about the rest of the GNU/Unix/Linux utilities in the same way. What is the ls program supposed to accomplish? Its only function is to list the files contained in a directory, remembering that directories themselves are nothing more or less than files. It can do this task in a number of different ways by using one or more of its several options – or no options at all.

Without options, the ls command lists only non-hidden filenames in the current directory (PWD), and as many as possible are listed on each line of output. The -l option is a long listing that shows the permissions, size, and other data about the files in a nice columnar listing that is easy to read. The -a option shows all files, including the hidden ones. The -r option lists files, recursing through each subdirectory and also listing the files in each of those as well. Without an argument, the ls command lists the files in the PWD. Using a different directory path as an argument, it can list the files in that other directory. Other variations of the argument let you list specific files.

The ls utility has a number of other interesting options and variations on the arguments that can be used with it. Read the man page for ls to see all of the possibilities.

Note that file globbing is handled by the shell and not by the ls command. Because the shell handles file globbing for all programs and scripts that take file names as an argument, none of those programs needs to do it. The shell expands the filenames that match the globs into a list of files on which the programs and scripts operate. This, too, is simplicity. Why include the file globbing capability into each program when it need only be in one place, the shell.

The thing you should observe about the ls utility is that every option, every argument variation, are all in aid of producing a list of files. That's it – that is all it does, list files. Therein lies its simplicity, that it does one thing and it does it very well. There is no point in adding more features to this program because it does not need them.

# Simplicity and the Philosophy

*At first I hoped that such a technically unsound project would collapse but I soon realized it was doomed to success. Almost anything in software can be implemented, sold, and even used given enough determination. There is nothing a mere scientist can say that will stand against the flood of a hundred million dollars. But there is one quality that cannot be purchased in this way — and that is reliability.* **The price of reliability is the pursuit of the utmost simplicity.** *It is a price which the very rich find most hard to pay.*[6]

— C. A. R. Hoare,[7] Writing about the development of the programming language PL/I[8] (Emphasis is mine.)

Many of the more interesting software problems I have encountered have involved the simplification of existing code – especially my own code. Adding new functions to a program increases its complexity. A quick new feature added to existing code and employed to meet a deadline increases complexity.

One of the hardest things to do is to reduce the complexity of code. But it pays dividends in the long run.

# Simplifying My Own Programs

One of my own programs, a bash shell script that I had written to perform a number of tasks after a basic Fedora installation has grown out of control more than once. I have already mentioned this post-installation program in Chapter 9, "Automate Everything." But now I need to discuss its darker side.

Due to the changes between Fedora releases, the needs of the program changed. The program needed to be modified to install some packages that are no longer installed during a default installation. Sometimes I needed to add code that would remove packages that were installed automatically because I did not want or need them.

Adding new code to do these things added to the complexity of the program. In some cases I added more options to be evaluated as the program initialized in order to leave my options open – as it were – with regard to the changes required to my program. Over a period of several years, this program grew to be quite large with plenty of cruft. I recently

---

[6]WikiQuote, *C. A. R. Hoare*, https://en.wikiquote.org/wiki/C._A._R._Hoare
[7]Wikipedia, *Tony Hoare*, https://en.wikipedia.org/wiki/Tony_Hoare
[8]Wikipedia, *PL/I*, https://en.wikipedia.org/wiki/PL/I

took some time to use the shellcheck utility and my own eyes on the code to remove cruft – mostly unused and no longer needed procedures – that reduced the size of the code by a few hundred lines.

# Simplifying Others' Programs

It is always more fun to talk about how I fixed other people's code. One of my past consulting jobs involved an almost complete rewrite of an interlocking set of existing Perl programs. There were around twenty-five or so of these programs running on a small Intel server. It was becoming impossible to maintain these programs to add new function and to locate and fix bugs due to the spaghetti code and lack of comments. My assigned task was to fix the bugs and add some additional function to these programs.

As I began trying to make sense of the frighteningly complex spaghetti code, it became clear that my first priority had to be simplifying the code. After commenting the code profusely and fixing a few bugs as I went,[9] I began to collect some code that had been inserted into two or more of these programs and collected them into Perl libraries. This made fixing problems easier because they only had to be fixed in one location – the library. I straightened out other code, simplifying the common execution paths.

The revised programs were faster, smaller, and easier to maintain. Problems could be located and fixed in hours and minutes rather than days.

# Uncommented Code

I scrounged around in my personal archives and found the code in Figure 18-1. I have no idea where it came from in the first place. I have no idea why I even kept it. It has no comments whatsoever. The few variable names are more than just a couple of characters in length, but they still tell us next to nothing about the purpose of the program or how it is supposed to work.

Even the "usage" procedure – apparently the "help" feature – in Figure 18-1 is not especially helpful because it shows a little about usage syntax, and it really still says nothing about the purpose of the program. Well – except for the program name. That indicates that it might have something to do with USB libraries. Is that even close to being understandable? I don't think so. I spent a good bit of time trying to figure it out.

---

[9]See Chapter 20, "Document Everything," for more information.

```sh
#!/bin/sh

prefix=/usr/local
exec_prefix=${prefix}
exec_prefix_set=no

usage()
{
        cat <<EOF
Usage: libusb-config [OPTIONS] [LIBRARIES]
Options:
        [--prefix[=DIR]]
        [--exec-prefix[=DIR]]
        [--version]
        [--libs]
        [--cflags]
EOF
        exit $1
}

if test $# -eq 0; then
        usage 1 1>&2
fi

while test $# -gt 0; do
  case "$1" in
  -*=*) optarg=`echo "$1" | sed 's/[-_a-zA-Z0-9]*=//'` ;;
  *) optarg= ;;
  esac
  case $1 in
    --prefix=*)
      prefix=$optarg
      if test $exec_prefix_set = no ; then
        exec_prefix=$optarg
      fi
      ;;
    --prefix)
      echo_prefix=yes
      ;;
    --exec-prefix=*)
      exec_prefix=$optarg
      exec_prefix_set=yes
      ;;
```

***Figure 18-1.*** *What does this code do?*

363

```
      --exec-prefix)
        echo_exec_prefix=yes
        ;;
      --version)
        echo 0.1.4
        exit 0
        ;;
      --cflags)
        if test "${prefix}/include" != /usr/include ; then
          includes="-I${prefix}/include"
        fi
        echo_cflags=yes
        ;;
      --libs)
        echo_libs=yes
        ;;
      *)
        usage 1 1>&2
        ;;
    esac
    shift
done

if test "$echo_prefix" = "yes"; then
        echo $prefix
fi
if test "$echo_exec_prefix" = "yes"; then
        echo $exec_prefix
fi
if test "$echo_cflags" = "yes"; then
        echo $includes
fi
if test "$echo_libs" = "yes"; then
        echo -L${exec_prefix}/lib -lusb
fi
```

***Figure 18-1.*** (*continued*)

The few variables I see are assigned in the second case statement and then used to determine the flow through the series of if statements at the bottom. In fact, this code could be refactored to make it simpler by deleting all the if statements and moving the echo statements up into the matching stanza of the case statement. This would eliminate the need for those variables in this code.

I copied the script to a VM and tried it a few times with various option combinations. The results are shown in Figure 18-2 and are not much more illuminating.

```
[root@testvm1 student]# ./libusb-config
Usage: libusb-config [OPTIONS] [LIBRARIES]
Options:
        [--prefix[=DIR]]
        [--exec-prefix[=DIR]]
        [--version]
        [--libs]
        [--cflags]
[root@testvm1 student]# ./libusb-config --version
0.1.4
[root@testvm1 student]# ./libusb-config --libs /usr/lib
Usage: libusb-config [OPTIONS] [LIBRARIES]
Options:
        [--prefix[=DIR]]
        [--exec-prefix[=DIR]]
        [--version]
        [--libs]
        [--cflags]
[root@testvm1 student]# ./libusb-config --prefix=/usr/lib
[root@testvm1 student]# ./libusb-config --prefix=/usr/lib --cflags
-I/usr/lib/include
[root@testvm1 student]# ./libusb-config --prefix=/var/lib --cflags
-I/var/lib/include
[root@testvm1 student]# ./libusb-config --prefix=/lib --cflags
-I/lib/include
[root@testvm1 student]# ./libusb-config --prefix=/lib
[root@testvm1 student]# ./libusb-config --prefix=/lib64
[root@testvm1 student]#
```

*Figure 18-2.* *The results from running this program are not helpful, either*

Nothing like crappy code. How could I fix this code without any idea what it is supposed to do? It *appears* that this code may be just a test or that it is the beginning of some larger script intended to do – something. The real problem with this code is that it takes valuable time to figure out that it apparently does nothing useful.

I eventually used the dnf command shown in Experiment 18-6, below, to discover that this script is part of the USB development library. I have no idea how it came to be in my personal ~/bin directory.

```
┌─────────────────────────────────────────────────────────────────┐
│                       EXPERIMENT 18-6                             │
└─────────────────────────────────────────────────────────────────┘
```

Files that are part of an RPM package in one of the repositories for which your host is configured can be located with the dnf command.

```
[root@david ~]# dnf whatprovides *libusb-config
Last metadata expiration check: 2:10:49 ago on Sat 24 Feb 2018 01:50:16 PM
EST.
libusb-devel-1:0.1.5-10.fc27.i686 : Development files for libusb
Repo        : fedora
Matched from:
Other       : *libusb-config

libusb-devel-1:0.1.5-10.fc27.x86_64 : Development files for libusb
Repo        : fedora
Matched from:
Other       : *libusb-config
```

We now know what RPM package provides this file, so let's see if that package is installed on our host.

```
[root@david ~]# dnf list libusb-devel
Last metadata expiration check: 2:11:35 ago on Sat 24 Feb 2018 01:50:16 PM
EST.
Available Packages
libusb-devel.i686              1:0.1.5-10.fc27                    fedora
libusb-devel.x86_64            1:0.1.5-10.fc27                    fedora
```

These RPMs are available, which means that they have not been installed.

In this case, the results indicate that the script is from an RPM that is not installed on my host. Because it is a development package, it is also unlikely that I would ever have installed it myself. The bottom line is that I can delete this script because – for me at least – it is cruft.

Of course this is all part of the SysAdmin's work, too. Finding these useless scripts in among the ones that perform some needed task and getting rid of them. It also involves finding useless variables, line of code that would never be executed, and other cruft, in otherwise useful scripts and getting rid of it. Identifying and removing cruft takes time and some level of dedication.

# Hardware

We have already talked some about hardware in Chapter 17, "Strive for Elegance." It is an appropriate topic when discussing simplicity, too. Hardware is, after all, the engines on which our software runs.

Hardware is not particularly complex these days. There are standard motherboard sizes, ATX, Mini ATX, Micro ATX, and Extended ATX. Most desktop and tower computer cases are standardized to accept any of these sizes, except perhaps the Extended ATX.

With a little research it is possible to purchase a CPU and RAM memory DIMMs that are compatible with any standard motherboard on the market. Additional adapters such as GPUs, SATA, and USB plug-in adapters, and others are facilitated by the standardized PCI Express bus common to the standard motherboards.

Power supplies are standardized and all fit in spaces specifically allotted to them. The only real difference being the total power wattage that they are capable of supplying. The power connectors have long been standardized as are the voltages that they supply.

USB and SATA connectors make attaching devices from hard drives to mice trivially easy and fast. Devices such as hard drives are standard sizes and fit easily in the space designed for them in today's cases.

I did say that hardware is not especially complex these days, but that is not strictly true. On the macro-level of motherboards, cases, adapters, power supplies, and so on, that is true. But each of those devices becomes more complex at the micro- and nano-levels. As the chips get smaller and more complex, they contain more and more of the logic necessary to make life simpler for the end user.

Perhaps you were not around in the early '80s when the original IBM PC was first released. Integrated circuits (ICs) could contain only a fraction of the components that they do now, and they ran at a tiny fraction of the speeds we now take for granted, let alone those speeds attainable by the extreme overclocking crowd.

In 1981, the Intel 8088 CPU with a single core held 29,000 transistors in an area of 33 square millimeters.[10] The 10-core Core i7 Broadwell-E, the latest of the Intel i-series processors listed on the Wikipedia page in footnote 10, contains 3.2 billion transistors in 246 square millimeters. This is more than 110 thousand times the number of transistors in only 7.5 times the area. All of this extra power makes it possible to do complex things within the CPU itself that used to be done by hand.

---

[10]Wikipedia, *Transistor count*, https://en.wikipedia.org/wiki/Transistor_count

In those early days, the ICs were simpler and had far fewer transistors. Jumper pins and DIP switches were common and confusing ways to configure the hardware. Today I can boot the computer into a BIOS configuration mode and make changes in a GUI environment. But in most cases, even this is not required as both the hardware and the operating system pretty much configure themselves.

# Linux and Hardware

Today's Linux brings amazing levels of simplicity to configuring hardware. Most of the time user intervention is not required. In the past it was often necessary for the Linux user to install device drivers for some hardware. In the present, Linux almost always does all of the work for us.

In Chapter 5 we looked at the Udev daemon and its mechanisms that enable Linux to identify hardware at boot time and when it is hot-plugged some arbitrary time after boot. Let's look at a somewhat simplified version of what takes place when a new device is connected to the host. I stipulate here that the host system is already booted and running at multi-user.target (run level 3) or graphical.target (run level 5).

1. The user plugs in a new device, usually into an external USB, SATA, or eSATA connector.

2. The kernel detects this and sends a message to Udev to announce the new device.

3. Based on the device properties and its location in the hardware bus tree, Udev creates a name for the new device if one does not already exist.

4. The Udev system creates the device special file in /dev.

5. If a new device driver is required, it is loaded.

6. The device is initialized.

7. Udev may send a notification to the desktop so that the desktop may display a notification of the new device to the user.

The overall process of hot-plugging a new hardware device into a running Linux system and making it ready is very complex – for the operating system. It is very simple for the user who just wants to plug in a new device and have it work. This simplifies things immensely for the end user. For USB and SATA hard drives, USB thumb drives, keyboards, mice, printers, displays, and nearly anything else, all I need to do as a user is to plug the device into the appropriate USB or SATA port and it will work.

## The Quandary

To me, the ultimate goal is to make things as simple for the end user as possible. We must not forget that we SysAdmins are also end users. I would much prefer getting actual work accomplished than fiddling with a new device for hours just to get it to work. That is the old way of doing things. But this new way of doing things moves the complexity from the human side of the equation to the software side. And that software complexity is aided by the manifold increase in hardware complexity.

So our quandary is that on the one hand we have been told that our programs should be simple, yet on the other hand that we should move complexity into the software or get rid of it entirely. Hopefully so that the user does not need to deal with it.

Reconciling this tension between complexity and simplicity is the task of both the developer and the System Administrator. The programs and scripts that we create to "automate everything" do need to be as simple as possible. But they also need to be able to perform the tasks at hand in order to simplify the end users' tasks as much as possible.

*Computers are unreliable, but humans are even more unreliable.*

— Gilb's Laws of Unreliability

When you have been a SysAdmin for a certain time, the truth of the preceding quote becomes obvious. Our users will, at some point, always find a way to do something unexpected, which will create more damage and havoc than anything we could possibly do in our programs and scripts. That means our objective must be to follow the basic tenets to write small programs that each do one thing well and interact using STDIO.

Let us not forget the ultimate irony – we SysAdmins are also humans, at least for now – and that makes us users of our own scripts. I have found that as a SysAdmin I am my own worst nightmare as a user. If I write my scripts to deal with the careless mistakes I know that I will make, they will be reasonably reliable. I ensure that my scripts are as reliable as possible by making them as simple as I can and continuously working to simplify them even further.

# The Last Word

*Fools ignore complexity; pragmatists suffer it; experts avoid it; geniuses remove it.*

— Alan Perlis[11]

_____

[11]Wikipedia, *Alan Perlis*, https://en.wikipedia.org/wiki/Alan_Perlis

# CHAPTER 19

# Use Your Favorite Editor

Why is this a tenet of *The Linux Philosophy for System Administrators*? Because arguing about editors can be the cause of a great deal of wasted energy. Everyone has their favorite editor, and it might not be the same as mine. So what?

I use vim as my editor. I have used it for years and like it very much. I am used to it. It meets my needs more than any other editor I have tried. If you can say that about your editor – whichever one that might be – then you are in editor nirvana.

I started using vi when I began learning Solaris over twenty years ago. My mentor suggested that I start learning to edit with vi because it would always be present on every system. That has proven to be true whether the operating system is Solaris or Linux. The vi editor is always there so I can count on it. For me, this works.

The vi editor can also used as the editor for bash command-line editing. Although the default for command editing is emacs, I use the vi option because I already know the vi keystrokes. The option to use vi style editing in bash can be set by adding the line "set -o vi" to the ~/.bashrc file for just your own use. For setting the vi option globally, a configuration file in /etc/profile.d/ is used, so that all users, root and non-privileged have that as part of their bash configuration.

Other tools that use vi editing are the crontab and visudo commands; both of these are wrappers around vi. Lazy SysAdmins use code that already exists, especially when it is open source. Using the vi editor for these tools is an excellent example of that.

There are many other editors available that are also great and powerful and fantastic. I still prefer vi or vim. You should use what you want and don't worry about what everyone else is using. Just because I use vim does not mean you have to use it also. Using the best editor for you is important for your productivity. Once you have learned the keystroke combinations and commands that you use most frequently in an editor, you can be very efficient in editing files of all types.

© David Both 2018
D. Both, *The Linux Philosophy for SysAdmins*, https://doi.org/10.1007/978-1-4842-3730-4_19

# More Than Editors

There is much more to this chapter than just editors. It is really about using the tools that work for you, and the discussions about the best editors are the archetype for those same types of discussions about all kinds of tools.

Discussions about which tools to use, whether about editors, desktops, shells, programming languages, or anything else, are normal and can be very helpful. Those discussions provide knowledge of new things or new information about how known things work and how to make them work better. Thoughtful and respectful discourse can be helpful and even critical to enhancing my knowledge and improving my skills as a SysAdmin. I hope it works that way for you, too.

The problem arises when those discussions degenerate into disrespectful and useless flame wars that only create anger and discord among the participants. I always try to exit those discussions in order to conserve my energies for more productive activities. Let's look at some examples.

# Linux Startup

SystemV and systemd are two different methods of performing the Linux startup sequence. SystemV start scripts and the init program are the old method and systemd using targets is the new method.

Just to ensure that we are all on the same page here, the Linux startup sequence begins after the kernel has loaded either init or systemd, depending upon whether the distribution uses the new or old startup, respectively. The init and systemd programs start and manage all of the other processes, that is, programs, and are both know as the mother of all processes on their respective systems.

Although many modern Linux distributions use the newer systemd for startup, shutdown, and process management, there are still some that do not. One reason for this is that some of the distribution maintainers and some SysAdmins prefer the older SystemV method over the newer systemd.

I think both have their advantages so let me explain my reasoning.

# Why I Prefer SystemV

The primary reason I prefer SystemV is that it is more open because startup is accomplished using bash scripts. After the kernel starts the init program, which is a compiled binary, init launches the rc.sysinit script, which performs many system initialization tasks. After rc.sysinit has completed, init launches the /etc/rc.d/ rc script ,which in turn starts the various services as defined by the SystemV start scripts in the /etc/rc.d/rcX.d, where "X" is the number of the runlevel that is being started.

All of these programs are open and easily knowable scripts. It is possible to read through these scripts and learn exactly what is taking place during the entire startup process. Each script is numbered so that it starts the service for which it is intended in a specific sequence. Services are started serially and only one service is started at a time.

Systemd is a single, large compiled binary executable that is not understandable without access to the source code. It represents a significant refutation of multiple tenets of the Linux philosophy. As a binary, systemd is not directly open to view or easy change by the SysAdmin.

# Why I Prefer systemd

I prefer systemd as my startup mechanism because it starts as many services as possible in parallel, depending upon the current stage in the startup process. This speeds the overall startup and gets the host system to a login screen faster than SystemV.

The systemd startup mechanism is open because all of the configuration files are ASCII text files. Startup configuration can be modified through various GUI and command-line tools, as well as adding or modifying various configuration files.

How many of us ever actually looked at, much less made changes to, rc.sysinit or rc programs? I did look at them but never would I have altered them in any manner. There are configuration files external to the code of these two scripts that enabled modification of the startup process as much as was ever needed.

# The Real Issue

Did you think I could not like both startup systems? I do and I can work with either one.

The real issue with SystemV vs systemd is that there is no choice on the SysAdmin level.[1] The choice of whether to use SystemV or systemd has already been made by the developers, maintainers, and packagers of the various distributions.

Despite the fact that this particular choice has been made for us, our Linux hosts boot up and work, which is what I usually care the most about. As an end user and even as a SysAdmin, my primary concern is whether I can get my work done: work such as writing this book, installing updates, and writing scripts to automate everything. So long as I can do my work, I don't really care about the start sequence used on my distro.

However, I do care when there is a problem during startup. Regardless of which startup system is used on any host, I know enough and am able to follow the sequence of events to find the failure and fix it. That is all that matters.

# Desktop

My preferred desktop is KDE Plasma. Several years ago, around 2008 with the release of Fedora 9, KDE moved from V3.x to V4 with significant changes that caused some serious problems. Some of my favorite KDE applications no longer worked because they had not yet been updated to work with the new version of KDE. I experienced frequent crashes of the desktop that made it impossible to get any real work done. Sometimes KDE would crash several times an hour. This was not good for productivity.

Fortunately I was able to switch to a different desktop and I used GNOME 2 for a year until KDE was usable again.

Then in late 2016 KDE underwent another set of changes that resulted in more instability. This time I made it a priority to learn more about several of the other desktop environments that are available. Starting in December of 2016, I used each of three different desktops for a month so I could really get a feel for how they worked. Just trying something out for a couple hours does not give you any real idea how a desktop works or how it can be configured to work more in line with your own style.

---

[1]OSnews, *"Editorial: Thoughts on Systemd and the Freedom to Choose,"* http://www.osnews.com/story/28026/Editorial_Thoughts_on_Systemd_and_the_Freedom_to_Choose

I tried Cinnamon, LXDE, and GNOME 3 and learned to like each for their own strengths. As a result of these trials, I wrote an article on each, "10 reasons to use Cinnamon as your Linux desktop environment,"[2] "8 reasons to use LXDE,"[3] and "11 reasons to use the GNOME 3 desktop environment for Linux,"[4] to match the one I wrote previously about KDE, "9 reasons to use KDE."[5]

I was able to turn a problem into an opportunity to try some new things: desktops, in this case. Each of these desktops has a number of strengths and each has some things that I found to be drawbacks when I used them.

Even KDE, my favorite desktop, has some issues. It does tend to go through cycles where it is unusable. It is large and takes a great deal of memory. Some of the default applications that it installs and which start when KDE is launched at login, suck up CPU cycles. My post-installation script has code to remove the more problematic KDE applications and turn off the background daemons of others so that my systems are not affected by them. And so I continue to use it when it is usable.

## sudo or Not sudo

I think that part of being a System Administrator and using your favorite tools is to use the tools we have correctly and to have them available without any restrictions. In this case I find that the sudo command is used in a manner for which it was never intended. I have a particular dislike for how the sudo facility is being used in some distributions, especially because it is employed to limit and restrict access by people doing the work of system administration to the tools they need to perform their duties.

   *[SysAdmins] don't use sudo.*

— Paul Venezia[6]

---

[2]Both, David, Opensource.com, *10 reasons to use Cinnamon as your Linux desktop environment*, `https://opensource.com/article/17/1/cinnamon-desktop-environment`

[3]Both, David, Opensource.com, *8 reasons to use LXDE*, `https://opensource.com/article/17/3/8-reasons-use-lxde`

[4]Both, David, Opensource.com, *11 reasons to use the GNOME 3 desktop environment for Linux*, `https://opensource.com/article/17/5/reasons-gnome`

[5]Both, David, Opensource.com, *9 reasons to use KDE*, `https://opensource.com/life/15/4/9-reasons-to-use-kde`

[6]Venezia, Paul, Nine traits of the veteran Unix admin, *InfoWorld*, Feb. 14, 2011, `www.infoworld.com/t/unix/nine-traits-the-veteran-unix-admin-276?page=0,0&source=fssr`

Venezia explains in his *InfoWorld* article that sudo is used as a crutch for SysAdmins. He does not spend a lot of time defending this position or explaining it. He just states this as a fact. And I agree with him – for SysAdmins. We don't need the training wheels in order to do our jobs. In fact they get in the way.

Some distros, such as Ubuntu, use the sudo command in a manner that is intended to make the use of commands that require elevated (root) privileges a little more difficult. In these distros it is not possible to log in directly as the root user so the sudo command is used to allow non-root users temporary access to root privileges. This is supposed to make the person a little more careful about issuing commands that need elevated privileges such as adding and deleting users, deleting files that don't belong to them, installing new software, and generally all of the tasks that are required to administer a modern Linux host. Forcing SysAdmins to use the sudo command as a preface to other commands is supposed to make working with Linux safer.

Using sudo in the manner it is by these distros is, in my opinion, a horrible and ineffective attempt to provide novice SysAdmins with a false sense of security. It is completely ineffective at providing any level of protection. I can issue commands that are just as incorrect or damaging using sudo as I can when not using it. The distros that use sudo to anesthetize the sense of fear that we might issue an incorrect command are doing SysAdmins a great disservice. There is no limit or restriction imposed by these distros on the commands that one might use with the sudo facility. There is no attempt to actually limit the damage that might be done by actually protecting the system from the users and the possibility that they might do something harmful – nor should there be.

So let's be clear about this – these distributions expect the user to perform all of the tasks of system administration. They lull the users – who are really System Administrators if you remember my list from Chapter 1 – into thinking that they are somehow protected from the effects of doing anything bad because they must take this restrictive extra step to enter their own password in order to run the commands.

# Bypass sudo

Distributions that work like this usually lock the password for the root user and Ubuntu is one of these distros. This way no one can log in to root and start working unencumbered. I have set up a VM with Ubuntu 16.04 LTS (Long Term Support) in it so I can show you how to set a password to circumvent the need to use sudo.

**Note**   Experiment 19-1 is optional. It is intended to guide you in using sudo to unlock the root account by setting a password for it. If the distribution you are using does not force you to use sudo, you should skip this experiment.

---

## EXPERIMENT 19-1

Let me stipulate the setup here so that you can reproduce it if you wish. I installed Ubuntu 16.04 LTS[7] and installed it in a VM using VirtualBox. During the installation I created a non-root user, student, with a simple password for this experiment.

Log in as the user student and open a terminal session. Let's look at the entry for root in the /etc/shadow file, which is where the encrypted passwords are stored.

```
student@ubuntu1:~$ cat /etc/shadow
cat: /etc/shadow: Permission denied
```

Permission is denied so we cannot look at the /etc/shadow file. This is common to all distributions so that non-privileged users cannot see and access the encrypted passwords. That access would make it possible to use common hacking tools to crack those passwords so it is insecure to allow that.

Now let's try to su – to root.

```
student@ubuntu1:~$ su -
Password:
su: Authentication failure
```

This fails because the root account has no password and is locked out. Let's use sudo to look at the /etc/shadow file.

```
student@ubuntu1:~$ sudo cat /etc/shadow
[sudo] password for student: <enter the password>
root:!:17595:0:99999:7:::
<snip>

student:$6$tUB/y2dt$A5ML1UEdcL4tsGMiq3KOwfMkbtk3WecMroKN/:17597:0:99999:7:::
<snip>
```

---

[7]Canonical Group LTD, Download web site, https://www.ubuntu.com/download/desktop

I have truncated the results to only show the entry for the root and student users. I have also shortened the encrypted password so that the entry will fit on a single line.

The fields are separated by colons (:) and the second field is the password. Notice that the password field for root is a "bang," known to the rest of the world as an exclamation point (!). This indicates that the account is locked and that it cannot be used.

Now all we need to do to use the root account as proper SysAdmins is to set up a password for the root account.

```
student@ubuntu1:~$ sudo su -
[sudo] password for student: <Enter password for student>
root@ubuntu1:~# passwd root
Enter new UNIX password: <Enter new root password>
Retype new UNIX password: <Re-enter new root password>
passwd: password updated successfully
root@ubuntu1:~#
```

Now we can log in directly on a console as root or su – directly to root instead of having to use sudo for each command. Of course, we could just use sudo su – every time we want to log in as root – but why bother?

---

Please do not misunderstand me. Distributions like Ubuntu and their up- and down-stream relatives are perfectly fine and I have used several of them over the years. When using Ubuntu and related distros, one of the first things I do is set a root password so that I can log in directly as root.

# Valid Uses for sudo

The sudo facility does have its uses. The real intent of sudo is to enable the root user to delegate to one or two non-root users, access to one or two specific privileged commands that they need on a regular basis. The reasoning behind this is that of the lazy sysadmin; allowing the users access to a command or two that requires elevated privileges and that they use constantly, many times per day, saves the SysAdmin a lot of requests from the users and eliminates the wait time that the users would otherwise experience. But most non-root users should never have full root access, just to the few commands that they need.

I sometimes need non-root users to run programs that require root privileges. In cases like this I set up one or two non-root users and authorize them to run that single command. The sudo facility also keeps a log of the user ID of each user that uses it. This might enable me to track down who made an error. That's all it does; it is not a magical protector.

The sudo facility was never intended to be used as a gateway for commands issued by a SysAdmin. It cannot check the validity of the command. It does not check to see if the user is doing something stupid. It does not make the system safe from users who have access to all of the commands on the system even if it is through a gateway that forces them to say "please" – That was never its intended purpose.

*Unix never says please.*

— Rob Pike[8]

This quote about Unix is just as true about Linux as it is about Unix. We SysAdmins log in as root when we need to do work as root and we log out of our root sessions when we are done. Some days we stay logged in as root all day long, but we always work as root when we need to. We never use sudo because it forces us to type more than necessary in order to run the commands we need to do our jobs. Neither Unix nor Linux asks us if we really want to do something, that is, it does not say "Please verify that you want to do this."

Yes, I dislike the way some distros use the sudo command.

# A Few Closing Words

It does not matter to me what tools you use and it should not matter to anyone else, either. What really matters is getting the job done. Whether you are vim or EMACS, systemd or SystemV, RPM or DEB, what difference does it make? The bottom line here is that you should use the tools with which you are most comfortable and that work best for you.

---

[8]Wikipedia, *Rob Pike*, https://en.wikipedia.org/wiki/Rob_Pike

It is of the utmost importance that the tools we choose to use are not restricted or hindered in any manner. The misuse of perfectly good tools to aid and abet this impediment is unconscionable and inimical with all of the freedoms that Linux and open source stand for. It should be resisted and circumvented whenever it is encountered.

One of the greatest strengths of Unix, Linux, and open source in general is that there are usually many options open for each task we need to accomplish. We have more open source word processors available to us than the three or so I remember at the height of the proprietary PC software age.

# CHAPTER 20

# Document Everything

*Real programmers don't comment their code, if it was hard to write, it should be hard to understand and harder to modify.*

— unknown

I, too, would want to remain anonymous if I had written that. It might even have been meant to be sarcasm or irony. Regardless, this does seem to be the attitude of many developers and SysAdmins. There is a poorly disguised ethos among some developers and SysAdmins that one must figure everything out for themselves in order to join the club – whatever club that might be. If you cannot figure it out, they imply, you should go do something else because you don't belong.

First, that is not true. Second, most developers, programmers, and SysAdmins that I know definitely do not subscribe to this view. In fact, the best ones, some of whom have been my mentors over the years, exemplify the exact opposite. The best of the best make documentation – good documentation – a high priority in everything they do.

I have used a lot of software whose creators subscribed to the philosophy that all code is self-explanatory. I have also been required to fix a lot of code that was completely uncommented and otherwise undocumented as well. It seems that many developers and SysAdmins figure if the program works for them, it does not need to be documented.

There are a number of quotes out there similar to the one above. They all tend to espouse the idea that documentation is neither needed nor should it be. Yet throughout my career, I have seen the disastrous results of this lack of documentation. I have been the SysAdmin assigned to fix uncommented code on more than one occasion. That is one of the least enjoyable tasks I have ever had to do.

Part of the problem is that many PHBs do not see documentation as a high priority. I have been involved in many aspects of the IT industry and fortunately most of the companies I worked for believed that documentation was not only important, but that it was crucial to the task at hand, regardless of what that task was.

D. Both, *The Linux Philosophy for SysAdmins*, https://doi.org/10.1007/978-1-4842-3730-4_20

I don't think I have ever heard anyone say, "This documentation is great." Mostly I hear how badly some specific documentation sucks. And I have repeated that refrain myself many times.

And yet there is a lot of really good documentation out there. For example, the documentation for LibreOffice is excellent. It includes several documents in multiple formats including HTML and PDF that range from "Getting Started" to a very complete user's guide for each of the LibreOffice applications.

The documentation for RHEL and CentOS, and that for Fedora – which are all very closely related distributions – are also among the best I have seen in my more than forty years of working in the IT industry.

Good documentation is not easy and takes time. It also requires an understanding of the audience – not only in relation to the purpose of the documentation, but also the technical expertise of the intended readers as well as the languages and cultures of the readers. Rich Bowen covered that quite nicely in his fine article at Opensource.com, "RTFM? How to write a manual worth reading."[1]

There is also the question of what constitutes good documentation for a SysAdmin. We explore these things in this chapter, which is mostly about documenting the scripts we write.

# The Red Baron

One of the more frustrating incidents in my IBM career as a Customer Engineer was to assist with resolving some problems on an IBM 1800[2] process control computer in an oil refinery.

This particular computer was connected to many sensors out in the refinery, and it was used to make adjustments to various components of the processes taking place. Based on the sensor readings, this computer would adjust things such as temperatures and flow rates to ensure that the products of the processes were correct and of high quality. But when things went wrong, it could have been disastrous. I mean, come on! This was process control for a freakin' oil refinery!

---

[1]Bowen, Rich, Opensource.com, *RTFM? How to write a manual worth reading*, https://opensource.com/business/15/5/write-better-docs

[2]Engineering and Technology Wiki, *IBM 1800*, http://ethw.org/IBM_1800

It seems that the programmer who wrote the code did not comment his code very well – or not at all as far as I could tell – not that I had direct access to his proprietary source code. That developer was apparently not a fan of informative error messages, either.

I do have to say that the code was good at detecting errors. It also seems to have been good at shutting off the affected processes out on the ground in the refinery. Nothing blew up, after all. However, to say that the program was deficient at communicating what was wrong was a gross understatement. No matter what the error, no matter what was wrong, the only message printed on the console was, "Curse you, Red Baron," along with a numeric error message that we had to look up in a very long list of error codes. The resulting message from the list was never much help, either.

Just to be fair to IBM, the programmer did not work for IBM.

# My Documentation Philosophy

My philosophy is one that has been drilled into me by my best mentors over the years, "The job is not done until the documentation is complete." This means that everything must be documented. And documentation is definitely not the place to skimp on typing. Still – good documentation means something different to a SysAdmin than it does to an end user.

In the context of the *Linux Philosophy for System Administrators*, we shall consider documentation for the intended audience of our code – ourselves and other SysAdmins. There are two primary types of documentation we SysAdmins need. Some form of decent command-line help option and well-commented shell code.

# The Help Option

The first place I go when looking for documentation to help me understand a shell script is the help facility because my most common need is to understand the syntax of the command that launches the program and available options and required or optional arguments to the command. This type of information is usually available by using the -h option for the desired command.

The bash script template we created in Chapter 10, "Always Use Shell Scripts," contains the template help facility shown in Code Listing 20-1. You have seen this before. Note that this is just a template, like the rest of the script template. All of the details required to provide usable help for the script need to be added and modified in this procedure as necessary. When adding a new option or function, that information should also be recorded in the help facility.

---

**CODE LISTING 20-1**

```
#########################################################################
# Help                                                                  #
#########################################################################
Help()
{
   # Display Help
   echo "Add description of the script functions here."
   echo
   echo "Syntax: template <option list here>"
   echo "options:"
   echo "g     Print the GPL license notification."
   echo "h     Print this Help."
   echo "v     Verbose mode."
   echo "V     Print software version and exit."
   echo
}
```

---

Simple help facilities like this one can answer most of the questions I have about what the script does and the various options available that can be used to modify its behavior. Between the description of the script's functions, the syntax diagram, and the list of options along with a short description of each, makes runtime questions easy to answer.

Good help is the first line of documentation for the scripts we write as SysAdmins. All of the operational documentation must be included in the help procedure. It also means that the user interface of the script should be blindingly obvious and extremely simple so that the need to refer to any form of help is minimized.

# Comment Code Liberally

Comments within code are a form of documentation. In fact, they should be the first and primary form of documentation for SysAdmins.

As part of my own need to document everything, I add many comments to my scripts. When tempted to cut back on comments, I think back to what it was like when I had to interpret and fix uncommented and undocumented code that was written by someone else.

I know many SysAdmins and other developers who think that their code is self-explanatory, even without comments. No matter how good our code is, and even with profuse and well-written comments, code will never be self-explanatory. We all think about problems differently, we write our code differently, and we solve problems differently. Because of the different ways in which we perceive things like code and its structure, the purpose of code that might be perfectly obvious to you even without comments, may be impenetrable to me.

Earlier in this book, we created first a bash script template and then we used the template to create a short script. The template and the script were both well-commented. The point of that is for me to remember to comment my own code as I build it. The comments I include in the script template are a good start.

I think that the first three sections are particularly important. These are the program description, the change history, and the license statement. I have included these here again in Code Listing 20-2 for ease of access.

---

## CODE LISTING 20-2

```bash
#!/bin/bash
###############################################################################
#                            scriptTtemplate                                  #
#                                                                             #
# Use this template as the beginning of a new program. Place a short          #
# description of the script here.                                             #
#                                                                             #
# Change History                                                              #
# 04/12/2017  David Both    Original code. This is a template for creating    #
#                           new Bash shell scripts.                           #
# 01/30/2018  David Both    Add an option for setting test mode.              #
#                                                                             #
#                           Add new history entries as needed.                #
#                                                                             #
```

```
#                                                                       #
#########################################################################
#########################################################################
#########################################################################
#                                                                       #
# Copyright (C) 2007, 2018 David Both                                    #
# LinuxGeek46@both.org                                                   #
#                                                                       #
# This program is free software; you can redistribute it and/or modify  #
# it under the terms of the GNU General Public License as published by   #
# the Free Software Foundation; either version 2 of the License, or      #
# (at your option) any later version.                                    #
#                                                                       #
# This program is distributed in the hope that it will be useful,        #
# but WITHOUT ANY WARRANTY; without even the implied warranty of         #
# MERCHANTABILITY or FITNESS FOR A PARTICULAR PURPOSE.  See the          #
# GNU General Public License for more details.                           #
#                                                                       #
# You should have received a copy of the GNU General Public License      #
# along with this program; if not, write to the Free Software            #
# Foundation, Inc., 59 Temple Place, Suite 330, Boston,                  #
MA  02111-1307  USA    #
#                                                                       #
#########################################################################
```

The program description defines the purpose of the program and a little about its primary functions and options. The change history tells future SysAdmins that may need to perform maintenance on the script, what features were added or removed, bugs that were fixed, who did the work, and when these things took place.

The license statement is used to document the license under which the script is distributed and made available for other users. This is important so that there can be no question about the conditions under which the script can be used, modified, and distributed.

Comments embedded in the code should describe the functions of the code segments to which they refer. They should also contain information about why things are done in a certain way, and explanations of logic where that might not be obvious. For example, the snippet of code in Code Listing 20-3 below has comments about its function, some assumptions I made, an indicator that a new method was used, and the old code was retained as a comment so that the difference could be evaluated.

386

---

**CODE LISTING 20-3**

---

```
#######################################################################
# Processing Intel CPU data
#######################################################################
# NOTE :This assumes certain data to be constant in /proc/cpuinfo based on
#       data from the chipsets.
if [ $verbose == 1 ]
then
    echo "This is an Intel box"
fi
CPUtype="Intel"
# Get number of CPU cores
# CPUs=`cat /proc/cpuinfo | grep "^processor" | wc -l`
# New method below
CPUs=`cat /proc/cpuinfo | grep "cpu cores" | uniq | awk -F: '{print $2}' |
sed -e "s/^ //"`
```

---

Also, the section of code in Code Listing 20-2 has a heading that helps to separate it visually from other sections of the code. This makes it easy to visualize the overall structure and functional flow of the code.

# My Code Documentation Process

Which came first? The program or the documentation. Ideally the documentation should be first. Then the code can be developed to meet the specifications outlined in the documentation. You do create specifications before you write code, don't you? That is another common problem I encounter: the lack of clear specifications for scripts.

As previously mentioned, I like to start coding by creating an outline of my proposed code using comments. This lets me see the structure of the program and determine whether it is clean and elegant, allowing me to change the structure if necessary before I have written any code. Whether I am writing new code or maintaining existing code, comments are the first thing I add. These comments become the specifications for the script I am writing or maintaining. Then I can write the code that enables the actions described in the comments.

But I don't always do all of the comments to begin with. I first create a basic outline containing a bare framework of comments describing the logic of the program. I create an outline of the main body of the program, as much as I can. If I envision using additional procedures, I create and name the empty procedure, then add comments to describe its internal functions.

I then create the code to implement that basic framework. I usually start with the main body of the program, adding new comments as it becomes necessary and then filling in the code to implement the comments. When I arrive at a call that branches to an incomplete function, I write that function and add any comments that might still be required, then write the code to implement the procedure.

This is the answer to the question I posed at the beginning of this section. For me, at least, the documentation comes first. I can hear the Agile proponents' keyboards typing their contrary opinions already. But in a very real sense, what I am doing is Agile, because I write just the documentation I need, just in time to write the code. And then the comments become the documentation as well.

Not everyone will want to work this way or will find it as well suited to their modus operandi as I do. There are as many ways of creating code and documenting it as there are people doing it. Do what works best for you but do it!

# Man Pages

Where do man pages fit into this philosophy of documenting everything? Frankly, not very well for scripts written by SysAdmins.

Early on we discussed the time constraints under which we SysAdmins work, and the fact that most of the scripts we write tend to start out as minimalistic solutions to operational problems. In this type of environment we have little or no time to spend on creating man pages. The bottom line is that I do not spend the time to create man pages.

# Systems Documentation

This type of documentation is not about documenting scripts or programs. It is about documenting the state of the network, the connected hosts, and any work I perform on them. This documentation is critical and important to the customers of my former consulting business, and to any employer where I have worked as a full-time employee or contractor.

At one time I owned a small LLC through which I used to do a bit of consulting on Linux and open source. I still do a bit of consulting for my church and a few friends.

When working with customers I always documented my interactions with them and the work I performed. Documentation like this serves me the same way that a doctor's notes of my visits serve her. It is a permanent record of the customer's environment that I can refer to when talking to them on the phone or engaging in email conversations. It provides me with a running commentary of the problems I find and what actions I take to resolve them.

In some cases, I have years of documentation that covers everything from my first contact with them to the information I discover about their network while I am working on projects for them, the details of hardware I install for them, details of my work on projects, and a record of each time I install updates. I include data in these records such as network diagrams, tables of network IP and MAC addressed with notes about the function of each node. I also keep the output from a script I have written that lists the hardware and some of the configuration details of each Linux host that I work on.

This information has multiple uses. It gives me a record so that I can go back and recall what I have done and the structure of my customer's environment – it is a memory aid for me. I can use it to support my recommendations for additional work when needed. Keeping detailed records also can be useful in the event of a dispute with a customer.

I always create a task list before performing work for a customer so that I do not forget anything that needs to be done. I take notes on that list and then, at the end of the work, the task list becomes part of the documentation of the work I have performed and is supplemented by the notes I took during my performance of the work. For some of my customers I have ended up with over forty pages of this type of documentation.

I typically use LibreOffice Writer for this type of documentation. Writer uses the Open Document Text (ODT) format, which is open and well-known and used by many word-processing programs. Even Microsoft Word can use the odt format.

Using a word processor for this type of documentation allows me to make it pretty so that it looks good when I give copies of it to my customers.

## System Documentation Template

I have created a template – really the outline for a template – that helps me document systems information for organizations I have performed work for in the past. The simplified outline below is what works for me, and it is my suggestion that you use it as a starting place if you do not already have a specification or template for this type of document. Feel free to use and modify it to meet your own unique needs.

1. Title Page.

2. Table of Contents.

3. Index of tables.

4. Index of Illustrations.

5. Index of Code Listings.

6. Introduction – A brief description of the document and the organization.

7. Administrators – A list of the current SysAdmins and their contact information.

8. Internet Connection – A description of the Internet connection and the ISP that provides it. This may include information about the contract dates and costs.

   - Cable run – A description of the physical cable location on the property as it runs from the ISP's street connection across the property, and to the demarcation point, which is usually the ISP's modem/router/switch.

   - External IP Addresses – A list of the external IP Addresses if static and General IP Address range if DHCP.

9. Internal Network – A description of the internal network.

   - Internal IP Address spaces for all internal networks.

   - Firewalls – A description of firewalls that belong to the organization and not the ISP.

   - Physical Description – This includes a text description, a network diagram, and an address map that lists each network node, its name, MAC address, IP address, whether network configuration is static or DHCP, and a very short description of its function.

10. Hardware – A list of each network node.

   - A description of the hardware. This can be created using the mymotd program created earlier in this book.

   - The operating system. For Linux, this includes the distribution and release.

   - A description of the functions provided by the network node.

11. Operating systems and software

   - A list of all operating systems and which hosts they run on.

   - A list of specific software on each host. This does not mean all of the software like the PHPs with no clue might request, but the primary software for which that host is intended. For example you might just say, "Desktop software," for a simple desktop. For servers, this might be, "DHCPD, HTTPD, NAMED," etc.

   - Licenses – Information about software licenses that might be pertinent such as renewal information and costs. Software with proprietary licensing should be listed with license IDs or numbers for reference in case a license compliance audit is required.

12. Host configuration – Common host configuration items such as network configuration in terms of DNS and DHCP servers, default gateway, Email servers, etc.

13. Administrative tasks – A list of various administrative tasks and the SysAdmin or user responsible for performing them or monitoring them if they are automated.

14. Contact lists – Include internal SysAdmin and management contacts and their responsibilities, as well as contacts for all vendors including the ISP, hardware and software vendors, HVAC, data center cooling, UPS, internal security, external security company, external emergency contacts such as fire and police, and anything else you might think of.

15. Activity log – This is my log of contacts with the customer and the work performed by me for the customer. This section should be as explicit as possible when describing problems and their solutions.

This template is a good place to start. Having this type of documentation is important as a memory aid – I always appreciated not having to ask the customer what I did for them because I could easily look it up. You may find it necessary to use a well-maintained document as evidence in a worst-case scenario where the customer or the PHB questions your actions. I was fortunate to never find myself in a worst-case scenario.

# Document Existing Code

Creating the documentation for existing code requires different approaches than any other type.

The first thing I do is read the source code, which is almost always Perl or bash scripts for me. Then I can use the comments as a starting point to create external documentation – if there are any comments and if the comments have any meaning at all.

One job I took a goodly number of years ago, I was to take over maintenance and fix a large number of preexisting bash scripts. Those scripts were part of a series of complex internal applications used by the company. The code worked – mostly – but was excessively convoluted spaghetti code, and it lacked usable comments and documentation of any kind.

My first task was to fix a few bugs in several of the scripts. I started reading these scripts to determine what they actually were supposed to do. As I determined what each section of code did, I added comments that would describe the code I had just read and interpreted. And just in the process of doing that, I was able to determine the cause of some the bugs and correct them.

During this initial stage I determined from reading the bash scripts and questioning the IT folks that the scripts were originally written by several different contractors and had been maintained over a period of years by a series of other contractors. Each of the contractors added on little sections of code that were obviously designed to circumvent the problems that they encountered. None of these add-on bits of code made any attempt to fix the root causes. Each contractor had their own way of doing things such as naming schemes for variables, indents, coding style, and comments. Those scripts were a complete disaster.

That project was a nightmare. It took me weeks to analyze the code and add appropriate, understandable, and useful comments to the code. That task was tedious and made more difficult by apparently random naming of the variables. That was one of the inevitable results of having so many different people working on the scripts without any type of guidance or oversight in terms of either the project objectives or programming style.

After I completed the task of commenting each of these scripts, renaming as many variables as I could, it became much easier to resolve the remaining problems.

Of course code written by others is not the only code with these problems. My own code, especially much of my older code, is subject to these same problems. This occurred because I had not yet learned about the Unix or Linux philosophy. My code did improve over time and when it becomes useful to revisit some of my old code to revise it of fix a problem, I revise it to follow the better programming practices I have learned since I was a baby SysAdmin.

# Keep Docs Updated

I have had a few issues with my own documentation. First among them is neglecting to update documentation in a timely or complete manner. This has caused problems when information I needed had not been properly recorded.

When I discover I have been lax in my documentation, I try to go back and correct it as soon as possible. This usually means correcting and updating the comments embedded in my scripts. It also means fixing the help procedures to be consistent with the changes made to the code.

Updating my customer documentation is also a task I need to keep up with. I sometimes forget to do this as I always seem to be rushing to my next task.

It takes discipline to keep my documentation current. Without constant upkeep, documentation can become hopelessly out of date.

# File Compatibility

File compatibility can also be an issue with external documentation – that is documentation that is outside of my code, such as customer documentation. For several years, I used some open source software that maintained my data in format that was not plain text and was proprietary in the sense that it was not documented and which no other software could access. This is at least in part because I was not aware of the data format and that was my own fault. It is also the fault of the developers of that program because they should have used open formats for the data.

In Chapter 13, "Store Data in Open Format Files," we looked at some of the reasons for using open formats. The emphasis there was on data used by the program itself. Now we are looking at data used by the SysAdmin to maintain various types of documentation such as records of customer visits and repair histories. These are important documents because they enable us to go back and review what has already been done and get a feel for the progress we have made in problem determination of current problems.

So when an upgrade to the program in question failed to properly upgrade the database in which the data was stored, I was unable to access customer notes from several years. Even returning to the previous version of the program did not recover my data because it had been corrupted. And, unfortunately, my backups were not as extensive as they now are, so I could not go back far enough to get a copy that was not corrupt.

I now store my notes in Open Document Format (ODF). ODF is a well-known, open, and documented format, and there are many applications that can work with it. Although that tenet specifically refers to program data, I believe that a corollary should be that documentation should be maintained in an open format such as ODF.

# A Few Thoughts

Documentation is very important to System Administrators. While executing our daily duties, we depend on the documentation that others have left for us. The quality and speed with which we can do our work is directly affected by the quality of that documentation. Here are some guidelines for documenting our scripts.

1. Scripts should be documented with lucid and meaningful comments.

2. Scripts should be easy to read. This is a form of self-documentation.

3. Scripts should have a useful and concise help feature.

4. Following these guidelines results in elegant scripts.

System documentation kept as a record of interactions with customers or as an internal record should always be kept up to date. Entries should be made as soon as the work is completed in order to ensure that the information is recalled as accurately as possible.

Whatever you do and however you choose to work, just remember that the job is not done until the documentation is complete.

# Back Up Everything – Frequently

Nothing can ever go wrong with my computer and I will never lose my data.
<Sarcasm>Right</sarcasm>.

I have experienced data loss for a myriad of reasons, many of them my own fault. Keeping decent backups has always enabled me to continue with minimal interruption. This chapter discusses some of the more common reasons for data loss and methods for preventing data loss and facilitating easy recovery.

## Data Loss

Without going into detail about my own stupidity, here are a few reasons why we may lose data at inopportune times. Of course, there is no opportune time to lose data.

**Self-inflicted** data loss comes in many forms. The most common form is erasure of one or more important files or directories.

Sometimes erasing needed files is accidental. I just erased a bunch of old files in a directory, and it turns out later that one or two are still needed. More often, for me at least, I actually look at the files and decide they are no longer needed. A day, or two, or a week after I delete them, it turns out that I still need at least some of the files I just deleted. I have also made significant changes to a file and saved it. Once again, I find at some time later I made changes and especially deletions that I should not have.

Clearly it is necessary to pay attention when deleting files or making changes to them. That still won't keep us from deleting data we may need later.

**Power failures** can occur for many reasons. This includes momentary power failures that can shut down the computer just as irrevocably as longer ones. Regardless of the reason for the power failure, there is the danger of losing data, especially from

© David Both 2018
D. Both, *The Linux Philosophy for SysAdmins*, https://doi.org/10.1007/978-1-4842-3730-4_21

documents that have not been saved. Modern hard drives and filesystems employ strategies that help to minimize the probabilities of data loss, but it still happens.

I have had my share of power failures. Back before modern, journaling filesystems like EXT3 and EXT4, I did experience some serious data loss. One way to help prevent data loss due to power failures is to invest in Uninterruptible power supplies (UPS) that maintain power on the hosts long enough to perform a shutdown, either manual or triggered by the power failure itself.

**Electromagnetic Interference, EMI**, is a various type of electromagnetic radiation from many different sources. This radiation can interfere with the correct operation of any electronic device, including computers.

When I worked for IBM in their PC customer support center in Atlanta, Georgia, our first office was about a mile from and directly on the centerline of the Dobbins Air Force base runway. Military aircraft of all types flew in and out twenty-four hours a day. There were times when the high-powered military radars would cause multiple systems to crash at the same time. It was just a fact of life in that environment.

Lightning, static electricity, microwaves, old CRT displays, radio frequency bursts on a ground line, all of these and more can cause problems. Good grounding can reduce the effects of all of these types of EMI, as we saw in Chapter 17. But that does not make our computers completely immune to the effects of EMI.

**Hard drive failures** also cause data loss. The most common failures in today's computers are devices that have moving mechanical components. Leading the frequency list are cooling fans, and hard drives are a close second. Modern hard drives have SMART capabilities that enable predictive failure analysis. Linux can monitor these drives and send an email to root indicating that failure is imminent. Do not ignore those emails because replacing a hard drive before it fails is less trouble than replacing one after it fails and then hoping the backups are up to date.

**Disgruntled employees** can maliciously destroy data. Proper security procedures can mitigate this type of threat, but backups are still handy.

**Theft** is also a way to lose data. Soon after we moved to Raleigh, North Carolina, in 1993, there was a series of articles in the local paper and TV that covered the tribulations of a scientist at one of our better-known universities. This scientist kept all of his data on a single computer. He did have a backup – to another hard drive on that same computer. When the computer was stolen from his office, all of his experimental data went missing as well and it was never recovered.

This is one very good reason to keep good backups separate from the host being backed up.

**Natural disasters** occur. Fire, flood, hurricanes, tornadoes, mud slides, tsunamis, and so many more kinds of disasters can destroy computers and locally stored backups as well. I can guarantee that, even if I have a good backup, I will never take the time during a fire, tornado, or natural disaster that places me in imminent danger to save the backups.

**Malware** is software that can be used for various malicious purposes, including destroying or deleting your data.

**Ransomware** is a specific form of malware that encrypts your data and holds it for ransom. If you pay the ransom, you may get the key that will allow you to decrypt your data – if you are lucky.

So, as you can see, there are many ways to lose your data. My intent with this list of possible ways in which data can be damaged or lost is to scare you into doing backups. Did it work?

# Backups to the Rescue

Recently, very recently – while I was working on this book, actually – I encountered a problem in the form of a hard drive crash that destroyed the data in my home directory. I had been expecting this for some time, so it came as no surprise.

## The Problem

The first indication I had that something was wrong was a series of emails from the S.M.A.R.T (Self-Monitoring, Analysis and Reporting Technology) enabled hard drive on which my home directory resided.[1] Each of these emails indicated that one or more sectors had become defective and that the defective sectors had been taken offline and reserved sectors allocated in their place. This is normal operation; hard drives are designed intentionally with reserved sectors for just this reason.

We will discuss curiosity in some detail in Chapter 22, "Follow Your Curiosity," but I put mine to use when these error messages started arriving in my email inbox several

---

[1]Your host must have a mail transfer agent (MTA) such as SendMail installed and running. The /etc/aliases file must have an entry to send root's email to your email address.

months ago. I first used the `smartctl` command to view the internal statistics for the hard drive in question. The original, defective hard drive has been replaced but – yes, I keep some old, defective devices for teachable moments like this. I installed this damaged hard drive in my docking station to demonstrate what the results of a defective hard drive look like.

You can perform this experiment along with me, but your results will be different – hopefully healthier than my defective drive.

The SMART reports used in Experiment 21-1 can be a bit confusing. The web page, "Understanding SMART Reports,[2]" can help somewhat with that. Wikipedia also has an interesting page on this technology.[3] I recommend reading those documents before attempting to interpret the SMART results; they can be very confusing.

---

**Note**   Be sure to perform this experiment on a physical host that is not in production use. The hardware status of a virtual hard drive is irrelevant.

---

---
**EXPERIMENT 21-1**
---

This experiment must be performed as root.

After installing the drive in the docking station and turning it on, the dmesg command showed the drive to be assigned as device special file /dev/sdi. Be sure to use the correct device special file for your hard drive. You can use any physical hard drive installed in your host, even if it is in use.

I have divided the results of the command into sections for easier reference during the discussion, and I have removed a large amount of irrelevant data.

```
[root@david ~]# smartctl -x /dev/sdi | less
smartctl 6.5 2016-05-07 r4318 [x86_64-linux-4.15.6-300.fc27.x86_64] (local
build)
Copyright (C) 2002-16, Bruce Allen, Christian Franke, www.smartmontools.org
```

---

[2]*Understanding SMART Reports*, https://lime-technology.com/wiki/Understanding_ SMART_Reports
[3]Wikipedia, *SMART*, https://en.wikipedia.org/wiki/SMART

```
=== START OF INFORMATION SECTION ===
Model Family:      Seagate Barracuda 7200.11
Device Model:      ST31500341AS
Serial Number:     9VS2F303
LU WWN Device Id: 5 000c50 01572aacc
Firmware Version: CC1H
User Capacity:     1,500,301,910,016 bytes [1.50 TB]
Sector Size:       512 bytes logical/physical
Rotation Rate:     7200 rpm
Device is:         In smartctl database [for details use: -P show]
ATA Version is:    ATA8-ACS T13/1699-D revision 4
SATA Version is:   SATA 2.6, 3.0 Gb/s
Local Time is:     Wed Mar 14 14:19:03 2018 EDT
SMART support is: Available - device has SMART capability.
SMART support is: Enabled
AAM level is:      0 (vendor specific), recommended: 254
APM feature is:    Unavailable
Rd look-ahead is: Enabled
Write cache is:    Enabled
ATA Security is:   Disabled, NOT FROZEN [SEC1]
Wt Cache Reorder: Unknown
=== START OF READ SMART DATA SECTION ===
SMART Status not supported: Incomplete response, ATA output registers missing
SMART overall-health self-assessment test result: PASSED
Warning: This result is based on an Attribute check.
```

The first section of results, shown just above, provides basic information about the hard drive capabilities and attributes such as brand, model, and serial number. This is interesting and good information to have. However, this section shows that this SMART data report must be taken with a bit of skepticism. Notice that my known defective drive has passed the self-assessment test. That appears to mean that the drive is not about to fail catastrophically even though it already has.

The data we are most interested in at present is in the next two sections. Notice that I have trimmed out a great deal of the information not essential to this experiment.

```
=== START OF READ SMART DATA SECTION ===
<snip - removed list of SMART capabilities.>
```

399

```
SMART Attributes Data Structure revision number: 10
Vendor Specific SMART Attributes with Thresholds:
ID# ATTRIBUTE_NAME           FLAGS    VALUE WORST THRESH FAIL RAW_VALUE
  1 Raw_Read_Error_Rate      POSR--   116   086   006    -    107067871
  3 Spin_Up_Time             PO----   099   099   000    -    0
  4 Start_Stop_Count         -O--CK   100   100   020    -    279
  5 Reallocated_Sector_Ct    PO--CK   048   048   036    -    2143
  7 Seek_Error_Rate          POSR--   085   060   030    -    365075805
  9 Power_On_Hours           -O--CK   019   019   000    -    71783
 10 Spin_Retry_Count         PO--C-   100   100   097    -    0
 12 Power_Cycle_Count        -O--CK   100   100   020    -    279
184 End-to-End_Error         -O--CK   100   100   099    -    0
187 Reported_Uncorrect       -O--CK   001   001   000    -    1358
188 Command_Timeout          -O--CK   100   098   000    -    12885622796
189 High_Fly_Writes          -O-RCK   001   001   000    -    154
190 Airflow_Temperature_Cel  -O---K   071   052   045    -    29 (Min/Max 22/29)
194 Temperature_Celsius      -O---K   029   048   000    -    29 (0 22 0 0 0)
195 Hardware_ECC_Recovered   -O-RC-   039   014   000    -    107067871
197 Current_Pending_Sector   -O--C-   100   100   000    -    0
198 Offline_Uncorrectable    ----C-   100   100   000    -    0
199 UDMA_CRC_Error_Count     -OSRCK   200   200   000    -    20
240 Head_Flying_Hours        ------   100   253   000    -    71781 (50 96 0)
241 Total_LBAs_Written       ------   100   253   000    -    2059064490
242 Total_LBAs_Read          ------   100   253   000    -    260980229
                            ||||||_ K auto-keep
                            |||||__ C event count
                            ||||___ R error rate
                            |||____ S speed/performance
                            ||_____ O updated online
                            |_____ P prefailure warning
```

The preceding section of results from the smartctl command displays raw data accumulated in the hardware registers on the drive. The raw values are not particularly helpful for some of the error rates; as you can see, some of the numbers are clearly bogus. The "Value" column is usually more helpful. Read the referenced web pages to understand a bit about why. In general, numbers like 100 in the Value column mean 100% good and low numbers like 001 mean close to failure – sort of 99% of the useful life is used up. It is really very strange.

In this case, 048 in the Value column for Reallocated_Sector_Ct – Reallocated Sector Count – sort of might mean that about half of the sectors allocated for reallocation have been used up.

The number 001 for Reported_Uncorrect – Reported defective sectors that are uncorrectable – and High_Fly_Writes – writes in which the heads were flying further off the recording surface of the hard drive than is optimal – means that the life of this hard drive is effectively over. This has been shown to be the case with empirical evidence.

This next section actually lists errors and information about them when they occur. This is the most helpful part of the output. I do not try to analyze every error; I simply look to see if there are multiple errors. The number 1350, in the first line below is the total number of errors detected on this hard drive.

```
<Snip>
Error 1350 [9] occurred at disk power-on lifetime: 2257 hours (94 days + 1
hours)
  When the command that caused the error occurred, the device was active
  or idle.

  After command completion occurred, registers were:
  ER -- ST COUNT  LBA_48  LH LM LL DV DC
  -- -- -- ==  -- == == ==  -- -- -- -- --
  40 -- 51 00  00 00 04 ed 00 14 59 00 00  Error: UNC at LBA = 0x4ed001459 =
  21156074585

  Commands leading to the command that caused the error were:
  CR FEATR COUNT  LBA_48  LH LM LL DV DC  Powered_Up_Time  Command/Feature_Name
  -- == -- ==  -- == == ==  -- -- -- -- --  ---------------  ------------------
  60 00 00 00  08 00 04 ed 00 14 58 40 00  11d+10:44:56.878  READ FPDMA QUEUED
  27 00 00 00  00 00 00 00 00 00 00 e0 00  11d+10:44:56.851  READ NATIVE MAX
                                                             ADDRESS EXT
                                                             [OBS-ACS-3]
  ec 00 00 00  00 00 00 00 00 00 00 a0 00  11d+10:44:56.849  IDENTIFY DEVICE
  ef 00 03 00  46 00 00 00 00 00 00 a0 00  11d+10:44:56.836  SET FEATURES [Set
                                                             transfer mode]
  27 00 00 00  00 00 00 00 00 00 00 e0 00  11d+10:44:56.809  READ NATIVE MAX
                                                             ADDRESS EXT
                                                             [OBS-ACS-3]
```

Error 1349 [8] occurred at disk power-on lifetime: 2257 hours (94 days + 1 hours)

When the command that caused the error occurred, the device was active or idle.

After command completion occurred, registers were:
ER -- ST COUNT  LBA_48  LH LM LL DV DC
-- -- -- == -- == == == -- -- -- -- --
40 -- 51 00 00 00 04 ed 00 14 59 00 00  Error: UNC at LBA = 0x4ed001459 = 21156074585

Commands leading to the command that caused the error were:

| CR | FEATR | COUNT | LBA_48 | | LH | LM | LL | DV | DC | Powered_Up_Time | Command/Feature_Name |
|----|-------|-------|--------|--|----|----|----|----|----|-----------------|----------------------|
| -- | == | -- | == | -- | == | == | == | -- | -- | -- | -- | -- | --------------- | ------------------- |
| 60 | 00 | 00 | 00 08 | 00 04 ed 00 14 58 | 40 | 00 | 11d+10:44:53.953 | READ FPDMA QUEUED |
| 60 | 00 | 00 | 00 08 | 00 04 f4 00 14 10 | 40 | 00 | 11d+10:44:53.890 | READ FPDMA QUEUED |
| 60 | 00 | 00 | 00 10 | 00 04 f4 00 14 00 | 40 | 00 | 11d+10:44:53.887 | READ FPDMA QUEUED |
| 60 | 00 | 00 | 00 10 | 00 04 f3 00 14 f0 | 40 | 00 | 11d+10:44:53.886 | READ FPDMA QUEUED |
| 60 | 00 | 00 | 00 10 | 00 04 f3 00 14 e0 | 40 | 00 | 11d+10:44:53.886 | READ FPDMA QUEUED |

Error 1348 [7] occurred at disk power-on lifetime: 2257 hours (94 days + 1 hours)

When the command that caused the error occurred, the device was active or idle.

After command completion occurred, registers were:
ER -- ST COUNT  LBA_48  LH LM LL DV DC
-- -- -- == -- == == == -- -- -- -- --
40 -- 51 00 00 00 04 ed 00 14 59 00 00  Error: UNC at LBA = 0x4ed001459 = 21156074585

Commands leading to the command that caused the error were:

| CR | FEATR | COUNT | LBA_48 | | LH | LM | LL | DV | DC | Powered_Up_Time | Command/Feature_Name |
|----|-------|-------|--------|--|----|----|----|----|----|-----------------|----------------------|
| -- | == | -- | == | -- | == | == | == | -- | -- | -- | -- | -- | --------------- | ------------------- |
| 60 | 00 | 00 | 00 08 | 00 04 ed 00 14 58 | 40 | 00 | 11d+10:44:50.892 | READ FPDMA QUEUED |
| 27 | 00 | 00 | 00 00 | 00 00 00 00 00 00 | e0 | 00 | 11d+10:44:50.865 | READ NATIVE MAX ADDRESS EXT [OBS-ACS-3] |
| ec | 00 | 00 | 00 00 | 00 00 00 00 00 00 | a0 | 00 | 11d+10:44:50.863 | IDENTIFY DEVICE |

```
ef 00 03 00 46 00 00 00 00 00 00 a0 00 11d+10:44:50.850   SET FEATURES [Set
                                                           transfer mode]
27 00 00 00 00 00 00 00 00 00 00 e0 00 11d+10:44:50.823   READ NATIVE MAX
                                                           ADDRESS EXT
                                                           [OBS-ACS-3]
```

Error 1347 [6] occurred at disk power-on lifetime: 2257 hours (94 days +
1 hours)
 When the command that caused the error occurred, the device was active or
 idle.

<Snip - removed many redundant error listings>

**These errors are indicative that something really is wrong with the disk.**

I decided I would wait to see what else occurred before I replaced the hard drive. The failure numbers were not as bad in the beginning. The error count rose to 1350 at the time of the catastrophic failure.

Some testing of over 67,800 SMART drives[4] by a cloud company named Backblaze provides some statistically based insight into failure rates of hard drives that experienced various numbers of reported errors. This web page is the first I have found that demonstrates a statistically relevant correlation between reported SMART errors and actual failure rates. Their web page also helped improve my understanding of the five SMART attributes that they found should be closely monitored.

In my opinion, the bottom line of the Backblaze analysis is that hard drives should be replaced as soon as possible after they begin to experience error reports in any of the five statistics they recommend monitoring.

My experience seems to confirm that although it was not even close to being statistically significant. My drive failed within a couple months of the first indications that there was a problem. The number of errors my drive experienced before failing beyond recovery is very high, and I had been very lucky to have been able to recover from several errors that caused the /home filesystem to switch to read-only (ro) mode. This only occurs when Linux determines that the filesystem is unstable and cannot be trusted.

---

[4]BackBlaze, Web site, "What SMART Stats Tell Us About Hard Drives," https://www.backblaze. com/blog/what-smart-stats-indicate-hard-drive-failures/

# Recovery

So that was all just a long way to say that the drive containing my home directory failed catastrophically. Recovery was straightforward if a bit time consuming.

I turned off the computer, removed the defective 320GB SATA drive, replaced it with a new 1TB SATA drive because I want to use the extra space for other storage later, and turned the computer back on. I created a physical volume (PV) that takes up all of the space on the drive, and then a volume group (VG) that fills the PV. I used 250GB of that space for a logical volume (LV) that was to be the /home filesystem. I then created an EXT4 filesystem on the logical volume and used the e2label command to give it the label "home" because I mount filesystems using labels. At this point the replacement drive was ready so I mounted it on /home.

As a result of the method I use to create my backups, it is only necessary for me to use a simple copy command, like that shown in Code Sample 21-1, to restore the entire home directory to the newly installed drive.

---

**CODE SAMPLE 21-1**

Note that to ensure that the data being restored would not be corrupted, I could not be logged in as any non-root user that has files in the /home filesystem. I logged in on a virtual console as root and used the following command to restore the data from my backup to the newly installed and prepared replacement hard drive.

```
cp -Rp /media/Backups/Backups/david/2018-03-04-RSBackup/home/ /home
```

The "R" option recurses through the entire /home directory structure and copies everything in the entire directory tree. The "p" option preserves the ownership and permissions attributes for the files.

---

After restoring the data to my /home directory, I logged in using my non-privileged user ID and checked things out. Everything worked as expected, and all of my data had been restored correctly, including the files for this book.

# Doing It My Way

My backups shell script is one of those programs that had the advantage of — well — being planned. This is because I wrote, used, and figured out what was wrong with a number of my own backup scripts prior to this one. I was able to more completely understand what I really needed in a backup system.

Once again, I started with a set of requirements. Ones I had been considering for several months. I already had a backup script that used tar to create backups in tgz files. But it was a good bit of work and took some time to deal with extracting single files or directories from the tar files. It also took over an hour each night to make the backups. And despite the gzip compression, the large files meant that only a few days history could be kept on the external USB hard drives I use for backups because everything was backed up completely multiple times.

I have a lot of files that I have accumulated over the years. Some of those files are very large, particularly the ones for my virtual machines. At this time, I have about 18 VMs that each have very large virtual disks associated with them. This takes up huge amounts of space.

So I wanted a backup solution that was fast, would easily and quickly handle very large files, which would allow more history on a single backup drive by saving space without creating some type of compressed archive, and that would be easy for me or my customers to access specific files when needed.

# Backup Options

There are many options for performing backups. In addition to old favorites like `tar`, most Linux distributions are provided with one or more additional open source programs especially designed to perform backups. There are many commercial options available as well.

None of these solutions fully met my needs and I really wanted to use another tool I had heard about, `rsync`.[5] Fancy and expensive backup programs are not really necessary to design and implement a viable backup program.

I had been experimenting with the `rsync` command, which has some very interesting features that I have been able to use to good advantage. My primary objectives were to create backups from which users could locate and restore files quickly without having to extract data from a backup tarball, and to reduce the amount of time taken to create and the backups.

---

[5]Wikipedia, *rsync*, `https://en.wikipedia.org/wiki/Rsync`

This section is intended only to describe my own use of `rsync` in a backup scenario. It is not a look at all of the capabilities of `rsync` or the many other interesting ways in which it can be used.

## rsync

The `rsync` command was written by Andrew Tridgell and Paul Mackerras and first released in 1996. The primary intention for `rsync` is to remotely synchronize the files on one computer with those on another. Did you notice what they did to create the name there? `rsync` is open source software and is provided with all of the distros with which I am familiar.

The `rsync` command can be used to synchronize two directories or directory trees whether they are on the same computer or on different computers, but it can do so much more than that. `rsync` creates or updates the target directory to be identical to the source directory. The target directory is freely accessible by all the usual Linux tools because it is not stored in a tarball or zip file or any other archival file type; it is just a regular directory with regular files that can be navigated by regular users using basic Linux tools. This meets one of my primary objectives.

One of the most important features of `rsync` is the method it uses to synchronize preexisting files that have changed in the source directory. Rather than copying the entire file from the source, it uses checksums to compare blocks of the source and target files. If all of the blocks in the two files are the same, no data is transferred. If the data differs, only the block that has changed on the source is transferred to the target. This saves an immense amount of time and network bandwidth for remote sync. For example, when I first used my `rsync` bash script to back up all of my hosts to a large external USB hard drive, it took about 3 hours. That is because all of the data had to be transferred because none of it had been previously backed up. Subsequent backups took between 3 and 8 minutes of real time, depending upon how many files had been changed or created since the previous backup. I used the `time` command to determine this, so it is empirical data. Last night, for example, it took 3 minutes and 12 seconds to complete a backup of approximately 750GB of data from 6 remote systems and the local workstation. Of course, only a few hundred megabytes of data were actually altered during the day and needed to be backed up.

The simple `rsync` command shown in Code Sample 21-2 can be used to synchronize the contents of two directories and any of their subdirectories. That is, the contents of the target directory are synchronized with the contents of the source directory so that at the end of the sync, the target directory is identical to the source directory.

---

### CODE SAMPLE 21-2

This is the minimum command necessary to synchronize two directories using `rsync`.

```
rsync -aH sourcedir targetdir
```

The -a option is for archive mode, which preserves permissions, ownerships, and symbolic (soft) links. The -H is used to preserve hard links rather than creating a new file for each hard link. Note that either the source or target directories can be on a remote host.

---

Now let's assume that yesterday we used `rsync` to synchronize two directories. Today we want to resync them, but we have deleted some files from the source directory. The normal way in which `rsync` would do this is to simply copy all the new or changed files to the target location and leave the deleted files in place on the target. This may be the behavior you want, but if you would prefer that files deleted from the source also be deleted from the target, that is, the backup, you can add the --delete option to make that happen.

Another interesting option, and my personal favorite because it increases the power and flexibility of rsync immensely, is the --link-dest option. The --link-dest option uses hard links,[6][7] to create a series of daily backups that take up very little additional space for each day and also take very little time to create.

Specify the previous day's target directory with this option and a new directory for today. The `rsync` command then creates today's new directory and a hard link for each file in yesterday's directory is created in today's directory. So we now have a bunch of hard links to yesterday's files in today's directory. No new files have been created or duplicated. Just a bunch of hard links to the files from yesterday have been created. After creating the target directory for today with this set of hard links to yesterday's target

---

[6]Wikipedia, *Hard Links*, https://en.wikipedia.org/wiki/Hard_link
[7]Both, David, DataBook for Linux, *Using hard and soft links in the Linux filesystem*, http://www.linux-databook.info/?page_id=5087

directory, rsync performs its sync as usual, but when a change is detected in a file, the target hard link is replaced by a copy of the file from yesterday and the changes to the file are then copied from the source to the target.

So now our command looks like that in Code Sample 21-3.

---

## CODE SAMPLE 21-3

This version of our rsync command first creates hard links in today's backup directory for each file in yesterday's backup directory. The files in the source directory – the one being backed up – are then compared to the hard links that were just created. If there are no changes to the files in the source directory, no further action is taken.

```
rsync -aH --delete --link-dest=yesterdaystargetdir sourcedir todaystargetdir
```

If there are changes to files in the source directory, rsync deletes the hard link to the file in yesterday's backup directory and makes an exact copy of the file from yesterday's backup. It then copies the changes made to the file from the source directory to today's target backup directory.

rsync also deletes files on the target drive or directory that have been deleted from the source directory.

---

There are also times when it is desirable to exclude certain directories or files from being synchronized. We usually do not care about backing up cache directories and, because of the large amount of data they can contain, the amount of time required to back them up can be huge compared to other data directories. For this there is the --exclude option. Use this option and the pattern for the files or directories you want to exclude. You might want to exclude browser cache files so your new command will look like Code Sample 21-4.

---

## CODE SAMPLE 21-4

```
rsync -aH --delete --exclude Cache --link-dest=yesterdaystargetdir sourcedir
todaystargetdir
```

Note that each file pattern you want to exclude must have a separate exclude option.

---

The rsync command can sync files with remote hosts as either the source or the target. For the next example, let's assume that the source directory is on a remote computer with the hostname remote1 and the target directory is on the local host. Even though SSH is the default communications protocol used when transferring data to or from a remote host, I always add the ssh option. The command now looks like this.

---

**CODE SAMPLE 21-5**

---

In this code segment the source directory is located on the remote host, remote1.

```
rsync -aH -e ssh --delete --exclude Cache --link-dest=yesterdaystargetdir
remote1:sourcedir todaystargetdir
```

This command backs up the data from the directory on the remote host to the local host.

---

The rsync command has a very large number of options that you can use to customize the synchronization process. For the most part, the relatively simple commands that I have described here are perfect for making backups for my personal needs. Be sure to read the extensive man page for rsync to learn about more of its capabilities as well as details of the options discussed here.

## Performing Backups

I automated my backups because – "automate everything." I wrote a bash script, rsbu, which handles the details of creating a series of daily backups using rsync. This includes ensuring that the backup medium is mounted, generating the names for yesterday and today's backup directories, creating appropriate directory structures on the backup medium if they are not already there, performing the actual backups, and unmounting the medium.

The end result of the method in which I employ the rsync command in my script is that I end up with a date-sequence of backups for each host in my network. The backup drives end up with a structure similar to the one shown in Figure 21-1. This makes it easy to locate specific files that might need to be restored.

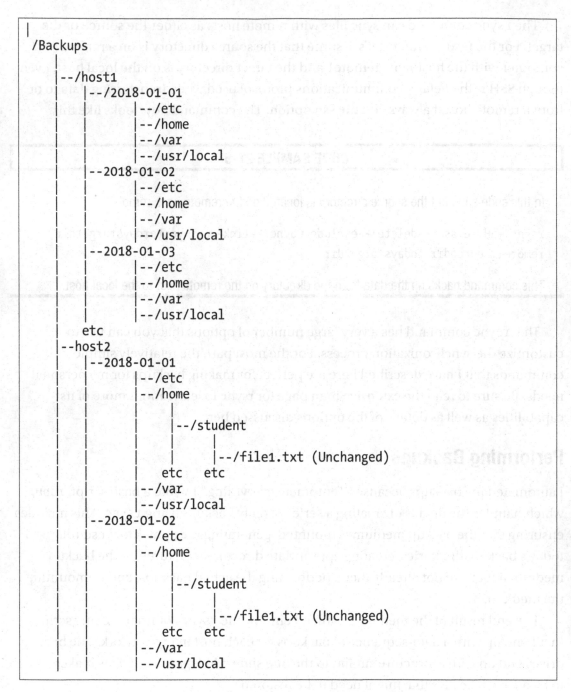

*Figure 21-1.* *The directory structure for my backup data disks*

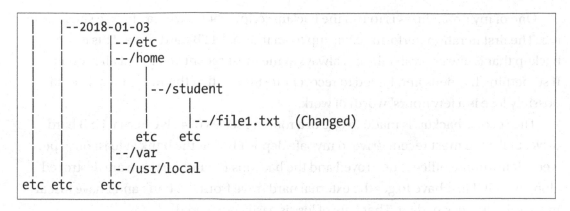

*Figure 21-1.* (*continued*)

So, starting with an empty disk on January 1, the rsbu script makes a complete backup for each host of all the files and directories that I have specified in the configuration file. This first backup can take several hours if you have a lot of data like I do.

On January 2, the rsync command uses the –link-dest= option to create a complete new directory structure identical to that of January 1, then it looks for files that have changed in the source directories. If any have changed, A copy of the original file from January 1 is made in the January 2 directory and then the parts of the file that have been altered are updated from the original.

After the first backup onto an empty drive, the backups take very little time because the hard links are created first, and then only the files that have been changed since the previous backup need any further work.

Figure 21-1 also shows a bit more detail for the host2 series of backups for one file, /home/student/file1.txt, on the dates January 1, 2, and 3. On January 2 the file has not changed since January 1. In this case, the rsync backup does not copy the original data from January 1. It simply creates a directory entry with a hard link in the January 2 directory to the January 1 directory, which is a very fast procedure. We now have two directory entries pointing to the same data on the hard drive. On January 3, the file has been changed. In this case, the data for ../2018-01-02/home/student/file1.txt is copied to the new directory, ../2018-01-03/home/student/file1.txt and any data blocks that have changed are then copied to the backup file for January 3. These strategies, that are implemented using features of the rsync program, allow backing up huge amounts of data while saving disk space and much of the time that would otherwise be required to copy data files that are identical.

One of my procedures is to run the backup script twice each day from a single cron job. The first iteration performs a backup to an internal 4TB hard drive. This is the backup that is always available and always at the most recent version of all my data. If something happens and I need to recover one file or all of them, the most I could possibly lose is a few hours' worth of work.

The second backup is made to one of a rotating series of 4TB external USB hard drive. I take the most recent drive to my safe deposit box at the bank at least once per week. If my home office is destroyed and the backups I maintain there are destroyed along with it, I just have to get the external hard drive from the bank and I have lost at most a single week of data. That type of loss is easily recovered.

The drives I am using for backups, not just the internal hard drive but also the external USB hard drives that I rotate weekly, never fill up. This is because the `rsbu` script I wrote checks the ages in days of the backups on each drive before a new backup is made. If there are any backups on the drive that are older than the specified number of days, they are deleted. The script uses the `find` command to locate these backups. The number of days is specified in the rsbu.conf configuration file.

Of course, after a complete disaster, I would first have to find a new place to live with office space for my wife and me, purchase parts and build new computers, restore from the remaining backup, and then re-create any lost data.

My script, rsbu, is available along with its configuration file, rsbu.conf, and a READ. ME file from `https://github.com/Apress/linux-philo-sysadmins/tree/master/Ch21`

# Recovery Testing

No backup regimen would be complete without testing. You should regularly test recovery of random files or entire directory structures to ensure not only that the backups are working, but that the data in the backups can be recovered for use after a disaster. I have seen too many instances where a backup could not be restored for one reason or another, and valuable data was lost because the lack of testing prevented discovery of the problem.

Just select a file or directory to test and restore it to a test location such as /tmp so that you won't overwrite a file that may have been updated since the backup was performed. Verify that the files' contents are as you expect them to be. Restoring files from a backup made using the rsync commands above simply a matter of finding the file you want to restore from the backup and then copying it to the location you want to restore it to.

I have had a few circumstances where I have had to restore individual files and, occasionally, a complete directory structure. I have had to restore the entire contents of a hard drive on a couple of occasions, as I discussed earlier in this chapter. Most of the time this has been self-inflicted when I accidentally deleted a file or directory. At least a few times it has been due to a crashed hard drive. So those backups do come in handy.

# Off-Site Backups

Creating good backups is an important first step in a backup strategy. Keeping the resulting backup media in the same physical location as your original data is a mistake.

We have seen that theft of a computer that has all its backups on an internal drive can result in the complete and irrecoverable loss of important data. Fire and other disasters can also result in the loss of original data and the backup data if it is stored in the same location. Fireproof safes are one option that can reduce the threat from both theft and disaster like fire. Such safes are usually rated in minutes at specified temperatures for which they are supposed to protect their contents. I guess my personal concern here is that I have no idea how long or hot a fire will burn. Perhaps the safe will hold out long enough, but what if it does not?

I prefer to do for my own backups what the large companies do. I keep current off-site backups. For me this is in the safe deposit box at my bank. For others this might be "in the cloud" somewhere. I like the end-to-end control I have with my safe deposit box solution. I know it is well protected. If my little home office is destroyed, the bank is likely far enough away that it will not be affected by whatever disaster occurred.

For large companies, there are services that store your backups in a remote, high security location with climate-controlled vaults. Most of these services will even send armored trucks to your facilities to pick up and transport your backup media. Some provide high-speed network connections so that backups can be made directly onto their own storage media at their remote locations.

Many people and organizations are making backups to the cloud these days. I have serious reservations about the so-called "cloud." First, "cloud" is just another word for someone else's computer. Second, considering the number of hacks into allegedly secure computing facilities that I have been reading about, I am not likely to trust my data to any external organization that maintains online backups accessible from the Internet. I would much prefer my remote backup data to be off line until I need it.

The concern I have with the cloud is that, aside from the marketing information the providers put on their web sites, there is no way for me to actually know whether their security measures are better than I can do for myself. Perhaps they can but as a SysAdmin I would like some proof of this. I have no doubt that a good portion of the cloud providers can do a better job of managing the security of the data entrusted to them than many businesses and individuals do. How do I know which ones those are? Remember that we are talking about cloud-based backup solutions, not application or web presence solutions.

What I think I can say with some level of confidence is that the established and recognized cloud providers, such as Amazon, Azure, Google, and others, are certainly more trustworthy when it comes to security than are many small or medium organizations. I am thinking about the ones don't have a full-time SysAdmin, or outsource IT to small, local companies that are not especially reputable. I also think that many less experienced SysAdmins are not ready to deal with the high level of security required on the Internet in today's world of constant cyberattack.

So for many organizations, the cloud may be a viable option. For others, an experienced and knowledgeable SysAdmin may be the best choice. As with many IT decisions, it is a matter of weighing the risk factors and determining how much you are willing to accept.

# Disaster Recovery Services

Taking backups a step further, some of the places I have worked maintained a contract with one or more disaster recovery services. This type of service is paid to maintain a complete computer and network environment that can replace your own on a moment's notice. This usually includes everything from mainframes down to Intel-based servers and workstations. This is, of course, in addition to keeping massive amounts of data in off-site backup storage.

At one of the places I worked, we had quarterly assessments of our disaster recovery plan. We shut down all of the computers from the mainframes through the Intel servers. We notified the disaster recovery company that we were conducting a test, and they prepared their site with the various computers we would require to get back up and operational. We had the backup storage service transport the latest backup media from their secure facility to the recovery site in Philadelphia.

A group of folks from our offices traveled up to the recovery site and restored all of the data from our backup media, brought everything online, and tested to ensure that everything was working properly.

There were always problems. Always. But that was the whole point of the exercise – to find the problems with our strategies and procedures. And then to fix them.

## Other Options

Not everyone needs a disaster recovery service or huge amounts of backup data storage. For some individuals and very small businesses with only a single computer, a couple USB thumb drives and a manual backup to one of those drives is more than sufficient. For others, a relatively small external USB hard drive works well.

It is all in what you need for your circumstances.

## What About the "Frequently" Part?

This is easy. Always make at least one backup every day. No matter what. If some file or files are particularly important and you have just created or altered them, make a backup of them right away.

The `rsbu` script will do this very quickly because it will only make backups for files that have changed. It does this in a way that still allows you to continue working on your computer.

## Summary

Backups are an incredibly important part of our jobs as SysAdmins. I have experienced many instances where backups have enabled rapid operational recovery for places I have worked as well as for my own business and personal data.

There are many options for performing and maintaining data backups. I do what works for me and have never had a situation where I lost more than a few hours' worth of data.

Like everything else, backups are all about what you need. Whatever you do – do something! Figure out how much pain you would have if you lost everything – data, computers, hard copy records – everything. The pain includes the cost of replacing the hardware and the cost of the time required to restore data that was backed up and to recover data that was not backed up. Then plan and implement your backup systems and procedures accordingly.

# CHAPTER 22

# Follow Your Curiosity

People talk about life-long learning and how that keeps one mentally alert and youthful. The same is true of SysAdmins. There is always more to learn, and I think that is what keeps most of us happy and always ready to tackle the next problem. Continuous learning helps to keep our minds and skills sharp, no matter what our age.

I love to learn new things. I was fortunate in that my curiosity led me to a lifetime of working with my favorite toys – computers. There are certainly plenty of new things to learn about computers; the industry and technology are constantly changing. There are many things on Earth and in this Universe to be curious about. Computers and related technology just seem to be the thing I enjoy the most.

I also assume that you must be curious because you are reading this book. But not everyone is as curious as we are.

## Charlie

Let's take a trip in my Wayback machine to 1970 in Toledo, Ohio. I was working at a chemical plant in a very boring job as a tester, along with seven or eight others. We would take chemical formulations dreamed up by our chemists, compound them into vinyl, and press it into various types of fabrics used in the automotive industry for seats and vinyl roofs. Our jobs were to test the resulting raw vinyl and coated fabrics to see if they met all of the specifications supplied by the auto company that had ordered them.

Never seen a vinyl roof on a car? Yeah, that long ago!

One of my coworkers, Charlie, was a negative sort of guy. His complaining was incessant. He would complain about the working conditions – we had lots of volatile chemicals around and it was pretty easy to get high and stay there if that is what you wanted, but it was also dangerous. He complained about the danger and about how boring the job was but we all did some of that – it was part of being in that type of job. But

© David Both 2018
D. Both, *The Linux Philosophy for SysAdmins*, https://doi.org/10.1007/978-1-4842-3730-4_22

Charlie complained about everything from the moment he walked in until the ending whistle blew in the afternoon.

One day we had a conversation that went something like this.

Charlie said to me one morning about 8:30 a.m., "I hate this job. Quitting time can't get here fast enough."

I was getting pretty fed up with his negativity, so I said, "Charlie, if you hate this job so much, why don't you find another job?"

"I don't know how to do anything else."

So I said, "Well, why don't you learn something new? I'll be going back to university next term and I'm not going to stay here for long after I get my degree. I plan to get a better job."

"That's easy for you – you're young. I'm old and you can't teach an old dog new tricks."

I asked him, "How old are you Charlie?"

"Thirty-six," he said.

Even then, in my early twenties and seemingly invulnerable and immortal in my own mind, I knew that thirty-six was not old. Right then I vowed to myself that I would never stop learning – that I would learn something new every day. And I have kept that vow. Of course, that vow has been pretty easy to keep what with both my vocation and avocation being computers for most of the last forty years.

# Curiosity Led Me to Linux

Curiosity got me into Linux in the first place but it was a long and winding road. You may skip this long and, perhaps to you, boring section, if you like. I do find that describing how my journey brought me to where I am today has been interesting and helpful to some people. It does show that the shortest distance between two points in life are not usually a straight line. In any event I will try to keep this as short as I can and still show the impact of curiosity on my life.

I was never a particularly good student in the standard sense of my school marks. I tended to follow my curiosity rather than the lesson plans. Most teachers don't like that. I was interested in electricity, electronics, math, and chemistry. I was fortunate to have good teachers for chemistry and math but in 1960 there were no high school classes in electronics unless I went to the vocational technical high school in Toledo. I wanted to go there but my parents convinced me that I could learn about electronics later.

During my early teen years, my interest in electronics was aided and abetted by my HO gauge model railroad, which required that I learn at least the basics of electricity. So I got books from the library to study. I also found college-level workbooks at the University of Toledo (UT) book store that I bought and studied. I wired my model railroad, and when I learned new things, I completely tore out the existing wiring and rewired it from scratch.

I also used to fix our TV when it broke. Eventually the neighbors started asking me to help them with their TVs and radios when they broke. It was easy in those days, because every electronic device came with a schematic and all I had to do was figure out which vacuum tube to replace. It helped that books were available that showed various symptoms in pictures and then listed the types of tubes that would cause those problems when they failed. It was also helpful that most every drug store and grocery had tube testers with a supply of tubes. That meant I could remove the tube or tubes I suspected of being the cause of the failure and walk to a place where I could test it and purchase a replacement.

I spent the summer of 1968 at an aunt's home in Los Angeles. My uncle worked as a computer programmer in the aerospace industry and I found a pile of old self-study manuals in their garage. Instead of going to the beach all the time as I had planned, I spent most of the summer learning about IBM mainframe computing from those old courses.

Then in late 1968 I was in a job that involved lots of number crunching and we were using very old mechanical calculators that could take several minutes to do a single multiplication. I suggested that we purchase one of the four-function electronic calculators that were just then beginning to hit the market. My supervisor thought this would be a good idea so he had me look into this possibility. Two of the vendors we contacted had these interesting new devices, desktop programmable calculators. Both were willing to let me use demonstrator models so I could test them out in our own environment with problems I knew we would be working on.

I was able to convince the financial people that this $3,500 calculator was worth the cost, so we purchased an Olivetti Programma 101.[1] I spent a few months programming that and wanted to learn more about programming in general.

I soon found that the university offered a single course in programming so I took a course in BASIC. This class was taught by the University of Toledo on a GE time sharing

---

[1]Wikipedia, *Programma 101*, https://en.wikipedia.org/wiki/Programma_101

system, probably a GE-600[2] series, located in Columbus, Ohio. Terminal access was through an ASR 33 teletype machine over dial-up phone lines at 300 baud.

I was then promoted from my job using the P-101 to working on the IBM 1401 as a night operator where I had my first direct contact with mainframe computers. I worked this job for a few months before moving on.

I got married in early 1969. Although this had no direct effect on my career path just yet, it would be critical later.

In my next job I had no direct contact with computers, but I also worked nights for a band as their sound technician and only roadie. The drummer for the band had a by-mail course in electronics that he had paid for but did not have time to take, so he offered it to me. I snatched at this opportunity and that electronics knowledge led me to a job at an audio sales and repair shop in Toledo where I learned even more.

By now it was around 1972 and my wife and I purchased a former rental house from my father-in-law. It turns out that one of our neighbors worked for IBM. He asked if I was interested in working at IBM, but I was happy where I was, so I said I was not interested.

The audio repair job led to another job as service manager of a new stereo shop where I also spent some time taking classes in electronics engineering. I excelled in these classes because I enjoyed electronics.

When I was laid off from my job at the new stereo shop, I asked my IBM friend if they were still hiring. He got me an interview and I started a 21-year career at IBM. My first job at IBM was as a Customer Engineer (CE) in the General Systems Division (GSD) repairing hardware. In 1978, IBM moved me to their facility Boca Raton, Florida, for a job-writing training courses for new products. In early 1981, I was assigned to write the training for the original IBM PC.[3]

In order to write the training course for the PC, I needed one in my office so I could have easy access to learn about it myself. Because it was so secret at the time, the security people had chicken wire installed in the ceiling of my office and a lock put on the door. I was the only non-manager in the building with a lock on my office door. I guess the chicken wire in the overhead was to prevent some nefarious thieves from climbing over the walls of my office and dropping down inside. Only after that could I have a PC in my office. I had serial number 00000001.

While writing the training course, I initially went with a more traditional IBM training strategy, but that was not working for the CEs in the Typewriter division who

---

[2]Wikipedia, *GE-600*, https://en.wikipedia.org/wiki/GE-600_series
[3]Wikipedia, *IBM PC*, https://en.wikipedia.org/wiki/IBM_Personal_Computer

were paid less than we were in GSD. Using CEs from the Typewriter division made it more cost effective, but it meant we had to familiarize those CEs in computer concepts and technology. I had to make sure they got hands-on during the training, but it was too expensive to have them travel to a training center.

So I rewrote the training completely. I wrote a complete computerized training program that would allow me to author the course content and then present it to the CEs in their local branch office on IBM PCs that we shipped to the branch office for the training. And then I wrote the course itself. Although this was most definitely not the first computerized training course, it was the first training software and courseware for the IBM PC.

In order to write this revised course and maintain our schedule with the PC release date, I requested that I be allowed to have a PC in my home so I could more easily work on the class at night. After dozens of sign-offs by various high-level executives I was given a PC to take home in addition to the one I had at the office. As far as I know, I am the first person to ever have an IBM PC at home.

Of course all of this got me very interested in personal computers. So I bought one for myself through the employee purchase program. This cost a bit over $5,000 after the employee discount. The system included a pair of 160KB 5.25" floppy drives, no hard drive, and 64K of RAM. I started hacking PC hardware when several of us at the office went together to purchase the parts for third-party memory cards that we had to build ourselves.

Following a couple of more career moves, my experience with the PC led to a job at the IBM PC Help Center in Atlanta, Georgia. I became very interested in operating systems during that time and eventually became one of the primary support people for OS/2.

After moving to Raleigh, North Carolina, in 1993, I left IBM in 1995 and started a consulting company that specialized in OS/2. By 1996 it was clear that OS/2 was not going to be around for much longer. I was appalled by the thought of learning Windows NT. I decided that the future for me was in Unix although I had not yet heard about Linux.

Around this time, an friend from IBM called me one day and asked if I knew anyone looking for a job who could help MCI, where he was now working, with their OS/2 computers. I took the job with the proviso that I get to learn Unix.

While at MCI, I was able to take some basic Unix classes that got me started. I also heard about this thing called Linux that was a lot like Unix and that I could install on one of my personal computers. I figured I needed to improve my Unix/Solaris skills, but

I could not afford to purchase a Sun computer and Solaris for home. So I purchased a copy of Red Hat 5.0 (not RHEL) at the local computer store and installed it on one of my several computers. I liked Linux and after learning more about it, I found that I was not progressing. I decided to make the leap and upgraded all but one of my home computers to Linux. The final step was when I migrated my web and email server from OS/2 over to Linux.

As a result of all this learning, I was able to find a job as a Unix engineer at a local ISP. They sent me to Solaris classes and I earned a Sun Certified System Administrator certification. This is where I met some of my best mentors.

About eighty of us were laid off from the ISP and I quickly found a job as a contractor. This is where I was responsible for fixing all of those Perl scripts running on a Red Hat Linux server. We also used some bash shell scripts that needed cleaning up. I learned a lot more about Linux and shell scripting in that job.

That led to a series of jobs that centered around Linux, in most of which I did at least some Linux training. I found that most places I worked had the need for someone to train other admins and users in various aspects of Linux. I put together several Linux classes and Lunch-and-learn sessions that were all well received.

I have found that I learn the most myself when I am teaching others whether in a classroom environment or in books and articles. I have to research things carefully in order to ensure that I get them right. I also have to answer questions from students about things I never considered when creating the materials. I have to research questions that I have no answers for.

And now here I am writing about Linux, which requires even more research, testing, and experimentation.

§

This is only a portion of my personal road to Linux and open source. There are a lot of side trips that affected some of my decisions and altered the timing of certain events in my life so that things were in place for the story above to unfold.

Getting a job in Linux was not something that could have been planned for while I was growing up or in school because neither Unix nor Linux nor open source existed when I was in high school and my early years at university. The choices I made, the people I met, the knowledge I gained, the places I lived, the series of jobs I had, all led to the place I am now because I chose over and over again to follow the things that I enjoyed and about which I had a deep curiosity, technology, computers, operating systems, and Linux. My choices, whether conscious or not, took me along a path that was driven by curiosity. It was enjoyable and rewarding in many ways.

If you are interested in reading the stories of some others who have found their way into Linux and open source, check out the list of articles tagged with "Careers"[4] at Opensource.com. They frequently publish stories of people who have found different ways to get here. Not all of the articles in the list are about "How I got a job in open source," but some are. You may find those and other articles with this tag interesting.

# Curiosity Solves Problems

There is an old – and I think incredibly stupid – saying that "curiosity killed the cat." I had this used on me as a kid, fortunately not by my parents. I think this dumb saying is used mostly to stifle kids when their questions and inquisitiveness takes them to places that some parents, teachers, and caregivers would rather not take the time to deal with. This is one of the way in which the boxes were built around us.

My personal saying is that "curiosity solves problems." Following our curiosity leads us to places that are outside the box, places that allow us to solve our problems in ways that we could not otherwise. Sometimes curiosity can lead me directly to the cause of a problem and other times the connection is indirect.

# Securiosity

Curiosity has led me to fix many problems, some of which I was initially unaware that even existed. In cases like these, the computer was still up and running and there were no noticeable symptoms such as crashes or programs failing. There were no observable problems and things seemed just fine. Security issues can be like that.

This particular adventure started one day many years ago when I decided to look at the security of my systems, particularly the firewalls between me and the outside world. I had already set up some firewall rules and some strong passwords on my firewalls. But I was curious about the state of my security and whether there might be some vulnerabilities that I could close. I don't mean code vulnerabilities, I mean procedural and security configuration vulnerabilities, things that I could do better than I was at that time. It all started with the logs.

---

[4]Opensource.com, *Tag Careers*, https://opensource.com/tags/careers

I like watching top, htop, iotop, glances, or any other system monitoring tool when things are working right so that I know when they look different that there might be a problem. I am this way with my log files, too. So I spent a good deal of time scanning my log files to see if I could spot any anomalies. It was always a very time-consuming chore and trying to interpret the hundreds and even thousands of lines on the log files each day was just too much, and it was difficult to boil the data down to something manageable. I needed to find a way to automate that task in a way that would alert me if there were a potential problem – yes, automate everything.

# Logwatch

I had read about Logwatch, which does just that, so I spent some time investigating that and other, similar tools that might work for me. Each day, Logwatch scans the log files for the previous day to look for anomalous entries that should be seen by the SysAdmin to determine whether there might be a problem. It is perfect for my needs.

I think I installed Logwatch on the Fedora host I was using for a firewall because it was not installed by default. It has been a long time so I do not remember for certain and my postinstall.sh script now installs `logwatch` if it is not already installed. Logwatch is most definitely not installed by default in current releases of Fedora workstation.

Logwatch is typically run by a cron job, `0logwatch`, in /etc/cron.daily and the 0logwatch script is configured to send the results as an email to the root user. I did not want the output from Logwatch to go to root, so I added a line to the /etc/aliases file on the firewall host and restarted sendmail. Now the emails would be sent to me.

The `logwatch` program can also be run directly from the command line. In this case, the default is for the output to be sent to STDOUT, so rather than wait for the next day to see what the cron job sent to me, I ran `logwatch` from the command line.

Experiment 22-1 installs Logwatch and then has you run it from the command line. I did this on my firewall, and there is a huge amount of data. I have removed large segments of some sections, leaving just enough for you to see

**EXPERIMENT 22-1**

This experiment must be performed as root. We will first install Logwatch and then run it from the command line.

```
[root@wally1 ~]# dnf -y install logwatch
Last metadata expiration check: 2:59:04 ago on Sat 07 Apr 2018 05:11:02 AM
EDT.
Dependencies resolved.
=====================================================================
 Package            Arch       Version          Repository Size
=====================================================================
Installing:
 logwatch           noarch     7.4.3-6.fc27     fedora     423 k
Installing dependencies:
 perl-Date-Manip    noarch     6.60-1.fc27      fedora     1.1 M
 perl-Sys-CPU       x86_64     0.61-13.fc27     fedora     19 k
 perl-Sys-MemInfo   x86_64     0.99-5.fc27      fedora     25 k

Transaction Summary
=====================================================================
Install  4 Packages

Total download size: 1.6 M
Installed size: 12 M
Downloading Packages:
(1/4): perl-Sys-CPU-0.61-13.fc27.x86_   49 kB/s |  19 kB     00:00
(2/4): perl-Sys-MemInfo-0.99-5.fc27.x  458 kB/s |  25 kB     00:00
(3/4): logwatch-7.4.3-6.fc27.noarch.r  776 kB/s | 423 kB     00:00
(4/4): perl-Date-Manip-6.60-1.fc27.no  1.8 MB/s | 1.1 MB     00:00
---------------------------------------------------------------------
Total                                  1.8 MB/s | 1.6 MB     00:00
Running transaction check
Transaction check succeeded.
Running transaction test
Transaction test succeeded.
```

```
Running transaction
  Preparing       :                                              1/1
  Installing      : perl-Sys-MemInfo-0.99-5.fc27.x86_64          1/4
  Installing      : perl-Sys-CPU-0.61-13.fc27.x86_64             2/4
  Installing      : perl-Date-Manip-6.60-1.fc27.noarch           3/4
  Installing      : logwatch-7.4.3-6.fc27.noarch                 4/4
  Running scriptlet: logwatch-7.4.3-6.fc27.noarch                4/4
  Running as unit:   run-r859e9a9c34c64b2280025d5d33b5a7ac.service
  Verifying       : logwatch-7.4.3-6.fc27.noarch                 1/4
  Verifying       : perl-Date-Manip-6.60-1.fc27.noarch           2/4
  Verifying       : perl-Sys-CPU-0.61-13.fc27.x86_64             3/4
  Verifying       : perl-Sys-MemInfo-0.99-5.fc27.x86_64          4/4

Installed:
  logwatch.noarch 7.4.3-6.fc27
  perl-Date-Manip.noarch 6.60-1.fc27
  perl-Sys-CPU.x86_64 0.61-13.fc27
  perl-Sys-MemInfo.x86_64 0.99-5.fc27

Complete!
```

After the installation we run the logwatch command with no options. I have snipped out a huge number of lines in some of the sections to save space. I have also inserted comments in the output to describe the results to some extent. Your results will be different from mine, but this will give you a good idea of why I let my curiosity take me to other aspects of security.

```
[root@testvm1 ~]# logwatch

 ################### Logwatch 7.4.3 (04/27/16) ####################
        Processing Initiated: Fri Apr  6 14:01:32 2018
        Date Range Processed: yesterday
                            ( 2018-Apr-05 )
                            Period is day.
        Detail Level of Output: 10
        Type of Output/Format: stdout / text
        Logfiles for Host: wally1.both.org
 ################################################################
```

The previous section is the header that describes the conditions, date, and time that the command was run. The next section contains kernel information, mostly start and stop entries for various services, and logins. Notice that Logwatch has already pruned this section from over 10,000 lines to only 100. I have cut it down even more.

```
-------------------- Kernel Audit Begin ------------------------

 **Unmatched Entries** (Only first 100 out of 10226 are printed)
   audit[1]: SERVICE_START pid=1 uid=0 auid=4294967295 ses=4294967295
   msg='unit=mlocate-updatedb comm="systemd" exe="/usr/lib/systemd/systemd"
   hostname=? addr=? terminal=? res=success'
   audit[1]: SERVICE_START pid=1 uid=0 auid=4294967295 ses=4294967295
   msg='unit=sysstat-collect comm="systemd" exe="/usr/lib/systemd/systemd"
   hostname=? addr=? terminal=? res=success'
   audit[1]: SERVICE_STOP pid=1 uid=0 auid=4294967295 ses=4294967295
   msg='unit=sysstat-collect comm="systemd" exe="/usr/lib/systemd/systemd"
   hostname=? addr=? terminal=? res=success'
```

<SNIP>

The next few entries are the result of some successful logins.

```
   audit[16590]: CRYPTO_KEY_USER pid=16590 uid=0 auid=4294967295
   ses=4294967295 msg='op=destroy kind=server fp=SHA256:e9:53:4c:65:7f:a4:
   cb:6d:42:0c:40:a3:a4:a2:a9:d3:05:dd:4f:41:3b:26:ed:f6:02:ec:2b:4f:f9:a2:
   9d:5c direction=? spid=16590 suid=0  exe="/usr/sbin/sshd" hostname=? addr=?
   terminal=? res=success'
   audit[16590]: CRYPTO_KEY_USER pid=16590 uid=0 auid=4294967295
   ses=4294967295 msg='op=destroy kind=server fp=SHA256:2d:39:44:81:f6:e0:
   47:1f:f3:b1:02:a1:76:73:2e:16:26:6f:d8:e5:7d:2a:4a:ab:76:17:dd:36:54:b1:
   e6:a5 direction=? spid=16590 suid=0  exe="/usr/sbin/sshd" hostname=? addr=?
   terminal=? res=success'
   audit[16590]: CRYPTO_KEY_USER pid=16590 uid=0 auid=4294967295
   ses=4294967295 msg='op=destroy kind=server fp=SHA256:c4:2a:24:f1:0b:14:
   d4:4e:eb:33:6b:90:e0:84:c5:64:72:ec:30:72:3c:84:28:72:88:14:e3:1a:9d:d7:
   de:a9 direction=? spid=16590 suid=0  exe="/usr/sbin/sshd" hostname=? addr=?
   terminal=? res=success'
```

```
audit[16589]: CRYPTO_SESSION pid=16589 uid=0 auid=4294967295 ses=4294967295
msg='op=start direction=from-server cipher=aes128-ctr ksize=128 mac=hmac-
sha2-256 pfs=diffie-hellman-group-exchange-sha256 spid=16590 suid=74
rport=54280 laddr=24.199.159.59 lport=22  exe="/usr/sbin/sshd" hostname=?
addr=109.228.0.237 terminal=? res=success'
audit[16589]: CRYPTO_SESSION pid=16589 uid=0 auid=4294967295 ses=4294967295
msg='op=start direction=from-client cipher=aes128-ctr ksize=128 mac=hmac-
sha2-256 pfs=diffie-hellman-group-exchange-sha256 spid=16590 suid=74
rport=54280 laddr=24.199.159.59 lport=22  exe="/usr/sbin/sshd" hostname=?
addr=109.228.0.237 terminal=? res=success'
```

<SNIP>

The next lines are only two of a huge number of login failures. This was my first indication of a high number of attacks. These are hard to find just by scanning visually, so I used the grep utility to find more. This method does not give a real sense of how bad the problem is, but there are other sections later, which do.

**audit[16589]: USER_LOGIN pid=16589 uid=0 auid=4294967295 ses=4294967295**
**msg='op=login acct="(unknown)" exe="/usr/sbin/sshd" hostname=?**
**addr=109.228.0.237 terminal=ssh res=failed'**

```
audit[16596]: CRYPTO_KEY_USER pid=16596 uid=0 auid=4294967295
ses=4294967295 msg='op=destroy kind=session fp=? direction=both spid=16597
suid=74 rport=41125 laddr=24.199.159.59 lport=22  exe="/usr/sbin/sshd"
hostname=? addr=221.194.47.243 terminal=? res=success'
```
**audit[16596]: USER_LOGIN pid=16596 uid=0 auid=4294967295 ses=4294967295**
**msg='op=login acct="(unknown)" exe="/usr/sbin/sshd" hostname=?**
**addr=221.194.47.243 terminal=ssh res=failed'**

<SNIP>

```
--------------------- Kernel Audit End ------------------------
```

The cron section shows how many times that each cron job was run in the previous 24-hour day.

```
-------------------- Cron Begin -----------------------

Commands Run:
    User root:
        /sbin/hwclock --systohc --localtime: 1 Time(s)
        run-parts /etc/cron.hourly: 24 Time(s)
        systemctl try-restart atop: 1 Time(s)

-------------------- Cron End -----------------------
```

The next section lists a very large number of authentication failures. It does this in a way that makes it clear how big the problem with unauthorized access attempts really is. It does this by listing the IP addresses from which the break-in attempts originate in order by the number of attempts.

```
-------------------- pam_unix Begin -----------------------

sshd:
    Authentication Failures:
        root (123.183.209.135): 21 Time(s)
        unknown (14.37.169.239): 10 Time(s)
        unknown (85.145.209.59): 10 Time(s)
        unknown (116.196.115.44): 8 Time(s)
        unknown (212.129.36.144): 6 Time(s)
        unknown (84.200.7.63): 5 Time(s)
        root (218.65.30.25): 3 Time(s)
        root (84.200.7.63): 3 Time(s)
        unknown (103.99.0.54): 2 Time(s)
        unknown (196.216.8.110): 2 Time(s)
        ftp (116.196.72.140): 1 Time(s)
        ftp (118.36.193.215): 1 Time(s)
        operator (5.101.40.81): 1 Time(s)
        root (103.26.14.92): 1 Time(s)
        root (103.89.88.220): 1 Time(s)
        root (103.92.104.175): 1 Time(s)
        root (103.99.2.143): 1 Time(s)
        root (118.24.28.246): 1 Time(s)
```

```
<SNIP>

        unknown (91.121.77.149): 1 Time(s)
        unknown (95.38.15.86): 1 Time(s)
    Invalid Users:
        Unknown Account: 163 Time(s)
    Sessions Opened:
        root: 2 Time(s)

 systemd-user:
    Unknown Entries:
        session opened for user root by (uid=0): 3 Time(s)

 --------------------- pam_unix End ------------------------
```

The line "Invalid Users" above, shows that there were 163 total attempts to crack into my firewall host system in the previous day. PAM is responsible for overall login security, and the previous section looks at the logins from the PAM point of view. The SSHD section below, does, too. It is is mostly the same information but presented a bit differently.

These two sections, where I could see the entire list of SSH attacks against my system really got me curious about their origins and how to prevent them.

```
 --------------------- SSHD Begin ------------------------

 Didn't receive an ident from these IPs:
    103.79.143.56 port 58313: 1 Time(s)
    103.79.143.56 port 61578: 1 Time(s)
    103.89.88.181 port 53906: 1 Time(s)
    103.89.88.181 port 57332: 1 Time(s)
    103.89.88.181 port 58951: 1 Time(s)

<SNIP>

    202.151.175.6 port 39552: 1 Time(s)
    217.61.5.246 port 44974: 1 Time(s)
    66.70.177.18 port 33668: 1 Time(s)
    87.98.251.208 port 56975: 1 Time(s)

 Failed logins from:
    5.101.40.81: 1 time
        operator/password: 1 time
    18.188.155.82 (ec2-18-188-155-82.us-east-2.compute.amazonaws.com): 2 times
```

```
        root/password: 2 times
    23.97.75.224: 1 time
        root/password: 1 time
    46.105.20.171 (vps16696.ovh.net): 1 time
        root/password: 1 time
    54.37.139.198 (198.ip-54-37-139.eu): 1 time
        root/password: 1 time

<SNIP>

    221.229.166.102: 1 time
        wp-user: 1 time

 Users logging in through sshd:
    root:
        192.168.0.1 (david.both.org): 2 times

**Unmatched Entries**
Disconnected from invalid user test 36.77.124.2 port 48914 [preauth] :
1 time(s)
Disconnected from invalid user ubnt 103.99.2.143 port 55522 [preauth] :
1 time(s)
Disconnected from authenticating user root 123.183.209.135 port 58498
[preauth] : 1 time(s)
Disconnected from invalid user ftpuser 36.36.201.21 port 46357 [preauth] :
1 time(s)

<SNIP>

Disconnected from invalid user avis 201.155.194.157 port 52769 [preauth] :
1 time(s)
Disconnected from authenticating user root 23.97.75.224 port 1984 [preauth] :
1 time(s)
Disconnected from authenticating user root 64.41.86.128 port 58134 [preauth] :
1 time(s)
Disconnected from invalid user sybase 188.187.55.243 port 36344 [preauth] :
1 time(s)
Disconnected from invalid user cron 221.145.180.62 port 37912 [preauth] :
1 time(s)

--------------------- SSHD End ------------------------
```

The rest of these sections are fairly self-explanatory and have nothing directly to do with security. Because of that, I have not added any further comments to this output. I have left these sections in so that you can see many of the sections that Logwatch might create from the logs of a typical firewall.

```
--------------------- Systemd Begin ------------------------

Reached target Shutdown: 3 Time(s)

Started:
    Cleanup of Temporary Directories: 1 Time(s)
    Generate a daily summary of process accounting: 1 Time(s)
    LVM2 metadata daemon: 1 Time(s)
    Network Manager Script Dispatcher Service: 103 Time(s)
    Update a database for mlocate: 1 Time(s)
    User Manager for UID 0: 3 Time(s)
    dnf makecache: 23 Time(s)
    system activity accounting tool: 144 Time(s)
    update of the root trust anchor for DNSSEC validation in unbound: 1
    Time(s)

User Sessions:
    root:  66 68 70

Slices created:
    User Slice of root 3 Time(s)

**Unmatched Entries**
    Closed D-Bus User Message Bus Socket.: 3 Time(s)

--------------------- Systemd End ------------------------

--------------------- Disk Space Begin ------------------------

Filesystem                      Size  Used Avail Use% Mounted on
devtmpfs                        3.9G     0  3.9G   0% /dev
/dev/mapper/fedora_wally1-root  9.8G  173M  9.1G   2% /
/dev/mapper/fedora_wally1-usr    35G  5.3G   28G  17% /usr
/dev/mapper/fedora_wally1-home  4.9G  262M  4.4G   6% /home
/dev/mapper/fedora_wally1-tmp    25G   45M   24G   1% /tmp
/dev/mapper/fedora_wally1-var    30G  6.2G   22G  23% /var
/dev/sda1                       2.0G  399M  1.5G  22% /boot

--------------------- Disk Space End ------------------------
```

```
--------------------- lm_sensors output Begin -----------------------

coretemp-isa-0000
Adapter: ISA adapter
Package id 0:   +82.0 C  (high = +85.0 C, crit = +105.0 C)
Core 0:         +79.0 C  (high = +85.0 C, crit = +105.0 C)
Core 1:         +83.0 C  (high = +85.0 C, crit = +105.0 C)
Core 2:         +80.0 C  (high = +85.0 C, crit = +105.0 C)
Core 3:         +80.0 C  (high = +85.0 C, crit = +105.0 C)

--------------------- lm_sensors output End -------------------------

###################### Logwatch End ########################
```

Logwatch extracts huge amounts of useful information about a Linux host from its logs. It reduces the amount of information a SysAdmin needs to look at from tens of thousands of lines to merely a couple thousand. The nice part is that it aggregates related log entries so they are all in one place in the final report, which makes it much easier to scan.

Some quick analysis of the Logwatch results indicated that the vast majority of the attacks are script kiddies. These are automated attacks using simple scripts that locate open SSHD ports by simply attempting to log in to a series of IP addresses. Once an IP with an open SSHD port is found, the script may spend a few minutes attempting to log in using random but known user IDs and dictionary-based passwords. The objective is to infect the computer with some malware if they can gain access.

Script kiddies are not especially serious about cracking into well-protected hosts. They are looking for easy pickings – the poorly administered hosts that are poorly protected or not protected at all. Serious crackers, those that target a specific person or business, are another story altogether. A cracker who is serious enough will eventually find a way into your computers.

In my case, these are not serious crackers. The Logwatch results showed that my firewall was being attacked hundreds and sometimes thousands of times per day. These attacks were random and never persistent. But I still needed to reduce the number of attacks to improve my security. Over time, I used multiple strategies to do this. At each step my curiosity was further flamed by new information, a new view of the problem, or simply by curiosity for its own sake.

## IPTables

The first place I turned for help in stemming the onslaught, because I was already familiar with it, is the iptables firewall. For a few weeks, I spent a good deal of time adding the IP Address of the most egregious offenders to my iptables firewall.

Out of curiosity I wanted to determine which part of the world the source IP Address was from using came from. So I started using `whois` to determine that. If the address was from someplace I knew I would never need to log in from myself, I simply blocked that whole range of addresses.

This was quite easy to do, but it did result in blocking some people who wanted to see one of my web sites. This method is overkill when blocking an entire A class of IP addresses, but it takes a huge amount of time to manually add individual addresses. So in the true manner of the lazy admin, and "automate everything," I grew curious about automating the addition of IP addresses to my firewall rules.

## fail2ban

After a good bit of exploring and research, I found fail2ban, open source software that automates what I was previously doing manually. "Use open source software."

Fail2ban has a complex series of configurable matching rules and separate actions that can be taken when attempts are made to crack into a system. It has rules for many types of attacks that include web, email, and many other services that might have vulnerabilities. Fail2ban works by detecting attacks and then adding a rule to the firewall that will block further attempts from that specific, single IP address for a specified and configurable amount of time. After the time has expired, it removes the blocking rule.

One of the methods that fail2ban uses to notify the SysAdmin when an IP address has been blocked is to send an email. The email is sent to root by default, but that can be configured, too. Rather than configure many different tools to send email to my personal address, I allow them to send to root and the /etc/aliases file, which I have already configured, reroutes all emails to root to be sent to me instead.

I spent some time out of curiosity adjusting the rules because Fail2ban will block an IP address after a specified number of cracking attempts in a specified period of time. I have found that – for my environment and needs – three attempts within any ten-minute period works exactly the way I want. I also discovered that blocking an IP address for at least twenty-four hours rather than the default of ten minutes, does tend to discourage repeat offenders. So the results in Sample Listing 22-1, below, are based on those filtering rules.

---

| SAMPLE LISTING 22-1 |
| --- |

---

A few days after installing fail2ban and configuring it according to my needs, I again ran logwatch and the `fail2ban` section looks like this.

```
-------------------- fail2ban-messages Begin ----------------------------
Banned services with Fail2Ban:                              Bans:Unbans
   my-sshd:                                                 [ 35:35 ]
      123.183.209.135                                         17:17
      84.200.7.63                                              4:4
      212.129.36.144 (212-129-36-144.rev.poneytelecom.eu)      3:3
      218.65.30.25 (25.30.65.218.broad.xy.jx.dynamic.          3:3
      163data.com.cn)
      18.188.155.82 (ec2-18-188-155-82.us-east-2.compute.      1:1
      amazonaws.com)
      66.70.177.18 (ns545339.ip-66-70-177.net)                 1:1

<SNIP>
      183.230.146.26                                           1:1

Fail2Ban hosts found:
   my-sshd:
      103.20.149.252 - 2018-04-05 11:01:55 (1 Times)
      103.20.149.252 - 2018-04-05 11:01:57 (1 Times)
      103.26.14.92 - 2018-04-05 07:43:26 (1 Times)
      103.26.14.92 - 2018-04-05 07:43:28 (1 Times)
      103.28.219.152 - 2018-04-05 05:17:57 (1 Times)
      103.28.219.152 - 2018-04-05 05:18:00 (1 Times)
      103.89.88.220 - 2018-04-05 11:57:17 (1 Times)
      103.89.88.220 - 2018-04-05 11:57:19 (1 Times)
      103.92.104.175 - 2018-04-05 02:23:13 (1 Times)
      103.92.104.175 - 2018-04-05 02:23:14 (1 Times)
      103.99.0.32 - 2018-04-05 16:15:59 (1 Times)
      103.99.0.32 - 2018-04-05 16:16:01 (1 Times)
      103.99.0.54 - 2018-04-05 04:17:38 (1 Times)

<SNIP>
      88.87.202.71 - 2018-04-05 01:31:22 (1 Times)
      90.84.44.20 - 2018-04-05 19:01:06 (1 Times)
```

```
        90.84.44.20 - 2018-04-05 19:01:08 (1 Times)
        91.121.105.20 - 2018-04-05 14:21:39 (1 Times)
        91.121.105.20 - 2018-04-05 14:21:41 (1 Times)
        91.121.77.149 - 2018-04-05 04:28:28 (1 Times)
        91.121.77.149 - 2018-04-05 04:28:29 (1 Times)
        95.38.15.86 - 2018-04-05 22:13:11 (1 Times)
        95.38.15.86 - 2018-04-05 22:13:13 (1 Times)

-------------------- fail2ban-messages End -------------------------
```

# Finding the Sources

Being curious about the sources of these attacks on my firewall, I started collecting these emails in order to analyze them. They typically look like that in Listing 22-2. This is the complete source of the email so you can examine it in detail.

---

**LISTING 22-2**

```
Received: from wally1.both.org (wally1.both.org [192.168.0.254])
        by bunkerhill.both.org (8.14.4/8.14.4) with ESMTP id w34E9NnR002675
        for <dboth@millennium-technology.com>; Wed, 4 Apr 2018 10:09:23 -0400
Received: from wally1.both.org (localhost [127.0.0.1])
        by wally1.both.org (8.15.2/8.15.2) with ESMTP id w34E9NTA013030
        for <dboth@millennium-technology.com>; Wed, 4 Apr 2018 10:09:23 -0400
Received: (from root@localhost)
        by wally1.both.org (8.15.2/8.15.2/Submit) id w34E9NBq013023
        for dboth@millennium-technology.com; Wed, 4 Apr 2018 10:09:23 -0400
Message-Id: <201804041409.w34E9NBq013023@wally1.both.org>
Subject: [Fail2Ban] SSH: banned 123.183.209.135 from wally1.both.org
Date: Wed, 04 Apr 2018 14:09:23 +0000
From: wally1 <wally1@both.org>
To: dboth@millennium-technology.com
X-Spam-Status: No, score=-48 required=10.6 tests=ALL_TRUSTED,BAYES_00,USER_
IN_WHITELIST
Content-Type: text/plain
MIME-Version: 1.0
X-Scanned-By: MIMEDefang 2.83 on 192.168.0.51
```

```
Hi,

The IP 123.183.209.135 has just been banned by Fail2Ban after
3 attempts against SSH.

Here is more information about 123.183.209.135:

GeoIP Country Edition: CN, China

Regards,

Fail2Ban
```

This is a typical example of the type of emails I get. The subject line contains the IP address of the source, the name of the host reporting the attack, and the Fail2ban rule, in this case SSH. I wanted to use the originating IP address to identify the country of origin. The Fail2ban ruleset includes an option to use GeoIP, a program that searches a database of IP addresses and their assigned countries to determine the country from which the attack originated. That was an interesting side excursion, and I installed it without too much difficulty. For Fedora, which is what I use for my firewall, GeoIP is located in the Fedora repository. For CentOS it is located in the EPEL[5] repository.

After collecting a large number of Fail2ban emails, I exported them from Thunderbird into a list of subject lines. I wrote a script that reads the list and uses GeoIP to identify the countries of origin and generate a list of countries by frequency.

The most frequent and persistent attacks seem to come from various regions of Asia, Eastern Europe, a couple of countries in South America, and the United States.

## Collecting the Emails

In order to collect these emails, I started by using the filters available in Thunderbird to identify the ones sent by Fail2ban and moving them to a specific folder. This worked ok, but I found that the Thunderbird filters were not always accurate. And this was not the only filter that was causing problems.

I decided I needed to something different for filtering and sorting my emails – all of them, not just the ones for Fail2ban.

---

[5]EPEL – Extra Packages for Enterprise Linux (Linux, RHEL, Fedora)

## procmail

I had heard of procmail before. It is installed on all Red Hat-based distributions as the default Local Delivery Agent (LDA). That made it a no-brainer for me to use procmail for this project. The project being, first, to sort emails sent by Fail2ban into a folder just for them, and second, to do some sorting on other emails as well.

There was also a technical problem I wanted to fix. Client-side email filtering relies on scanning messages after they are deposited in the inbox. For some unknown reason, sometimes the client does not delete (expunge) the moved messages from the inbox. This may be an issue with Thunderbird (or it may be a problem with my configuration of Thunderbird). I have worked on this problem for years with no success, even through multiple complete reinstallations of Fedora and Thunderbird.

To solve these multiple problems, I needed a method for filing emails (i.e., sorting them into appropriate folders) that was server-based rather than client-based. This would mean that it would not be necessary to keep Thunderbird – or any email client – running in order to perform email sorting.

After doing some research on procmail, I was able to create a procmail rule that sorted the incoming Fail2ban emails to a specific folder for that purpose. I also created some other rules that sorted other types of emails into various folders.

Although I use SpamAssassin for identifying spam, I now use a procmail rule to file spam emails into my spam folder. There are also a few spams I get that SpamAssassin rules never seem to identify. At some point soon, whenever the disgust of seeing those particular spam emails in my inbox sets in, I will create a rule or rules to filter those as well. I am also curious about the efficacy of my spam filtering so, rather than delete spam, I store it for a few days in case I need to view the SpamAssassin scores in order to improve those rules.

In November of 2017, I wrote an article[6] for Opensource.com about using SendMail, SpamAssassin, and procmail to classify and sort email. It goes into more detail than I have here, about solving multiple problems, not just sorting Fail2ban emails into a specific folder.

---

[6]Both, David, *SpamAssassin, MIMEDefang, and Procmail: Best Trio of 2017*, Opensource.com, https://opensource.com/article/17/11/spamassassin-mimedefang-and-procmail

## rkhunter

After seeing how many attempts to crack into my firewall were happening each day, I got a bit more concerned. So my curiosity about how to proceed led me to discover root kits. I decided to start looking specifically for root kits, which are software packages installed on hosts that have been compromised by the crackers. They allow the cracker to access the host and control it for their own purposes.

Ensuring that there are no root kits installed – at least no known ones – is a task performed by a software tool called rkhunter, for root kit hunter. I installed rkhunter and run it on a regular basis to ensure that no known root kits are installed.

Of course that last sentence is indicative of the problem with any software that is designed to scan a computer system for any type of malware – it can only find the malware that is already known and for which a signature has been developed. By the time you detect a root kit, the damage is already done and it is time to wipe out everything and start over.

I do use rkhunter but I do not depend solely upon it for the security of my network.

## SSH

The attacks I am trying to prevent are simple scripted password hacks. So the obvious step is to ensure that the passwords are essentially uncrackable and use SSH with Public/Private Key Pairs (PPKP) for inter-system communications inside my network.

So I set up moderately long passwords for all of my internal systems and extremely long passwords for my firewall hosts. I have always used SSH and PPKPs for logins to other hosts on my network so there was no significant change in my operational procedures there. I will not describe the specifics of this setup on my firewalls because it might provide some assistance to a serious cracker. Besides, this section is more about the directions that my curiosity has taken me than about the details of all the steps I have taken to secure my systems.

§

So this odyssey into the security of my firewall host system was very enlightening. I had been doing some pretty basic security to start with but did not fully understand the scope of the problem until I really looked at it. Step by step, my curiosity took me further into the world of securing my systems. I used this knowledge to secure the rest of my systems and those of my customers as well.

Had the problem not been laid out so clearly by Logwatch, I would probably not have had my curiosity piqued enough to cause me to explore security and firewalls. As a result, my systems are all much safer.

I also looked at some other options for security on my systems but things like various forms of intrusion detection tend to be after the fact and the administrative load they impose was more than I felt was required for my own systems. In this case the risk reduction did not justify the cost of the effort required to enable and maintain it.

SELinux[7] is also installed by default on all Red Hat-based distributions, and my curiosity has also taken me down that path several times in the past. I found – that for me in my environment – it was not appropriate for use on all of my hosts. I did enable it in restrictive mode on my firewalls because that is where I get the most results for the effort. Any serious attackers would need to breach the firewalls first so that would trigger warnings that someone was serious about cracking into my network. I could then take appropriate actions before the breach actually occurred. Remember, though, that there is no such thing as perfect security. The object of any set of security precautions is to make cracking in to your systems more expensive in time and effort than the bad guys are willing to exert. It boils down to the question of how much risk can you afford.

This all started from my curiosity. I originally intended to ease the task of checking log files for potential issues. That took me in some very interesting directions, and the primary one was the security of my network, especially the firewalls. It also took me some other places that I have not even covered here just because you should already see the point.

# Follow Your Own Curiosity

I have already mentioned more than once that you should explore the many aspects of Linux and go wherever your curiosity leads you. It was only by following my curiosity, first about electronics, then computers, programming, operating systems, OS/2, Linux, servers, networking, and more, that I have been able to do so many fun and interesting things.

You may have specific personal and career goals in mind and that may fuel your curiosity by taking you to places that can help you meet those goals. You may also be an innately curious person and more inclined to be curious about things that are of particular interest to you without being attached to a specific goal. It does not matter how your curiosity is driven. It just matters that you follow it and that you not allow anyone or anything to dampen that curiosity.

---

[7]Binnie, Chris, *Practical Linux Topics*, Apress 2016, 91,

## Be an Author

I currently write many articles for Opensource.com[8] and, no matter what I write about, I always learn something new, even about things I am already familiar with. Every article I have ever written, be it for *Linux Journal*, *Linux Magazine*, or Opensource.com has been an opportunity to indulge my curiosity and learn more about Linux.

Writing this book has not been an exception to that. Even as I research various aspects of this book, I have learned more about commands that I already know and I have learned some new commands. I have allowed my curiosity to take me down paths that would never show up in this book just because it is fun to learn new things about Linux and there is so much to learn.

Finding topics about which I want to write is almost never a problem. I typically use recent events as the subjects of my articles. Things to write about are always happening. It is just a matter of recognizing them and putting the story into words. A number of things happened during the writing of this book that became part of it; I have mentioned those in several chapters.

Sometimes, as I occasionally struggle to translate into words this philosophy of mine, I learn more about The Philosophy and about how I have used it and how it has helped and guided me. I have learned that in many ways, my Philosophy is about more than just Linux.

## Failure Is an Option

*I have not failed. I've just found 10,000 ways that won't work.*

—Thomas A. Edison

Although the failure of thousands of specific combinations of individual materials and fabrication technologies during testing did not lead to a viable light bulb, Edison continued to experiment. Just so, the failure to resolve a problem or create code that performs its defined task does not mean that the project or overall goal will fail. It means only that the specific tool or approach did not result in a successful outcome.

I have learned much more through my failures than I have in almost any other manner. I am especially glad for those failures that have been self-inflicted. Not only did I have to correct the problems I caused myself, but I also still had to find and fix the

---

[8]Opensource.com, `https://opensource.com/`

original problem. This always led to a great deal of research that caused me to learn much more than if I had solved the original problem quickly.

This is just my nature, and I think it is the nature of all good SysAdmins to look upon these situations as learning opportunities. As mentioned previously, I have spent many years as a trainer and some of the most fun experiences were when demonstrations, experiments, and lab projects would fail while I was teaching. Those were fantastic learning experiences for me as well as for the students in my class. Sometimes I even incorporated those accidental failures into later classes because they enabled me to teach something important.

# Just Do It

Everyone learns best in their own way. As a trainer I saw this every time I taught a class, regardless of the subject. Following our curiosity is the same – we all have that spark that leads us to discover more. Our methods may not be the same, but they will lead us all to greater knowledge and skill.

I started by installing Linux on all of my computers at home. This forced me to learn Linux and not look back. So long as I had a means to go back to my old and well-known way of doing things, it was never necessary for me to truly learn Linux. This is what I did when I decided I wanted to learn Linux, and it has taught me a large part of what I know. I had several computers and created a complete internal network in my home office. Over the years my network has grown and changed, and I have learned more with every alteration. Much of this was driven by my curiosity rather than any specific need.

I have static IP addresses from my ISP and two firewalls to provide outside access and protect my internal network. One of these firewalls is a Raspberry Pi with CentOS on it. I have had Intel boxes with Fedora and CentOS on them over the years. I learned a lot about using both in roles as a firewall and router.

I have a server that runs DHCP, HTTP, SMTP, IMAP, NTP, DNS, and other services to provide them to my internal network, and to make some of those services available to the outside world, such as my web site and incoming email. I have learned a great deal about using Linux in a server role in general. I have learned an incredible amount about implementing and managing each of these services.

I have a couple of desktop workstations, a laptop, an EeePC, all connected to my wired network. The EeePC and laptop can also connect using one of my wireless routers; I don't use the wireless provided by my ISP due to the monthly cost and it does not give me the opportunity to learn about configuring wireless routers. I also have a couple of smartphones, a Kindle, and an iPad. Learning how to set up my email server to best work with these tools while doing my best to provide those services in a secure manner has been challenging.

To me, curiosity is the driving force behind learning. I can't just sit in a classroom because someone says I need to learn a particular thing and be successful at it. I need to have some interest in the subject and something about it needs to pique my curiosity. That propensity to work harder on the subjects I liked was very evident during my school years as I did well in the subjects that intrigued me.

## Summary

By using my home network for indulging my curiosity, I had lots of safe space in which to fail catastrophically and to learn the best ways to recover from that. And there are lots of ways to fail so I learned a lot. I learned the most when I accidentally broke things, but I also learned a great deal when I would intentionally bork things. In these instances, I knew what I wanted to learn and could target the breakage in ways that would enable me to learn about those specific things.

I was also fortunate because I had a few jobs that required, or at least allowed me, to take classes on various aspects of Unix and Linux. For me, classroom work is a way to validate and reinforce what I learn on my own. It gave me the opportunity to interact with – for the most part – knowledgeable instructors who could aid and clarify my understanding of the bits and pieces that I could not make sense of on my own.

Be the curious SysAdmin. It worked for me.

# There Is No Should

This had not really been one of my tenets until I began writing this book and especially the part about the contest I created for Opensource.com. It struck me as I was writing that section that I had already used the phrase, "There is no should," more than once. I even discussed it briefly way back in Chapter 2, so I started thinking about this in a new way and decided that it really should be a tenet.

This tenet is about possibilities. It is also the most Zen of all of the chapters in this book. It is more about how our minds work to solve problems than it is about specific technology. It is also about overcoming or at least recognizing some of the obstacles that prevent us from fully utilizing the potential we have in ourselves.

## There Are Always Possibilities

Each of the tenets covered in this book reveals some basic truth about Linux and how you as a SysAdmin can interact with it. I am not saying that these truths are about how you "should" interact with Linux. With Linux there is no "should."

```
 _____
/ There are always  \
\ possibilities.     /
 -------------------
        \   ^__^
         \  (oo)_____
            (__)\       )\/\
                ||----w |
                ||     ||
```

In "The Wrath of Kahn," Spock says, "There are always possibilities." With Linux there are always possibilities – many ways to approach and solve problems. This means that you may perform a task in one way while another SysAdmin may do it in another. There is no one way in which tasks "should" be done. There is only the way you have done it. If the results meet the requirements, then the manner in which they were reached is perfection.

I have included an excellent example of this in "The Pipeline Challenge" section of Chapter 4, "Transforming Data Streams." More than eighty SysAdmins from around the world submitted their solutions to a problem I posed in the form of a contest on Opensource.com. A few of the solutions were very close to being alike, but no two were exactly alike and many were very different. Each of those SysAdmins had a unique, creative solution that met the requirements of the contest.

How can a single problem, when presented to so many different people, result in such a wide range of solutions? There are two factors in play here. It is because what at first glance is the seeming complexity of Linux is, in actuality, its incredible flexibility. The many diverse solutions to this one specific problem is the direct result of the many different commands and utilities available to the Linux System Administrators.

The second factor is that which Linux SysAdmins have learned Linux in many different ways and our experiences are so different. It is also the fact that these experiences have allowed us to realize that the unrestricted nature of Linux and open source software allows us to more fully understand and reason about the operating system. Even when using the exact same commands, we can find different ways to apply them to the problem at hand.

# Unleashing the Power

I read and hear a lot of people who talk about "harnessing the power of..." whatever they are promoting today. These are many times marketing campaigns. Many self-help gurus talk about harnessing the power of the mind, or "the power within," although within what is never exactly defined and neither is the "power" being referred to.

I did a Google search on "Harnessing the power of Linux" and found about fourteen articles with that phrase. I Googled "Unleashing the power of Linux" and got six results. This illustrates to me a problem in perspective. When we talk about harnessing something, we imply that we want to contain something or to bring it under control; and when we talk about unleashing something, we are thinking from the perspective of setting it free.

In some ways this is about semantics[1] because semantics is indicative of how we think. Semantics is the study of meanings, and it considers things like word selection and its effects on meaning. The words we use have meanings to speakers or writers that may be different from the meanings assigned to them by the hearers and readers. I consider the selection of unleash vs. harness in the context of computing and particularly Linux to be quite revealing.

My very unscientific observations have led me to theorize[2] that those of us who are Linux SysAdmins tend to think more in terms of "unleashing," "releasing," or "setting free" the power of Linux. I believe that we Linux SysAdmins approach solving Linux problems with fewer restraints on our thinking than those who appear to think more in terms of "harnessing" and "restrictions." We have so many simple yet powerful tools available to us that we do not find ourselves constrained by either the operating system or any inhibitive manner of thinking about the tools we use or the operational methods with which we may apply them.

There is power beyond measure available when the imaginations of thousands of people can be unleashed on the problems that can be solved with open source software.

# Problem Solving

Most of us have little awareness of how we solve problems. and this can impair our ability to do so. Problem solving is an art that relies heavily on the scientific method and critical thinking. Understanding this concept can free us from cognitive limits imposed upon us by institutionalized thinking.

We are taught to think in specific ways by educational systems that seem to preach the method du jour for solving problems. For example, I was taught my math basics with so-called traditional methods. I learned the number system, algorithms for calculating sums and differences including positional values, the concepts of carry and borrow; I memorized multiplication tables, specific algorithms for division, and much more. My children learned math using different methods that was probably "new math." Today, my grandkids are learning with the "new" new math.

---

[1]Wikipedia, *Semantics*, https://en.wikipedia.org/wiki/Semantics
[2]I have no scientific basis for drawing a conclusion of any kind, but I can certainly theorize based on what I have observed.

Having read a bit about the current methods of teaching math, I wish I had learned this way. I like the fact that the students are being taught well-defined, repeatable, and teachable processes for solving math problems.

In a 2017 article in the *Journal of Physics: Conference Series*, "The Increase of Critical Thinking Skills through Mathematical Investigation Approach,"[3] the authors established a positive correlation between an investigative approach to learning math and an increase in critical thinking skills. Critical thinking is a key skill for SysAdmins when solving problems.

The thing is, I like doing math the way I was taught. It is easier for me than the more recent methods even though I now understand those methods a bit better as the result of my research for this chapter. I have watched my grandkids solve math problems, and I have no idea what they were doing or how they arrived at the correct results. Checking their results using my "old math" methods, I arrived at the same results – except for the ones on which they made mistakes. Or I made the mistakes. Mostly it was my results that were wrong. But when we both got it right, the answer was definitely the same.

So, who was right? Which of us was using the right methods for solving these problems? While we are in school, getting the right answer is only part of solving the problem. The other part is using the correct algorithms, the ones being taught today, to arrive at the correct answer. It is the algorithms and how we choose the correct algorithm and apply it to the math problem at hand that are being taught. Outside of the educational system, in the so-called real world, the only thing that counts is that the numeric result of the calculation is correct.

In the realm of Linux and computers in general, the thing that counts is fixing the problem at hand. It does not matter whether that turns out to be a hardware problem, a software problem, or something else. Fixing it is the measure of success for the SysAdmin.

Breaking out of the "shoulds" taught to us by institutional instruction methodologies, particularly rote memorization and algorithms that we blindly follow, can free us to think about solving problems in new ways. This does not mean that those methods are wrong, only that other methods might also be considered and that they might be better suited for particular situations, especially for solving technical problems.

---

[3]N Sumarna, Wahyudin, and T Herman, *The Increase of Critical Thinking Skills through Mathematical Investigation Approach*, Journal of Physics: Conference Series, Volume 812, Number 1, Article 012067, http://iopscience.iop.org/article/10.1088/1742-6596/812/1/012067/meta

It is not only institutions that have caged me with "should." Many times, it is myself. I find myself thinking inside the box because that is where I think I "should" be. There are ways of preventing this and of recovering when I find myself trapped by "should."

In Chapter 24, "Mentor the Young SysAdmins," we will explore in some detail one algorithm for solving problems that is rooted in the Scientific Method. For now, let's look at two important skills that are required for problem solving and avoiding the box of limited thinking – critical thinking and reasoning.

## Critical Thinking

Way back in Chapter 1, I briefly mentioned my participation in interviews with potential new hires at some of the places I worked. We would start by asking the interviewees some basic questions and then move on to more difficult ones that were intended to explore the limits of their knowledge. Most of the people we considered were able to get through this stage of the interview fairly easily.

Our concerns with many of the prospective new hires arose when we started asking questions that required them to look at problem situations and reason through a sequence of steps that would enable them to determine the cause of a hypothetical problem. Most could not do this. Their standard approach to solving problems was to reboot the computer without doing any real problem analysis. Then their normal methodology was to use a specific set of scripted actions in a sequence designed to, hopefully, resolve the problem based on a set of probabilities that specific symptoms would be fixed by specific actions. There never was any attempt to understand the reasoning behind why specific actions should be taken or to locate the root cause of the problem.

I call this the "symptom – fix" method. It is basically a script – a series of choices – that can be followed with little or no knowledge of how the underlying systems work. This is a common approach to fixing broken computers and other devices when restrictive systems are involved. It is the only way that really works because the restrictive and closed systems cannot be truly known in the same way as open systems, particularly operating systems like Linux.

The vast majority of those who were able reason through the trouble scenarios we set for them tended to have significant experience with Unix and Linux. In my opinion, this is because Unix and Linux users and SysAdmins think about solving problems differently from those who use more restrictive operating systems. Using and administering Unix and Linux systems require a higher level of reasoning skills. The unconstrained natures of both Unix and Linux also invites us to learn and improve those skills. Armed with a deep knowledge of a powerful operating system, a thorough understanding of the available tools, and well-developed critical thinking skills,[4] Linux SysAdmins are capable of resolving problems quickly and with great freedom in their choice and use of tools.

Critical thinking is a key component of what makes Linux and Unix SysAdmins so good at what we do. It gives us the ability to look at the symptoms of the problem, to determine what is important and what is not, to connect those symptoms to previous experiences or knowledge we have, and to use that to determine one or more possible root causes of the problem.

Please do not misunderstand me. There are many very smart SysAdmins who work with Windows and other closed and proprietary operating systems. All of these very smart SysAdmins also use critical thinking and reasoning to solve problems. The real issue is the closed nature of the systems on which they work and that it restricts the possibilities that are available to them.

# Reasoning to Solve Problems

Another skill that contributes to the ability of SysAdmins to solve problems is reasoning.[5] After our critical thinking has enabled us to look at the symptoms of a problem, we can use different forms of reasoning to determine some possible root causes of the presenting symptoms in order to determine the next steps.

There are four widely recognized forms of reasoning, and we SysAdmins use all of them to help us resolve problems. We use inductive, deductive, abductive, and integrated reasoning[6] to lead us to a conclusion that points to one or more possible causes for the observed symptoms. Let's briefly look at these forms of reasoning and see how they apply to problem solving.

---

[4]Skills You Need web site, *Critical Thinking Skills*, https://www.skillsyouneed.com/learn/critical-thinking.html

[5]Wikipedia, *Reason*, https://en.wikipedia.org/wiki/Reason

[6]Butte College, *Deductive, Inductive, and Abductive Reasoning*, http://www.butte.edu/departments/cas/tipsheets/thinking/reasoning.html

# Deductive Reason

This is the most common form of reason that most of us are aware of. It is used to draw conclusions about specific instances from large numbers of more general observations that result in a general rule. For example, the following syllogism illustrates deductive reasoning – and its primary flaw.

**General rule:** Elevated temperatures in a computer are caused by the failure of a mechanical device, a fan.

**Observational instance:** My computer is overheating.

**Conclusion:** The fan in my computer is failing.

Many times this line of deductive reasoning has been successful at resolving problems with overheating. However, the conclusion is entirely dependent upon the accuracy of both the rule and the current observation.

Consider the other possibilities. The ambient temperature in the computer room may be extraordinarily high resulting in higher temperatures inside the computer. Or the heat radiator fins on the CPU may be clogged with dust, which reduces the airflow thus reducing the efficacy of the cooling system. I can think of other possible causes as well.

There is a huge fallacy in this syllogism as in all deductive reason. The rule and the assertion must always be correct for the conclusion to be true. This fallacy does not make it wrong to use this type of reasoning, but it does inform us that we do need to be careful.

# Inductive Reason

Inductive reason flows in the other direction. The conclusions are arrived at to create a general rule from a few observations, sometimes only a single one. This sample of inductive reason also shows the potential for built-in fallacies.

**Observations:** The failure of a fan caused my computer to overheat.

**Conclusion:** Computers always overheat because of fan failures.

Actually, there are more equally bad conclusions that could be drawn from this. One is that all fan failures cause computers to overheat, which is also not true. Another is that all computer fans fail. Yet another is that all computers will overheat due to fan failures.

Here again, we must be careful of the conclusions we reach. In this type of inductive reasoning, we are very likely to synthesize a general rule that can lead us astray when we apply the rule as an assertion in a deductive syllogism.

# Reason Fails

Both deductive and inductive reason contain the seeds of their own failure due to the incorrect assumption that all of the evidence is available and that all of the assertions are true. Both of those types of reasoning are rigid and inflexible. Neither deductive nor deductive reasoning allow for possibility, probability, incomplete data, incorrect assertions, randomness, intuition, or creativity.

Let's explore this for a moment. First, I stipulate that in this thought experiment we have no experience or training of any kind to help us determine the cause of the problem.

My computer is overheating. I can feel the top of the case and it is much hotter than it ever has been in my past experience. I turn the computer off, and after opening the case, I turn it back on for a moment. I can now see that a large case fan is not rotating.

Because I have no basis on which to reason that the failing case fan is the problem, I just take a chance and replace it with a new working one. This fixes the problem and the computer no longer overheats.

I use a bit of inductive reasoning as follows.

**Observation:** I fixed an overheating computer by replacing the case fan.

**Rule:** Replacing the case fan will fix computer overheating problems.

I have taken a single instance and generalized it into a rule. Now let's look at another problem. In this case a different computer is overheating. Here is my deductive logic.

**Rule:** Replacing the case fan fixes computer overheating problems.

**Assertion:** The computer is overheating.

**Conclusion:** I should replace the case fan.

In this bit of deductive logic, I have taken the rule I created from my single experience with overheating and applied it to a second instance of a computer overheating. I have taken a general rule and applied it to a specific instance. The logic is correct. There is no fault in the logic but replacing the case fan does not solve the problem. Why? Because in this second instance the power supply is overheating because the air intake is clogged with dust from the environment.

The difficulty here lies first in the fact that the rule we generated by our first overheating experience was faulty because it was too general. The second problem is that, based on this single faulty rule and the rigidity imposed by this form of reasoning, if forced me to a conclusion that could be the only possible cause of the problem and so I stopped looking for other root causes. The logic caused me to not even bother to check to see of the fan was working or not.

Another problem with this set of rigid logic is that there is no flexibility for other possibilities. Our rule set was too limited to solve the problem. This raises the questions of whether we can aver have a rule set large enough to solve all possible problems or that any single rule can be complex enough to resolve even a single symptom all the time. You see where I am going with this?

## Abductive Reason

Abductive reasoning is a third recognized form of reasoning and it is more complex while being more flexible. It allows for incomplete information and probabilities that specific relationships are present. It also allows that sometimes the best way to proceed is with an educated guess based on the available information.

Abductive reasoning takes the full body of whatever data is available – our observations – and allows us to draw conclusions that point to one or more of the most likely root causes of the observed symptoms. Abductive reasoning works regardless of whether we have all of the information or not. It allows us to draw conclusions based on the best information we have on hand. It allows flexibility because any rules we have put in place from previous inductive reasoning and any conclusions that we draw from those rules using deductive reasoning are not rigidly enforced.

With abductive reasoning, we need not accept the conclusion as the only possible result as inductive and deductive reason do. We are then free to adjust our body of rules, to restart our reasoning process with new data, that is, that the previous line of reason was incorrect – *in this case*. Thus, the freedom we now have to reason is the foundation for integrated reason.

## Integrated Reason

I believe that SysAdmins use all three of those previously discussed forms of reasoning to resolve problems. In fact, we do it so seamlessly that it is difficult to identify the specific portions of our thought processes that represent one of the three recognized forms of reasoning. In fact, this type of combinatorial reasoning is what successful SysAdmins use rather than a single style. This is called Integrated reason.

For example, I already have rules in place about overheating that I use to deduce possible causes. That example illustrates flexibility and the use of limited information to analyze the problem and use additional testing to obtain more data. It also allows for the inductive process that can add more rules to the rule set we use in our deductive process. It is also possible to disregard and discard rules that are clearly incorrect, outdated, or no longer needed.

Integrated reasoning feels seamless to me and perhaps it seems that way to you as well. I barely know that I am doing it and there is little or no indication when I switch from deductive to abductive reasoning, for example, as I progress in the process of problem solving. Integrated reasoning, intentional or not, conscious or not, helps me to avoid the pitfalls of "should." Not always but certainly most of the time. By understanding my own reasoning process, I can more easily recognize when I do get stuck in the "should" trap and more easily find my way out of it. For our overheating computer, this might mean a reasoning process more like this.

The computer is overheating, and I know from previous experience that there are at least two possible causes. I check over the computer and discover that none of the fans are failing and that the power supply is not overheating. Since neither of the two possible causes that I already know about are not the source of the current problem, I do some further checking using both the hddtemp command and the touchy-feely method, both of which show the fact that one hard drive is very hot.

I could replace the hard drive, but I noticed that there is no airflow around that hard drive. Further exploration reveals that there is a place to install a fan that would create a cooling flow of air over that hard drive. I install a new fan. I then check the hard drive and its temperature is now much cooler.

In the case of this actual problem, I did not just blindly replace the overheating component. The hard drive itself was not the cause of the problem despite the observable fact that it was very hot. The lack of a fan to provide cooling airflow was also a culprit, and there were other contributing factors. First, even though the fan provided enough airflow to cool the drive down to normal levels, I was curious, so I checked its usage patterns using System Activity Reporter – SAR. The SAR logs showed that the drive was in constant heavy use. Additional investigation using htop and glances showed that the /home filesystem was being heavily accessed by a program called baloo.

My filesystems were spread out over two physical hard drives, but the two most used, /home and /var were on the same drive. My first step, in order to reduce the stress on that hard drive, was to install a new hard drive as a means to spread the load and moved the most heavily used /home filesystem to that new drive. Then, I did some research on baloo, which turns out to be a file indexer that is a part of the KDE desktop environment. I figured out how to turn that off and that reduced the disk activity in /home to nearly zero except for my own work.

In reality, there were multiple causes for this single symptom of overheating and all of the fixes I implemented were appropriate. The root cause was a rogue program that produced heavy activity in a single filesystem. This caused a high level of disk activity, which overheated the disk drive. The lack of airflow over the drive due to the absence of a cooling fan only exacerbated the problem.

Yes, this was a real incident and not especially uncommon. Following the rigid logic forms could never bring us to the place where we would truly solve that problem and reduce the chances of it occurring again. Abductive reasoning allows us to be logical as well as creative and to think outside the alleged box. It also allows us to take preventative measures to ensure that the same or related problems do not recur.

Abductive reasoning allows us to learn from our experiences. This is true not just when things go right and we solve the problem but also, and especially, when things go wrong and we do not get it right.

# Self-Knowledge

Of course, these styles of reasoning are artificial structures that are intended to enable philosophers, psychologists, psychiatrists, and cognitive scientists to have a vocabulary and common structural referents to enable discussion and exploration of how we think.

These purely artificial structures should not be construed as limits on how SysAdmins should work. They are merely tools to enable us to understand ourselves and how we think. A little introspection can go a long way in helping us to become better at what we do.

# Finding Your Center

As a student of yoga, the first thing I do when starting my (almost) daily practice, whether in my own little yoga room or in a class, is to find my center. This is time to just be, and to use my mind to explore the physical aspects of my being while opening up to the experience of just existing.

Having done it myself, I suggest that this is an excellent method for exploring our thinking and reasoning as SysAdmins. That is not to say I use this technique to solve problems, but rather to explore my own methods for problem solving.

Many times, after solving a problem, particularly a new or especially difficult one, I spend some time just thinking about the problem. I start with the symptoms, my thinking process, and where those symptoms led me. I take time to consider what finally led me to the solution, things I might have done better, and what new things I might want to learn.

It gives me an opportunity to, as an individual, perform what we used to call a "lessons learned" meeting at one of my former places of employment. That was an opportunity to look at what we as a team did right and what we could have done better. The best and yet hardest part now is that I don't have others to help me understand what I could have done better. That makes it all the more important for me to do this as much as possible.

It is not necessary to practice yoga in order to do this. Just set aside some time, find an empty space where you won't be interrupted, close your eyes and contemplate. Breathe, relax, and calm your mind before trying to review the incident. Start from the beginning and think your way through the incident. Review the complete sequence of events and the steps you used to ultimately find the solution. The things you need to know and learn will make themselves clear to you. I find that this form of self-evaluation can be quite powerful.

I also like to take a moment before I start to work on a new problem to center myself. This opens my mind to the possibilities. First there are the possibilities that represent the likely causes of the problem. Then there are the possibilities that represent the methods and tools I have to locate the causes of the problem. Finally, there are the possibilities that represent the ways that there are to fix the problem.

# The Implications of Diversity

As individuals, our reasoning processes are complex and diverse. We each have different experiences that form the basis for the structures and processes we use in reasoning. No two of us will approach the task of solving a problem in the same way because of these differences.

I could not have asked for a better illustration of this particular tenet, "There is no should," than the command-line challenge I created for Opensource.com that we explored back in Chapter 4, "Transforming Data Streams." The incredible diversity of thought, creativity, and problem-solving approaches is staggering in its range and heartening in its implications.

The results from that challenge illustrate the huge variety of ways in which a few small, common utility programs can be combined to produce a correct result. This is an important point to remember when working with Linux. There are as many correct ways to solve a problem as there are SysAdmins, developers, DevOps, or whatever. What counts is the result.

## Measurement Mania

*Technology is dominated by two types of people: those who understand what they do not manage, and those who manage what they do not understand.*

—Archibald Putt, *Linux Journal*

I still hear PHBs talk about KLOCs,[7] keystrokes, error counts, and other types of numerical measurements designed so that they can be used by lower-level PHBs to report results to higher level PHBs and which are intended to show that progress is being made. These attempts to quantify the quality and volume of work performed by developers and SysAdmins completely miss the point and can lead to code bloat for developers. If you pay me to write X number of lines of code per day, I will, regardless of whether they are needed to perform the task the program is designed to do.

For SysAdmins, such attempted quantification results in symptom fixes and not fixing the root causes of problems. The number of tickets taken and resolved in a specified time period is a disgustingly ignorant way to measure performance. Productivity measurement concepts are based on time and motion study[8] practices developed by Taylor, Gilbreth, and Gilbreth in the mid-1800s and made popular with the industrialist management of those times. Wikipedia has a short but interesting article on time and motion.[9]

Using measurement strategies that are more than 150 years old, like these are, devalue the work being performed by SysAdmins and developers. They focus on the wrong things. They create the boundaries that are supposed to contain us in a manner that is comprehensible to the PHB who does not know how else to deal with us.

---

[7]KLOC is an acronym for "thousand (K) Lines of Code" that has been used by IT managers to measure performance.

[8]Time and motion study. BusinessDictionary.com. WebFinance, Inc. http://www.businessdictionary.com/definition/time-and-motion-study.html (accessed: April 01, 2018).

[9]Wikipedia, Time and motion study, https://en.wikipedia.org/wiki/Time_and_motion_study

Throughout this book we have looked at the lazy SysAdmin. It is impossible to measure the productivity of a thinking mind. I hope that such a thing never does become possible. Yet the results of the thinking SysAdmin can be indirectly measured in terms of the productivity achieved by the conclusions that resulted from that contemplation. For example, each new script – scripts that were conceived in our contemplative state, each new and improved method of installing and managing computers and their operating systems, and each failure mode analyzed for better methods, enhances overall productivity and results in diminished need for future intervention from SysAdmins and others. This results in more time for the SysAdmin to engage in unfettered thinking.

I have talked about the PHBs in a very derogatory manner throughout this book. Thanks to the Dilbert comic strip, PHB is now a common synonym for a really bad manager. I have had a few of these managers and they are destructive to good teams and to creative and successful SysAdmins. I have seen many good SysAdmins leave an organization because of toxic managers.

# The Good Manager

Despite the many PHBs in the real world, there are also a lot of really good managers, and I have been fortunate to have some of those in my career. The good ones – the ones that understand the technology and who understand how to manage those who deal directly with the technology – those are usually the few who have come up from the ranks. They were CEs, developers, SysAdmins, testers, or even hackers in previous jobs.

These amazing managers know that the best way to deal with those of us now doing the work is to ask a few knowledgeable questions to understand the situation and then step out of the way to let us fix whatever is wrong, while keeping the higher-level managers and PHBs informed as much as possible. They understand that we work best without constant micromanagement and that the freedom to do what is necessary is the hallmark of such a manager.

# Working Together

So now that I have you convinced that "there is no should" and it's all good just to do everything your own way, that leaves us with a question. How do all of us widely disparate SysAdmins all work together in teams?

Teams?! What teams? We don't need no stinkin' teams.

Actually, we do need teams, and we do need to work together in those teams. We have some excellent examples of teams and their results in pretty much every bit of open source software that exists.

Teams comprised of developers from around the planet work together to produce the open source software we all use and appreciate. Some of the team members may be paid but most are not and volunteer their time and energy to work on code. Other volunteers perform in the role of SysAdmins to help keep development systems up and running. Others test the resulting code and still others develop documentation.

Teams are as diverse geographically as the individuals comprising the teams are unique in the way they work best. This geographic dispersal of talent imposes some interesting and important constraints on working as a team.

In 2012, Ryan Tomayko wrote a blog post based on his experiences as an early employee at GitHub. Entitled, "Your team should work like an open source project,"[10] The premise of this post is that teams that are geographically compatible and that can work in the same office space, will work better if the same types of constraints on communication and interpersonal interactions that are imposed by geography on widely dispersed open source teams. According to Tomayko, "...processes designed to conform to open source constraints results in a project that runs well, attracts attention, and seems to be self perpetuating where the same project structured more traditionally requires much more manual coordination and authoritative prodding...[it] creates the possibility of cooperation without coordination. ..."

I strongly suggest that you read Tomayko's post. It has some interesting things to think about. He lists the constraints and says that the office, as a working space, is on the decline and will be mostly used as a space designed specifically for the mobile worker, providing those same services needed to work from places like your favorite cafe.

As SysAdmins we are often required to work across time zones and with team members we know only through electronic interactions. My own experience is in line with Tomayko's and shows that this can work better than when everyone is local and traditional alleged management is applied. Clearly, most open source projects are excellent examples of this success.

---

[10]Tomayko, Ryan, *Your team should work like an open source project*, https://tomayko.com/blog/2012/adopt-an-open-source-process-constraints

# Silo City

I was involved for about a year at one organization which is a fantastic example of the failure of the traditional team methodology taken to its extreme. The worst part is that it was also a horrible daily commute.

In this organization – which shall remain nameless – management had created very narrow, very tall silos to contain everything. There were multiple teams, the Unix team, the application team, the network team, the hardware team, the DNS team, the rack team, the cable team, the power team – pretty much any team you can think of.

And the procedures were mind boggling. For example, one of my projects was to install Linux on several servers that were to be used for various aspects of the organization's web site. The first step was to order the servers, but the request took weeks to work its way through the administrative bureaucracy.

Once the servers were delivered, the Unix team would rack them in the installation lab and install the operating system. We had that part down very nicely. But first we had to request an IP address. We could not do that before we had the servers delivered, because the request for IP address required the serial numbers of the servers and MAC addresses of the NICs.

The issue here was that each silo had to have a Service Level Agreement (SLA) with every other silo and the response time defined by the SAL was a minimum of two weeks. And every silo took no less time to respond than that specified in the SLA.

However, we could not get the IP address until we had a rack location assigned in the server room because IP addresses were assigned by rack and location in the rack. So we had to send a request for a rack assignment and wait two weeks for that to be provided.

So the next step after getting the IP address was to send that to the silo that handled DHCP configuration. Then it was at least two weeks after getting the IP address that we had to wait before the DHCP was set up.

Only when the network configuration data for the server was configured on the DHCP server could the request for moving the server from our rack to the server room be sent. Another two-week turnaround.

After the move request was approved – and only after – we could then send a request to install the computer in the rack. After the installation was complete, then we could send the request to cable the server with network and power. Only when that was completed could we send a request to power on the server.

Except for installing the operating system, we could not touch the server. We were not even allowed to enter the server room. Ever.

Needless to say, it took months to install each server and get it running and ready for the production teams to take over. I could go on about many more ways in which this place was a functional disaster, but I think you get the idea. Their alleged teams were just political fiefdoms, protected by silos that were impenetrable.

## The Easy Way

I had a much better experience at Cisco with BRuce. You will learn more about BRuce in the next chapter. He and I had a really great system worked out.

The servers were usually delivered less than a week after we ordered them. BRuce and I would rack four of them in the morning, assign IP addresses, configure the switches to which they were connected, add them to DNS and DHCP servers and install Linux on them. We would do four more in the afternoon.

The difference is that all of the teams worked together. The teams that dealt with network addressing and configuration had written scripts – automate everything – and gave us access so that we could use those scripts to do all of the network configuration for DHCP and DNS. The script that I wrote was used to perform the Linux installations.

BRuce and I were totally responsible for the racks and everything in them that had to do with getting the servers up and running. He and I worked well as a team because we took a bit of time each day to determine what needed to be done and decide which of us would take on each of the various tasks that we needed to accomplish. This was not a meeting; there was nothing at all formal about it. No one assigned us tasks based on some arbitrary criteria. Both BRuce and I were SysAdmins with strong personalities. When left alone to do our jobs, we did so quickly and with ease. We simply split the tasks between us as we both felt appropriate and went about our business. Many times we required the assistance of other SysAdmins, both local and remote, and we would simply continue to have our little morning discussions to determine the work for the day, splitting it up between three or four of us, depending upon how many we were. We worked well with the other teams and would usually turn over the servers to the developers or testers by late the same day they were delivered to the lab.

Management cooperated in this methodology. We were simply told that a new project was starting up or that there were changes that needed to be made to an existing one. We would confer with the project leaders to determine what their needs and objectives were. As you will see in the next chapter, sometimes BRuce and I had to work at it to get the information we needed, but once we had it we took care of the rest with little or no intervention or oversight from management.

# Thoughts

Those of us who are successful at Unix and Linux System Administration are by our very nature inquisitive and thoughtful. We take every opportunity to expand our knowledge base.

We like to experiment with new knowledge, new hardware, and new software out of curiosity and "because it is there." We relish the opportunities that are opened to us when computer things break. Every problem is a new possibility for learning. We enjoy attending technical conferences as much for the access to other SysAdmins they afford as for the amazing amount of new information that we can gather from the scheduled presentations.

Rigid logic and rules do not give us SysAdmins enough flexibility to perform our jobs efficiently. We don't especially care about how things "should" be done. SysAdmins are not easily limited by the "shoulds" that others try to constrain us with. We use logical and critical thinking that is flexible and that produces excellent results. We create our own ways of doing things with independent, critical thinking, and integrated reasoning, which enables us to learn more while we are at it.

We SysAdmins are strong personalities – we need to be in order to do our jobs and especially to do things the "right" way. This is not about how we "should" perform the tasks we need to do, rather it is about using best practices and ensuring that the end result conforms to those practices.

We don't just think outside the box. We are the ones who destroy the boxes that others try to make us work inside. For us, there is no "should."

# CHAPTER 24

# Mentor the Young SysAdmins

I have taken many training courses over the years and most have been very useful in helping me to learn more about Unix and Linux as well as a host of other subjects. But training – as useful and important as it is – cannot cover many essential aspects of performing SysAdmin duties.

All of the classes I have attended were a few days in length, usually four or five. There is just too much information to be able to cover everything you need to know just with respect to commands, procedures, filesystems, processes, and many of the things we have touched on in this book. And not everything can be taught in the classroom. Some things can only be taught by a good mentor in a real-world environment, usually while you are under extreme pressure to fix a critical problem.

There is nothing like having the PHB or one or more minions looking over your shoulder and criticizing your every move and decision. It happens. These pressures to provide hourly progress reports, to answer dumb questions like, "when will it be fixed," to resist the PHB's attempts to add three more people to a one-person task, and much more, not only wastes our time, it also breaks our train of thought and reduces our overall efficiency. Most of the time we know what to do and how to do it, we just need an environment that will allow us to work in relative peace.

A good mentor will allow you to do the actual work in these situations so you can have a valuable learning experience while keeping the wolves at bay, taking the heat while you work uninterrupted. A great mentor will also be able to create a learning opportunity from every situation no matter how critical.

© David Both 2018
D. Both, *The Linux Philosophy for SysAdmins*, https://doi.org/10.1007/978-1-4842-3730-4_24

When I first started, I was a young and innocent SysAdmin. I was fortunate because I worked at a couple different jobs where other, seasoned SysAdmins were willing to mentor me and encourage me. None of them laughed at me when I asked what must have seemed to them to have answers that were blindingly obvious. None of these patient SysAdmins ever told me to RTFM.

# Hiring the Right People

Mentoring the right people is never simple or easy; mentoring the wrong people is impossible. With that in mind, let's take a look at how to hire the right people.

As a SysAdmin, particularly if you are a senior SysAdmin, part of your job should be to help hire the right people as part of your team. If your PHB isolates you from the hiring process, you should do everything in your power to change that. Fortunately, this has seldom been a problem in most of my work life. The smart managers will get their entire team involved with hiring new members.

One of the best and most enjoyable interviews I ever had was when I applied for a job as a tester and part-time lab SysAdmin at Cisco. I spent a little time with the manager, and then the rest of the people in the department tag-teamed me for about five hours. They came in groups of two or three and asked me all kinds of questions. Each group gave me hypothetical situations to solve, they asked me technical questions, and they tested my patience. I actually had fun in that interview because every one of the people who interviewed me was the right person for the job they had been hired to do. I did get that job. I did not know everything. I did tell the interviewers that fact when it was true.

There are many methods that can be used to hire the right people, but there is no foolproof method for doing so. I have, however found that the right interviewers and the right questions can go a long way to making that happen.

As I have previously mentioned, a lot of people who interview for SysAdmin types of positions are not ready because they have no idea how to solve problems. Sometimes you cannot tell this until you hire the person, and it may be difficult to "unhire" them at that point. One place I worked used a hands-on test. Our test was simple. We set up a Linux host with three specific but fairly simple problems that the applicant had to fix within a specified amount of time.

Although this test was about finding and fixing the problems, we also looked at the manner in which the applicant approached the task. Those who panicked or who proceeded more or less randomly, thrashing about with little direction were quickly eliminated from our consideration. Even if they did not resolve all of the problems, those who proceeded with some sense of purpose, with a well-developed problem-solving algorithm, those were the ones we considered most likely to be successful in the jobs we had available. We could easily teach the technology, but we could not easily teach the problem-solving techniques and Zen.

There can be legal issues with testing but, if the test is truly representative of the type of work the applicants will be doing, and all of the applicants are required to take the test, then (check with your lawyers) it should be fine to use a test.

# Mentoring

How does one mentor a young SysAdmin? How many stars are there in the galaxy? Every SysAdmin has their own way of mentoring, and each young SysAdmin needs different knowledge and a different approach.

It was easier to learn when I had an excellent teacher, but I found that when I enjoyed a subject and had interest in it, the quality of my teachers made little difference. The best mentors allowed and even encouraged me to follow my curiosity. They rewarded me when I experimented even when I failed to accomplish my goal.

However, a really bad teacher can destroy not only the desire to learn but also the ability to learn. One nontechnical example was my high school English literature teacher. It was quite obvious that she really enjoyed the books, stories, poems, and other literature that we were supposed to learn. Unfortunately, she had no idea how to teach or how to transmit that love of the subject to we students. We studied Shakespeare, among others, and I was bored out of my skull.

The next summer, because I had been in some school plays, and the drama teacher liked my work, she recommended me to a recruiter for the Irish Hills Playhouse, a summer stock theater doing Shakespearean repertory in southern Michigan. Wow! A whole summer of Shakespeare? Yes, and I loved it. As an apprentice that summer, I learned more about Shakespeare than I would ever have in a classroom environment with teachers like the one I had for that lit class.

I had a couple good mentors that summer. They held training sessions for all of us. They helped us learn the meaning of the material as well as the mechanics of acting. For me, it was the understanding that was the most helpful. I think that understanding is one of the most important things that a mentor can help with. Rote memorization is not the key – understanding and critical thinking and problem solving skills are the most important things that my technical mentors bestowed upon me.

# BRuce the Mentor

I was fortunate in having a number of very fine and patient mentors who allowed me to fail so that I might learn. One person in particular, BRuce, as he liked to sign his emails, ensured that I had the necessary training, but he also allowed me put that training to use very quickly. He assigned me to difficult tasks right away, ones that forced me to use my newfound knowledge and to break through the boundaries of my own comfort and self-imposed limitations.

BRuce and I worked together at two different companies over the years, both of which required deep Unix/Linux knowledge and skills. We worked together well because we were both very good at what we did. He understood that I did not start with the same skill level that he had, but he respected the skills I did have and gave me plenty of opportunity to use those skills and learn new ones.

In many ways, BRuce was the quintessential grumpy SysAdmin – and with good reason. What I mean by this is that, when dealing with less-technical people such as marketing people and the PHBs about things they wanted to do in the labs for which we were responsible, his first response was almost always a flat, definite, "no." This was always because the projects, whatever they were, would cause problems in the lab as they were initially conceived because they were all poorly thought out with no concept of what could and could not be done. BRuce then asked the persons who made the request a series of questions that eventually led us to what they really wanted to do. It seems that most of the people making these requests were also trying to design the infrastructure to support those projects and that was our area of expertise, not theirs. They were also not very thoughtful about how their projects might affect others using the lab to test their projects.

BRuce was not being a jerk like some people thought. He was doing his job, which was to ensure that the lab was fully functional for everyone who used it. Most of the initial requests that we received were significantly flawed. It was our responsibility to ensure that those flaws did not affect the rest of the lab. BRuce was just very blunt because we did not have the time to deal with problems caused by other people when it was just the two of us dealing with more than 15 rows with 24 racks each in the lab, all of them full of equipment running tests that would have had to be restarted if the Lab network were to be compromised by someone's experiments run amok.

In that type of environment, there was no tolerance for errors. BRuce and I were simply enforcing lab guidelines that had been designed to protect all of the users. As my mentor, this is also something that BRuce was trying to help me understand – that this is one of those times when the good of the many outweighs the good of the few. The lab had to be run in a manner that prevented some users from impinging upon the work of the rest.

# The Art of Problem Solving

One of the best things that my mentors helped me with was the formulation of a defined process that I could always use for solving problems of nearly any type. As I look at it, it is very closely related to the scientific method.

During my research for this book, I discovered a short article entitled, "How the Scientific Method Works,"[1] that describes the scientific method using a diagram very much like the one I have created for my Five Steps of Problem Solving. So I pass this on as a mentor and it is my contribution to all of you young SysAdmins. I hope that you find it as useful as I have.

Solving problems of any kind is art, science, and – some would say – perhaps a bit of magic, too. Solving technical problems, such as those that occur with computers, requires a good deal of specialized knowledge as well.

Any approach to solving problems of any nature – including problems with Linux – must include more than just a list of symptoms and the steps necessary to fix or circumvent the problems that caused the symptoms. This so-called "symptom-fix" approach looks good on paper to the managers, but it really sucks in practice. The best way to approach problem solving is with a large base of knowledge of the subject and a strong methodology.

# The Five Steps of Problem Solving

There are five basic steps that are involved in the problem solving process as shown in Figure 24-1. This algorithm is very similar to that of the Scientific Method referred to in footnote 1 but is specifically intended for solving technical problems.

---

[1]Harris, William, *How the Scientific Method Works*, https://science.howstuffworks.com/innovation/scientific-experiments/scientific-method6.htm

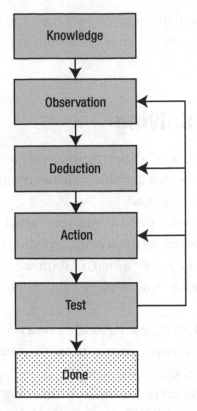

**Figure 24-1.** *The Five Steps of Problem Solving are much like those of the Scientific Method*

You probably already follow these steps when you troubleshoot a problem but do not even realize it. These steps are universal and apply to solving most any type of problem, not just problems with computers or Linux. I used these steps for years in various types of problems without realizing it. Having them codified for me made me much more effective at solving problems because when I became stuck, I could review the steps I had taken, verify where I was in the process, and restart at any appropriate step.

You may have heard a couple other terms applied to problem solving in the past. The first three steps of this process are also known as problem determination, that is, finding the root cause of the problem. The last two steps are problem resolution, which is actually fixing the problem.

The next sections covers each of these five steps in more detail.

# Knowledge

Knowledge of the subject in which you are attempting to solve a problem is the first step. All of the articles I have seen about the scientific method seem to assume this as a prerequisite. However the acquisition of knowledge is an ongoing process, driven by curiosity and augmented by the knowledge gained from using the scientific method to explore and extend your existing knowledge through experimentation. This is one of the reasons I use the term "experiment" in this book rather than something like "lab project."

You must be knowledgeable about Linux at the very least, and even more, you must be knowledgeable about the other factors that can interact with and affect Linux, such as hardware, the network, and even environmental factors such as how temperature, humidity and the electrical environment in which the Linux system operates can affect it.

Knowledge can be gained by reading books and web sites about Linux and those other topics. You can attend classes, seminars, and conferences. You can also just set up a number of Linux computers in a networked environment and through interaction with other knowledgeable people. Knowledge is gained when you resolve a problem and discover a new cause for a particular type of problem. You can also find new knowledge when an attempt to fix a problem results in a temporary failure.

Classes are also valuable in providing us with new knowledge. My personal preference is to play – uh, experiment – with Linux or with a particular piece such as networking, name services, DHCP, Chrony, and more, and then take a class or two to help me internalize the knowledge I have gained.

Remember, "Without knowledge, resistance is futile," to paraphrase the Borg. Knowledge is power.

# Observation

The second step in solving the problem is to observe the symptoms of the problem. It is important to take note of all of the problem symptoms. It is also important to observe what is working properly. This is not the time to try to fix the problem; merely observe.

Another important part of observation is to ask yourself questions about what you see and what you do not see. Aside from the questions you need to ask that are specific to the problem, there are some general questions to ask.

- Is this problem caused by hardware, Linux, application software, or perhaps by lack of user knowledge or training?

- Is this problem similar to others I have seen?

- Is there an error message?

- Are there any log entries pertaining to the problem?

- What was taking place on the computer just before the error occurred?

- What did I expect to happen if the error had not occurred?

- Has anything about the system hardware or software changed recently?

Other questions will reveal themselves as you work to answer these. The important thing to remember here is not the specific questions, but rather to gather as much information as possible. This increases the knowledge you have about this specific problem instance and aids in finding the solution.

As you gather data, never assume that the information obtained from someone else is correct. Observe everything yourself. This can be a major problem if you are working with someone who is at a remote location. Careful questioning is essential, and tools that allow remote access to the system in question are extremely helpful when attempting to confirm the information that you are given. When questioning a person at a remote site, never ask leading questions; they will try to be helpful by answering with what they think you want to hear.

At other times the answers you receive will depend upon how much or how little knowledge the person has of Linux and computers in general. When a person knows — or thinks they know — about computers, the answers you receive may contain assumptions that can be difficult to disprove. Rather than ask. "Did you check...," it is better to have the other person actually perform the task required to check the item. And rather than telling the person what they should see, simply have the user explain or describe to you what they do see. Again, remote access to the machine can allow you to confirm the information you are given.

The best problem solvers are those who never take anything for granted. They never assume that the information they have is 100% accurate or complete. When the information you have seems to contradict itself or the symptoms, start over from the beginning as if you have no information at all.

In almost all of the jobs I have had in the computer business, we have always tried to help each other out and this was true when I was at IBM. I have always been very good at fixing things, and there were times when I would show up at a customer when another CE was having a particularly difficult time finding the source of a problem. The first thing I would do is assess the situation. I would ask the primary CE what they had done so far to locate the problem. After that I would start over from the beginning. I always wanted to see the results myself. Many times that paid off because I would observe something that others had missed. In one very strange incident, I fixed a large computer by sitting on it.

## Sitting Down on the Job

This took place while I was an IBM CE in Lima, Ohio, in about 1976. Two of us were were installing an IBM System 3, which was smaller than an IBM mainframe, like a 360 or 370, but still large enough to need a room of its own, high voltage power, and significant air cooling.

We had assembled the main CPU and had started to attach the IBM 1403 line printer controller when we ran into the problem. The printer controller was contained in a slightly lower than desktop-height unit to the left of the CPU. That nice large work surface is just the right height to sit on.

We had just bolted the printer controller to the frame of the CPU and were doing one of the very many checks built into the installation instructions. We connected the leads of an Ohm meter between the frame of the CPU and a specific terminal on the power supply of the printer controller. The result was supposed to be an open circuit, that is, infinite resistance, which would indicate that the hot leads of the power supply were not shorted to the frame. In this case there was a short – zero resistance – which was bad. There would not have been a spectacular display of noise and fireworks like you see on TV, but it would have been a problem as it would prevent the computer from powering up. Best to catch this while it was still being assembled rather than later.

After an hour of trying to find the problem, we were unable to do so. We called the support center for the System/3 in Boca Raton, Florida, and were guided through several further problem determination steps that were unsuccessful.

A bit frustrated, I sat on the printer control unit. Out of the corner of my eye, I saw the needle on the Ohm meter swing to indicate an open circuit. I mentioned this to the other CE and to Vern in Boca Raton, who would later be one of my own mentors when I went down there for a few years as a Course Development Representative (CSR).

We removed the top, where I had perched, from the controller and with a bit of luck, found that one of the bolts holding the top to the frame of the printer controller had come loose and fallen into the power supply and caused the short. When I sat on the top of the controller, the frame moved just enough to cause the bolt to no longer make the contact required to produce the short. Removing that loose bolt from the power supply fixed the problem.

Vern, who was responsible for the System/3 support at that time, made some changes to the instructions to cover this problem in case it happened again. He also worked with the manufacturing people to *ensure* that it did not happen again, putting in place a check to ensure that the bolt was properly tightened during the build process.

The thing to remember is to really observe what is going on in all parts of the system. Pay attention to everything and don't ignore the slightest clue. Sometimes watching top or one of the other utilities used to monitor the internal functioning of the kernel or the network can provide a momentary glimpse of something – a clue – that gets us started in the right direction.

And sometimes it takes just a bit of luck like sitting on the printer control unit.

# Reasoning

Use reasoning skills to take the information from your observations of the symptoms, your knowledge to determine a probable cause for the problem. We discussed the different types of reasoning in some detail in Chapter 23. The process of reasoning through your observations of the problem, your knowledge, and your past experience is where art and science combine to produce inspiration, intuition, or some other mystical mental process that provides some insight to the root cause of the problem.

In some cases this is a fairly easy process. You can see an error code and look up its meaning from the sources available to you. Or perhaps you observe a symptom that is familiar and you know what steps might resolve it. You can then apply the vast knowledge you have gained by reading about Linux, this book, and the documentation provided with Linux to reason your way to the cause of the problem.

In other cases it can be a very difficult and lengthy part of the problem determination process. These are the types of cases that can be the most difficult. Perhaps symptoms you have never seen or a problem that is not resolved by any of the methods you have used. It is these difficult ones that require more work and especially more reasoning applied to them.

It helps to remember that the symptom is not the problem. The problem causes the symptom. You want to fix the true problem, not just the symptom.

## Action

Now is the time to perform the appropriate repair action. This is usually the simple part. The hard part is what came before – figuring out what to do. After you know the cause of the problem, it is easy to determine the correct repair action to take.

The specific action you take will depend upon the cause(s) of the problem. Remember, we are fixing the root cause, not just trying to get rid of or cover up the symptom.

Make only one change at a time. If there are several actions that can be taken that might correct the cause of a problem, only make the one change or take the one action that is most likely to resolve the root cause. The selection of the corrective action with the highest probability of fixing the problem is what you are trying to do here. Whether it is your own experience telling you which action to take, or the experiences of others, move down the list from highest to lowest priority, one action at a time. Test the results after each action.

## Test

After taking some overt repair action, the repair should be tested. This usually means performing the task that failed in the first place but it could also be a single, simple command that illustrates the problem.

We discussed testing in Chapter 11 in conjunction with writing code for shell scripts and the process is the same here. We make a single change, taking one potential corrective action and then testing the results of that action. This is the only way in which we can be certain which corrective action fixed the problem. If we were to make several corrective actions and then test one time, there is no way to know which action was responsible for fixing the problem. This is especially important if we want to walk back those ineffective changes we made after finding the solution.

If the repair action has not been successful, you should begin the procedure over again. If there are additional corrective actions you can take, return to that step and continue doing so until you have run out of possibilities or have learned with to a certainty that you are on the wrong track.

Be sure to check the original observed symptoms when testing. It is possible that they have changed due to the action you have taken and you need to be aware of this in order to make informed decisions during the next iteration of the process. Even if the problem has not been resolved, the altered symptom could be very valuable in determining how to proceed.

# Example

One example of solving a problem from my own experience occurred in my role as a part-time Linux System Administrator. It is fairly simple but is useful to illustrate the process flow of the steps I have outlined.

I received an email from one of our testers indicating that an application he had installed as part of a test was crashing. It was giving error messages indicating that it was out of swap space. This is the initial **Observation** performed by the user and transmitted to me.

My **Knowledge** told me that the system that was being used for testing this application had 16GB of RAM and 2GB of swap space. Previous experience **(Knowledge)** told me that swap space in these computers is almost never used and RAM usage is typically far below 25% of the 16GB of RAM in these boxes.

At this point I **Reasoned** that the problem was not really a problem with swap space as that would seem highly improbable. I could still hold that possibility open, though only very slightly. You will find that many error messages provided by programs can be quite misleading and user observations can be even more so.

I made some **Observations** of my own. I logged into the box and used the **free** command as a tool to view memory and swap space. I could **Observe** that there was lots of free RAM and swap space usage was at zero. I **Know** that if swap space usage is actually zero, then it is very likely that none of the available swap space has never been allocated and no paging has occurred since the last boot.

I also **Reasoned** from previous experience **(Knowledge)** that there might be a kernel of truth in that error message. That being it was very likely to be out of some resource or other. The other primary consumable resources are CPU cycles and disk space.

This did not seem like a CPU problem so I **Observed** disk space using the **df** command, which showed that the /var filesystem was full. I **Reasoned** that the full filesystem was the cause of the problem. A little exploration of /var indicated that the tester's software was indeed located there and had filled the filesystem.

All of the systems were kickstarted with a /var filesystem of 1.5GB. The policy was to install application programs in /opt, which is where the ones we were supposed to test were designed to be installed, and which was configured to take all remaining disk space so can easily be 100GB or more in size – more than enough for any of the applications that were being tested.

I discussed this with the tester and was told that he had indeed installed the application in /var. I told him to uninstall the new program from there and install the application in /opt where it belonged. After taking this **Action**, I had him **Test** the corrective action by performing the operation that had previously failed. The test was successful and the problem solved.

## Iteration

As you work through a problem, it will be necessary to iterate through at least some of the steps. If, for example, performing a given corrective action does not resolve the problem, you may need to try another action that has also been known to resolve the problem in the past. Figure 24-1 shows that you may need to iterate to any previous step in order to continue.

It may be necessary to go back to the observation step and gather more information about the problem. I have also found that sometimes it was a good idea to go back to the Knowledge step and gather more basic knowledge. This latter includes reading or rereading manuals, man pages, using Google, whatever is necessary to gain the knowledge required to continue past the point where I was blocked.

Be flexible and don't hesitate to step back and start over if nothing else produces some forward progress.

## Concluding Thoughts

In this chapter we have looked at one way to approach fixing problems that applies to many non-technical things as well as to computer hardware and software. What we have discussed here is how specific reasoning methods can be used within the framework of an algorithm for problem solving. The flexibility of this particular combination is extremely powerful.

I am not telling you that you "should" use this method. However, if you go all Zen and analyze your own method for solving problems, you will very likely find that it is already very close to the algorithm I describe here. As a mentor, I am suggesting that you do take the time to analyze your own methods. I think you will find it a productive use of time that will be quite enlightening.

I also implore you to mentor others. Pass along the knowledge, skills, and your own philosophy. There is very little that can be more important than this for experienced SysAdmins. Our skills are amazing and we did not achieve them all by ourselves. We are amazing because of those who mentored us and the fact that they thought we had what it takes to be great SysAdmins. It is our responsibility to pass that along to the younger SysAdmins.

Finally, I had some amazing mentors who understood what it takes to learn – to really learn – and who allowed me to do so. You all gave me the opportunity to learn through failure. You helped my figure out where I went wrong and got me back on track. You are my heroes. Here's to you, Alyce, BRuce, Vern, Dan, Chris, Heather, Ron, Don, Dave, Earl, and Pam. And to all of you unsung mentors out there – You rock! Thanks for your support and guidance.

# CHAPTER 25

# Support Your Favorite Open Source Project

Linux and a very large proportion of the programs that we run on it are open source programs. Many of the larger projects, such as the kernel itself, are supported directly by foundations set up for that purpose, such as the Linux Foundation, and/or by corporations and other organizations that have an interest in doing so.

As a SysAdmin, I write a lot of scripts and I like doing so, but I am not an application programmer. Nor do I want to be because I enjoy the work of a SysAdmin, which allows for a different kind of programming. So, for the most part, contributing code to an open source project is not a good option for me. There are other ways to contribute and I use those options. This chapter will help you explore some of the ways in which you might contribute.

## Project Selection

Before we discuss the different ways in which we can contribute to open source projects, we will look at how to select a project to which we want to contribute. This may seem daunting because of the many projects that need support of one kind or another.

My primary considerations are whether I use the software or hardware produced by the project. For example, I use LibreOffice daily. I depend upon it and find it incredibly useful to my productivity. So one of the projects I support is LibreOffice.

I also support high-level organizations, ones that oversee certain aspects of open source such as the Linux Foundation, which supports and encourages the use of open source software and which supports many different open source communities.

Pick some project that has some meaning for you and support it. But do not forget about the "hidden" projects. Some of those projects are critical to the success of

477

open source software yet nobody knows about them and so they get no support. The Heartbleed[1] vulnerability from a few years ago is an example of this type of project. With only one maintainer at that and a tiny budget, the OpenSSL software that is used in virtually every Linux distribution and other operating systems as well, had a bug – a vulnerability – that endangered every computer that used OpenSSL. This vulnerability had been around since 2012[2] but had not been discovered until 2014.

The vulnerability was quickly fixed, and some organizations contributed to the project to ensure that the developers could continue work on it and to help ensure that no additional vulnerabilities existed in the code.

Whatever you choose, find some project that you can support and do so in some way that makes sense to you and that is fun. It should always be fun!

# Code

Just because I choose not to contribute code to open source projects does not mean that you should avoid it also. I know that many SysAdmins are excellent programmers and could be very helpful to one or more of the hundreds of open source projects out there. Without the coders, there would be no projects in the first place.

Many projects have large teams of developers and others are quite small, sometimes with only a single developer who works on their open source project as a second, non-paying job. Other developers work for larger organizations that pay them to code for open source projects, usually because the organization has some specific interest in that project. A new developer for a small project would be very welcome in most cases, but larger projects are also very grateful to have new developers.

Different coding languages are used in different projects. Many projects are coded in C or C++ while others use interpreted languages such as Perl, PHP, Python, Ruby, bash, or other shell scripting languages.

Whatever your skill level, you can find a project that has plenty of tasks for you to work on.

---

[1]Heartbleed web site, `http://heartbleed.com/`
[2]Wikipedia, *Heartbleed*, `https://en.wikipedia.org/wiki/Heartbleed`

# Test

After the code is written, someone needs to test it. Testing is just as important as writing the code is in the first place. We discussed testing in detail in Chapter 11, "Test Early, Test Often," assigning it a chapter to itself because of its importance.

Some projects need dedicated testers who take code as soon as it is completed by the developer and run it through a series of formal tests. This is very similar to half of my responsibilities when I worked at Cisco. This type of testing requires writing a formal test plan and then systematically working through the plan. Failed tests are reported back to the developers to fix.

You can also download and test beta versions of many common and popular software packages. Most of these beta versions are put out to the world with the explicit intent of eliciting bug reports – and fixes if you are so inclined. This type of testing is usually less rigorous. The project leaders make the product available for use in the real world and may provide some direction such as to test a specific feature. You use the product just as you would a final version, but when you find a bug, you report it to the project for fixing.

# Submit Bug Reports

Submitting bug reports is a very important way to support an open source project. I have done a few of these and it is easy to do.

Most projects have well-defined and documented methods for reporting bugs. Many projects use Bugzilla for reporting bugs and some use other tools including some homegrown ones, or even just emails to the developers. The details of how to submit bugs are usually found through a link on the project home page.

In this case we are not talking about beta testing as in the previous section. Here we are using final release code that has passed all of the alpha and beta testing that could be devised to test it. This is real world, "test in production," type of testing; because production is the best and final test.

When we find a bug in a production product, even though this is not part of an official test program of any type, it is incumbent upon us to submit a bug report to the project. Almost every project as some means of reporting bugs.

Requests for more information from the developers are common so that they might narrow down the source of the problem. These requests are important and quick responses are very helpful. Much of the time these requests are to clarify the conditions under which the error occurred such as the operating system version, or the amount of free memory, swap, and disk space available at the time of the failure. In one case I was asked by a kernel developer to install a kernel version with checkpoints designed to help the developer locate the portion of code in which the problem existed.

Reporting bugs in production software helps to make it better for all users, not just ourselves.

# Documentation

Documentation is an area where many of us can participate regardless of whether we code or not. Although there are many jokes about people not reading the documentation (RTFM), the documentation is very important.

There are different types of documentation. These range from man pages for command-line utilities and tools, to complete online manuals for large applications such as that for LibreOffice. LibreOffice has a series of well-written manuals that can be downloaded as PDF files or used online with your browser.

LibreOffice also has an excellent help facility with a table of contents, an index, and a search utility. Figure 25-1 shows the first page of the LibreOffice help facility. It has clear directions for using it and different methods for finding information. It is one of the best help facilities I have seen.

For those of us who like to write, creating and maintaining documentation can be an excellent way to contribute.

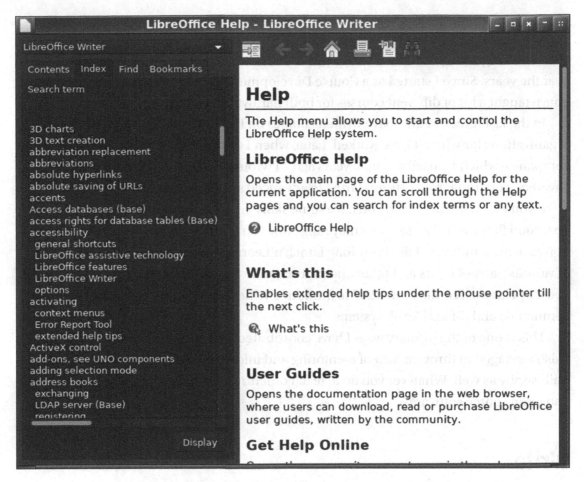

*Figure 25-1.* *The main page of the LibreOffice help facility offers multiple options for locating information about the current application. David Both, CC-by-SA.*

# Assist

Assisting others is another great way to support open source software. This type of participation offers many different options.

One option is to participate in local meetups where open source enthusiasts discuss the advantages of open source with people who are unfamiliar with it. In many of these meetups, sometimes called install fests, the experienced users help the noobs install Linux and get started with the basics. Another option is to simply introduce your friends and family to Linux and help them get started. Some Linux users like to hang out on various forums and IRC chat rooms to help people by answering questions.

I do this sometimes, but it is not what I do best.

# Teach

I like teaching. I am good at it according to the course evaluation forms I have received over the years. Since I started as a Course Development Representative at IBM in 1978, I have taught a lot of different courses for both hardware and software.

In the last fifteen years I have written courses on Linux and taught them for various organizations for which I have worked. Later, when I started my own Linux consulting company – which I closed a couple years ago – I wrote three multi-day courses that covered everything from getting started to advanced system administration.

If you are so inclined, and you have some skills in doing presentations, teaching may be a good fit for you. The sessions may range from an hour in length or a week. At two of my employers I did hour-long Lunch'n'Learn sessions that were just overviews of various parts of Linux and other open source software. At other places I did one- or two-day classes that were intended to introduce Windows admins to some basic Linux commands and things like filesystems.

This is one of the primary ways I have contributed – by spreading my knowledge. I also managed to throw in a bit of mentoring and information about my Linux Philosophy as well. Whatever you do to teach others is helping them to learn about Linux and open source software.

# Write

I also like to write. This book is only one of my writing projects, the others being my frequent articles for Opensource.com[3] and my own web sites, especially the Linux DataBook[4] web site. The DataBook web site is my attempt to record things I have learned that were hard to find.

The DataBook web site began life back in my days at IBM as a database of information about OS/2.The database was designed to allow me and the other OS/2 support personnel to locate information about OS/2 quickly. I also used it to ensure that once I had discovered how to do something, or found a particularly elusive bit of information, that I would not have to reinvest the time spent obtaining it. It was basically a memory aid for me. Much of that information on OS/2 also appeared as Chapter 6,

---

[3]Opensource.com, https://opensource.com/
[4]DataBook for Linux, http://www.linux-databook.info/

"File Systems," and Chapter 22, "Troubleshooting," in the hardcopy book, *Inside OS/2 Warp.*[5]" After I left IBM, this information became the basis for the *DataBook for OS/2*, which like its predecessor, was a memory tool for me in my independent consulting company.

After OS/2 was dropped by IBM, I started writing two new books, *The DataBook for Linux Administrators* and the *DataBook for Linux Users.* These two new(er) books are collection of data about Linux, particularly about Fedora Linux, for System Administrators and users, respectively. They contain information that I have discovered over the years I have been using Linux and that I need to maintain for myself – again as a memory aid. I also wanted to make this information available to everyone so I put it all up on my web site.

I have written many articles for Opensource.com that are mostly deep dives into some important subjects such as filesystems, various server software, desktops, and other Linux and open source software.

Writing articles and books that help SysAdmins and others who want to be SysAdmins is my own primary means to give back to the open source community and also to provide some level of mentoring even if it is at somewhat of a remove from the intended recipients.

Here again, if you are good with the written word, you may find that writing about Linux and open source is a good way for you to help.

# Donate

Finally, most projects accept monetary donations. At first glance, this would seem to be a rather crass, hands-off way of providing support for an open source project, but all projects need monetary support. I have chosen three to which I contribute a bit of money from time to time.

Because of its importance in my day-to-day work, I support LibreOffice[6] with small donations. I also support a couple of the high-level organizations. I donate to the Linux Foundation[7] because they support Linux infrastructure, they directly support Linus

---

[5]Mark Minasi, et al, *Inside OS/2 Warp*, New Riders Publishing, 1995
[6]LibreOffice web site, *Support LibreOffice*, https://www.libreoffice.org/donate/
[7]Linux Foundation, *Donate to The Linux Foundation*, https://www.linuxfoundation.org/about/donate/

Torvalds by paying him to continue his work on the kernel, and they support other open source communities that are important to its well-being and growth. I also donate to the Open Source Initiative,[8] which is responsible for approving various licenses and certifying that they comply with open source principals.

There are many other open source organizations and projects that are in need of funding. Your monetary donation can directly support the work of those who at the forefront of the open source movement.

# Thoughts

Open source is all about contributing in one way or another. My primary contributions have been in teaching and writing. I like doing both of those things and I am good at them.

I am not going to list a bunch of projects here. The primary reason is that there are too many and I would certainly miss some. Any such list printed here would be a snapshot at a point in time – even if I could list them all – and would be obsolete before I submitted the first draft to my publisher. I have simply listed a very few that I support at the time of this writing.

So if you want to support a project, pick one that you are familiar with and that has made a difference for you, locate its home page, and find out there how to contribute in some way that makes sense for you.

Then contribute!

---

[8]The Open Source Initiative, *Donate*, https://opensource.org/civicrm/contribute/transact?reset=1&id=2

# Reality Bytes

We have had our heads in the clouds for most of this book. It is, after all, a book of technical philosophy that would not normally be very practical. I just want to take this opportunity to bring us back down to the real world before the book ends.

There is "truth" here. Reality imposes itself upon SysAdmins every day in a multitude of ways. It is possible always to be able to follow each of the tenets previously set forth in this book – but it is quite improbable. In the "real" world, we SysAdmins face some incredible challenges just to get our assigned work completed. Deadlines, management, and other pressures force us to make decisions many times a day about what to do next and how to do it. Meetings usually waste our time – not always but usually. Finding time and money for training is unheard of in many organizations and requires selling your SysAdmin soul in others.

Finding the time to remember and employ the Philosophy is challenging at best. Yet adhering to the Philosophy does pay high-value returns in the long run.

Still, reality always intrudes on the ever-so-perfect philosophical realm. Without room for flexibility, any philosophy is merely doctrine and that is not what the *Linux Philosophy for System Administrators* is about. In this chapter, we explore how some aspects of reality affect us as System Administrators.

## People

*Computers are easy – people are hard*

—Bridget Kromhout

SysAdmins must work and interact with people. It can be difficult, but we do need to do so from time to time.

One thing I have always liked about computers from the very first time I sat down at one in 1969 was the fact that is did exactly what I told it to do when I wrote the program.

© David Both 2018
D. Both, *The Linux Philosophy for SysAdmins*, https://doi.org/10.1007/978-1-4842-3730-4_26

I could make it do anything I wanted – within its capabilities – by typing in a series of commands that formed a program. If I wanted to change what it did, all I had to do was change the program. Very simple.

People are not simple at all. Not only don't I have access to their programming, they don't always pay attention to the programming they have – or that others think they have. People are not at all simple. If I were the boss of everyone, they would all do it my way and then things might be simple. But it does not work that way.

So in our striving to be the most Zen SysAdmins possible we run into people. They are usually well meaning, even most of the PHBs. The problem is that many don't understand technology.

# The Micromanager

I once had a situation where someone with a position of some authority at a place I do some volunteer work for sent me an email saying I needed to get a document up on the web site news feed as soon as possible. They also said that the hard copy was on the desk at the office. They wanted me to scan the hard copy and put that up as an image. I responded that I wanted to see the file, and I could put it up before I would have a chance to look at the hard copy.

This person responded back to me that they (meaning more than two people by now) wanted me to see the hard copy because it was an odd size and they did not want it "to be too big." Whatever that meant. But, oh, by the way, they did have a copy of the PDF that was sent to the printer. Unfortunately that PDF was not attached. To which I responded that I do not care about the size of the hard copy because I would make it an appropriate size for the space available on the web site news feed and please send me the PDF.

The next email I received had a copy of the PDF attached and a few words to the effect that, if the document was too big on the web site, a lot of people would be very upset. What?!

I did a copy and paste from the PDF to the WordPress post on the web site and added a copy of the image they wanted on the document. It looks really good, but it will be gone by the time you read this so I won't tell you where to look for it.

But wait! There's more!

So far, this has taken about three days. I could have had the document up on the news feed twenty or thirty minutes after receiving it had they sent the PDF in the first email.

In the interest of ensuring harmony among the people involved, I spoke to the writer of the emails the next time we met in person, indicating that I was not thrilled with their tone. I then briefly explained four good reasons why I was doing it the way I did and why the use of a PDF directly on the web site was not nearly as good as using the raw text I copied from it. I am sure you can think of multiple reasons why, so I won't even go into that here.

The person I spoke to looked quite perplexed at all of this and said, "I don't understand anything about what you just said." I said that I was just trying to make sure that the document looked as good as possible on the web site, and left the conversation at that point, leaving unsaid a few things that I was thinking by then.

§

That is dealing with people. It is our reality.

I know that the people involved in this just wanted everything to look good and make a good impression on visitors to the web site. I *know* that. But knowing it does not make it easier to deal with the frustration of having multiple people trying to micromanage a task that needed no management at all.

## More Is Less

*If you can't blind them with brilliance, baffle them with bullshit.*

—W.C. Fields

I used to have this old, ugly t-shirt that had the saying above printed in very bold letters on the front. I have heard many SysAdmins say similar things about the nontechnical people they work with. This attitude might work for a t-shirt but it is inappropriate for a truly professional SysAdmin.

We SysAdmins must interact with other people whether they be users, technical professionals on other teams, our peers, or management. We need to discuss our work with other people who have differing levels of knowledge. Knowledge is not a binary condition; it is analog. People have a wide disparity in the amount of knowledge that they have about computers and technology. This ranges from seemingly less than none to very knowledgeable. Their level of knowledge is important in how we interact with them.

One thing I have found is that, regardless of the knowledge level people have about computers and technology, they almost always respond well when I explain things in some detail. In this situation, I make the assumption that the person to whom I am explaining things is smart enough to understand everything I say and that they will ask for clarification if they do not understand something I say.

There are two different types of reaction when I do this. The first type of reaction is from the person who really does not understand much about technology. Before I get very far, they usually just say that they don't understand. In this case I summarize as best I can and let it go at that. In many cases these people are confused by what I have tried to tell them but feel good because I have made the assumption that they deserved to be treated as knowledgeable. This goes a long way to generating goodwill and setting the stage for a positive experience for both of you. The second type of reaction is from people who are knowledgeable. They appreciate that I am willing to give them the detailed explanation but usually just want to cut to the chase fairly quickly.

This approach leaves the other person to set their own limits on the conversation. They are free to tell us they want more or less information at any time. I find that giving people more information means less hassle in the long run.

# Tech Support Terror

I am a people, too. When I call for tech support for my Internet connection when something is not working, I don't even let the first-level support person ask me the first question on their script before I say, "I did reboot the modem. I did not reboot my computer because it is Linux and does not need rebooted. I want to speak to the third level support."

They hate when I call. I know they talk about me for days after I call them. And yet when I call I have already done all of the things that they would try to have me do during the scripted conversation with the level-one support people. I cannot stand having to work my way up through various levels of support. It takes time away from me getting my work done.

Yet, sometimes, they can get it fixed right away. Sometimes the person on the other end of the conversation actually has some pertinent knowledge.

So I asked myself, "self – how do others see me when they need help from me?" The answer was not good. I asked my wife and she did not hesitate. It was not pretty. I can be arrogant, condescending, brusque, and a real jerk all at the same time. That is certainly not my intent, but there it is.

For me this can be the result of frustration at something else entirely, that I was interrupted, that I hear the same problems many times over, that I am just tired, or whatever. All of this emotional response to whatever is happening then gets in the way of fixing the problem.

This is my reality – in both directions. So my personal tasks are to be nicer to people who need my help and also to the people from whom I am trying to get help.

## You Should Do It My Way

I can't count how many times I have said in this book that there is no one right way to do anything in Linux. I even wrote a chapter entitled, "There Is No Should," to get the point across.

Yet everything would be so much simpler if I just gave in to my urges and tell people to do it my way. I just know that everything would be fine if they just did it my way. It can be frustrating and hard to watch a new SysAdmin struggle with something that I can fix quickly. It is very difficult for me as a mentor to let them make mistakes. I think this is the hardest thing for me, to watch and let the young ones learn the hard way.

I learned how to do this from my flight instructor. Many years ago I took flying lessons. I was about halfway through this process, which took several months, and I was preflighting a Cessna 152 prior to a training flight with my instructor. I had completed the entire checklist for the exterior and had gotten in the plane and seated myself in the left-hand seat. I went through the checklist for the cabin and the startup checklist. Checklists are big things for pilots. All this time, my instructor just sat in the co-pilot's seat and watched.

At the end of the checklist, I released the parking brake and advanced the throttle a bit. The airplane did not move. I advanced the throttle a bit more and still nothing happened. There was only one reason this might occur. I looked out the side window to verify that I had indeed left the chocks in place. That plane was not going to go anywhere – that is exactly what the chocks are supposed to do.

I went through the shut-down checklist, exited the aircraft, pulled the chocks, got back in, and went through the startup checklist for the second time. This time, the aircraft did move freely. I taxied to the end of the runway and took off to start our training flight.

My instructor never said a word about it. She did not have to because I knew I had missed a step on the checklist. I learned that lesson well. It was my instructor's job to teach me how to fly *by myself* and not to do things for me. How would I ever learn if she did the things that I forgot for me? I don't fly any longer, but when I did, I always, *always* remembered to perform every item on the list and to be sure I checked that the chocks had been pulled.

These are absolutely the best teaching moments. When you can see that the young SysAdmin is clearly in the process of making a mistake, and you let them continue without saying a word.

There is something else to watch for in these situations. Observe the demeanor of the SysAdmins you are training. If they get frustrated and angry and blame you for not telling them what they know you saw, if they blame someone else for their problems, they may not be suitable for the job of SysAdmin.

# It's OK to Say No

Sometimes a SysAdmin just has to say no. A flat, straight, there are no alternatives, no. BRuce and I had to completely reject a couple projects that wanted to use our lab. Those projects would have produced great upheaval in our smoothly running lab, destroying the work of several other projects while they were about it.

I mean, we did explain why we could not take on those projects. We spent some time with the engineers who proposed those projects and helped them understand why their projects were incompatible with the work already being done in our lab. They were not happy, but they ultimately understood why we could not do what they needed in our lab. In both cases we suggested alternatives including building their own labs, but I have no idea what they ultimately did.

Sometimes a strong "no" is the right answer whether it is appreciated or not.

# The Scientific Method

We have looked at using an algorithm based on the Scientific Method to perform problem determination and resolution. It works. Your algorithm may be somewhat different from mine, but if you are successful with it stick to it. Using some form of this algorithm will make problem solving more rigorous and repeatable.

However, some problems are just intractable. Although they could probably be solved given enough time and iterations of the various loops in the algorithm, it may make more sense to start over from the very beginning. It is, after all, necessary to keep downtime to a minimum when working in a production environment.

I have on occasion moved the hard drive from a failing system to a working one. The way Linux deals with hardware these days using dbus and udev to automatically add device special files in /dev makes this an easy move and the system with the transplanted hard drive just came up and ran without a problem. Once the new system was up and running, I could install another hard drive in the failing one and try to find the root cause of the problem on it. In other cases, the fastest solution was to reinstall the operating system.

Sometimes, even with having all the time I need available to me, and plenty of Googling, I still have not been able to resolve an issue. This is another of those times that I find it necessary to reinstall the operating system in order to go back to doing more productive work. I dislike doing this because I may never figure out the root cause of the problem.

Just to be clear, the Scientific Method does work. However, sometimes the need to fix the computer and get it productive again means that we just need to suck it up and do whatever is necessary to get it running again. If we can later figure out the root cause, that is great and can help us in the future. If not, we can only move forward with our curiosity unsatisfied.

# Understanding the Past

I find it both fun and informative to learn about the history of Unix and Linux. Earlier in this book, I have referred to two books in particular that I have found helpful in my understating of Linux and its philosophy.

*Linux and the Unix Philosophy*[1] by Mike Gancarz has been particularly interesting in terms of the philosophy. The second book, *The Art of Unix Programming*[2] by Eric S. Raymond, provides fascinating insider historical perspective on Unix and Linux programming and history. This second book is also available in its entirety at no charge on the Internet.[3]

I recommend reading both of these books if you have not already. They provide a historical and philosophical basis for much of what I have written in this book.

---

[1]Gancarz, Mike, "Linux and the Unix Philosophy," Digital Press – an imprint of Elsevier Science, 2003, ISBN 1-55558-273-7

[2]Eric S. Raymond, Eric S. "The Art of Unix Programming," Addison-Wesley, September 17, 2003, ISBN 0-13-142901-9

[3]Raymond, Eric S. "The Art of Unix Programming," http://www.catb.org/esr/writings/taoup/html/index.html/

# Final Thoughts

This has been a fun book to write. When I first outlined the chapters, I thought that I might not find very much to say about some of them. It seems that I really did have a lot to say. So I will keep this last part brief.

- Computers break.

- SysAdmins fix broken computers.

- People are hard.

- SysAdmins deal with all types of people.

- Read the books I have referred to in this book. They are amazing resources and can provide powerful insights into being a Linux System Administrator.

- Never stop learning new things. There is so much to learn with more every day.

- Follow the philosophy.

- Use the algorithm. It works.

And lastly, the only "should" that you should find in this book.

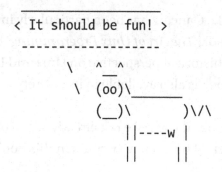

```
   _____
 < It should be fun! >
   -------------------
         \   ^__^
          \  (oo)_____
             (__)\       )\/\
                 ||----w |
                 ||     ||
```

# Bibliography

## Books

Binnie, Chris, Practical Linux Topics, Apress 2016, ISBN 978-1-4842-1772-6

Gancarz, Mike, Linux and the Unix Philosophy, Digital Press – an imprint of Elsevier Science, 2003, ISBN 1-55558-273-7

Kernighan, Brian W.; Pike, Rob (1984), The UNIX Programming Environment, Prentice Hall, Inc., ISBN 0-13-937699-2

Libes, Don, Exploring Expect, O'Reilly, 2010, ISBN 978-1565920903

Nemeth, Evi [et al.], The Unix and Linux System Administration Handbook, Pearson Education, Inc., ISBN 978-0-13-148005-6

Matotek, Dennis, Turnbull, James, Lieverdink, Peter; Pro Linux System Administration, Apress, ISBN 978-1-4842-2008-5

Raymond, Eric S., The Art of Unix Programming, Addison-Wesley, September 17, 2003, ISBN 0-13-142901-9

Siever, Figgins, Love & Robbins, Linux in a Nutshell 6th Edition, (O'Reilly, 2009), ISBN 978-0-596-15448-6

Sobell, Mark G., A Practical Guide to Linux Commands, Editors, and Shell Programming Third Edition, Prentice Hall; ISBN 978-0-13-308504-4

van Vugt, Sander, Beginning the Linux Command Line, Apress, ISBN 978-1-4302-6829-1

Whitehurst, Jim, The Open Organization, Harvard Business Review Press (June 2, 2015), ISBN 978-1625275271

© David Both 2018
D. Both, *The Linux Philosophy for SysAdmins*, https://doi.org/10.1007/978-1-4842-3730-4

BIBLIOGRAPHY

# Web Sites

BackBlaze, Web site, What SMART Stats Tell Us About Hard Drives,
https://www.backblaze.com/blog/what-smart-stats-indicate-hard-drive-failures/

Both, David, 8 reasons to use LXDE, https://opensource.com/article/17/3/8-
reasons-use-lxde

Both, David, 9 reasons to use KDE, https://opensource.com/life/15/4/9-reasons-
to-use-kde

Both, David, 10 reasons to use Cinnamon as your Linux desktop environment,
https://opensource.com/article/17/1/cinnamon-desktop-environment

Both, David, 11 reasons to use the GNOME 3 desktop environment for Linux,
https://opensource.com/article/17/5/reasons-gnome

Both, David, An introduction to Linux network routing, https://opensource.com/
business/16/8/introduction-linux-network-routing

Both, David, Complete Kickstart, http://www.linux-databook.info/?page_id=9

Both, David, Making your Linux Box Into a Router, http://www.linux-databook.
info/?page_id=697

Both, David, Network Interface Card (NIC) name assignments, http://www.
linux-databook.info/?page_id=4243

Both, David, Using hard and soft links in the Linux filesystem, http://www.
linux-databook.info/?page_id=5087

Both, David, Using rsync to back up your Linux system, https://opensource.com/
article/17/1/rsync-backup-linux

Bowen, Rich, RTFM? How to write a manual worth reading, https://opensource.com/
business/15/5/write-better-docs

Charity, Ops: It's everyone's job now, https://opensource.com/article/17/7/
state-systems-administration

Dartmouth University, Biography of Douglas McIlroy, http://www.cs.dartmouth.
edu/~doug/biography

DataBook for Linux, http://www.linux-databook.info/

Digital Ocean, How To Use journalctl to View and Manipulate Systemd Logs, `https://www.digitalocean.com/community/tutorials/how-to-use-journalctl-to-view-and-manipulate-systemd-logs`

Edwards, Darvin, Electronic Design, PCB Design And Its Impact On Device Reliability, `http://www.electronicdesign.com/boards/pcb-design-and-its-impact-device-reliability`

Engineering and Technology Wiki, IBM 1800, `http://ethw.org/IBM_1800`

Fedora Magazine, Tilix, `https://fedoramagazine.org/try-tilix-new-terminal-emulator-fedora/`

Fogel, Kark, Producing Open Source Software, `https://producingoss.com/en/index.html`

Free On-Line Dictionary of Computing, Instruction Set, `http://foldoc.org/instruction+set`

Free Software Foundation, Free Software Licensing Resources, `https://www.fsf.org/licensing/education`

gnu.org, Bash Reference Manual – Command Line Editing, `https://www.gnu.org/software/bash/manual/html_node/Command-Line-Editing.html`

Harris, William, How the Scientific Method Works, `https://science.howstuffworks.com/innovation/scientific-experiments/scientific-method6.htm`

Heartbleed web site, `http://heartbleed.com/`

How-two Forge, Linux Basics: How To Create and Install SSH Keys on the Shell, `https://www.howtoforge.com/linux-basics-how-to-install-ssh-keys-on-the-shell`

Kroah-Hartman, Greg , Linux Journal, Kernel Korner – udev – Persistent Naming in User Space, `http://www.linuxjournal.com/article/7316`

Krumins, Peter, Bash emacs editing, `http://www.catonmat.net/blog/bash-emacs-editing-mode-cheat-sheet/`

Krumins, Peter, Bash history, `http://www.catonmat.net/blog/the-definitive-guide-to-bash-command-line-history/`

Krumins, Peter, Bash vi editing, `http://www.catonmat.net/blog/bash-vi-editing-mode-cheat-sheet/`

Kernel.org, Linux allocated devices (4.x+ version), `https://www.kernel.org/doc/html/v4.11/admin-guide/devices.html`

LibreOffice, Portable Versions, `https://www.libreoffice.org/download/portable-versions/`

LibreOffice, Home Page, `https://www.libreoffice.org/`

LibreOffice, Licenses, `https://www.libreoffice.org/about-us/licenses/`

Linux Foundation, Filesystem Hierarchical Standard (3.0), `http://refspecs.linuxfoundation.org/fhs.shtml`

Linux Foundation, MIT License, `https://spdx.org/licenses/MIT`

The Linux Information Project, GCC Definition, `http://www.linfo.org/gcc.html`

Linuxtopia, Basics of the Unix Philosophy, `http://www.linuxtopia.org/online_books/programming_books/art_of_unix_programming/ch01s06.html`

LSB Work group - The Linux Foundation, Filesystem Hierarchical Standard V3.0, 3, `https://refspecs.linuxfoundation.org/FHS_3.0/fhs-3.0.pdf`

Microsoft, The Windows Subsystem for Linux, `https://docs.microsoft.com/en-us/windows/wsl/about`

N Sumarna, Wahyudin, and T Herman, The Increase of Critical Thinking Skills through Mathematical Investigation Approach, Journal of Physics: Conference Series, Volume 812, Number 1, Article 012067, `http://iopscience.iop.org/article/10.1088/1742-6596/812/1/012067/meta`

Opensource.com, `https://opensource.com/`

Opensource.com, Appreciating the full power of open, `https://opensource.com/open-organization/16/5/appreciating-full-power-open`

Opensource.com, David Both, SpamAssassin, MIMEDefang, and Procmail: Best Trio of 2017, Opensource.com, `https://opensource.com/article/17/11/spamassassin-mimedefang-and-procmail`

Opensource.com, Feb 6, 2018, Power(Shell) to the people, `https://opensource.com/article/18/2/powershell-people`

Opensource.com, Tag Careers, `https://opensource.com/tags/careers`

Opensource.com, What is open source?, https://opensource.com/resources/what-open-source

Opensource.com, What is The Open Organization, https://opensource.com/open-organization/resources/what-open-organization

The Open Source Initiative, Donate, https://opensource.org/civicrm/contribute/transact?reset=1&id=2

Opensource.org, Licenses, https://opensource.org/licenses

opensource.org, The Open Source Definition (Annotated), https://opensource.org/osd-annotated

OSnews, Editorial: Thoughts on Systemd and the Freedom to Choose, http://www.osnews.com/story/28026/Editorial_Thoughts_on_Systemd_and_the_Freedom_to_Choose

Peterson, Christine, Opensource.com, How I coined the term 'open source', https://opensource.com/article/18/2/coining-term-open-source-software

Petyerson, Scott K, The source code is the license, Opensource.com, https://opensource.com/article/17/12/source-code-license

PortableApps.com, Home page, https://portableapps.com/

Princeton University, Interview with Douglas McIlroy, https://www.princeton.edu/~hos/frs122/precis/mcilroy.htm

Raspberry Pi Foundation, https://www.raspberrypi.org/

Raymond, Eric S., The Art of Unix Programming, http://www.catb.org/esr/writings/taoup/html/index.html/

Wikipedia, The Unix Philosophy, Section: Eric Raymond's 17 Unix Rules, https://en.wikipedia.org/wiki/Unix_philosophy#Eric_Raymond%E2%80%99s_17_Unix_Rules

Raymond, Eric S., The Art of Unix Programming, Section The Rule of Separation, http://www.catb.org/~esr/writings/taoup/html/ch01s06.html#id2877777

SourceForge, Logwatch repository, https://sourceforge.net/p/logwatch/patches/34/

Time and motion study. BusinessDictionary.com. WebFinance, Inc. http://www.businessdictionary.com/definition/time-and-motion-study.html

BIBLIOGRAPHY

Understanding SMART Reports, `https://lime-technology.com/wiki/Understanding_SMART_Reports`

Unnikrishnan A, Linux.com, Udev: Introduction to Device Management In Modern Linux System, `https://www.linux.com/news/udev-introduction-device-management-modern-linux-system`

Venezia, Paul, Nine traits of the veteran Unix admin, InfoWorld, Feb 14, 2011, `www.infoworld.com/t/unix/nine-traits-the-veteran-unix-admin-276?page=0,0&source=fssr`

Wikipedia, Alan Perlis, `https://en.wikipedia.org/wiki/Alan_Perlis`

Wikipedia, Christine Peterson, `https://en.wikipedia.org/wiki/Christine_Peterson`

Wikipedia, Command Line Completion, `https://en.wikipedia.org/wiki/Command-line_completion`

Wikipedia, Comparison of command shells, `https://en.wikipedia.org/wiki/Comparison_of_command_shells`

Wikipedia, Dennis Ritchie, `https://en.wikipedia.org/wiki/Dennis_Ritchie`

Wikipedia, Device File, `https://en.wikipedia.org/wiki/Device_file`

Wikipedia, Gnome-terminal, `https://en.wikipedia.org/wiki/Gnome-terminal`

Wikipedia, Hard Links, `https://en.wikipedia.org/wiki/Hard_link`

Wikipedia, Heartbleed, `https://en.wikipedia.org/wiki/Heartbleed`

Wikipedia, Initial ramdisk, `https://en.wikipedia.org/wiki/Initial_ramdisk`

Wikipedia, Ken Thompson, `https://en.wikipedia.org/wiki/Ken_Thompson`

Wikipedia, Konsole, `https://en.wikipedia.org/wiki/Konsole`

Wikipedia, Linux console, `https://en.wikipedia.org/wiki/Linux_console`

Wikipedia, List of Linux-supported computer architectures, `https://en.wikipedia.org/wiki/List_of_Linux-supported_computer_architectures`

Wikipedia, Maslow's hierarchy of needs, `https://en.wikipedia.org/wiki/Maslow%27s_hierarchy_of_needs`

Wikipedia, Open Data, `https://en.wikipedia.org/wiki/Open_data`

Wikipedia, PHP, https://en.wikipedia.org/wiki/PHP

Wikipedia, PL/I, https://en.wikipedia.org/wiki/PL/I

Wikipedia, Programma 101, https://en.wikipedia.org/wiki/Programma_101

Wikipedia, Richard M. Stallman, https://en.wikipedia.org/wiki/Richard_Stallman

Wikipedia, Rob Pike, https://en.wikipedia.org/wiki/Rob_Pike

Wikipedia, rsync, https://en.wikipedia.org/wiki/Rsync

Wikipedia, Rxvt, https://en.wikipedia.org/wiki/Rxvt

Wikipedia, Semantics, https://en.wikipedia.org/wiki/Semantics

Wikipedia, SMART, https://en.wikipedia.org/wiki/SMART

Wikipedia, Software testing, https://en.wikipedia.org/wiki/Software_testing

Wikipedia, Terminator, https://en.wikipedia.org/wiki/Terminator_(terminal_
emulator)

Wikipedia, Time and motion study, https://en.wikipedia.org/wiki/Time_and_
motion_study

Wikipedia, Transistor count, https://en.wikipedia.org/wiki/Transistor_count

Wikipedia, Tony Hoare, https://en.wikipedia.org/wiki/Tony_Hoare

Wikipedia, Unit Record Equipment, https://en.wikipedia.org/wiki/Unit_record_
equipment

Wikipedia, Unix, https://en.wikipedia.org/wiki/Unix

Wikipedia, Windows Registry, https://en.wikipedia.org/wiki/Windows_Registry

Wikipedia, Xterm, https://en.wikipedia.org/wiki/Xterm

WikiQuote, C._A._R._Hoare, https://en.wikiquote.org/wiki/C._A._R._Hoare

WordPress, Home page, https://wordpress.org/

# Index

## A

Anacrontab file, 183, 189, 191

ASCII, 73, 102, 130, 156, 195, 201, 257, 259, 268, 270–271, 294, 309, 356, 373

ASR 33, 420

## B

Backblaze
  study of hard drive failure rates, 403

Backup
  cloud, 413
  off-site, 413–414
  procedures, 412
  recovery testing, 412
  shell script, 405

Bash
  configuration files
    ~/.bash_history file, 140
    ~/.bashrc, 135, 270, 371
    /etc/bashrc, 135, 260, 263
  global configuration, 265–268
  history, 139, 223
  sourcing files, 263
  tab completion, 137–138
  user configuration, 268–270

Binary
  executable, 373

Bogdanovic, D., 57

## Book

The Art of Unix Programming, 3–4, 335, 491

Linux and the Unix Philosophy, 3–4, 491

The Open Organization, 319

Producing Open Source Software, 319

The Unix Philosophy, 3, 27

Boot record, 34–36, 60, 74–75, 77–78

Bourne again shell, 110, 118

Bowen, R., 382

BRuce, 461, 466–467, 476, 490

Bug reports, 479–480

## C

Chase, T., 56

Cisco, 5, 218, 223, 327, 335, 461, 464, 479

Classroom, 167, 422, 443, 463, 465

Code sharing, 201, 318–319

Command-line
  history, 143
  interfaces, 12, 110–111
  recall and editing, 139

Command-line interface (CLI), 10, 12, 31, 33, 44, 78, 82, 85, 87, 109–130, 134, 137, 145, 182, 198–200, 340, 354

Command list
  adventure, 357
  alias, 134–135, 263

501

© David Both 2018
D. Both, *The Linux Philosophy for SysAdmins*, https://doi.org/10.1007/978-1-4842-3730-4